IMPLOSION

IMPLOSION

India's Tryst with Reality

JOHN ELLIOTT

HarperCollins *Publishers* India

First published in India in 2014 by
HarperCollins *Publishers* India

Copyright © John Elliott 2014

ISBN: 978-93-5029-735-3

2 4 6 8 10 9 7 5 3 1

John Elliott asserts the moral right
to be identified as the author of this work.

The views and opinions expressed in this book are the author's own and
the facts are as reported by him, and the publishers are not in
any way liable for the same.

HarperCollins *Publishers*
A-53, Sector 57, Noida, Uttar Pradesh 201301, India
77-85 Fulham Palace Road, London W6 8JB, United Kingdom
Hazelton Lanes, 55 Avenue Road, Suite 2900, Toronto, Ontario M5R 3L2
and 1995 Markham Road, Scarborough, Ontario M1B 5M8, Canada
25 Ryde Road, Pymble, Sydney, NSW 2073, Australia
31 View Road, Glenfield, Auckland 10, New Zealand
10 East 53rd Street, New York NY 10022, USA

Typeset in 11/14 Adobe Garamond
by Jojy Philip, New Delhi 110 015

Printed and bound at
Thomson Press (India) Ltd.

Contents

Acknowledgements

I've wanted to write a book about India since the end of my *Financial Times* posting in Delhi in the 1980s, but there never seemed to be any time. Eventually my *Riding the Elephant* blog, which I have written since 2007, provided me with a platform to develop ideas and assemble material that I have gathered during twenty-four amazing and eventful years writing about a range of subjects in South Asia.

None of this would have happened if Geoffrey Owen and Nico Colchester, then the editor and foreign editor of the *FT*, had not been willing to break with the convention that only foreign correspondents could be foreign correspondents and post me, then the paper's industrial editor and formerly the labour editor, to India in 1983 to open the *FT*'s bureau. Many thanks to them for launching a family adventure – years later, the careers of my three sons, Mark, Nick and Charlie, have all been linked at various times in banking, advertising and construction, to India.

Thanks next to Bill Emmott, editor of *The Economist*, for helping me to settle back in India by giving me part-time jobs on that great magazine (newspaper as they call it) in 1995 and again in the 2000s. Then to Rik Kirkman, who hired me for *Fortune* magazine, and especially to Robert Friedman, my patient and instructive international editor in the late 2000s, who asked me in 2007 to write *Riding the Elephant*, which *Fortune* had just created. Remembering Robert's constructive editing, I turned to him to sort out a muddled draft of the introduction to this book. Thanks also to James Lamont of the *FT* for organising the blog, after *Fortune* had handed it over to me, onto the FT.com website, and to Andy Buncombe of *The Independent* who quickly arranged for it to move to his newspaper's blog site after it left the FT. Now it also appears as articles on the Hong Kong-based *Asia Sentinel*.com news site, thanks to John Berthelsen, the editor.

Ravi Singh, then at Penguin India, and Namita Gokhale, who writes novels and co-directs the Jaipur Literature Festival, first encouraged me to think about turning the blog into a book, and both of them have kept me focused over several years. She, and novelist and BBC journalist Humphrey Hawksley, have constantly given advice, reading and re-reading long drafts, with Humphrey in particular prodding me into conclusions that I was trying to duck. They both helped with the title, which could have been the name of the blog, though that would not have indicated the line I was taking. I was always tempted to include the words 'Because of the Gods' as a counter-point to *FT* journalist Ed Luce's *In Spite of the Gods: The Rise of Modern India* (published eight years ago) to indicate that 'the gods' in the broadest sense of culture, customs, and habits are now slowing that rise down. But I've had IMPLOSION as a working title for a year or two, and that won through.

Without Belinda Wright, this book may never have been completed because of the distractions of trying to work in Delhi. She lent me her tranquil forest home near her family's 'Treading Softly in the Jungle' Kipling Camp on the edge of Kanha National Park in Madhya Pradesh on three occasions. With cheetal and monkeys, and the famous elephant Tara wandering by, and the prospect of tigers, leopards and bears not far away, I did a lot of writing over the twelve weeks I was there – well looked after by Babulal and all the staff. Thanks also to my old friends Diana and Horace Mitchell for letting me retreat to the quiet top floor of their home near Newbury to finish the chapters.

I've been helped to explore and learn about India by many people over the years, and a lot of them appear in this book. I'm grateful to friends and contacts who have given me their time and advice, some also reading drafts, especially those listed here (roughly in the order of the chapters where they were most involved): Anand Mahindra, Sudarshan Maini and his family, Pavan Varma, Montek Singh Ahluwalia, Rakesh Mohan, S.L. Rao, Ashok Desai, Hugh Sandeman, Madhukar Khera, Lord (Nigel) Lawson, Shylashri Shankar, Vikram Singh Mehta, Ravi Kaimal, Sudeshna Chatterjee, Subrata Gupta, Ravinder Kaur, Dipankar Gupta, Nandan Nilekani, Biswajit Mohanty, Sachin Pilot, Mani Shankar Aiyar, Amitabha Pande, Nitin Bhayana, B.K. Synghal, Kalyan Bose, Arun Shourie, Anvar Alikhan, Ram Karan, V.K. Srinivasan, Manoj Joshi, Ajai Shukla, Rahul Chaudhry, Khutub Hai, Stephen P. Cohen, Sunil Dasgupta, Naresh Chandra, Tariq A. Karim, Shivshankar Menon, K. Shankar Bajpai, G. Parathasarathy, Kanwal Sibal, T.C.A. Rangachari, Navtej Sarna, Rob Young, Bob Blackwill, David Sloan and Arun Kapur.

Keshav Choudhary, a young graduate, did some valuable research, and I'm grateful to Samir Saran and C. Raja Mohan at the Observer Research Foundation for hosting me at countless seminars and networking vegetarian lunches. At Harper Collins, thanks to Krishan Chopra, my editor Karthika V.K., and also to Shantanu Chaudhuri and all the staff.

Going back in history, Abid Hussain, along with Tarun Das and others, helped me to begin to understand India in the 1980s, and encouraged me to return in 1995 when Abid gave me a visiting fellowship at the Rajiv Gandhi Institute of Contemporary Affairs, which he was then running. Later, he often gave ideas and encouragement but sadly died in June 2012, just as we were about to meet and talk, so could not advise me as much I had hoped on this book. Others I have also sadly missed include S.K. Singh, Hari Shankar Singhania, Vijay Shankardass and David Gore-Booth. The many other contacts and friends over the years are far too numerous to name but include Pran Chopra, Salman Haider, Vijay Kelkar, Bimal Jalaan, Peter Hassan, Bim Bissell, Gautam Thapar, Jamshyd Godrej, Rahul Bajaj, R.C. Bhargava, V. Krishnamurthy, Talmiz Ahmad, Arvind Singhal, Pradip Shah, Sanjoy Bhattacharyya, Jairam Ramesh, Mark Tully,

Dinesh Trivedi, Sushil Premchand, Rejeev Gupta, Aditi Phadnis, Tony Jesudasan, Mike Knowles, Michael Carter, Marcus Winsley and William Knight.

A tribute to Geoffrey Goodman, my old colleague, mentor and friend, to whom this book is dedicated, appears at the end of the Introduction.

JOHN ELLIOTT

January 2014
Delhi

Introduction

The Risk of Implosion

India punches below its weight, failing to achieve what it could and should be doing. It has the vast potential of a population of over a billion people, abundant natural resources and an ancient culture, yet it constantly disappoints admirers and validates the views of critics. Most recently, with declining economic performance, poor governance and endemic corruption, people have begun to ask, 'Why is India proving such a failure?'

The purpose of this book is not so much to look at the most recent short-term failures, but at how and why more has not been achieved since independence in 1947. During these years, India has largely muddled through, turning confusion and adversity into varying degrees of success – initially building a new nation, and then a new economy after 1991, when the country took historic steps to open up internationally. This approach has worked, untidily, erratically, argumentatively, and corruptly, as far as it has gone, but an economy and society can no longer survive, let along thrive, with such lack of focus and drive in times of increasingly rapid change.

At the heart of this national approach is what is known as *jugaad* (sometimes spelt *jugaar*), which means making do and innovating with what is available, and *chalta hai*, which means 'anything goes' and hoping for the best. The private sector generally works on more positive lines, driven by increasing competition since 1991, but jugaad and chalta hai fit with a culture where public debate is more important than the conclusion, where 'introspection' (a much loved word) is celebrated more than any outcome, and where it is easier to argue than to listen. Being seen to know something is more important than turning that information into coordinated analysis and action. Decisions – especially those that are conveniently 'holistic' (another favourite) – are an end in themselves, without concern for implementation.

Maybe some of that stems from the Indian caste system's brahminical approach to learning rather than action, but it also fits with politicians and others who want the glory and tamasha of laying foundation stones, metaphorically and actually, without caring about what, if anything, is then implemented or achieved. Jugaad is a brilliant patchwork solution for a deprived and underdeveloped society, but it is not enough for a country in India's state of development because it deters efficiency and innovation and destroys institutional structures. In the past few years, India's pace of events has overwhelmed jugaad, making it impossible for the country to cope with basic services, projects and development – and that is now leading to the risk of implosion.

Every country has a similar approach to a greater or lesser degree, and many other countries have failed to face up to endemic problems. Brazil has a word, *jeitinho*, from the Portuguese, which is an improvised fix to a problem (sometimes illegal),[1] and *vai dar*, which means something like 'it will work out all right'. But these traits are so deeply ingrained into how India's people and institutions function that performance crumbles. Individuals can, of course, do well, as they demonstrate in their own endeavours and as part of many successful Indian companies. This is also evident in the way they thrive abroad as traders and businessmen in Africa, shopkeepers and bankers in the UK, and software entrepreneurs and space scientists in the US. But the country as a whole is failing and, in so doing, has lost the drive of fast economic growth that it enjoyed in the first decade of this century.

A sense of preordained karma, where one's path is laid out,

coupled with deep religious traditions and beliefs in the power of the gods, contributes to the fatalism and inevitability of chalta hai. People pray regularly for a variety of things, not least success at work. The owner of a shop in my local market stands outside in the morning bustle, praying for several minutes before entering and starting work. A bureaucrat who used to be in charge of a chaotic public office that I sometimes have to visit in Delhi, stood at his desk when he arrived in the morning and prayed, hands clasped, a personal island of serenity amid the impatience and frustrations around him. Big tycoons and politicians seek success by donating large sums of money and other valuables to temples, such as the majestic Lord Venkateswara temple in Tirupati in Andhra Pradesh. Vijay Mallya, a flamboyant businessman, donated three kilograms of gold there in December 2012 when his Kingfisher Airways was floundering – it did not recover.[2]

Antonio Armellini, a former Italian ambassador in Delhi, has written that 'no other country has India's capacity to project the future into the present'.[3] This was a neat way of saying that India enthusiastically takes forecasts and projections for granted, projecting them as instant reality, while largely ignoring the need to work and make them come about. The best and most serious example of this is how India has revelled for the past few years in its 'demographic dividend', with about half the population (560m people) being under the age of 25, including 225m between 10 and 19. But little has been done to harness the potential with good education, adequate skills training and suitable job opportunities, especially in the underperforming manufacturing industry. The dividend now risks becoming a demographic disaster with the number of unemployed semi-educated youth climbing rapidly. 'If we get it right, India becomes the workhorse of the world. If we get it wrong, there is nothing worse than unemployable, frustrated youth,' says Shashi Tharoor, a central government minister with responsibilities for education, and also a writer and former senior United Nations official.[4]

It is difficult to live in India for long without becoming deeply sceptical and even cynical about the future of the country, and its leaders and society. I travelled to a jungle camp near Kanha National Park in the middle of India, to write part of this book.[5] As I was driven from Jabalpur, an old city that has been an important military and regional centre since before independence, I wondered whether the great rolling countryside would change my basic views and moderate my criticisms. I needn't have worried. Over the next few days, the local newspaper, *The Hitavada*, kept me on track. One day, a senior forestry official's residence had been raided and 'disproportionate property' worth over Rs 40 crore had been discovered.[6] Two days later, police wielding lathis charged at a crowd in the state's capital city, beating people who were protesting against the killing and alleged rape of an eight-year-old girl.

Inspiration in the '80s

India's massive potential captured me when I first came to the country in 1982, writing articles on industry for the *Financial Times*. I had been reporting Britain's industrial decline for 15 years and I was struck, as I travelled from Bengaluru northwards to Bombay, Pune and Delhi, by the contrast with India's economy that was just beginning to open up, albeit extremely slowly.[7] Black-and-white televisions were beginning to appear in rural villages, though urban markets sold video players, not recorders, because nothing was being broadcast that was worth recording. A government-owned company, Maruti Udyog, was looking for a foreign partner to make cars (it eventually linked up with Suzuki) to run on roads crowded with 30-year-old derivatives of British Morris Oxfords and Fiat 1100s alongside the bullock carts and auto-rickshaws. Japanese two-wheeler and light commercial vehicle companies were setting up joint ventures. Operation Flood was building a network of thousands of milk cooperatives that would make India self-sufficient in milk. Indira Gandhi, the prime minister, had just begun to decontrol cement prices, an arcane but seminal initiative.

A couple of years later, after I had come to live in Delhi, there was a young prime minister who had dreams of opening people's eyes to the potential of a new India. Rajiv Gandhi gave business a much needed sense of respectability and inspired interest among the young in the stock market. He started initiatives to loosen up industrial controls, introducing high technology and entrepreneurial drive into a government-dominated economy. Pepsi Cola was soon demonstrating how a foreign company could help agriculture by pulping and exporting tomatoes as well as selling its cola. Opponents of reform were regularly pushing Gandhi off course, but the foundations of new India were being prepared. The potential was already visible.

Hopes were pinned on what were seen as India's acclaimed advantages as an investment destination – notably its stable parliamentary democracy, deep-rooted cultural and social traditions in a free and open society, with established legal, accounting, and financial systems and institutions, and a respect for private property. One could also include a firmly based private sector, high quality technicians with good analytical brains, a strong base of competent managers, and English as the main language of business and government'.[8] Together, that gave India a distinct edge over China though, even then, India was frequently regarded as a problem, and suffered internationally from "a bad image as an 'unpredictable, unreliable, and even difficult place to do business'.

The *Financial Times* posted me to Hong Kong in 1988 at the end of five years based in Delhi, so I did not report on the economic reforms introduced in 1991 that opened up the economy and sharpened the focus on developing a modern India. I returned in 1995, expecting to find an even greater sense of the enormous potential that I had felt in the 1980s. Instead, I found a society and a government that were unsure about the benefits and political viability of economic liberalization. Leaders at all levels had found new ways to milk the country of its riches, encouraged by greedy foreign as well as big Indian companies and banks that were only too willing to pay for out-of-turn contracts, mandates and licences.

There was even a new willingness to gossip openly about corruption, which had not been evident in the 1980s. The names of top officials in some ministries (even the finance ministry, as I had heard in Hong Kong) were being attached to major projects and financial mandates. India was emerging into what it has now become – a place where many deals have an illicit price, and where politicians and bureaucrats link with businessmen to plunder the country's wealth, deprive the poor of sustenance and aid, steal natural resources that range from land and coal to wildlife, and secure future wealth through layers of political dynasties.

The March of Corruption

Corruption plays a vital role in the country's failings. It prevents central and state governments adequately addressing key issues, and leads both the public and private sector to assume that they can buy their way into contracts and out of problems. It oils the wheels for businessmen and politicians, and helped create a pre-2011 economic boom by exploiting the country's natural resources, while also greasing the wheels of inefficiency and poor performance. Until recently, society knew it was happening but did little to stop it. The fraud and extortion are now beginning to unravel though, partly because of India's right to information (RTI) laws that are publicizing widespread corruption, and partly because of public anger and protest movements, aided by hyperactive and inquisitive television and the growing power of social media.

'Everyone seems to assume that advancement – whether it is admission to a college for a child who has failed its exams, the award of a contract for mending a road, fixing a court case, or winning a top public sector job – can be bought,' I wrote in 2001.[9] 'State chief ministers regard state electricity boards as their personal fiefdom, and the rich and powerful – plus the poor – steal electricity and refuse to pay bills. Politicians regard India's forests as places to be plundered for their personal and party finances. Public sector projects are commissioned to create both kickbacks for officials and over-invoiced work for contractors. Inevitably, the people who benefit from this illicit wealth do not want economic reform.'

These problems must however be seen in the context of the massive economic, political and social changes since independence, and especially the most dramatic period of transition and adjustment in the past 10 to 15 years. This was when the 1991 reforms fed through into the lives of at least a third of the population, triggering unimagined consumerism and availability of jobs. New technologies brought satellite television, 24-hour TV news and the internet, opening the eyes of rural as well as urban communities to lifestyles they had never seen. All this led to a breakdown of old family bonds and awakened new social attitudes, ambitions and awareness, plus an impatience with corrupt and ineffective politicians – all coming together in three decades instead of sequentially, over the far longer periods that it took other developed economies.

The Opposite Is True

India has its own form of logic and many contradictions so that virtually everything and its opposite are true. Indian people are kind and generous, but it is often a cruel, ruthless society. They can be honest but without conventional Western-style ethics, proud of an established rule of law but with scant interest in abiding by it, hard-working yet indolent in a laissez faire way, with clean homes yet without concern about filthy environments. There is enormous energy and creativity, yet the influence of chalta hai is pervasive. There is a respect for animals from the sacred cow to the revered tiger, yet the natural heritage is plundered, and there is reverence for frugal lives, yet tolerance of arrogant displays of wealth and huge waste. Perhaps the biggest and most important contradiction of all is the failure to rise to the expectations that stem from the combination of a rich, deep culture with an apparent openness and accessibility, plus an unrealized potential in terms of people and natural resources.

Realism is now setting in as people see that many things cannot be taken at face value, especially when cultural factors affect openness and honesty. As Kris Gopalakrishnan, co-chairman and one of the founders of Infosys, a leading Indian information technology company, said in a newspaper interview, 'In Indian culture, people often leave important things unsaid, while people from abroad are more transparent. So they assume that if something is not said, it doesn't matter. But in India if something isn't said, it really does not mean it doesn't matter'.[10] That rhymes with what a neighbour in Delhi said when I asked a question about Indian politics: 'What are you to me that I should tell you the truth?' He was probably half joking, and was enjoying teasing a foreign journalist, but there was a revealing undercurrent of reality. K. Shankar Bajpai,[11] a veteran diplomat, once told me, 'Hinduism does not believe in conversion, so we make assertions without trying to persuade anyone else to our point of view.' Namita Gokhale, a novelist and publisher, explained that 'The Hindu religion leads you to seek individual salvation, so you have little place for community and ethical values, and that leads to a moral ambivalence and acceptance of corruption in one's mindset.' A former top official in the defence services had this to offer: 'We are a feudal society, so if a minister says, "Do something in five years", we will say, "No sir, we'll do it in three years" and then we will not do it at all.'

In 1995, I wrote a comparative study of India and China's liberalization policies[12] and searched for a way of explaining why China always seemed to be given the benefit of the doubt, whereas India would be quickly criticized. 'The problem for India is that foreigners expect more of it than China,' I wrote. 'Its apparent openness, with the English language and a suave elite, make it look easy, westernised and welcoming – though noisy. Only later does it emerge as a complex and often difficult challenge. China, on the other hand, is shrouded in mystery and looks intriguingly remote and orientally challenging, though in reality it is more orderly than India. China is therefore almost always given the benefit of the doubt. Whatever businessmen manage to achieve in China is notched up as a success. Whatever they don't quickly achieve in India is a black mark.' Foreigners still continue to expect more of India, not only because of the English language and apparent similarities with their own countries, but because of the hopes released in the 1980s, and especially after 1991.

Aspirational India

Despite the criticisms, it is the upside of a new aspirational India that gives the country hope. New generations of ambitious young people, ranging from the poor to the elite, have been freed from many of the social and economic restrictions and shortages of earlier generations. Urban India is now almost unrecognizable from 30 years ago in terms of transport, consumer goods, entertainment and lifestyles, though there is still widespread hardship and poverty, and the chaotic and dangerous clutter of unauthorized construction and urban decay. Mobile telephones have transformed communications – there are over 700m active connections (though many people have more than one) compared with less than 30m mostly land line (and inefficient) telephones 10 to 20 years earlier.

Aspirational India has emerged in other ways too, affecting traditional values. Arranged marriages continue, for example, but those looking for partners no longer focus on the safety of caste and community links but look for educational and business qualifications and possibly the opportunity to live abroad. In the 1980s, matrimonial advertisements in newspapers focused on complexion, caste and education, but now it is 'MNC' for multinational corporations and 'MBA' for a business degree, demonstrating a growing concern for material success. Instead of just advertising in the classified pages of weekend newspapers, the hunt for a partner happens on the internet too, and there is even a website for second marriages that demonstrates an acceptance of divorce that would have been unthinkable when I first came to India.[13]

'Every successful economy needs a tangible celebration,' Rajeev

Sethi, a veteran promoter of India's arts and artists, said a few years ago when I was writing an article on the then booming Indian modern art market for London's *Royal Academy* magazine.[14] He was referring to the huge success being enjoyed by Indian artists, famous and not-yet-famous, who were slowly generating interest abroad. International art fairs and auctions were being staged in Delhi and Mumbai,[15] opening up access to art for people young and old, many of whom would have been reluctant to walk into the forbidding arena of the formal art gallery.

The market has since slumped, partly because prices for contemporary art rose irrationally high, but mainly because – rather revealingly – buyers were looking at their purchases primarily as financial investments rather than works of art.

Another tangible celebration that would have been unthinkable in the 1980s is an annual literature festival in the Rajasthani city of Jaipur that has grown haphazardly from a few hundred people in 2006 to one of the world's biggest such events, spawning other festivals across India and in neighbouring Pakistan, Nepal, Bhutan and Myanmar.[16] In January 2012, there were 15,000–20,000 people at Jaipur every day for four or five days, with 260 writers, including famous Indian and foreign literary names, mixing with masses of book lovers and schoolchildren.

Aspirational India and corrupt India merged in another very tangible celebration with the fast-paced Twenty-20 cricket matches of the Indian Premier League (IPL) that was launched in 2008, fetching over $1bn for television rights and $723m for regional franchises that were bought by flashy Indian businessmen and film stars. This had grown by 2010 to a massive $4bn wealth-creating brand of sponsorships, broadcasting and other franchises, fees and other takings.[17] Apart from the very poor in remote rural areas who had no access to television, everyone seemed to relish the tournament, despite massive allegations of corruption. Never before had a scam been enjoyed and celebrated by such a massive proportion of Indian people.[18]

The national celebration of the lucky few getting rich in a poor country is one of India's many curious contradictions. The poor have (up to a point) always admired the massive illicit personal wealth of some politicians because it shows what can be achieved from a deprived background. Similarly, the successes of the IPL organizers, cricketers and team owners were enjoyed as a symbol of hope for what might be. Some of the scams did catch up with the IPL though, and the brand value had dropped to $2.92bn in 2012.[19] Its image crashed in 2013 when a huge match-fixing scandal was exposed by a television sting operation that caught players looking for large bribes, generating police investigations and charges.[20]

'Exasperation and Exhilaration'

International criticism has hardened in recent years as India's less favourable systems have come to the fore with the connivance, after 2004, of a somnolent and corrupt coalition government nominally led by Manmohan Singh as prime minister but effectively controlled by Sonia Gandhi as head of the ruling Congress party. Singh had been put on too high a pedestal for his role as finance minister in the 1991 reformist government that was led by Narasimha Rao, the prime minister. The decline of such an icon as Singh has epitomized India's failure to sustain the potential of the 2000s when growth neared nine or ten per cent.

I wrote a spoof piece on my blog in September 2010 about an un-named country that was obviously India.[21] Left-wing rebels controlled a quarter of the country's districts. There were two tiresome neighbours, one riven with religious extremism and terrorism that the perpetrators wanted to export. The other, far bigger, neighbour had for years been encouraging the smaller neighbour to do its worst. The prime minister was a nice, well-meaning, elderly guy run by a foreign-born lady whose main interest seemed to be making sure her son became prime minister one day. The prime minister could not control many of his ministers, who mainly wanted to make money for themselves and their regional political parties, thus undermining key areas of the economy for which they were responsible – such as airlines and airports, telecoms and mining, and sometimes industrial and other policies relating to foreign direct investment, special economic zones, petroleum, agriculture and food supplies.

In my story, most parliamentarians – a meaningless title since most of them did little constructive parliamentary work – were dynastically getting their sons, daughters, wives and even mistresses into politics, presumably not for the good of parliament or the country. Personal greed seemed to govern sport, ranging from chaotic preparations for some imminent regional games to a lucrative private sector cricket league. Businessmen and politicians were conniving to plunder the country's mineral wealth with scant regard for the environment or the law. And you could not believe what you read in the newspapers because several newspapers printed what they were paid to print, and at least one of them had got commercially involved with its advertisers by investing in their stocks and managing their advertising budgets. When I told this story at a small business dinner party before it went up on the blog, the first comment, from a foreign executive, was, 'Yet we keep coming – India takes you to exasperation and to exhilaration at the same time. That's the way it is.'

This book does not attempt to cover all aspects of this exasperation and exhilaration, but tries to look at how India works and where it goes wrong – and right – by examining how things are done or not done. It mainly focuses on subjects that I have written about on my blog since it started in April 2007, initially on the *Fortune* magazine website, plus other articles – from 1983 to 1988 in the *FT*, and after 1995 at various times in *The Economist, The New Statesman,* India's *Business Standard* and *Fortune.*

In the course of my reporting, I've been involved in the creation of two internationally recognized words or phrases, and both are in the book. I'm credited in Bhutan as the first foreign correspondent to be told (for the *FT* in 1987) by the then King Jigme Singye Wangchuck about his plans for Gross National Happiness or GNH, which later became an international theme. I was also the first journalist (again for the *FT* but in 1979, before I came to India) to write about privatisation, a word which had not appeared before in a newspaper – it sounded so odd that the newspaper's features editor refused to put it in the story's headline, saying no one would understand it!

To some extent, it is easy to write a book pointing out the faults when India is on a downward trend, as it has been for the past few years. Indeed, what I have written here will probably be more acceptable in the current mood than it would have been five or ten years ago when audiences sometimes found my stories too negative.

The word 'implosion' has various connotations. It usually conjures up dramatic images of buildings and glass shattering inwards, and of objects collapsing violently. What is happening in India is not that sort of massive one-off event but a more insidious and equally dramatic inward collapse. Internal forces are gradually eating away at institutions, organizational procedures and the functioning of authority that are needed to run a country.[22] Contributing to this creeping implosion are self-serving politicians and government officials, plus widespread and endemic corruption, and a lack of interest in tackling problems. When such developments swamp and begin to destroy the political process, the judiciary and the media, implosion has begun.

When I was about to come to India in the early 1980s, friends had suggested I should read V.S. Naipaul's celebrated books *An Area of Darkness* and *A Wounded Civilisation*. I began them but gave up, deciding I did not want to start reporting on a country with such depressing negative introductions. A veteran journalist friend, Geoffrey Goodman, then gave me *An Indian Summer* by James Cameron, a great reporter and writer whom he knew well. Geoffrey wrote in the book that he hoped it would 'help nourish your interest in, and love for, a great land'. Well, it did, because I found that Cameron's mixture of admiration and frustration for all India's contradictions matched my first instincts and later experiences. To mark that gift and his continuing sound advice and encouragement till he sadly died in

September 2013, this book is dedicated to Geoffrey, in memory of one of Britain's most dedicated and committed industrial correspondents and one of the finest political commentators of his generation.

Notes

1. 'Brazil's monetary *jeitinho*', *Financial Times*, 15 January 2013, http://blogs.ft.com/beyond-brics/2013/01/15/brazils-monetary-jeitinho/#axzz2idTH2e1O

2. http://www.indiatimes.com/more-from-india/vijay-mallya-donates-3kg-gold-to-tirupati-%5Btwitter-reacts%5D-50681.html

3. Antonio Armellini, *If the Elephant Flies: India Confronts the Twenty-first Century*, p. 407, Har-Anand Publications, Delhi 2012

4. Thomas L. Friedman, 'India vs. China vs. Egypt', *The New York Times*, 5 February 2013, http://www.nytimes.com/2013/02/06/opinion/friedman-india-vs-china-vs-egypt.html?_r=0

5. http://ridingtheelephant.wordpress.com/2012/11/26/writing-in-the-wild-at-kipling-camp/

6. 'Madhya Pradesh Lokayukta raids forest official, uncovers assets worth Rs. 40 crore', *Mail Today*, 6 February 2013 – with photographs of the raid including a suitcase with bundles of 1,000-rupee notes, http://indiatoday.intoday.in/story/madhya-pradesh-lokayukta-raids-forest-official-uncovers-assets/1/249088.html

7. John Elliott (JE), 'Celebrating the Vested Interest Raj', 'Bystander' column, *Business Standard*, 29 June 2001, http://www.business-standard.com/india/storypage.php?autono=94193&

8. *India and China – Asia's New Giants: Stepping stones to prosperity* by JE, page 3, Rajiv Gandhi Institute of Contemporary Studies, Delhi 1995

9. John Elliott (JE), 'Celebrating the Vested Interest Raj', 'Bystander' column, *Business Standard*, 29 June 2001, http://www.business-standard.com/india/storypage.php?autono=94193&

10. 'Go east, entrepreneurs – with Indian partners', *Financial Times*, 14 February 2013, http://www.ft.com/intl/cms/s/0/c24607ac-7689-11e2-8569-0144feabdc0.html#axzz2SKxZeg65

11. K. Shankar Bajpai in conversation with JE, October 2012

12. JE, 'India and China: Asia's New Giants: Stepping Stones to Prosperity', Rajiv Gandhi Institute of Contemporary Studies, Delhi, 1995.

13. http://www.secondshaadi.com/

14. 'Made in India: Contemporary Art in India', http://www.royalacademy. org.uk/ra-magazine/winter2006/features/made-in-india,49,RAMA. html

15. http://ridingtheelephant.wordpress.com/2011/01/27/delhi% E2%80%99s-art-summit-a-huge-international-success-with-128000-visitors-and-good-sales/ and http://ridingtheelephant.wordpress. com/2012/10/02/ratan-tata-and-mahatma-gandhi-reflected-in-anamorphic-cylinders/

16. http://ridingtheelephant.wordpress.com/2011/01/30/incredible-india%E2%80%99s-literary-woodstock/

17. 'IPL brand value doubles to $4.13bn: Brand Finance', PTI, http:// www.business-standard.com/article/companies/ipl-brand-value-doubles-to-4-13-bn-brand-finance-110032200177_1.html

18. http://ridingtheelephant.wordpress.com/2010/04/24/india% E2%80%99s-scam-ridden-ipl-cricket-is-a-national-celebration/

19. 'Profits still elude some IPL teams', *Mint*, 2 April 2013, http://www. livemint.com/Consumer/Vx82Oge7kJ5nYt6rylf5FM/Profits-still-elude-some-IPL-teams.html

20. 'Betting scandal deepens in India cricket league', *Financial Times*, 23 May 2013, http://www.ft.com/intl/cms/s/0/d635c988-c39a-11e2-aa5b-00144feab7de.html

21. http://ridingtheelephant.wordpress.com/2010/09/10/india-as-it-is-%E2%80%93-a-spoof%E2%80%99s-eye-view/

22. http://www.macmillandictionary.com/thesaurus/british/implosion# implosion_4

I

JUGAAD/CHALTA HAI

1

India's Master Plan

One of the magical things about India is its unpredictability and its ability to turn muddle and adversity into success. This is true of many countries, of course, especially developing economies, but in India it has been turned into an art form and governs the way that vast areas of the country operate. In the days of the pre-1991 Licence Raj, when government controls restricted what companies could do and people could buy, this approach enabled the country to work, creakily, until systems and machinery broke down and were patched up again to judder on inefficiently.[1] Hindustan Motors' Ambassador car, which is still being produced,[2] is an archetypal example of such patchwork. Its 60-year-old (British Morris Oxford) body has been remoulded on the edges and smartened up with chrome strips, and the engine, gearbox and other parts have been replenished over the years, while the basic car has remained the same.

This kind of jugaad, which means making do and innovating with what is available, can be many things, both good and bad. It is the knack of turning shortages, chaos and adversity into some sort of order and success, and it enables the poor in India to benefit from low-cost adaptations and innovations with fixes such as using a belt from a motorbike wheel to run an irrigation pump, using a Pringles potato crisps container to bridge a piping gap in a car engine, and applying turmeric powder to fix a radiator leak.[3] It leads to the innovation that drives entrepreneurial activity – for example, in slums like the world-famous Dharavi in Mumbai where, in filthy conditions, there is an informal and unregulated $750m–$1bn a year parallel economy with businesses ranging from the manufacture of good-quality leather goods to recycling of plastics and electronic hardware. Some 60,000 families live there, tightly packed amid the squalor.

The positive aspects of jugaad are being lauded internationally because of what some auto industry executives and others call India's 'frugal engineering', where the best is made of minimal resources for the lowest cost. This has appeared over the past decade as India's manufacturing industry has begun to shed an image of inefficiency and poor workmanship, proving that internationally competitive products can be produced. Jugaad has consequently become a management fad and is being praised outside India as a great Indian invention. The BBC made a 30-minute radio programme revelling in jugaad's canny inventions,[4] and management books are putting jugaad on a pinnacle of achievement.

Jugaad Innovation[5] by Navi Radjou, Jaideep Prabhu and Simone Ahuja, published in 2012 when the world's economy was in a downturn and many companies were strapped for cash, called it a 'breakthrough growth strategy'. It argued that jugaad is a better low-cost method of innovation than international companies' high-budget, structured research and development programmes which, the book says, lack flexibility and are elitist and insular. The authors suggested six jugaad principles: 'seek opportunity in adversity, do more with less, think and act flexibly, keep it simple, include the margin, follow your heart'. They say that jugaad is about developing a 'good enough solution that gets the job done'.

That is fine for management theory, and it might encourage companies to take a fresh look at their innovation programmes, but the reality is that India has for decades relied on jugaad instead of looking for new levels of performance and excellence. It has linked this with the more negative attitude of chalta hai, which literally means 'it walks' and is broadly interpreted as 'anything goes'. Together this means that, like an archetypal Indian wedding, delays and organizational chaos will give way to razzmatazz and a great tamasha on the day, providing sufficient jugaad has been spread around. Kaam chalao is another rather negative rendering of the same theme, meaning 'will make do' in a makeshift and improvised way, without the innovation of a clever jugaad.

Such a culture intuitively sees no need for rigid structures and rules and, where they do exist, instinctively fudges and evades them, trusting that eventually all will be well, which of course it increasingly often is not. The laid-back approach has support through another phrase – Ram bharose, 'trusting in god', or more specifically, 'leaving it to Lord Ram' – Ram, or Rama, being the Hindu god who is worshipped as a legendary king as well as a deity.

This was fine – indeed constructive – when independent India was building a new nation. 'The concept of quality used to be that if it works somehow, it's okay, but it doesn't need to work all the time,' Baba Kalyani, chairman of Pune-based Bharat Forge, which has grown into one of the world's biggest forgings companies, told me in 2007 for a *Fortune* magazine article.[6] That concept stemmed from the decades before 1991 when the government's industrial licensing system created shortages and restricted competition, making it both difficult and unnecessary to produce quality goods. 'No one could create a high-technology, high-capital-cost business. You waited a year for an equipment-import licence, got less than you wanted, then paid 80 per cent import duty – and interest rates were at 18–20 per cent,' said Kalyani.

These attitudes should have become less universal when India began developing a new economy after 1991, but they are still in place and continue to harm the country. Jugaad no longer works effectively because the pace and complexity of rapidly changing events and communication make it impossible for India to run its basic services, projects and development on the basis of quick fixes, comforted by the faith that something will turn up to save the day.

This was graphically demonstrated when the country was held up to international ridicule over corrupt and slothful preparations for

the 2010 Commonwealth Games in Delhi. There are many other
examples with less satisfactory outcomes. The most evident involve
public sector infrastructure, ranging from annual monsoon flooding
that cripples Mumbai and inadequate services in Delhi's shiny new
satellite city of Gurgaon to unhealthy water supplies emanating from
Delhi's polluted and sewage-ridden Yamuna river, building collapses,
and outdated defence equipment. Incredibly, radioactive steel scrap
was found in a Delhi recycling yard in 2010.[7]

Together, jugaad and chalta hai contribute to a matrix of factors
that prevent India from excelling. While jugaad provides for the
Ambassador car's longevity and Dharavi's successes, chalta hai means
that companies, both Indian and foreign, tolerate the urban chaos
around their office towers. There is tolerance of poor maintenance
of India's massive railway system; when serious crashes lead to loss of
life, government ministers silence criticism and avoid the need for
follow-up action by handing out financial compensation to victims'
families. Jugaad leads to cannibalization of spare parts of fighter jets
and army tanks, while chalta hai has over the years led to depleted
defence preparedness and a failure to tackle urgent security issues
with new organizational and other arrangements. 'India's capacity
for self-deception is extreme, and this constitutes the gravest threat
to national security,' says the Institute for Conflict Management.
'Counterterrorism policies have been based principally on political
posturing, and not on objective and urgent considerations of strategy
and response ... creating an illusion of security has been given far
greater priority than giving real muscle and substance to the country's
terrorism apparatus'.[8]

In another dimension, foreign executives talk about staff trying
to disrupt established management procedures and structures so
that jugaad can come into play (maybe, or maybe not, to facilitate
extortion and bribes). A European finance director marvels with
frustrated bewilderment at the way his Indian taxation staff fudge and
ignore established procedures and work with the taxation authorities
in impenetrable ways that eventually produce acceptable results.[9]

Jugaad therefore does more harm than good. While often solving problems, it leads to complacency and acceptance of things as they are. It encourages and facilitates the undermining and corruption of institutions, which has become a serious problem. As a result, much of the country is in a constant state of unstable and sometimes fatal underperformance that often benefits those in authority because they can bypass the failures and gain from the chaos. This situation is exacerbated by widespread corruption, with both the public and private sectors assuming they can buy their way into contracts and out of poor quality performance and consequential problems. Officials place contracts that (appear to) sort out the chaos with companies that are adept at playing the game. Why build a good road that could last years if you can bribe officials to accept substandard work at inflated overinvoiced prices, and then bribe them again to let you do the repairs, again with substandard materials charged at overinvoiced prices? The same disregard applies to hygiene. This was demonstrated tragically in July 2013 when 27 children died after eating food – possibly contaminated by insecticide – provided by a government midday meal scheme at their primary school in Bihar.

It often seems that life in India is not valued highly. Public services are allowed to decay, and there is scant concern for public safety. The narrow streets of areas such as old Delhi, mostly inaccessible in an emergency, are full of overcrowded, unlawfully extended buildings of poor quality construction, strewn with jumbles of low-hanging electrical wires and potentially dangerous equipment. Mumbai's chief fire officer said in March 2013 that, out of 1,857 buildings inspected for fire safety facilities, only 237 – just 13 per cent – fully complied. The service had issued notices to over 1,000 buildings for not following fire safety norms, and there were over 5,000 high-rise buildings yet to be inspected.[10]

In Kolkata, at least 20 people were killed in February 2013 in a market fire, while 93 had died in a hospital fire 14 months earlier and there were 45 deaths in a fire in a block of flats in March 2010. Some of the people responsible were arrested, including businessmen who owned the hospital, but that was primarily a political gesture by the state government to appease public criticism and nothing basic was done to improve fire services and clear unsafe buildings. It was reported in Delhi in April 2013 that there were only ten inspectors for the city's 30,000 licensed lifts, none of which had ever lost their licences.[11] This is, of course, not just an Indian problem. One of the most tragic results of faulty construction and irrelevant safety regulations was reported from Dhaka, the capital of Bangladesh, in April 2013 when an eight-storey factory building collapsed, causing the deaths of over 1,100 people who had been working in appalling conditions. Over the previous decade, more than 700 textile and apparel industry workers had died in fires and building disasters.[12]

Such problems are just too enormous to be tackled in the foreseeable future, and the basic attitudes pose greater risks as the economy grows with new technologies. In the light of Japan's Fukushima Daiichi nuclear plant disaster in March 2011, one wonders if India can be relied on to ensure sustained safety standards if it goes ahead with its planned series of nuclear power plants.[13] Union Carbide's pesticide plant disaster in the city of Bhopal in 1984 was basically caused by a disregard for safety and management procedures, as I discovered on a series of visits at the time. The Indian management had ignored a warning issued two years earlier by experts from the US parent company about 'the adequacy of the tank relief valve to relieve a runaway reaction'.[14] That led to the death of over 5,000 people and continued ill health of over 500,000 in one of the world's worst industrial calamities. Nearly 30 years later, the 70-acre site has still not been cleared and cleaned up, and the ground is contaminated with dangerous chemicals at over 500 times the Indian standard levels.[15] Gaunt rusting steel structures and dilapidated factory buildings stand as a grim reminder of poor company management and inadequate government control, and nothing has been learned.

Notes

1. http://ridingtheelephant.wordpress.com/2012/02/14/thinkers-ponder-whats-amiss-in-india-is-it-jugaad/

2. 'Lauded by the World', *Business Standard*, 27 July 2013, http://www.business-standard.com/article/beyond-business/lauded-by-the-world-113072601051_1.html

3. 'Thinkers ponder what's amiss in India – is it jugaad?' *Riding the Elephant*, http://wp.me/pieST-1AI

4. 'Jugaad: The Rise of Frugal Innovation, BBC Radio 4, 18 October 2013, *http://www.bbc.co.uk/programmes/b03cv473*

5. Navi Radjou, Jaideep Prabhu and Simone Ahuja, *Jugaad Innovation: A Frugal and Flexible Approach to Innovation for the 21st century*, Random House India, 2012, http://jugaadinnovation.com/

6. JE, 'Manufacturing takes off in India', *Fortune* magazine, 19 October 2007, http://money.cnn.com/2007/10/18/news/international/India_manufacturing.fortune/index.htm

7. Jason Overdorf, *India: Radioactive in Delhi, GlobalPost*, 20 April 2010, http://www.globalpost.com/dispatch/india/100419/india-garbage-delhi-radiation

8. 'India Assessment: 2013', South Asia Terrorism Portal, http://www.satp.org/satporgtp/countries/india/index.html

9. Conversation with JE

10. 'Hands full with highrise checks, BMC fire brigade to expand', *Indian Express*, 25 March 2013, http://www.indianexpress.com/news/hands-full-with-highrise-checks-bmc-fire-brigade-to-expand-cell/1043853

11. 'Delhi has only 10 inspectors for 30,000 lifts', *The Times of India*, 17 April 2013, http://timesofindia.indiatimes.com/eity/delhi/Delhi-has-only-10-inspectors-for-30000-lifts/articleshow/19588179.cms

12. Bangladesh Institute of Labour Studies assessment reported in 'Bangladesh building collapse unlikely to spur reform, experts say'. Mark Magnier, *Los Angeles Times*, describes the disaster and the background. 25 April 2013, http://www.latimes.com/news/nationworld/world/la-fg-bangladesh-collapse-20130426,0,1747667.story

13. http://ridingtheelephant.wordpress.com/2011/03/15/india%E2%80%99s-jugaad-means-its-nuke-power-plans-should-be-dumped/

14. JE, 'Indian plant management warned of safety risks, *Financial Times*,

11 December 1984 – one of a series of *FT* reports by JE from Bhopal on the disaster

15. http://ridingtheelephant.wordpress.com/2009/12/01/serious-chemical-contamination-25-years-after-bhopal%E2%80%99s-lethal-gas-leak-new-study/

2

Fixes and Frugal Benefits

The word jugaad is used for many things. Traditionally, it is the name of a rough pick-up truck type of vehicle assembled in India's northern states of Punjab and Uttar Pradesh with a front end often made from half a motorbike and the rest from a few planks of wood on wheels. It rumbles through towns and villages, belching noisily, overladen with people, animals, farm produce and other goods. Its owners do not usually pay taxes and are in violation of motor vehicle laws, despite occasional government and court attempts to curb its use.[1]

The vehicle was created some 70 years ago in the city of Ludhiana, in Punjab, which has always been a centre for innovation and has grown into one of the world's biggest cycle producing centres – and India's most polluted city.[2] Alongside small fume-generating engineering workshops, Ludhiana's big companies include Hero Cycles and Atlas Cycles, which are among the world's biggest bicycle manufactures and account for 60 per cent of India's sales. 'Originally, the small workshops just produced components, then they gradually assembled them into finished products, generating what is now widely recognized as jugaad,' says Sudarshan Maini, who runs a company in southern India that excels in fine engineering.[3]

Jugaad can also mean fixing a bribe. 'Is there a jugaad?' suggests to a policeman that a payment is being offered to erase a traffic offence. It was used scathingly by a politician in 2012 to describe what he saw as the coalition government's incompetence at 'managing' its continuation in power.[4]. The meaning has been extended to cover frugal or flexible ways of thinking and a whole range of innovative ideas. For example, farmers and fishermen send traders missed mobile phone calls as a signal that they need information on market prices (the caller cancels the call before the other party picks up, so does not have to pay).

When I started to write this book, I needed a new desk chair. I found a smart black mesh reclining model in one of the many shops that have sprung up haphazardly along M.G. Road, a busy highway and metro railway route between Delhi and the new satellite city of Gurgaon. 'The base and arms come from China, the mesh back from Malaysia and the hydraulics and seat are from India,' said G.S. Arora, the owner. 'We put them together in our local factory – that's jugaad, a cheaper chair. Go and buy a branded chair and you'll pay twice as much'. He was proud of the way he cobbled together his chairs, visiting China and Malaysia to source the parts, while his mother managed the shop. His is just one of many companies across the world assembling components from various sources – the booming economy of southern China's industrial coastal zones between Hong Kong, Shenzhen and Guangzhou was built in the 1980s doing just that, but he sees it as part of a national trait.

His price was just over Rs 9,000, so I went to Godrej & Boyce, one of India's largest groups and the best known producer of office furniture, to compare prices. A similar branded chair was Rs 17,000 and would have taken a week or two to deliver, so I went back to M.G. Road and drove away with my jugaad chair. The finish could have been better – rough metal edges on the base needed filing smooth – but it was good value, even though Arora failed to send a mechanic to boost the gas pressure that controls the seat's height adjustment. Someone told me that the height problem was caused by hot weather, and so it proved – when the winter came, the seat stopped sliding downwards. Chalta hai!

There are countless examples of more innovative jugaad-inspired design. In Rajasthan, a small thriving family business is producing handmade paper from elephants' high-fibre dung.[5] A potter in

Gujarat developed a low-cost refrigerator called Mitticool (*mitti* means earth) that is not made of metal and uses no electricity but cools with water seeping through the gadget's clay walls.[6] In a rather upmarket version of the original jugaad vehicle, a farmer in Gujarat developed a small low-cost three-wheeler tractor called the Santi around a Royal Enfield Bullet motorbike, enabling him to replace his costly bullocks for a variety of tasks such as ploughing.[7]

Anvar Alikhan, a senior corporate executive, points to jugaad's roots in what he describes as 'the austere, socialistic India of the 1970s, when we were deprived of everything, and had to make do with whatever we could'. Giving a personal example, he says, 'When I was a teenager, I was shopping for my first music system and the only thing available was a very mediocre Philips system – which in any case was beyond my budget. So I finally bought an ingenious music system put together by an IIT engineer friend, which had its bass speaker placed inside an earthenware matka [terracotta pot]. The sound was terrific.'

People often joke that 'it's jugaad' when they innovate to solve a problem. At Kipling jungle camp on the edge of Kanha National Park in the middle of India, I saw people burning leaves at the bottom of a freshly dug pit, prior to planting a tree. When I asked why, they replied, 'To burn out the termites – it's jugaad.' Another day, a plumber said the same thing when he temporarily nailed a vice, which would normally be fixed on a work bench, into a tree trunk to hold pipes that he needed to bend.

Business in the DNA

This sort of basic industrial innovation comes more naturally to artisanal, farming and other production-oriented communities than to India's mostly trading-based businessmen, according to Harish Damodaran, a business journalist who has studied the caste and regional origins of modern Indian business. He argues that conventionally organized production has never been part of the

DNA of most of India's business class because the people come from bazaar and trading backgrounds and not from manufacturing or laboratories.[8] While these businessmen have been adept at evolving sophisticated trading and financing arrangements, they are not instinctively attuned to assembly lines and machinery. Manual workers, however, in both rural and urban areas, have the ability to innovate, says Damodaran, though they 'lacked the capital to convert any of their raw manufacturing innovations – jugaad – into reliable, marketable products'.

He argues that the resulting divide has had huge implications for innovation in India. 'Indian business innovation has been mostly restricted to marketing and finance, producing for example the hundi system (an indigenous discountable and negotiable bill of exchange enabling seamless movement of goods and money across the subcontinent), fatka (futures transactions rarely resulting in actual delivery of the underlying commodities), teji-mandi (put-and-call-option contracts), goladari (warehouse receipt financing) or even rotating savings-and-credit schemes like nidhis, kuries and chit funds.'

Damodaran's article was pegged to Ranbaxy, a Delhi-based Indian pharmaceutical company, which developed Syniram, India's first original drug, and was taken over in 2008 by Daiichi-Sankyo of Japan. Apart from this malaria treatment, the mainstream pharmaceutical industry, led by Ranbaxy, has mostly grown by developing generic variations of internationally patented drugs. There are a few other examples where Indian manufacturers have proved exceptions to the general lack of manufacturing innovation – almost all are in the auto industry. As Damodaran notes, all the machinery for rice mills and dairy products is imported.

The Jugaad Trap

India's top managers now fear that the jugaad adulation has gone too far. Anand Mahindra, chairman of the Mumbai-based Mahindra

Group, which is strongly focused on innovation, is worried that respect for jugaad and frugal engineering is being overdone. 'Jugaad can be the death of us if we carry on extolling its virtues,' he says.[9] 'It was a point on a trajectory of evolution, giving us technological confidence and self-esteem. That was okay in an economy of scarcity – making do without stuff we didn't have because of shortages, but it is not an end in itself and it perpetuates a lack of self-esteem … It is good to do brainstorming, asking how would we do this if we didn't have what we have. But the rule in a California garage start-up is frugal innovation, so we need to be brutal and realize we didn't invent this and move on, as they do in California to the frontiers of technology.'

Mahindra talks about the 'jugaad trap' of equating different ways of thinking with what used to be known as 'appropriate technology'. This, he says, 'is the most dangerous phrase ever invented – appropriate technology is an act of condescension and makes you think the consumer will make do with lower quality finish, features or aesthetics.'[10] That reminded me of the fashion for appropriate technology in the 1980s, when foreign companies would ship old production lines to India to make products ranging from cars to steelworks and pulp mills – and India would be grateful and inefficient.

Carlos Ghosn, head of Renault and Nissan, is credited with bringing the phrase 'frugal engineering' to India, where consultants and the media seized on it as a simple headline-grabbing concept. Ghosn was about to make a saloon car, the Logan, with the Mahindra group and was impressed, at the launch in 2006, that the procurement costs were 15 per cent below budget. 'He asked me how we did it, and said we must be emulating "frugal engineering",' Anand Mahindra told me.[11] (The two companies did not follow through on their joint venture plans. Like many other foreign companies' entry products in the past 20 years, the Logan looked too boring for the price and did not meet the demands of India's aspirational market. Mahindra relaunched it as the lower-priced Verito.)

The Nano Story

Ravi Kant, vice chairman and former managing director of Tata Motors, describes jugaad as a 'quick and dirty solution to problems, not an ideal solution but one that works'. A juggaru, he says, is a person who has been able to do this. 'It's positive that he has done it, but negative that it may have been done through short cuts and not be ideal.'[12] He says that the tiny but spacious 624cc Tata Nano, launched as the world's cheapest car in 2009 when he was Tata Motors' managing director, is 'an example of frugal engineering which reduces costs, but unlike jugaad, does not compromise on quality'.

The Nano has indeed often been praised as an example of low-cost manufacturing, but its price was made possible partly by substantial state government loans, tax subsidies, and other state government concessions that were initially agreed for a site at Singur in West Bengal.[13] The terms were later matched and even improved, when Tata moved the factory to Gujarat[14] after the Singur site became a trailblazer for violent social and political protests against the use of rich agricultural land for industry. Tata also cut costs, and the eventual price, by squeezing component suppliers' profit margins.

The vehicle development story is well told in a Tata-promoted book, *Small Wonder: The Making of the Nano*.[15] It tracks the excitement of the car's evolution, watched over by Ratan Tata, whose interest in design and cars led him to be more personally involved in Tata Motors than most other companies in the group when he was chairman of Tata Sons from 1991 to the end of 2012. He encouraged revolutionary ideas for the Nano that were eventually abandoned, such as having a plastic body and no doors, and assembling the car at small franchised workshops around the country.

Eventually, the car, though stylish, did not break significant new ground. It made manufacturing savings by being very small – 10ft long and just over 5ft wide – and by cutting a four-cylinder engine from an earlier Tata car, the Indica, in half. It has three nuts instead of four on tiny wheels, and one large windscreen wiper instead of two. The tail-gate does not open, so access to luggage and the radiator is from behind the rear seats, as is the all-aluminium rear engine that can only be accessed by unscrewing six butterfly nuts and lifting off the cover.[16] These economies made frugal engineering an end in itself,[17] whereas many engineers would argue that it should be used to develop new ideas at a low cost. (Tata Motors now has more interesting plans for car bodies made of composite materials[18] along with other innovations, but that is for the future.)

Sadly, the Nano turned out to be a misguided concept and the launch, which was staged as a mega media event, was preceded for several years by a grossly overdone worldwide public relations blitz. There was even a pop-star-style unveiling of the 'Peoples' Car' at Delhi's biennial auto show in January 2008.[19] The extent of the unreal hype was illustrated by a blog on the *Financial Times* website written by Suhel Seth, a Delhi-based television pundit who runs a brand marketing company and has been an adviser to some Tata companies. He wrote excitedly about 'the launch of a million possibilities' under the headline 'Why India Needs a Nano'. He wrongly, as later events showed, described it as 'a vehicle for Indian aspirations' and one that was 'a car for the people'.[20] He claimed that it would be seen 'with awe and pride', and had 'many firsts' to its credit. 'From a marketing perspective, it has already gone into the lexicon of India's people and the fact that Tata called it a people's car is even more suggestive of the transfer of ownership of the brand from a company to its users: the people,' wrote Seth. Rarely has the *FT* been so far removed from reality.[21] I wrote a rejoinder to Seth's article on my 'Riding the Elephant' blog headlined 'Tata's "One-Lakh" Nano: Let's Cool the Hype' which appeared on FT.com alongside his piece.

Cost increases meant that Tata could only sell a very basic no-frills version (without air conditioning) at the 'one lakh car' (Rs 100,000) price that Ratan Tata originally promised, so the slogan became a marketing drag. Aspirational Indian families, who Tata dreamed of upgrading from unsafe overloaded scooters, did not want to own the world's cheapest product. Many would not have had space to park it near their homes in cramped narrow streets.

Production of the Nano was initially held up because of the move from West Bengal to Gujarat. The launch had to be delayed and Ravi Kant and his team had the monumental task of setting up a temporary production line at another Tata plant in five months. 'That was a nightmare. I don't think any auto company in the world has done that,' says Kant. Output recovered after a new factory was established in Gujarat, but the combination of the price, customer apathy and slow production build-up (plus some electrical fires in the cars) meant that only 175,000 were sold in the first two years compared with a production capacity of 250,000 a year. Later, the Nano was revamped with stylish colour schemes and a bigger engine with the aim of becoming an iconic low-priced car that would appeal to the middle class, not mass buyers.

While the Nano remained frugal, a family engineering company in Bengaluru was showing how to develop new engineering at low cost with plastic-bodied electric cars.

The Reva Dream

'Frugal engineering is jugaad plus innovation,' says Sudarshan Maini, an engineering enthusiast and perfectionist. 'When you see that jugaad is not producing the right quality and quantity for what you need, you innovate further to achieve it. That makes it a stepping stone to both innovation and frugal engineering.'

On my first visit to India in 1982, Maini held up a small precision-tuned automotive component between his fingers. 'This is what we can produce in India,' he proudly told me, standing in the Bengaluru factory of Maini Precision Products, a company he had set up nine years earlier to prove he could turn out international quality engineering components to micro tolerances and attract export customers. The finely machined and ground component was a cast iron lapping mandrel with a tolerance of 1 micron which, Maini explained, ensured the fine internal finish needed for fuel injection systems. Such levels of precision were all but unknown in

India. Maini became motivated at the beginning of his career in the 1960s at Guest Keen & Williams (part of the British GKN group) in Kolkata. 'So much was being talked about poor quality, but I knew we could produce the best quality in the world,' he says.[22]

Maini's memories illustrate the problems that the manufacturing industry faced in the early decades of independence. He was frustrated by the standards of work and by 'lots of wasteful scrap and poor production' at the Koltata factory when he took over as the company's first Indian assistant manager. Employees were work-shy and management was weak. He tells a story about a man who had been given two weeks' leave every year for the previous five years after producing telegrams that said his father had died.

'I called him and asked, "How many fathers do you have?",' says Maini. 'He was very upset and said he was going to kill the personal officer who had taken 500 rupees every year for getting the leave sanctioned.'

In the mid 1990s, General Motors (GM) started buying components from India and selected Maini, which became the American company's smallest supplier. The components that GM needed were difficult to make because machining operations left complicated burrs (rough edges) on the metal surface. The order was for 8,000 pieces a day, which required 45 women just to remove the burrs. Jugaad came into play when the Mainis thought of a simple low-cost solution – a small device that enabled the burrs to be seen through a 45-degree mirror, making removal easy and reducing the number of workers involved to two.

'If General Motors tells us it needs a special component in 30 days, we do a jugaad solution for that sort of fast development and production, maybe making it manually,' says Sandeep, Maini's eldest son, who now heads the group. The second stage is to put in a process to make the component reliably, and that means producing it by appropriate technology that is not jugaad – the process equals reliability.

Maini's enthusiasm for perfection led the group to expand sales from Rs 1 crore in 1982 to Rs 350 crore in 2012, with 70 per cent of the production being exported and a product range that was diversified from automobile components to higher levels of precision engineering for the defence and aviation industries. Companies like Bosch, BAE, Boeing, Volvo and GE have become customers and the group is also into specialist vehicles and plastics, and is looking at automated logistics systems and warehousing.

Maini's youngest son, Chetan, expanded the family's engineering traditions by spending 15 years pioneering electric cars, which culminated in March 2013 in the launch of the latest 'e20' version of a car called the Reva.[23] Chetan Maini's interest in electric cars began with model vehicles when he was a child. While studying at the University of Michigan in the US, he worked, in 1990, on General Motors' award-winning Sunracer solar-powered racing car, and in 1994, he co-founded the Reva Electric Car Company (RECC).

The Reva was first developed with an American company and the Mainis saved costs by sending some components from India, including a dashboard instrument panel from an established manufacturer in Coimbatore, the jugaad capital of southern India. 'We designed and developed the testing equipment for a variety of components, including batteries, which on an average cost us less than 1 per cent of what we would normally pay if we bought the same in the market – a typical jugaad example,' says Sudarshan Maini. Assembly of the electric cars started in 2001, with five people producing the first seven vehicles in Bengaluru. To avoid having to build an assembly track for the small quantities, the car's tubular metal frame was put on wheels and pushed down the production line.

Eventually, to become a global brand, Reva needed more funds than the family was prepared to risk, and in 2010, the Mahindra auto-based group bought a 56 per cent stake in a new company, Mahindra Reva Electric Vehicles. Mahindra put in a total investment of Rs 100 crore and the Maini family holds a 24.6 per cent stake.[24] The e20 is being produced at a new factory where 35 per cent of the energy needs are solar powered. The factory can produce 30,000 cars a year, a relatively small number by auto industry standards, but it is substantial for electric vehicles and a huge increase from the 4,000 older Revas sold till 2012. The 2013 sales target was a modest 400–500 vehicles, priced at around Rs 6 lakh, so it is not cheap.

It seems sad for a family that put so much effort and money into the project for 15 years to have to lose control. 'We had mixed emotions about letting go,' says Sandeep, explaining the catch-22 situation that they could not get financial backing till they produced a viable model and production line, which could not be done without funds. 'We didn't have deep pockets – we were technical creators, and we also needed competence to develop markets and car manufacturing processes.' Mahindra met those requirements. Anand Mahindra is committed to using frugal engineering to drive innovation and, having talked to various other companies, the Mainis felt that he had the most commitment to electric vehicles and appreciation of what Chetan, who is still in charge as Mahindra Reva's chief executive, had been trying to achieve.

In recognition of his work, Chetan was awarded *The Economist* magazine group's Innovation Award for Energy and the Environment in 2011.[25] The dream is that the e20 could become the first electric car in the world to make a profit, but that will be difficult, given the price and the lack of demand for such vehicles. Sudarshan has told the story of the Reva in a book published in 2013.[26]

The family is proud of its frugally engineered innovation, which has broken new ground with all-electric power, zero emissions and solar power battery-charging ports. Drivers can have access to the car from a smart phone app that can control air conditioning and locking controls, and trigger a remote emergency battery charge system. 'It's definitely been worthwhile as a pioneering effort that doesn't come along every day,' says Gautam, Sudarshan's middle son. 'We gained a lot of respect because people know we put our own money at stake,' says Sandeep.

Notes

1. 'SC brakes on road "menace"', *The Telegraph*, 16 May 2013, http://www.telegraphindia.com/1130516/jsp/nation/story_16904625.jsp#.UfjbXqyfouQ

2. 'Ludhiana fails to shed most-polluted city tag', *Tribune,* http://www.tribuneindia.com/2012/20121004/ldh1.htm

3. Sudarshan Maini, founder of Maini Precision Products of Bangalore, in conversation with JE.

4. 'UPA is a "jugaad" expert: Nitish Kumar', *The Times of India*, 18 September 2012, http://articles.timesofindia.indiatimes.com/2012-09-18/india/ 33925129_1_upa-allies-fdi-decision-upa-government

5. 'The Scoop on Poop', *Business Today*, 19 August 2012

6. Described in Navi Radjou, Jaideep Prabhu and Simone Ahuja, *Jugaad Innovation*

7. 'He bit the Bullet, turned it into farm equipment', *The Times of India*, 23 May 2012, http://www.nif.org.in/dwn_files/Print.pdf

8. 'Why "Made in India" is just a slogan', Harish Damodaran, *Business Line,* 8 May 2012, http://www.thehindubusinessline.com/opinion/columns/harish-damodaran/article3397771.ece

9. Anand Mahindra in conversation with JE, March 2012

10. 'Thinking Differently: The state of Indian innovation', *Fortune India,* April 2012

11. Anand Mahindra in conversation with JE, March 2012

12. Ravi Kant in conversation with JE, March 2012

13. Tata Motors' West Bengal package of loans, tax concessions and other benefits for the Nano site, which matched an earlier offer from the state of Uttarakhand, is available on http://www.wbidc.com/images/pdf/Agreement%20between%20TML,%20WBIDC%20and%20Government%20of%20West%20Bengal.pdf; Tata requested in 2008 that it should not be publicized and obtained a court order to keep it secret.

14. 'Ratan Tata announces Nano plant in Gujarat', 19 January 2009, 'Asked about the overall deal offered by the Gujarat government, Tata said, "It is as good as or slightly better than the one we had previously," (in West Bengal)' http://www.timesnow.tv/Nano-to-roll-out-of-Sanand-Gujarat/articleshow/4312189.cms; In 2010, Tata disputed Gujarat's estimate of the size of a substantial soft loan, the first instalment of

which was eventually paid in February 2013, http://timesofindia. indiatimes.com/business/india-business/Tata-Motors-get-first-part-of-assured-funds-from-Gujarat/articleshow/18652120.cms

15. *Small Wonder – the making of the Nano*, http://www.westlandbooks.in/ book_details.php?cat_id=5&book_id=209

16. 'Nano test drive review', *AutoCar India*, 19 August 2009, http://www. autocarindia.com/Review/269238,tata-nano-old.aspx

17. http://ridingtheelephant.wordpress.com/2012/12/29/ratan-tata-indias-sensitive-and-visionary-tycoon-steps-down/

18. 'Tata Motors bets on series of launches, including a low-cost composite car', *Economic Times*, 24 February 2013, http://economictimes. indiatimes.com/news/news-by-industry/auto/automobiles/et-exclusive-tata-motors-next-gen-for-road-ahead--a-prototype-of-low-cost-car/articleshow/18648578.cms

19. http://ridingtheelephant.wordpress.com/2008/01/10/nano-achieves-ratan-tata%E2%80%99s-dream/

20. 'Why India needs a Nano', Suhel Seth, FT.com, 22 March 2009, http:// www.ft.com/cms/s/0/8003d9f8-16a9-11de-9a72-0000779fd2ac. html

21. 'Tata's "One-Lakh" Nano – let's cool the hype, *http://ridingtheelephant. wordpress.com/2009/03/23/tata%E2%80%99s-%E2%80%9Cone-lakh%E2%80%9D-nano-%E2%80%93-let%E2%80%99s-cool-the-hype/ and FT.com 23 March 2009 http://www.ft.com/cms/s/0/2b47c97e-178f-11de-8c9d-0000779fd2ac.html*

22. Sudarshan Maini and his sons Sandeep and Gautam in conversation with JE, Bangalore, December 2012.

23. http://ridingtheelephant.wordpress.com/2013/03/19/indian-engineering-excellence-produces-a-new-reva-electric-car/

24. 'Why Mahindra & Mahindra needs Reva', *Forbes India*, 10 June 2010, http://forbesindia.com/article/big-bet/why-mahindra-mahindra-needs-reva/14052/0 and Chetan Maini interview, same date, http:// forbesindia.com/interview/magazine-extra/chetan-maini-spells-out-the-rationale-behind-selling-reva/14062/0

25. http://www.economistconferences.co.uk/innovation/energyandtheenviron mentwinner2011

26. Dr S.K. Maini with Sandhya Mendonca, *Reva EV: India's Green Gift to the World*, Random House India, 2012, http://www.randomhouse. co.in/BookDetails.aspx?BookId=toXun7mSaq0%3d

3

Fault Lines

Jugaad and chalta hai do India more damage on a macro level. They build fault lines that undermine and erode established institutional systems that are central to the functioning of a society and economy. They contribute to India's failures to operate efficiently and instil a lack of responsibility that stretches from opposition parties blocking parliamentary proceedings to failure to mend broken roads and tackle public health risks. The self-centred focus of society comes into play here. For example, if chalta hai will keep the country functioning at a tolerable level, the opposition parties in parliament need have no qualms about pursuing their own interests and stymieing the government's attempts to pass legislation. Parliament lost between 70 per cent and 80 per cent of available working time in the 2012 monsoon session because of opposition demonstrations and about 50 per cent was similarly lost in the 2013 Budget session,[1] up from a third in 2011 and over 40 per cent in 2010.[2]

Similarly, if jugaad and chalta hai together keep the country's defence forces equipped and operating at what appears to be a tolerable level, the defence establishment (which includes grossly inefficient public sector corporations) can afford to look after its own interests with comfortable jobs, patronage and the luxury of dealing with foreign suppliers and their agents, while restricting the ambit of the more efficient private sector. Similarly, the aviation ministry and government-owned Air India can wallow in the luxury and spoils of crony patronage while the airline declines and airports are developed

largely for the benefit of the companies involved. There are similar
self-serving examples across the public sector.

'Total inadequacy of our politico-administrative apparatus to our
needs is our single worst peril,' says K. Shankar Bajpai.[3] 'It comes
from the sort of considerations, or thinking, that nowadays shape our
decision-making and behaviour – what Marx called *kleinburgerlich* –
ignorant, pettily self-seeking, parochial, inappropriate if not wholly
irrelevant, of course with no thought of India.'[4]

Gautam Ahuja, professor of business administration and strategy
at the University of Michigan, has suggested that India's 'limited
institutional capital and inadequate or poorly functioning institutions'
have boosted the development of jugaad. By institutional capital
he means formal and informal organizations, rules and norms that
have 'broad acceptance in a society and that facilitate and enable the
productive activities of that economy'.

In a speech in Delhi in 2011,[5] he painted a picture of modern India
without naming it, saying: 'When the ordinary people in a society
adopt an approach that is openly dismissive of those rules and laws,
or if the government applies the laws in a fitful, selective or capricious
manner, you have a society in which institutional capital is lacking.
In such a society, contracts are not binding, corruption and bribery
are an accepted fact of social life, and the laws and norms are followed
when it suits an individual. It is in such a society that teachers do
not teach, students are not trained, and health-care is not provided
because the resources "leak" away before they reach their intended
recipient ... If unchecked, this lack of institutional capital spreads
from one sphere of activity to another – from business to education
to politics, the society becomes a nonchalant accepter of this way of
life.' This links with the fact that the way to get things done in India
– especially if a government is involved – is not to follow a process or
a procedure but to find someone who can fix something.

Ahuja acknowledged that India had learned to innovate frugally
but said that 'quick fix' represented three failures. The first was the
system not working. Second, the more often a system failure was

solved through a jugaad, the more likely it was that the system would completely break down. 'Systems work through processes and routines being followed, not by exceptions being created,' he wrote. 'Every jugaad introduces an exception into the system. With sufficient jugaad over time, there is no worthwhile process left and the system eventually collapses to ineffectiveness.' The third failure was that 'a person who gets used to jugaad, or short-circuiting one given system, often then moves down the slippery slope and loses respect for other systems too', and that led to the collapse of other systems. 'Thus the practice of jugaad can lead to a vicious cycle, in which institutions are steadily undermined.'

'Master of Jugaad'

In the private sector, the licence and quota-based controlled economy introduced by Nehru after independence in 1947 made it inevitable that companies would look for jugaad-style ways around the controls, setting Ahuja's 'vicious cycle' trend that continues today in a partially liberalized economy. The Reliance conglomerate, which was founded in 1966 by Dhirubhai Ambani and is now run by his sons Mukesh and Anil as two separate businesses (Reliance Industries and Reliance Group), has been a leading practitioner in Ahuja's cycle of using jugaad to undermine institutions.

Reliance Industries is one of India's biggest groups with interests stretching from polyester, petrochemicals, oil and gas exploration and refining to retail stores. It has thrived through well-placed contacts, as Hamish McDonald, an Australian journalist, has recounted in a revealing book, *Ambani and Sons*.[6] By 1980, Dhirubhai Ambani 'had a close and sympathetic friend as minister of commerce, the Bengali politician Pranab Mukherjee'.[7] (Mukherjee became finance minister in 1982, a post he returned to between 2009 and 2012, having also been external affairs and defence minister in a career that culminated in him becoming President of India in 2012.) Earlier, McDonald reported, Prime Minister Indira Gandhi had given 'a parting gift' to Ambani just before her government lost power in 1977 when she exempted all polyester yarn imports from customs duty. That was 'a gift of Rs 37.5m to Dhirubhai'.[8] McDonald also wrote that Dhirubhai had 'put his resources' behind Gandhi's efforts to split India's coalition government that took office in 1977. In the late 1980s, he 'swung the appointment' of a Reserve Bank of India deputy governor. The book revealed how the government was suborned and policies bent, stock markets manipulated, competitors unethically harassed and undermined, opponents pursued with vendettas, and business partners and suppliers treated roughly.[9]

Dhirubhai Ambani combined this with excellent project management, which has been widely recognized, but he also enjoyed displaying his inside knowledge. A public relations executive told me how he had once offered him a job, saying that a major part of the role would be to discover in advance what big stories were being prepared by leading newspapers and magazines. When asked why, he replied, 'So that I can say to someone when I meet them at an airport, "I hear that so-and-so magazine is doing a big article on you – congratulations." He will then be impressed with my good information.' A parallel story is told by Anand Giridharadas, an American journalist, in *India Calling*.[10] He recounts how a former Reliance manager told him that a woman executive from Enron, the now-defunct fraud-ridden American power company, told Dhirubhai in the 1990s that Enron had become as powerful in India as Reliance. Dhirubhai's reply, according to the manager, went something like this: 'Yesterday at 2.19 p.m., you arrived at the finance ministry to meet so-and-so official. You talked about this issue and that issue. You left the office at two-thirty-five.' The Enron official, stunned, muttered, 'OK, maybe almost as powerful.' (The reference was presumably to Rebecca Mark, a flamboyant executive based in the company's Houston head office, who was in charge of Enron in India.)

Mukesh Ambani stressed to Giridharadas that the focus was on continuity of relationships when doing business, rather than being 'transactional' on individual deals. Asked about helping bureaucrats' children find and pay for places in American colleges, he acknowledged that an executive or a company foundation could have paid. Giridharadas was told by an unnamed source that, with Reliance, 'once you join, you're there for life'. This included both active and retired journalists and bureaucrats. When I was researching an article for *Fortune* magazine in 2002, shortly after Dhirubhai Ambani had died, a rival businessman told me, 'They don't listen to stories about their bad public image because they think they can buy their way out of any problem.' I tackled Mukesh on the allegations in an interview and he claimed there was 'a difference between image and reality' and added: 'In the '80s I used to get upset – now I realize they [the criticisms] are natural in a democracy where people are going to say this sort of thing – this is not China.'

The fixing has been lauded by at least two leading writers – Arun Shourie, originally a campaigning newspaper editor and then an MP and BJP government minister, and Swaminathan Aiyar, a leading political commentator and journalist. At a meeting in 2003 to commemorate the first anniversary of Dhirubhai's death, Shourie paraphrased Friedrich Hayek, a Nobel prize-winning economist. Previously a critic of Reliance's business ethics, Shourie surprisingly praised the Ambanis for undermining government policy. 'By exceeding the limits in which restrictions sought to impound them', companies such as Reliance had 'helped create the case for scrapping regulations', he said.[11] (There are many other examples of companies 'exceeding limits' in this book, but few of them can be seen in the same pioneering light as Reliance.)

Aiyar perceptively tied what the Ambanis did directly with jugaad, and applauded them because they broke through restrictions that were impeding their business growth. In an article headed 'Jugaad Is Our Most Precious Resource',[12] Aiyar wrote in 2010 that 'Dhirubhai Ambani was the master of jugaad. The licence-permit raj made it impossible for him to progress legally, so he exploited the corruption and cynicism of the system. He exported junk to get profitable import entitlements. He created industrial capacities vastly in excess of licensed capacity. He imported huge textile machines as "spare parts". He engineered highly profitable changes in rules for polyester imports and telecom licences. The jugaad he used to overcome hurdles was not distinguishable from crony capitalism.' Yet, Aiyar added, when the licence-permit raj gave way to a more open and deregulated economy, Dhirubhai used the same jugaad 'to scale dizzying heights of productivity' and become world class. 'He showed that manipulation and world-class productivity are two sides of the same coin called jugaad. If governments create business constraints through controls and high taxes, jugaad will be used to overcome those hurdles. But if deregulation abolishes these hurdles, the main business constraints become lack of quality and affordability, so jugaad shifts to improving productivity, quality and affordability. That ultimately makes you world class.'

Using jugaad to become 'world class', of course, also undermines basic ethics as well as institutions, so once companies had less need to bypass controls after 1991, many moved on to bribing politicians and officials for favourable allocation of natural resources, sometimes investing jointly with them. As Ahuja wrote, 'the practice of jugaad can lead to a vicious cycle, in which institutions are steadily undermined.'

In an era of growing corruption and collusion between politicians and businessmen, this reduction in the role of institutional systems weakens accountability, notably of parliament and the government. This was particularly evident in 2011 and 2012 when popular anti-corruption movements led by two social rights campaigners, Anna Hazare and Arvind Kejriwal, challenged the authority of the government and, backed by access to right to information legislation, began to expose the depths to which the ethics of the country had sunk.

The erosion of institutions and the practice of fudge have also contributed to an absence of strategy across many areas. George Tanham, who was a respected South Asia and security specialist at America's Rand Corporation policy think tank, controversially wrote in 1992 that 'Indian elites show little evidence of having thought coherently and systematically about national strategy'.[13] He suggested that the situation might have been changing, but what he went on to say is as true today as it was then: 'Few writings offer coherent, articulate beliefs or a clear set of operating principles for Indian strategy. Rather, one finds a complex mix of writings, commentaries and speeches, as well as certain actions that cast some light on Indian strategy. The lacunae and ambiguities seem compatible with a culture that encompasses and accommodates readily to complexity and contradiction. They also seem more confusing to Westerners than to Indians who accept the complexities and contradictions as part of life.'

He was referring mainly to foreign policy and security strategy, but the point is valid far more widely. On foreign affairs, few people – or foreign countries – understand where India stands, and there is no think tank of a top international standard. On economic and industrial policy, there is little overall strategy or consensus covering, for example, economic liberalization or foreign investment. 'One of the biggest weaknesses affecting India's economic liberalization is the way that industrial and allied policies are made,' I wrote on my blog in 2009.[14] 'Changes affecting industries that range from telecoms and banks to aviation and retail stem far more from the pressures of vested interests and lobbies than from reasoned analysis and debate.' The reforms of 1991 were introduced because of a financial crisis and, though they have not been reversed, widening them is highly controversial and they are not underpinned as part of an overall strategy of public policy.

There has also been no clear view on the role of dynasty in politics, and in particular on the role of the Nehru-Gandhi family at the top of the Congress party. Sonia Gandhi, as president of the Congress and head of the ruling UPA coalition after the 2004 general election, pulled strings, jugaad-style, from behind the walls of her Delhi house at 10 Janpath without any clear institutional delineation of her powers in relation to the prime minister. The official line was that Gandhi was in charge of party politics while

Manmohan Singh was in charge of the government, but in practice Gandhi dictated government policy when it suited her. Would such a vague, undemarcated relationship have been possible at the top of a democracy with a strong institutional base?

The leadership vacuum from 2004 was in marked contrast to the previous government when Atal Bihari Vajpayee, the BJP prime minister from 1998, presided with the stature of a statesman and with strong central authority. A brilliant orator but slow speaker who was not given to discursive interviews, Vajpayee did not lead in an outgoing, inspirational sense, but he ruled with authority, mainly through Brajesh Mishra, his national security adviser and principal secretary. Vajpayee was 73 when he became prime minister and relied on Mishra to implement his wishes. Part of his strength was that he always seemed to know what was happening, says Arun Shourie, who was disinvestment and telecoms minister in the Vajpayee government.[15] 'If something was stuck, sometimes Mishra would speak to the Minister concerned directly – a mere indication from him would be enough. But in general, Mishra worked through the secretaries,' says Shourie, referring to the top-ranking civil servants at the top of ministries. 'People heeded him because they knew he was speaking with the full backing of his boss. They knew that he would almost always have sought the prime minister's view before intervening and that, in the rare case in which he may not have done so, would do so the very day he had talked to the minister or secretary.'

'Cracks in the Social Structure'

Traditionally, fault lines in India have involved caste rivalries, clashes between religions and communities, the activities of secessionist groups (at various times, in areas of the north-east, Punjab and Kashmir) and insurgencies. Of these, by 2013, the most serious was the Naxalite movement, but new ones were emerging, especially over the use of land, which were increasing the risks of social unrest and political upheaval while also creating uncertainty and new risks for business. Yogendra Yadav, a social scientist and political analyst who became a founder member of the new anti-corruption Aam Aadmi Party (AAP), has talked about 'how the plunder of natural resources will affect the existing fault lines' and worries 'there are some cracks in the social structure that could take democracy apart'.[16]

The growing role of the states has been changing their relationship with the centre in India's federal system, opening up fault lines in the way the country is run. The relationship is laid down in the country's Constitution but, in practice, regional parties have gained enormous additional ad hoc political clout in recent years since they became members of central government coalitions. Their power was particularly apparent in the 2004 and 2009 Congress-led coalition governments that depended on the support of regional political leaders for their survival. This virtually allowed these regional leaders to dictate what the coalition could or could not do – for example, on land and tax reforms, foreign investment in supermarkets, a river water sharing agreement with Bangladesh.

Pressure on the use of land and rapacious profiteering by real estate and other speculators when land became available for development, have led to bottlenecks that affect economic development and growth. Small landowners, mostly rural and including tribal groups, have opposed their lands being used for mining and industrial development. This, along with the growing impact of the Naxalite rebels, has led to social unrest and protests in both rural and urban areas.

Legislation conferring a right to information that was passed in 2005 has opened up a new fault line – albeit a very constructive one – because, as in other countries, governments can no longer assume that deliberations will remain confidential. Coupled with rising popular pressure against corruption, it has made politicians vulnerable to sudden and unforeseen exposure of corrupt dealings and has undermined the image and authority of the government and of politicians. It has also slowed down decision-making because politicians and bureaucrats have become nervous of being accused, rightly or wrongly, of corruption. This combination of jugaad, chalta hai and emerging fault lines has led to increasingly dramatic and extensive project failures in recent years that have compounded India's traditional crab-like approach to decision-making and execution. The best-documented and most shaming events were the Commonwealth Games preparations in 2010, and a day in July 2012 when power supplies to half of India's population were cut for up to eleven hours – said to be a world record.

All international games have their moments of crises before they start, but Delhi's went to an extreme with its inefficiency, bad governance, shoddy work and corruption. This led to international rejection of 'filthy and uninhabitable' conditions at the athletes' village, just 13 days before the games were due to begin, which coincided with the collapse of a new steel arch footbridge near the main sports stadium. Among many other problems, the flats were incomplete or had quickly become dilapidated after being invaded by construction workers (and stray dogs) seeking refuge from their grossly inadequate labour camps in unusually heavy monsoon rain. The basic problem was that there were too many people nominally in charge, with no top-down coordination and leadership. Those responsible for various aspects of the preparations and operations included Delhi's chief minister and the central government's ministers for urban development and sports, none of whom had the calibre or authority to lead such a mega event, especially not Suresh Kalmadi, chairman of India's Commonwealth Games Organizing Committee. Manmohan Singh and his Prime Minister's Office (PMO) should have taken an early lead, but he played his usual role of standing back from the fray, and the PMO lacked punch. Singh should have been encouraged to step in by Sonia Gandhi, but nothing happened, and Sonia and her son and heir Rahul did not deign – or dare – to become involved.

In 1982, Sonia's husband, Rajiv Gandhi, who was then a Congress party general secretary, had taken charge of preparations for Delhi's Asian Games when they had fallen behind schedule.[17] As in 2010, there were 'vast numbers of overlapping government committees and over-spends, with construction workers leading miserable underfed lives,' wrote Ved Mehta in *Rajiv Gandhi and Rama's Kingdom.*[18] 'The whole exercise is being transformed by unscrupulous entrepreneurs with political pull into a money spinning operation,' Mehta wrote, quoting *The Hindu* newspaper. 'It has led to widespread hoarding and black-marketing of construction material. pushing up costs and, in the process, filling the pockets of the privileged few...' Yet, 26 years later, India had learned no lessons and the Gandhis stayed away – though, ultimately, the games went well and India won 38 gold medals, coming second to Australia.[19] Chalta hai!

Multiple accusations of corruption and extortion led to court cases against officials led by Kalmadi, a flamboyant, wealthy and well-connected politician in the Congress party. He had made a career out of heading sports administrative bodies, including the Indian Olympic Association, and was the chairman of the games' organizing committee. He was booed at the opening ceremony because he was seen as the leader of all that had gone wrong. The boos reflected the pent-up anger and frustration of Delhi-ites who saw this blustering responsibility-dodging part-time politician as the focal point for failures that had blackened India's international image.[20] He was jailed, pending trial, for ten months in 2011. He was then released on bail and was, unsurprisingly, rehabilitated into some activities of the Congress party though he was no longer socially acceptable. In February 2013, he was put on trial along with nine others on charges linked to a Swiss firm's contract for the games' timing, scoring and results system, but there was no sign of action against many others in the Delhi government and elsewhere who were suspected of involvement in corrupt deals.

The other major breakdown of infrastructure occurred when the national power grid failed in July 2012. It was overloaded by at least three states drawing more than their authorized share of electricity. A few days earlier, there had been a similar shutdown affecting a quarter of the population. About one-third of the 174 gigawatts of electricity generated in India annually is either stolen or lost in the conductors and transmission equipment that form the country's distribution grid, contributing, along with slow project development, to a shortfall of close to 10 per cent in supplies.[21] Jugaad usually solves the problem, partially and expensively, with power generated by large private power plants in factories and portable generators in individual homes and shops.

On the same night as the biggest black-out, a fire on an express train killed 32 people. Two months earlier, 29 people had died in two train collisions.[22] Although very different occurrences, these infrastructure failures stemmed from the country's generally laid-back approach to tackling and curing problems, in the hope that they would go away. In both cases, there was a lack of focused political management. The railway minister at the time was Mukul Roy, a minor politician from West Bengal, who spent most of his time in the state, doing the bidding of his political boss, Mamata Banerjee, the chief minister, who herself had earlier been an absentee railways minister. Like Banerjee, Mukul rarely visited his railways ministry office in Delhi.

Sushilkumar Shinde, who had been minister of power for three years, was not wholly responsible for the grid failures because power supplies are managed by individual states. He should, however, have put more effort into tackling India's overall energy crisis, which had been left to fester by the government, from the prime minister downwards. In particular, insufficient effort had been made to speed up delayed coal deliveries from the badly run government-owned Coal India, which had caused power stations to cut output and even shut down. Management of coal production had also been disrupted by a crisis over corrupt mining licenses. Shinde could have used his political clout to demand more action on these fronts.

Notes

1. Parliament Session Wrap, PRS Legislative Research, http://www.
    prsindia.org/parliamenttrack/parliament-updates/parliament-session-
    wrap-budget-2013-2746/
2. http://www.prsindia.org/parliamenttrack/vital-stats/
3. K. Shankar Bajpai in conversation with JE, October 2012
4. K. Shankar Bajpai, 'The closing on the Indian Mind', *The Hindu*, 29
    May 2012, http://www.thehindu.com/opinion/lead/article3466593.
    ece
5. 'Inclusive Growth for the Bottom of the Pyramid', The C.K. Prahalad
    Memorial Lecture by Prof Gautam Ahuja, 9 January 2011, http://
    www.pravasitoday.com/prof-c-k-prahalad-memorial-lecture-by-prof-
    gautam-ahuja-at-pbd-2011-complete-text-and-video
6. The Ambani story was told by Hamish McDonald, an Australian
    journalist, in *The Polyester Prince*, Allen & Unwin NSW, Australia
    1998, which the Ambanis arranged to have withdrawn from
    publication in India. It was reprinted in two modified and extended
    2010 editions: *Ambani & Sons*, Roli Books, Delhi, and *Mahabharata
    in Polyester*, University of New South Wales Press, Sydney.
7. *The Polyester Prince,* Allen & Unwin NSW, Australia 1998, p. 52.
8. Ibid., p. 47.
9. 'An Ambani Story gets a makeover', *Mail Today,* pp. 20–21, by JE,
    3 October 2010, http://epaper.mailtoday.in/epaperhome.aspx?issue=
    3102010 and on http://ridingtheelephant.wordpress.com/2010/10/03/
    ambani-sons-%E2%80%93-revived-from-the-polyester-prince-they-
    pulped/
10. *India Calling,* Anand Giridharadas, HarperCollins India 2011, http://
    www.harpercollins.co.in/BookDetail.asp?Book_Code=2740
11. 'Indian telecoms – The right connections', *The Economist*, 18
    December 2003, http://www.economist.com/node/2304669
12. S.A. Aiyar, 'Jugaad is our most precious resource', *The Economic
    Times*, 15 August 2010, http://articles.economictimes.indiatimes.
    com/2010-08-15/news/27567823_1_jugaad-frugal-engineering-
    innovation
13. George Tanham, *Indian Strategic Thought*, Rand Corporation, 1992,
    http://books.google.co.in/books?id=sOsCAAAACAAJ&dq=Tanham

+%E2%80%9CIndian+strategic+thought%22&hl=en&sa=X&ei=A
qarUNraCMHprAfWkoDQDA&ved=0CDIQ6AEwAg

14. *http://ridingtheelephant.wordpress.com/2009/02/18/india%E2%80%
    99s-fdi-changes-reveal-weaknesses-in-industrial-policy-making/*

15. In conversation with JE, September 2013

16. Yogendra Yadav, speaking on 'Fault Lines of Democracy', at a King's
    College India Institute (London) conference, 'Making Sense of India',
    in Delhi, September 2012

17. http://ridingtheelephant.wordpress.com/2010/07/19/history-
    repeated-as-delhi-judders-leaderless-towards-the-commonwealth-
    games/

18. Ved Mehta, *Rajiv Gandhi and Rama's Kingdom*, Penguin Books India,
    1995; *Yale* University Press, 1996, *http://www.amazon.com/Rajiv-
    Gandhi-Ramas-Kingdom-Mehta/dp/0300068581*

19. 'The games end well – in a week of other incredible India scams', Riding
    the Elephant blog, 15 October 2010, http://wp.me/pieST-15y

20. http://ridingtheelephant.wordpress.com/2010/10/04/boos-and-
    cheers-clear-the-air-for-a-vibrant-commonwealth-games/

21. 'World's Greatest Power Thieves Keep 400m Indians in Dark',
    Bloomberg TV, 1 June 2011, Power Secretary P. Uma Shankar gave
    the statistics in an interview. http://www.bloomberg.com/news/2011-
    05-31/world-s-greatest-power-thieves-keep-400-million-indians-in-
    dark.html

22. http://ridingtheelephant.wordpress.com/2012/07/31/creaking-india-
    hit-by-power-and-railway-failures/

4

Planning the Unplanned

India's cities have a rich architectural and cultural legacy. It ranges from the Mughal tombs and British-era imperial government buildings of New Delhi to the Rajput palaces and forts of Rajasthan, and the Hindu temples of the eastern coastline. But the legacy is being lost in modern India because of a lack of planning controls and corruption. This is partly a result of the lucrative powers of patronage and a laid-back approach that assumes planning can be fixed when the need arises.

Huge swathes of India's towns and cities have grown unlawfully without official permissions, especially in the 2000s, to meet the needs of rapid economic growth. They have done so without the necessary infrastructure of roads, water and power supplies, and sewage and drainage facilities. About 75 per cent of the country's cities have no master plan,[1] and there are few sustained programmes of infrastructure development and maintenance. This has brought India to the brink of a national crisis. Between 30 per cent and 50 per cent of water supplies are lost in transit in most Indian cities, and less than 30 per cent of officially recorded sewage is treated in adequate facilities.[2]

Since the days of Mahatma Gandhi, who regarded the 'growth of cities as an evil thing',[3] populist political focus has been on rural development and financial support for the rural poor, not the needs of urban areas. Urban planning was started by Jawaharlal Nehru in the early days of India's independence, but it provided a restrictive framework that failed to inspire orderly urban expansion and has been exploited for decades by well-connected developers. Few government officials seem to care about urban decline. Those that are aware of what is needed can do little to ensure that state governments draw up and implement plans, though a start was made in 2007 with a government aid scheme, the Jawaharlal Nehru National Urban Renewal Mission (JNNURM), which has yet to have a significant impact.

Nehru envisaged 300 planned cities by the end of the twentieth century. Instead, there are now only a handful, led by Chandigarh, a grid-based city planned by Le Corbusier, the French architect who also designed the city's raw concrete government buildings in the international brutalist architecture style of the period. Only two major planned cities have appeared in the past 50 years – a state capital for Gujarat at Gandhinagar in the 1960s, and a state capital for Chhattisgarh at Naya Raipur, which is under construction. More are now planned as part of the Delhi-Mumbai Industrial Corridor project which envisages nine new cities.

'India's Urban Awakening'

In 2010, McKinsey Global Initiative produced a report, 'India's Urban Awakening',[4] which warned that India was in 'a state of deep inertia about the urgency and scale' of necessary urban reforms. It said that India's infrastructure required capital expenditure investment of $1.2 trillion by 2030 in roads, railways, water supplies, sewage, drainage and affordable housing. That was equivalent to $134 per capita, but only $17 was being spent in 2010, a figure that was likely to double to $34 on current trends. China, by comparison, spent $116 and New York $292 in 2010. 'Despite the perilous state of many Indian cities and the impending wave of urbanisation, there seems to be comfort with the status quo, resistance to change, and a lack of recognition of the urgent need for change,' said the report. Like many such dire forecasts about India's future, the report hit the headlines for a short time, but has been forgotten in the three years since it was published.

Current performance shows that there is no chance of such a massive programme being implemented without basic changes in the way India is governed. The report said that, contrary to public perception, there need be no real shortage of funds to build the infrastructure, provided various sources were tapped. This would include developing government land and introducing realistic property taxes and user charges that could provide the government with market-value revenue from real estate as values increased, plus private sector participation. The report was not explicit about the sensitive politics that would be required to accomplish this, but it was in effect calling for a total change in the relationship between developers and governments so that maximum payments stopped going to politicians and political parties with smaller amounts reaching the government and city authorities.

One of the report's authors, Ajit Mohan, hinted at what this involved in a *Wall Street Journal* blog in 2011 when he wrote that 'in a political system built around patronage, and where the rapid rise in the cost of elections forces political parties to look for substantial sources of funding from private interest groups, chief ministers and state leaders are reluctant to devolve power over such decisions to city governments and systematic urban planning processes'. He added that 'in the arbitrariness of urban land allocation lie power, wealth, and the possibility of political patronage'.[5]

Nandan Nilekani, one of the founders and a former chief executive of Infosys, the Bengaluru-based information technology company, who went on to set up India's country-wide personal biometric database, traces the post-independence story in his book *Imagining India*. Tracking the decline of city institutions, he says that political power was 'amputated at every level' and, in the absence of powerful elected bodies, 'city resources became prizes to be quartered among powerful interest groups'.[6] By the 1970s, with a series of restrictive laws, 'a pork-barrel politico could not have had it better!'

Amitabh Kundu, a professor at Delhi's Jawaharlal Nehru University, explains that the meticulous planning of the 1960s 'did not take vested interests into account' so, in later decades, there were only 'vision documents that leave things open for the actors to do as they want'.[7] The actors include politicians and bureaucrats who run city administrations and are, more often than not, in league with real estate and other companies. Ravi Kaimal, a Delhi-based architect and partner in an urban design firm, Kaimal Chatterjee & Associates, deplores the system of administration because, he says, it is in the hands of 'intelligent amateur bureaucrats on short-term appointments' plus 'nominal control' by politicians.[8]

Since there is 'no downside for being inactive', the bureaucrats mostly look after themselves and protect their careers by pleasing the politicians above them, says Kaimal. The politicians owe primary allegiance to slum dwellers who, because of middle-class apathy, make up the vast majority of their vote-banks and are content with their semi-legal lifestyle where they pay little or nothing for services. There is therefore little or no pressure on politicians to improve urban planning and facilities, while the bureaucrats, generally speaking, have no stake in improving the situation or services, but often show initiative in the awarding of contracts, though not in the completion of the contracts, says Kaimal. (The initiative, of course, though he does not say it, is receipt of bribes and other favours at the start of contracts and while they are in progress.) 'Till the current governance structure of cities changes to more empowered [for decision-making and for revenue] and locally accountable city governments, the concerns of the middle class for long-term vision and planning are likely to be ignored,' he adds.

Crumbling Mumbai

India's commercial capital of Mumbai is one of the worst examples of urban decline, both in terms of its physical infrastructure and its governance, despite being touted in the 2000s as a potential international and regional financial centre conveniently located between Singapore, Hong Kong and Japan to the east, and Dubai, Europe and the US to the west. It does, of course, serve India well, with top businessmen and financial services executives thriving in the sophisticated seclusion of well-furnished and efficiently equipped islands of excellence in what are often scruffy, ill-maintained office blocks surrounded by the chaos of traffic, broken roads and footpaths and a general lack of public services.

It also functions well in its slums where eight million people run a huge parallel and informal economy that demonstrates India's ability to make the best of dreadful conditions. Flying into Mumbai airport, many visitors' first view of the country is of a mass of corrugated-roofed slums clustered on hillsides around the end of the main runway.[9] But there is another image crouching below the aerial view, which was painted in the colour, drama, fun and cruelty of the Oscar-winning film *Slumdog Millionaire*. The film was set in a slum in Juhu, though the most famous of the slums in Mumbai is Dharavi, which is also one of the biggest in Asia, covering over 500 acres. Up to one million people live and work in unhealthy cramped conditions, fuelling a highly entrepreneurial informal economy. Alleyways a few feet wide lead to bakeries, metal workshops and sheds that recycle discarded plastic goods ranging from medical syringes to telephones and computers. Lorries crammed with buffalo, goat and other skins collected from abattoirs push through narrow lanes to grimy tanneries. Nearby, workers in a series of tiny workshops spray-paint, cut and press strips and sheets of leather and vinyl with varying degrees of expertise and branding authenticity.[10]

Slums like these, which are surrounded by high-value business and residential areas, have defied planners and real estate firms' redevelopment schemes. Many of the people working and living there would like to legitimize their unauthorised occupancy of land and premises and maybe move to better conditions, but few have legal titles to their premises and they currently gain by evading taxes and other official payments. There is also an established business momentum and order amidst the apparent chaos. If they were moved out, these people would probably switch to another slum rather than try to adapt to the new economic realities of redevelopment. This in many ways is the story of modern India – so many people have vested interests in life as it is, however awful it may be, that there is strong resistance to change.

The slums are among the least of Mumbai's serious worries – while they are bad for the city's image, they are part of its success too. A government committee listed the main priorities in 2007 – they included 'crumbling housing in dilapidated buildings pervading the city; poor road/rail mass transit as well as the absence of water-borne transport in what is essentially an island-city; absent arterial high-speed roads/urban expressways; poor quality of airports, airlines and air-linked connections domestically and internationally; poor provision of power, water, sewerage, waste disposal, as well as a paucity of high-quality residential, commercial, shopping and recreational space that meets global standards of construction, finish and maintenance.'

The 'high powered' committee was reporting on what Mumbai needed to do to become an international financial centre.[11] It comprised top Indian businessmen and public figures, headed by Percy Mistry,[12] a former World Bank economist and Hong Kong banker who now runs a consultancy in the UK. In addition to financial and other policy reforms that included the creation of a single financial services regulator and privatisation of banks, it named a devastating range of infrastructure deficiencies that applied not just to Mumbai but, in varying measure, to every Indian city and town: 'Lifestyle facilities that concern human welfare will need to be brought up to world standards and run on world-class lines in terms of their management and growth.' Hospitals, public and private health care, and educational, recreational and cultural facilities were needed. The greatest challenge was likely to be raising 'the quality of municipal and state governance, the provision of personal security and of law enforcement' that would need to 'improve dramatically from third-world to first-world standards'. Mumbai would also 'need to be seen as a cosmopolitan metropolis that welcomes and embraces migrants from everywhere – from India and abroad' with 'more user-friendly visa/resident permit mechanisms, making all arms of government expatriate-friendly, and exhibiting a gentle, tolerant, open and welcoming culture'.

The committee might have simply said, 'forget the idea'. Instead, it correctly noted that an international finance centre was 'too small a tail with which to wag the much larger urban development dog'.

There have been individual improvements since the report, but they are fragments compared with what needs to be done. There are new airport terminal buildings, with a new airport under construction, plus a part-completed expressway with an elegant cable-stayed bridge called the Bandra–Worli Sea Link across a bay on the urban coast. There is a new financial district of good modern buildings adjacent to the city's airport highway. Mumbai is not however tackling the macro problems, and it is failing to monetize large-scale up-market residential, office and retail development, thus missing a big opportunity to harness the government-funding suggestions made by McKinsey. It is also failing to make significant progress on clearing Dharavi and the other slums, while Navi Bombay, a satellite city that was planned in the 1970s, is only half-built and has a massive slum problem.[13]

Perhaps the committee was doomed from the start. Its 'high powered' title predictably had the opposite effect, and its report called for action 'on a war footing', which is a public relations line, not a clarion call for action. Such is life in India where, perhaps more than in other countries, when one thing is said, the opposite is meant.

Crony Delhi

Now regarded as a hive of corrupt crony capitalism, the Delhi Development Authority (DDA) was set up in 1957 when Jawaharlal Nehru's government merged the capital's planning and development agencies. It was given sole responsibility for the city's development with 'public purpose' powers (dating from an 1894 legislation) to acquire land forcibly below market prices. Delhi's Nehru Place office centre on the city's southern outer ring road, which was proudly built by the DDA in the 1970s and 1980s, is a monument to all that is wrong with bureaucratic control. It is a dreary multistorey concrete jungle of offices and scruffy shops with unmade roads and broken pavements. Car parking is pure jugaad, with touts using every possible space to squeeze in vehicles. It was a blot on the capital city's landscape when I used to go there in the 1980s to visit companies like the Modi family group and the National Thermal Power Corporation. Today it is best known as the computer hardware equivalent of a flea market.

'Such physical rot is an outward indication of the enormous corruption that gripped the DDA in its heyday of the 1970s and 1980s,' Rana Dasgupta, a writer, reported in *Granta*, the UK-based quarterly magazine in 2009.[14] The DDA would keep the supply of land low and developers would claw back the cost of their bribes with poor-quality construction. 'This racket was big business, and some of the largest fortunes in the city were made by mid-level DDA engineers whose job it was to rubber-stamp new projects – and many of them resisted promotion out of these lucrative positions for years.'

Delhi's municipal authorities' tight grip, which is supported by the Ministry of Urban Development, has continued across the city. This creates even greater rewards for corrupt bureaucrats who sanction unauthorized developments that include conversion of houses and flats to shops and offices, addition of extra floors and other extensions to existing buildings, increased building densities, commercial redevelopment of old traditional villages as the city envelops them, and construction of palatial 'farm' residences and weekend retreats on large plots of land around the city's perimeter. As with virtually every Indian city, there is little or no control of building standards, nor any effective safety measures such as fire precautions. Many bazaars and other crowded areas are unsafe.[15] Colonies (as residential districts are called in India) have sprung up all over the city, teeming with as many as 250,000 residents in broken narrow lanes, crudely erected concrete and brick buildings, and a jumble of low-hanging electricity cables that typify India's poorer urban areas.

Such haphazard development, often without public services, has of course fuelled the economic expansion of the capital, without which India's growth in the 2000s could not have happened. From time to time, various areas are regularized[16] – sometimes as a political gesture before elections – but only enough to bring a glimmer of order and not so much, or so precisely, as to reduce the power of extortion and inflow of bribes. That was evident in 2012–2013 during the preparation of a new Delhi master plan. The same is true of towns and cities across the country.

Purges of unlawful construction often have ulterior motives. In 2005 and 2006, the Municipal Corporation of Delhi (MCD) blitzed and sealed the fronts of shops, homes and other buildings across the city with mechanical diggers and bulldozers, provoking violent scenes and near riots that had to be controlled by security forces. Officially, this was a drive to clear illegal extensions that had been allowed, in most cases, because MCD officials had been bribed. Four small shopping malls on the Mahatma Gandhi (M.G.) Road, a major highway from Delhi to Gurgaon, were included in the partial demolitions in a move that illustrated cruel authoritarianism and a lack of care for the environment. The buildings housed up-market designer fashion shops and restaurants, which were well-built and were less at fault than thousands of other illicit structures across the city.

It was suggested at the time that the owners were being forced out in order to make them move to a new mall that was being built nearby. Later, it was alleged that the then chief justice of India had authorized the demolition 'around the time that his sons got into partnerships with mall and commercial complex developers, who stood to benefit from his sealing orders'.[17] The MCD, which is famous for being riven by corruption, did nothing to tidy up the sites after the front of the buildings had been hacked by its mobile cranes and diggers. Seven years later, the buildings still stand semi-demolished on a major highway, looking as though bombs had hit them.[18]

Buccaneering Gurgaon

Restrictions on development in Delhi led to growing pressure for office space and homes in authorized developments, which eventually burst outside the city to what are now the satellites of Gurgaon in Haryana, Noida in Uttar Pradesh, and beyond. Noida began as an industrial development by the Uttar Pradesh state government, which drew up an overall master plan that provided fast highways and open areas, plus good water supplies because it lies in the relatively water-rich Gangetic flood plain. Diverting from the planners' intentions, it rapidly expanded into residential and commercial development, and is now a thriving though chaotic conurbation providing jobs and homes for over 650,000 people. Like Delhi itself, it is beset by predictable crony capitalism on land deals, poor governance, and law and order problems.

Gurgaon should be a showpiece for modern India. It epitomizes the country's rapid growth and economic success with stylish buildings housing top multinationals as well as Indian information technology and industrial businesses. There are masses of blocks of flats to accommodate the aspirational young, plus shopping malls, night clubs and golf courses, and Delhi airport is nearby. But it is not a showpiece. Instead it is an unplanned, uncoordinated concrete and plate glass jungle. A total lack of infrastructure planning has led to failing water supplies and drainage and sewerage systems, plus a lack of organized parking facilities, all spelling disaster in the next decade unless there is a dramatic change.

Originally there was just an old village here, together with (since the end of the 1970s) the factories of Maruti, India's largest car manufacturer. A mixed bag of developers, with varying degrees of ethics (or lack of them), moved into what till then had been undeveloped farmlands, buying up and agglomerating small plots from the locals, and getting together with local politicians to bully landowners and obtain permissions. It started with residential developments for people to escape from Delhi, followed by modern office blocks of a quality that Delhi lacked, and then mushroomed with mixed developments. A master plan was superimposed, but it came too late to solve water and sewage problems.

The most successful of the private sector developers was Kushal Pal Singh, a businessman then in his forties, who worked for Delhi Land and Finance, now called DLF. The company had run out of land in New Delhi, having developed what became prosperous middle-class suburbs such as South Extension, Hauz Khas and Greater Kailash, so Singh moved out to what is now Gurgaon. There he began the urbanizing of rural settlements of the agricultural Ahir and Jat castes and, in the process, turned DLF into the country's leading real estate company.

He illustrated the original buccaneering spirit in a *Business Standard* interview in 2005.[19] 'I did everything it took to persuade these farmers to trust me. I spent weeks and months with their families. I wore kurtas, sat on charpoys, drank fly-infested milk from dirty glasses, attended weddings, visited the sick. To understand why this was important, it is necessary to understand the landholding pattern. The average plot size in Gurgaon was four to five acres, mostly held by Hindu undivided families. Legally, to get clear titles, I needed the consent of every adult member of these families. That could be up to thirty people for one sale deed. Getting the married daughters to sign was often tricky because the male head of the family would refuse to share the proceeds of the sale with them. So I would travel to their homes and pay the daughters in secret. Remarkably, Gurgaon's farmers sold me land on credit. I would pay one farmer and promptly take the money back as a loan and use that to buy more land. The firm's goodwill made them willing to act as bankers for DLF. But it also meant I had to be extra careful about interest payments. Come rain or shine, the interest would be hand-delivered to each farmer on the third of every month at ten a.m.

We bought 3,500 acres of land in Gurgaon, more than half of it on credit, without one litigation against DLF.'

In 2007, Singh listed the company on the Indian stock exchange and five months later *Forbes* magazine estimated him to be India's fourth richest man, worth $35bn.[20] Dramatic falls in DLF's stock market prices had reduced that figure by October 2013 to just $3.4bn.[21] Saddled with heavy debt, DLF sold hotels, wind farms and other diversifications while maintaining its core activities. It was also hit by controversies that included a deal with Robert Vadra, husband of Sonia Gandhi's daughter Priyanka, whose sudden wealth and business activities (which included DLF) had begun to lead to criticisms of the ruling dynasty. The deal exposed widely suspected and gossiped-about links between businessmen, politicians and bureaucrats in Haryana. A Vadra company called Sky Light Hospitality had bought a 3.53 acre plot in February 2008 in Manesar-Shikohpur near Gurgaon for Rs 7.5 crore from a local real estate company that was owned by a businessman said to be close to the chief minister of Haryana's Congress state government.[22] The following month, the state's town and country planning department issued a housing development licence for 2.7 acres of the land and, within 65 days, Vadra entered into an 'agreement to sell' to DLF for Rs 58 crore.[23] The land value had gone up nearly eight times in two months because of the change-of-use licence, allegedly due to Vadra's political connections.[24]

DLF has built impressive-looking office blocks, some of which would not look out of place on the Hong Kong waterfront. But, along with other developers and Haryana's state government, it did not provide the basic infrastructure needed for an area that grew to a population of 1.5m by 2011, with 3.7m forecast by 2021. In an interview in 2011, Singh admitted that 'the city is based on archaic planning norms', adding (apparently to deflect the criticism) that there were 'big roads, golf courses' in later phases of DLF's developments.[25] There was no mention of providing basic amenities. The city was 'thinking malls and high-rises, but not water or sewage', the Centre for Science and Environment (CSE) said in 2012.[26]

'Gurgaon is drowning in its own excreta,' warned the centre's director general, Sunita Narain. In 2021 Gurgaon would need 666m litres of water a day, she said, but would on present plans only be able to treat and supply 573m litres. It would be generating 533m litres of sewage daily, but have a capacity to treat just 255m litres. Chalta hai?

Notes

1. 'Three-fourths of Indian cities functioning without a Master Plan', Sudhir Krishna, Urban Development Secretary, reported in *The Hindu*, 30 September 2012
2. 'Excreta Matters', Centre for Science and Environment (CSE), Delhi 2012, http://urbanindia.nic.in/programme/uwss/slb/Septage PolicyPaper.pdf, and http://www.cseindia.org/content/excreta-matters-0
3. 'Back to the Village', http://www.mkgandhi-sarvodaya.org/momgandhi/chap76.htm
4. 'India's Urban Awakening – building inclusive cities', McKinsey Global Institute, April 2010
5. Ajit Mohan, 'Weekend Panorama: Who Will Champion India's Cities?', 'India RealTime', 10 September 2011 http://blogs.wsj.com/indiarealtime/2011/09/10/weekend-panorama-who-will-champion-india's-cities/>
6. Nandan Nilekani, *Imagining India*, pp. 209-232, Penguin 2008
7. In conversation with JE, March 2013
8. In conversation with JE, April 2013
9. 'Inside the slums, Light in the darkness', *The Economist*, 17 January 2005, http://www.economist.com/node/3599622
10. Ibid.
11. 'Report of the High Powered Expert Committee on Making Mumbai an International Financial Centre', http://finmin.nic.in/the_ministry/dept_eco_affairs/capital_market_div/mifc/fullreport/execsummary.pdf

12. Ibid. Mistry resigned from his High Powered Committee just before the report was published, apparently because he disagreed with public sector bankers on the committee who were insisting that the report's criticisms of their operations should be watered down.

13. 'Slum & the city: How "planned" Navi Mumbai lost the plot', Firstpost.com, 29 May 2013, http://www.firstpost.com/mumbai/slum-the-city-how-planned-navi-mumbai-lost-the-plot-825695.html?utm_source=mail&utm_medium=newsletter

14. Rana Dasgupta, *Capital Gains*, *Granta* 107, Summer 2009, http://www.granta.com/Archive/107/Capital-Gains/1 and http://www.ranadasgupta.com/texts.asp

15. 'Most East Delhi buildings are unsafe', National Institute of Disaster Management survey, *The Times of India*, 13 December 2012, http://articles.timesofindia.indiatimes.com/2012-12-13/delhi/35796550_1_nidm-lalita-park-new-structures

16. '91 more illegal colonies to be regularised', *The Hindu*, 23 January 2013, http://www.thehindu.com/news/cities/Delhi/91-more-illegal-colonies-to-be-regularised/article4335069.ece

17. 'A former Chief Justice defends his honour', *The Times of India*, 2 September 2007, http://epaper.timesofindia.com/Repository/ml.asp?Ref=Q0FQLzIwMDcvMDkvMDIjQXIwMTAwMA==&Mode=HTML. But the allegations continued later in September 2007, as these two reports show: 'How true is Justice Sabharwal? Probe demanded'. Merinews.com, 20 September 2007, http://www.merinews.com/article/how-true-is-justice-sabharwal-probe-demanded/126536.shtml; 'Justice Sabharwal's Defence Gets Murkier – Senior advocate Prashant Bhushan, part of the eminent panel that framed allegations against former Chief Justice of India Y.K. Sabharwal, rebuts the retired judge's rejoinder point by point', *Tehelka*, 22 September 2007, http://archive.tehelka.com/story_main34.asp?filename=Ne220907JUSTICE.asp

18. 'MG Road buildings to rise from the debris', *Indian Express*, 11 September 2012, http://www.indianexpress.com/news/mg-road-buildings-to-rise-from-the-debris/1001343

19. 'Building on a dream – How illiterate farmers helped K.P. Singh create India's biggest real estate firm', Interview with K.P. Singh of DLF, *Business Standard*, 22 March 2005, http://www.business-standard.com/article/management/building-on-a-dream-105032201044_1.

html and also on http://www.dlf.in/dlf/DLF-Chairman/chairmans_
profile_link3.htm

20. 'K.P. Singh in the *Forbes* Rich List', 14 November 2007, http://www.
forbes.com/lists/2007/77/biz_07india_Kushal-Pal-Singh_0UU7.
html

21. 'K.P. Singh in the *Forbes* Rich List', October 2013, http://www.forbes.
com/profile/kushal-pal-singh/

22. *First Post,* 17 November 2012, http://www.firstpost.com/business/
robert-vadras-got-vision-rest-of-the-world-wears-bifocals-526787.
html

23. 'Deal between DLF and Vadra Cancelled', NDTV (with timeline),
16 October 2012, http://www.ndtv.com/article/cheat-sheet/58-crore-
deal-between-dlf-and-robert-vadra-cancelled   -by-ias-officer-ashok-
khemka-280411; Ashok Khemka, a senior bureaucrat in Haryana,
was transferred three days after he cancelled DLF's purchase of 3.5
acres and also ordered an inquiry into all land deals within the state
between Vadra and DLF – see chapter on corruption

24. 'Senior official probing Vadra-DLF land deal shunted out', *The Hindu*,
16 October 2012, http://www.thehindu.com/news/national/senior-
official-probing-vadradlf-land-deal-shunted-out/article4000137.ece

25. 'Gurgaon was envisaged as another Chandigarh', *Mint*, 3 December
2011,   http://www.livemint.com/Companies/9FsmGo7MbA0W
PNWSLv9RDI/KP-Singh--Gurgaon-was-envisaged-as-another-
Chandigarh.html

26. 'Gurgaon is growing, but for how long?' Centre for Science and
Environment, 12 April 2012, http://www.cseindia.org/content/
gurgaon-growing-how-long

5

Getting Things Done and
Who Can Do It

Every 12 years, tens of millions of people gather over a period of several weeks to bathe in the sacred river Ganga at a Hindu festival called the Kumbh Mela. This is the biggest assembly of people anywhere in the world, and there are similar, smaller festivals at other locations every three years. Naked sadhus covered in ash and adorned with garlands of flowers mix with rich and poor pilgrims, self-conscious politicians and tourists to enter the water at auspicious times as near as possible to the confluence of the Ganga with the river Yamuna at Allahabad, in the northern Indian state of Uttar Pradesh.

In early 2013, around five million people lived there for 55 days in a vast tented camp covering 6,000 acres. As many as 30m to 50m more people visited every day. Equipped with electricity and water supplies, sanitation and emergency services, the mela was run by the state government jointly with religious organizations and other voluntary bodies. There were no disasters at the site, though 36 people were killed in a stampede at Allahabad railway station.

The successful organization of this complex mega event, with all its potential for chaos – and in one of India's most corrupt states – belies the failures of jugaad and chalta hai. 'It shows that the system is capable of saying "we know we have to do this",' says Montek Singh Ahluwalia, who runs the Planning Commission.[1] This is also a significant and rare example of a government learning from a disaster – in 1954, several hundred people were killed when there was a sudden surge in the crowds. (Another example of disaster triggering a new approach came in Orissa in October 2013, when fewer than 25 people died in a massive cyclone – the state and central governments had learned lessons from a cyclone in 1999 when 10,000 people were killed because of a lack of planning and effective administration.)[2]

The significant point about the Kumbh Mela is that one senior official from the Uttar Pradesh government was in sole charge. He reported to top state bureaucrats and to the chief minister, but he had overall administrative powers based on the authority of a district magistrate. Akhilesh Yadav, the state's young chief minister, was inevitably quick to welcome plaudits when he led a delegation to Harvard University to discuss how it was organized,[3] but basically, politicians did not interfere. 'It only goes on for a short time, so it is not a threat to political authority, and its success is important politically because of the problems if something went wrong,' says Rahul Mehotra,[4] a Mumbai architect[5] and Harvard University urban design professor.

Mehotra led a Harvard group to the mela in 2013 to see what could be learned for the organization of temporary cities that house refugees from conflict areas and natural disasters. He reckons the success is partly due to a 'common purpose and clarity' about what is needed, with clearly defined objectives, and without the sort of conflicting aims and tensions that develop over time in a community. The absence of prestige-conscious politicians also lessens demand for the best spaces, once the needs of the akhara (sect of Hindu Sadhus) leaders have been met. Mehotra says that order is helped by the site having a strict grid layout, which in 2013 included consumer goods outlets and corporate marketing displays. 'For many who participate in the melas, these huge human gatherings are opportunities for the practice of commerce, politics, services of many kinds, or public health,' he says.[6]

This story demonstrates what officials can achieve when they are not fettered by politicians, and shows that there are ways through India's corrupt political and bureaucratic quagmire, though both the

Kumbh Mela and the Orissa cyclone were one-off events that did not require sustained and effective administration over a long period. Mehotra graphically explains that the 'Indian wedding syndrome' ensures that 'differences are put aside to make it happen' for a short time. 'It would be different if it went on for five years.'

Such success needs a precisely defined focus in the way that government and the public sector work, plus people committed to achieve change and excellence. Use of information technology for communication and storage of records and other purposes can also help, though this is only effective when it is accompanied by a will to perform and, where necessary, change procedures. Strong political leadership, which has been lacking at a national level in India since 2004, is also needed, and the will to stand aside to let things happen.

One of the examples of effective administration is the Election Commission, which runs India's national and state elections with overall authority that includes the freedom, for example, to reprimand even a cabinet minister for breaking election rules by making a policy announcement, or removing senior officials and police commanders who favour one party. Like the Kumbh Mela, India's general election is the biggest event of its kind in the world with over 700m voters – more than all the countries of Europe or the Americas taken together – and over 8,000 candidates. It harnesses modern technology by using 1.2m electronic voting machines. The Commission consists of three commissioners with just 30 officials and 300 supporting staff, plus 11m civil servants who are seconded from their regular jobs at election time. 'This shows the bureaucracy can perform. All we need to do is to insulate what we do from political pressure,' says S.Y. Quraishi, the chief election commissioner from 2010 to 2012.[7]

Possibly the best early example of the will and determination of one person implementing change is the success of Verghese Kurien, a single-minded and stubborn metallurgist-turned-dairy manager, who set up Operation Flood, the National Dairy Development Board's cooperatives-based milk scheme, and ran it for 33 years from 1970, making India self-sufficient in milk. Another possible candidate is the Delhi Mumbai Industrial Corridor (DMIC) project, run by Amitabh Kant, an extrovert bureaucrat with a sound administrative track record in developing tourism. This project aims to reverse the lack of urban planning and infrastructure by constructing nine new cities along a 1,483-km dedicated freight railway track. It is at a very early stage and the strong central leadership will be inevitably diffused as the action moves down to individual states, where powerful political and business interests will wade in.

Three more examples demonstrate what can be achieved with a firm government and leadership – the 1998–2004 BJP government's Golden Quadrilateral highway programme, the construction of the Delhi Metro in the 2000s, and the Unique Identification Authority of India (UIDAI) Aadhaar biometric identification scheme launched in 2010.

People with direct experience in such projects say that, without a powerful and determined politician as a sponsor or patron, it is almost impossible to break away from political and bureaucratic blockages and then stay clear of the constant attempts to invade and suborn. 'You cannot do a project of this scale and magnitude without very strong support from the prime minister and lot of other people who matter,' says Nandan Nilekani.[8]

Vajpayee's Golden Quadrilateral

In 2000, Atal Bihari Vajpayee, then the prime minister, provided political backing for the construction of the first stages of India's 5,800-km Golden Quadrilateral highway under the direction of Major General B.C. Khanduri, a retired army-engineer-turned-politician who was already in his early seventies. Running in an erratic square or diamond shape around the bulk of the country, the Quadrilateral was part of a new, mostly four-lane, national highways programme and it linked the capital of Delhi with three other big metros – Mumbai, Chennai and Kolkata.

With Vajpayee's personal authority backing him – and with

adequate government funding and a general acceptance of the urgent need for new roads – Khanduri became a hands-on minister for road transport and highways. 'The message went out that I was interfering – interfering to help the contractors, the National Highways Authority and consultants – so it was accepted,' Khanduri told me in 2005 for a *Fortune* magazine article.[9] 'No one thought India had the construction industry, the funds, or the management expertise to do such a programme.' Khanduri proved the sceptics wrong. 'We changed the mindset because I set targets that looked unreasonable and impossible,' he said. 'Gradually people realized what could be achieved.' Highway contracts awarded while the BJP was in power, mostly on the Quadrilateral, led to some 6,000 km being completed by the end of 2005. (Khanduri later became chief minister of the state of Uttarakhand where he found it more difficult to be effective in state-level politics.)

When the BJP unexpectedly lost the 2004 general election, the road-building programme lost top-level sponsorship and direction, and it has never fully recovered. Sonia Gandhi and her ministers did not seem to want to draw attention to one of their predecessor's spectacular successes, especially after the BJP had personalized it before the election with pictures of Vajpayee on banners strung across completed highways. Manmohan Singh was an enthusiast and ordered widespread six-laning of four-lane highways, but T.R. Baalu, his minister of road transport, shipping and highways, was more interested in promoting a shipping canal between his home state of Tamil Nadu and Sri Lanka than in building highways elsewhere.[10]

There was also extensive infighting between the highways authority and ministry and the Planning Commission, which wanted the private sector to replace the BJP government's substantial public funding and unwisely insisted on complex contractual arrangements that slowed down project awards. As frequently happened in the Manmohan Singh government, no one took ministerial responsibility for making decisions that would cut through the lethargy, contract and funding rows, and corrupt aspirations. There were also inevitable delays because of slow land acquisition and extortion by gangsters and Naxalite rebels. By the end of April 2009, the total completed road had only gone up to just over 11,000 km, and awards of new contracts had slowed to such an extent that work was only started on 9,700 km compared with a five-year target of 16,000 km.[11] It picked up again but the single-minded momentum of the Vajpayee-Khanduri period was not recovered, though there was a successful government-funded rural roads programme that opened up access to villages and led to improved health and education services as well as access to markets for farm produce.[12]

Sreedharan's Delhi Metro

Around this time, Delhi's highly successful metro railway was being built by Elattuvalapil Sreedharan, a former Indian Railways engineer. He was 65 in 1997 when he became managing director of the government-owned Delhi Metro Corporation and he stayed in charge till 2012 when he turned 79. He was backed by Sheila Dikshit, Delhi's chief minister, and by other city authorities including Vijay Kapoor, who was the lieutenant-governor when the project began. They saw the urgent need for the railway, which was substantially funded by Japan, though Dikshit also gave surprisingly enthusiastic support to a rival ill-planned and chaotic Bus Rapid Transit (BRT) System.[13]

Sreedharan became internationally recognized for his achievements. A slim, rather austere-looking man, he had earned his reputation as a top project manager during a long career with the railways, finishing as a board member. From 1990, he was in charge of building the 760-km Konkan Railway on India's west coast. Cutting through difficult terrain, across the mountains and rivers of the Western Ghats, with nearly 150 bridges and 92 tunnels,[14] the railway runs from Mumbai through Goa to Mangalore in Karnataka.

At the Delhi Metro, Sreedharan used his authority to insist, before he was appointed in 1997, that he would have full autonomy and would be free from any political interference – which, he was, apart from an early battle over whether the track should be broad or standard gauge, which he lost. He was able to insist on that independence, he told me in 2005, because at his age he had no career ambitions and could walk out at any time.[15] That meant he could set new parameters for public project management in a country where politicians and bureaucrats routinely interfere and demand favours from public sector corporations.

Before Sreedharan was appointed, it had seemed as though the metro would be doomed to go the same way as other major projects. After years of talk, the corporation (jointly owned 50–50 by the governments of India and Delhi) was registered in 1995, but nothing much happened, partly because of problems finding someone to head it. 'That's how government works,' said Sreedharan. 'No one wants to take responsibility for an action.' He was appointed when Japan threatened to withdraw substantial soft loan funding, without which the project would not have been feasible. 'People have to become aware that delay means money,' he said. The first stage of the system was built within budget and opened in 2002, three years ahead of schedule – a dramatic change from India's only other metro railway, which had taken 23 years to build in Kolkata.

Sreedharan applied private-sector methods that most public-sector bosses would never dare attempt, starting with a work culture that encouraged executives to take 'fast and transparent' decisions. Faced with the need to divert complex services such as communication cables and sewers, Sreedharan insisted that the corporation should take the work away from Delhi's state government departments. 'We did in a few days what they would have taken months to do,' he told me. When construction of an underground section was running eight months late after four-and-a-half-years of work, he gave contractors acceleration payments to speed up their pace. 'I'll get that back in one month's revenues,' he said. Corruption was also significantly reduced. Sreedharan says he selected senior staff for their integrity, introduced strict systems, and did not allow agents to come between the corporation and its contractors. Government officials often delay paying suppliers in order to demand bribes for sanctioning partial payments, so Sreedharan insisted bills were paid quickly – 80 per cent were paid within 24 hours of falling due.[16]

The metro is now a huge success, running – profitably – for 190 km on six lines with 142 stations, and carrying two million people a day. Extensions are on the way to bring the total to 330 km by 2016. It has been modelled on the Hong Kong Mass Transit Railway (MTR) metro and the rolling stock has the same style and feel, with open carriages stretching the length of a train. The only downside is poor construction maintenance at many stations, plus an Airport Railway that was run unsuccessfully as a public–private partnership (PPP) by the Reliance Group controlled by Anil Ambani till it was taken over by the metro corporation.

Overall, the metro has done more to develop Delhi than any other initiative, opening up new areas and changing society and working patterns. It has improved lifestyles and boosted aspirations for people living in the crowded alleyways of old Delhi, the comfortable colonies of central areas, and new multistorey flat developments in the suburbs, including Gurgaon and Noida,[17] as it extends into neighbouring areas. Sreedharan's success story has also led about ten other Indian cities to plan and build networks, some with him appropriately as the adviser.

Nilekani's Aadhaar

Another project which shows the importance of strong political support is the Unique Identification Authority of India (UIDAI), whose chairman is Nandan Nilekani. The task is to set up a country-wide personal biometric database and issue hundreds of millions of people with a 12-digit unique identification number called an aadhaar (foundation stone). Estimates have for years suggested that 70 per cent or more of such aid is lost on its way down to rural recipients. By early 2013, the system was beginning to be used for a direct cash transfer scheme to deliver aid money via Aadhaar-validated bank accounts.

There were, inevitably, technical glitches when the scheme was being rolled out, but Nilekani's ambitious aim is to have enrolled more than 50 per cent of the population by 2014. He was appointed by Manmohan Singh with the rank of a central cabinet minister in 2009 to set up and run the UIDAI. That provided him with the status he needed to be effective, but his strength in cutting through political and bureaucratic blockages has stemmed from the backing of Sonia and Rahul Gandhi. P. Chidambaram, the finance minister, has called the identification number a 'game changer' in the delivery of corruption-prone aid money and a 'massive re-engineering of the system'. Pranab Mukherjee and Montek Singh Ahluwalia were also supporters, but the Gandhis' backing was crucial in the project's early days when Chidambaram was home minister (2008–2012) and favoured his ministry's rival scheme that was focused more on catching illegal immigrants.

Nilekani, a politically savvy and cautiously media-friendly technocrat, says he was looking for a public role where he could make a difference with his technology knowledge when he was invited by Manmohan Singh to lead the UIDAI.[18] He was attracted to the challenge and simple definition of success – to build the biometric database and enrol hundreds of millions of people. Aadhaar is intended to include the poor in India's growth by giving them an identity and easier access to opening bank accounts, obtaining mobile phones and gas connections and, most importantly, protecting the delivery of their aid funds. 'This enhances access of the common man to public services while reducing the hassle he or she faces in accessing the service,' says Nilekani.[19]

Nilekani sees this as a first step in a continuing programme to bring know-how metaphorically from his old base of Bengaluru to Delhi, using information technology to streamline and improve government operations ranging from national information programmes to taxation. 'Needless to say, active political support and civil society engagement is a sine qua non for this to happen', he says.[20] He envisages combining technology with regulatory and institutional reform to change the way the government relates with the private sector as a buyer on defence and other equipment and services, as a seller such as on licences for natural resources, and as a regulator in areas such as telecoms.[21] He has been advising the government on the formation of a not-for-profit company called Goods and Services Tax Network (GSTN), jointly owned by central and state governments, with additional private sector equity, that could provide a country-wide technology infrastructure for the new tax.

Notes

1. Interview with JE, June 2013
2. http://ridingtheelephant.wordpress.com/2013/10/14/odishas-cyclone-shows-india-can-handle-disasters-but-longer-term-action-is-needed/
3. 'Harvard to get Kumbh lesson from Akhilesh', *Indian Express*, 13 April 2013, http://m.indianexpress.com/news/harvard-to-get-kumbh-lesson-from-akhilesh/1101841
4. In conversation with JE, May 2013
5. Rahul Mehotra's architecture firm website http://rmaarchitects.com/
6. 'Lessons of a temporary city – Researchers from across Harvard share findings from India's Kumbh Mela festival', *Harvard Gazette*, 4 April 2013, http://news.harvard.edu/gazette/story/2013/04/lessons-of-a-temporary-city/
7. Speaking at the British Council in Delhi, May 2013
8. '"Direct cash transfer facility for UID cardholders": Nandan Nilekani', PTI, 26 November 2012, http://articles.economictimes.indiatimes.com/2012-11-26/news/35364892_1_uid-project-uid-numbers-nandan-nilekani
9. JE, 'On the Road to Repair', *Fortune* magazine, 31 October 2005
10. http://ridingtheelephant.wordpress.com/2007/07/19/hastening-slowly-on-india%E2%80%99s-highways/
11. http://ridingtheelephant.wordpress.com/2009/06/02/nath-inherits-a-muddy-murky-highways-programme/
12. Clive Bell and Susanne van Dillen, 'How Does India's Rural Roads

Program Affect the Grassroots? Findings from a Survey in Orissa', World Bank, August 2012, http://elibrary.worldbank.org/docserver/download/6167.pdf?expires=1379402806&id=id&accname=guest&checksum=AEDB7F1E5FDEB9CFF94647C0E6D0F2C9

13. https://ridingtheelephant.wordpress.com/2009/01/02/sheila-dikshit-gets-it-wrong-and-now-plans-a-%E2%80%9Cflexi-brt%E2%80%9D-muddle/

14. 'E. Sreedharan: More Than the Metro Man', *Forbes India*, 5 October 2012, http://forbesindia.com/article/leaderhip-award-2012/e-sreedharan-more-than-the-metro-man/33847/1#ixzz2OjIjaBOF

15. JE, 'Delhi's Delight', *Fortune* magazine, 31 October 2005

16. Anuj Dayal, *35 Management Strategies for Delhi Metro's Success: The Sreedharan Way*, published by Delhi Metro Rail Corporation, Delhi, 2012

17. A series of articles on the *Wall Street Journal's* 'India RealTime' blog reported in 2012 on the impact of the Delhi Metro: http://blogs.wsj.com/indiarealtime/2012/05/30/metrocity-journal-delhis-changing-landscape/, http://blogs.wsj.com/indiarealtime/2012/05/31/metrocity-journal-the-new-trade-routes/, http://blogs.wsj.com/indiarealtime/2012/u06/01/metrocity-journal-public-vs-private-space/?mod=WSJBlog&mod=irt, http://blogs.wsj.com/indiarealtime/2012/06/02/metrocity-journal-up-up-and-away/

18. Conversations with JE, 2012

19. Nandan Nilekani, 'Tackling Corruption: Some Alternative Approaches', The 19th Lovraj Kumar Memorial Lecture, 1st November 2012, http://uidai.gov.in/images/tackling_corruption_01112012.pdf

20. Ibid.

21. Nandan Nilekani, 'Passing a law can't solve the corruption problem', CNN-IBN, 22 October 2012; video trailer of interview: http://ibnlive.in.com/news/nilekani-slams-kejriwal-says-passing-a-law-cant-solve-the-corruption-problem/301655-37-64.html and http://ridingtheelephant.wordpress.com/2012/10/23/corruption-tamashas-and-gossip-flood-india-but-change-will-be-very-slow/

II

Opening Up

6

Clearing the Cobwebs

'We have got to get rid of the cobwebs,' Prime Minister Narasimha Rao told top officials on 21 June 1991, the day he formed his new Congress government. Go away to your office, he said to Manmohan Singh, and work out some details. Thus was born, with a classic understatement, India's biggest burst of economic liberalization that, over the past 25 years, has touched almost every corner of this vast country and affected the lives of virtually everyone in the billion-plus population. Chalta hai had been pushed aside by a dire financial crisis, but none of the officials in Rao's office that morning could have dreamed of the long-term effects of the measures they would be launching, and nor could he. They knew they were about to remove industrial, trade and financial controls that would help to solve the crisis by freeing up economic activity and generating international trade.

What happened, however, was far more dramatic. The moves they initiated gradually unleashed previously repressed entrepreneurial drive, skills and aspirations. This was accelerated by unpredictably rapid expansion of information technology and the internet, plus India's growing involvement in international business and trade.

Manmohan Singh was at the meeting because he was about to be named finance minister – he was sworn in later in the day with the rest of the cabinet. The country's financial plight was desperate. A collapse of international confidence in the rupee had caused capital flows to dry up. Foreign exchange reserves had plunged so far that they only covered two weeks of imports, which was not viable. Talks

83

were in progress with the International Monetary Fund for a rescue package. The rupee was devalued in two 10 per cent tranches a few days later on 1 and 3 July, and dramatic trade reforms were quickly introduced to coincide with the second devaluation. Two weeks after that, 47 tonnes of gold were ignominiously flown to the capital of India's former colonial ruler and deposited in the vaults of the Bank of England to cover a desperately needed bridging loan. Major reforms were announced in a 'New Industrial Policy' on the same day as Singh's first budget speech on 21 July, which made it clear that real and not cosmetic change was happening.[1]

The Beginnings

The ground for all this had been well prepared, and there were plenty of ideas ready for Singh to pick up. Plans for reform had emerged in various debates and policy papers over several years, notably in the 1980s when Rajiv Gandhi was prime minister, and then during two years of unstable coalition rule between his defeat in a 1989 general election and the formation of Rao's government.

The reforms really began at the start of the 1980s after Indira Gandhi was returned (in 1980) as prime minister, having recovered politically from a controversial two-year state of Emergency that she had declared in 1975. She had a new approach on economic policy, as L.K. Jha, her top adviser and a veteran bureaucrat, used to explain to me, sitting in the study of his home at the 10 Janpath bungalow in New Delhi where Sonia Gandhi now lives.[2] His task, he said, was to begin to reverse some of the state controls and protectionist policies that Indira Gandhi (and he) had introduced and extended in the 1960s and 1970s, building on the centralist economic doctrine of her father, Jawaharlal Nehru.

It was her initiatives and Jha's work, not the 1991 reforms, that marked the turning point in the history of India's two phases of development since independence, as Arvind Virmani, a former chief economic adviser to the Indian government, has explained.[3]

The 30 years from 1950 to 1980 saw India's version of socialism, which aimed to block imports and force the purchase of India-made goods (known as import substitution). The freedom of the private sector to compete was restricted in many industries, and government ownership and controls were extended into as many areas as possible. The second phase, which started in the early 1980s and was boosted in 1991, still continues. Virmani calls this the phase of 'market experimentation', in which the oppressive control regime set up during the first phase was gradually modified and removed. (Many controls however still remain, enabling companies involved with natural resources, land and infrastructure to impede development and encourage corruption.)

One of Indira Gandhi's first initiatives, in February 1982, was to begin to remove controls on the cement industry (in response to a corruption scandal involving the exploitation of cement shortages by, among others, a leading Congress politician).[4] I was on my first visit to India at the time, writing articles for a *Financial Times* country survey on India, and remember meeting my colleagues, Alain Cass and K.K. Sharma, on the terrace of the Taj Mahal Hotel in Mumbai. Cass, who was the Asia editor, asked Sharma, then our India correspondent, if this heralded real change and how we should reflect that in the overall approach of the survey. Little did we realize the significance of the question.

Gandhi had by this time lost some of her antipathy for the private sector and had also developed an unexpected enthusiasm for importing foreign technology. Alcatel of France had just started work on modernizing parts of India's telephone system, which was so antiquated that Plessey of the UK donated two electronic exchanges in 1983 for use by a Commonwealth heads of government meeting in Goa.[5] (Critics suggested that Gandhi had been influenced by Dhirubhai Ambani, founder of the rapidly growing Reliance Industries, who had a close political connection with her government, to swing in favour of the private sector. The acceptance of foreign technology controversially led to the award of fertiliser projects to

Snamprogetti of Italy. Ottavio Quattrocchi, the company's Delhi representative, and his wife had become friends of Italian-born Sonia Gandhi and Rajiv, and he was later embroiled in a notorious 1980s corruption scandal over a Bofors gun contract.)

More significant initiatives were taken by Rajiv Gandhi when he became prime minister after his mother was assassinated in October 1984. He opened India's eyes to a modern world beyond the frugality, shortages and controls of the Nehru and Indira Gandhi years, and also beyond the khadi, home-spun traditions of Mahatma Gandhi. He started a debate between 1985 and 1988 about dismantling controls, forcing virtually every government department to examine how they could reduce restrictions on economic and business plans. In practical terms, his government rationalized and reduced taxation levels in various areas, produced a long-term fiscal policy, and pushed through tentative relaxations in the country's tortuous industrial licensing system. He instigated significant activity in India's electronics and associated industries, allowing imports and foreign joint ventures that helped to pave the way for India's software successes in the information technology revolution of the 1990s and 2000s. The stock markets came to life for the first time in decades with a series of share issues that resulted in what was recognized abroad as well as in India as the launch of an 'equity culture'.[6]

Unfortunately, India was not ready for such a vision of the twenty-first century, driven by 'sunrise' industries, modern cars, computers and electronics, and Rajiv Gandhi did not have enough time to learn how to politicize and implement his enthusiasm and drive.[7] Consequently, he was not able to achieve as much as he had hoped, and what he did do remained under-recognized as his government floundered with corruption and other crises. Referring to vested interests and his political opponents, he told a bureaucrat in 1988 that he was not pushing reforms in foreign direct investment because 'after Bofors they'd accuse me of selling out to foreigners'.[8] Nevertheless, he did point to a more sensible way of managing the economy and he inspired reformers, who continue to have influence today, as well as a young generation of entrepreneurs and managers who still talk about how he made business a respectable occupation.

The 'M' Document

The 1991 reforms first appeared publicly on 11 July 1990 as an unsigned article headed 'Towards a restructuring of industrial, trade & fiscal policies' that was spread across a page and a half of the *Financial Express* newspaper. A note by the editor (A.M. Khusro) said that there had been 'some controversy' over a government policy paper that was being considered by a committee of secretaries, so the *Express* was publishing it 'to generate a public debate on matters raised in the document'.

No one knew for sure who wrote the document, but Montek Singh Ahluwalia, one of India's leading economic policy makers who now runs the Planning Commission as deputy chairman, has revealed to me that he was the author.[9] Who leaked what was later dubbed the 'M' document – with the title page removed to hide its source – remains a mystery. Maybe it was Ahluwalia himself! I tracked down the article because I was convinced that Manmohan Singh was not the architect of the reforms and had heard that Ahluwalia was said to have written something called 'What's left to be done' at the end of Rajiv Gandhi's 1984–89 government. I followed the trail till Ahluwalia told me in June 2013 about the 'M' document and admitted authorship, though he did not have a copy. *The Indian Express* then searched its Chandigarh archives and later in the year found it and I passed a photostat to Ahluwalia, who said, 'it takes me really down memory lane'.[10]

Ahluwalia confirmed that he initially wrote the ideas as an overview of 'what needed to be done' late in Gandhi's government when he was an economic adviser in the prime minister's office. He then turned the ideas into a presentation for V.P. Singh, formerly the finance minister, who became prime minister of a minority eleven-month National Front government in December 1989 (after breaking away from the Congress party). The ideas were discussed by a high-level committee of secretaries (the top level of the civil service) and that became the *Financial Express* leak. 'The note he [Ahluwalia] wrote for the prime minister in 1990 ... contained most of the ideas which were subsequently implemented. He was, thus, a pioneer as far as economic reforms are concerned,' says C. Rangarajan, who was deputy governor of the RBI at the time[11] and later became the governor and top economic adviser to the prime minister from 2004.

Ahluwalia says that the paper was specially significant because it pulled together a comprehensive approach for tackling India's economic problems and set out a five-year plan with firm objectives – though it acknowledged it was bound to create more controversy. 'Even if you do things gradually, you must emphasize the end result – that is needed for any reforms,' says Ahluwalia,[12] citing initiatives in recent years on energy pricing as an example. He says it was also significant because it linked the reduction in import tariffs with reduction in the rupee exchange rate so that increased imports could be balanced by a growth in exports.

The paper began by setting the scene: 'Our ability to compete is likely to be significantly impaired if our industry continues to operate in an environment which is much more restricted, and less amenable to various types of international linkages than our competitors.' It covered five areas: 'achievement of macro-economic balance with high investment levels; reform and redefinition of the role of public sector; reducing and restructuring domestic controls over production and investment licensing; reducing the degree of protection to Indian industry; opening up to foreign investment'. There were detailed proposals for tackling the country's mounting fiscal crisis, followed by plans for public sector reforms (but not privatisation), drastically reducing industrial licensing and trade protection, and opening the country up to foreign investment. The need for financial and labour reforms were mentioned without any details.

Another policy document had been prepared at the industries

ministry during V.P. Singh's time by Amar Nath Verma, the industry secretary (the ministry's top civil servant), and Rakesh Mohan, then the ministry's economic adviser and later the finance secretary and a deputy governor of the RBI. The industry minister at the time (later aviation minister from December 2011) was Ajit Singh, who was new to politics. He had returned to India in 1981 with plans to set up his own company after 17 years in the US working as a software systems trouble-shooter with IBM, Xerox and others. His father, Chaudhary Charan Singh, a prominent farmers' leader in Uttar Pradesh and briefly prime minister in 1979–80, died in 1987 and this swept Ajit into politics to inherit a mass-base legacy. Accustomed to life in America, he was impatient for reforms and was appalled by the huge number of approvals and files that crossed his desk. 'The industries minister was the most powerful in the government – I had seven secretaries handling licensing for everything,' he told me.[13] In January 1990, V.P. Singh (no relation) told him to go to the World Economic Forum in Davos, which was just beginning to grow into an annual Swiss alpine jamboree for world leaders and businessmen, and talk about how India could be changed by reforms. 'We had to brief him on policy and that was the trigger for putting together a presentation on what had to be done,' says Mohan,[14] adding: 'That gave me the opportunity to see the whole picture on control mechanisms that were in place including industrial licensing, phased manufacturing, monopolies regulations, controlling capital issues and export-import controls.' But a day or two before Ajit Singh was due to fly to Davos, V.P. Singh decided to send someone else who did not have an industries' brief.

The ideas continued to be developed and, in the middle of 1990, Ajit Singh placed a new industries policy in the Rajya Sabha. This included measures that appeared in the 'M' document and proposed, perhaps most controversially, raising the permissible level of heavily restricted foreign direct investment (FDI) to 51 per cent of a company's equity, and opening some public sector industries to the private sector. It also proposed relaxing controls on monopolies and industrial production, and changing the way that import and export trade classifications were listed. There was widespread opposition, and the ideas had not progressed by the time the V.P. Singh government fell in November. Next came a coalition government led by Chandrashekhar (his second name was Singh but he was always known by this one name), a respected veteran socialist politician with a broad enough base to be chosen as leader of a fractured coalition. India was heading into a deep financial crisis and there was some interest in reforms, but there was strong resistance from politicians, bureaucrats and the private sector, who regarded the ideas as too controversial, so nothing was done. Eventually, the Chandrashekhar government collapsed in June 1991 after just seven months in office, triggering the election of Rao's administration.

1991: Ten Hours to a New Policy

After Narasimha Rao had told Manmohan Singh to go and assemble reform policies, he prepared for a television address that he made to the nation at 9.45 the next evening, 22 June. He returned to his cobwebs theme and said there was 'no time to lose' because the government and the country could 'not keep living beyond their means'. With 'no soft options left ... this government is committed to removing the cobwebs that come in the way of rapid industrialisation'.[15] Major announcements were planned for Singh's Budget speech on 21 July, but the schedule was suddenly upset on the morning of 3 July when it became clear that a second devaluation would be needed by the end of that day. Singh rang Ahluwalia, who was secretary for commerce, to say that he should brief Chidambaram, the commerce minister, on the need to announce, simultaneously with the devaluation, that expensive export incentives would be abolished. (Called the cash compensatory scheme, these incentives, which gave exporters arbitrarily, and potentially corruptly, authorized tax rebates, would no longer be necessary because the devaluation would give exporters sufficient incentive without compensation.)[16]

That phone call triggered one of the most rapid exercises ever seen in policy development and implementation, with major policy restructuring being written and approved by two ministries, as well as the prime minister, in just ten hours. Ahluwalia suggested to Chidambaram that grumbles from exporters about losing the rebates could be offset if a new liberalized trade policy, which the ministry was working on, was also announced at the same time.[17] Chidambaram was new to economic policy making but, as a lawyer and one of the best brains in government, he quickly bought the idea.[18] He and Ahluwalia said the policy could be ready in a few hours and suggested to Singh that it should be announced that evening. Singh agreed, overruling objections from top officials who were against the reforms.

'We returned to the Commerce Ministry and worked feverishly to outline the proposals,' says Ahluwalia. Late in the afternoon, the papers were taken to the prime minister, who signed the file without the customary scrutiny by his office staff. Jairam Ramesh, who was posted in the PMO and was involved in drafting the policies, was 'asked to ensure it received wide publicity'. That evening, Singh announced the second devaluation, and the new trade policy was launched by Chidambaram, who eulogistically told the media, 'We have always had wings, but suffered a fear of flying. We should now soar in the high skies of trade.' He said he wanted to achieve full convertibility of the rupee on the trade account in three to five years – it was done in two years.

After the trade reforms, industrial licensing was tackled in the new industrial policy on Singh's first Budget Day. The moves were so dramatic and extensive that they sent out a strong reform message, even though they had been opposed behind the scenes by some cabinet members, as well as senior civil servants. Chidambaram says the opponents 'shot them down as a betrayal' of the Congress party's early leaders. He overcame that opposition with some neat drafting that confounded the critics by harking back to the origins of independent India. He says he inserted a tribute to Nehru's original goals in the first lines of the policy document, and wrote that the new policy was 'inspired by these very concerns, and represents a renewed initiative towards consolidating the gains of national reconstruction at this crucial stage'.[19] Another key factor was that Narasimha Rao himself held the industry minister's portfolio, so he did not have to persuade another, possibly reluctant, politician to give up a host of discretionary powers.

All but 18 nationally important and sensitive industries (such as defence, coal, pharmaceuticals, railways and sugar) were freed from industrial licensing, and the number of core industries reserved for the public sector was reduced to eight, including railways, defence equipment, atomic energy and coal.[20] Rules that limited foreign investment primarily to technology projects were abolished, and automatic approval was announced for foreign equity stakes up to 51 per cent (up from a 40 per cent basic limit) in 35 industries, with faster approval-vetting above that level, and 24 per cent stakes in small-scale industries.[21] Transfer of technology was eased, and revision of mergers and monopolies legislation was announced along with plans for a new foreign investment promotion board. Also removed were restrictions on the location of industry and price controls in various sectors such as steel and aluminium. Foreign companies were allowed into some infrastructure areas (up to 100 per cent ownership in power projects), and the financial services' primary and secondary markets. Foreign stock brokers' activities were boosted by Indian companies gaining access to global capital markets. Other major decisions taken with or shortly after the New Industrial Policy included allowing the use of foreign brand names, and the abolition of the finance ministry's Controller of Capital Issue who presided over stock market affairs.

Other changes followed, but the pace slowed when the approach of a general election due in 1996 led Rao to decide that reforms were not good electoral politics. There were, however, some more gradual changes such as the opening up of telecom and aviation to the private sector, trade and electricity reforms and licensing of private sector banks and these have continued, haltingly, through successive governments.

From 1996, when the Rao government was defeated, India had a series of coalitions and it became difficult for the leading party to obtain agreement from its often more populist regional partners. The Bharatiya Janata Party-led National Democratic Alliance (NDA) coalitions from 1998 to 2004 did continue with reforms, but parliamentary oppositions became increasingly irresponsible and negative. Arun Shourie, the NDA's minister for disinvestment, put it neatly when he told me in 2001 that his government's implementation problems stemmed from 'a fractured electorate that leads to a fractured legislature' and an opposition that had a 'perverse concept of what it means to be out of office'.[22] This was a reference to the Congress-led opposition that was disrupting parliament over rows ranging from corruption on defence contracts and the collapse of the country's largest unit trust to controversial anti-terrorism legislation. As a result, there was a backlog of more than 40 bills.

'Everyone has enough power to block everything and no one has enough power to see anything through,' said Shourie, highlighting a failing of India's parliamentary democracy which became even more true with the 2009–2014 UPA coalition. During those years, the BJP and other opposition parties behaved even more irresponsibly in parliament than Congress had done earlier. It wasted weeks of parliamentary time and impeded urgently needed legislation such as land ownership compensation, banking and insurance regulations and labour laws, while the government dithered on opening up the defence industry and other areas.

The opposition also played havoc with overhyped plans to allow foreign investment into supermarkets and other parts of the retail business, which Manmohan Singh and his commerce minister, Anand Sharma, unwisely allowed to become a litmus test of reform success.[23] This was a typical example of the government avoiding difficult basic issues and policy debate with headline-grabbing reforms. Singh and Sharma hoped that foreign companies would invest in supermarket supply chains and would then force through state-level reforms in public sector-dominated and inefficient marketing arrangements for farm produce. Instead, the policy foundered and foreign supermarket companies were put off partly by muddled and complex regulations and ministerial hubris, and partly by entrenched opposition from vested interests in the distribution system, supported by populist and anti-Congress regional political parties.

Gandhi Sops, Not Growth

The main blockage to reforms between 2009 and 2014 came from divided government leadership. It was caused by Sonia and Rahul Gandhi favouring the provision of expensive and wasteful sops and aid schemes for the poor rather than pushing growth-oriented reforms favoured by Manmohan Singh. I heard in London in June 2012 that Rahul had told a friend on a recent visit that the way for Congress to stay in power and win elections was through the aid scheme route, not reforms.[24] 'Has the domination of economic policy by Sonia and Rahul Gandhi, together with regional members of the governing coalition ... become so established that there is now no room for reformers to be heard? Is the government so much under the spell of these forces that India's leadership has gone back to the 1970s when the private sector profit was frowned on [except when it lines the pockets of politicians]?' I asked on my blog in August 2012.[25]

Raghuram Rajan, who became governor of the Reserve Bank of India in 2013, criticized the Gandhis' favourite aid project, the National Rural Employment Guarantee Scheme (NREGS, renamed the Mahatma Gandhi National Rural Employment Guarantee Act, MNREGA, in 2009). The scheme guaranteed at least 100 days' employment a year to those volunteering for unskilled manual work. In a 2010 interview, he said it was 'a short-term insurance fix' for dealing with problems of the poor, but added: 'If it comes in the way of creating long-term capabilities, and if we think NREGS is the answer to the problem of rural stagnation, we have a problem'.[26] The scheme helped to boost rural wages in many (though not all) states, but was inefficiently and corruptly run, with money being siphoned off on the way down to villages. It also frequently involved unproductive projects. In April 2013, the Comptroller and Auditor General (CAG) condemned extensive misuse of funds and incomplete projects.[27]

Similar criticisms were made of food security legislation[28] that was passed at the insistence of Sonia Gandhi, who led the final debate in parliament despite opposition from senior government ministers and the Reserve Bank of India.[29] Aimed at providing five kilograms of subsidized rice per family, wheat and other food grains every month to tackle widespread hunger among the poor, it ranged far wider and was gifted to a total of 810m people (75 per cent of the rural population and 50 per cent in urban areas). This brought the total cost of subsidized food aid to $21bn a year, which could not be afforded when the country was facing a growing current account deficit. Surjit Bhalla, an economics commentator, put the cost at 3 per cent of GDP.[30] There would inevitably be massive waste as funds leaked and food was diverted or rotted in India's inefficient food distribution system; experts also argued that the balance of protein was inadequate. But such concerns were not a priority for Sonia Gandhi, who regarded the scheme as a potential vote winner at the 2014 general election. Incredibly, Gandhi insisted on going ahead with the scheme and announcing it on Rajiv Gandhi's birth anniversary, even though the country was in the middle of a financial crisis with a mounting current account deficit and a plunging rupee.[31] Later, in order to keep the scheme running, the government even disrupted World Trade Organisation negotiations on an international food security agreement that was supported by other developing nations.[32]

The Gandhi family had however shelved some of their

ambivalence about reforms by the end of 2012 and publicly backed various measures when India faced a run on the rupee and a sharp decline in its international image as an investment destination. They allowed Chidambaram, reappointed as finance minister in 2012, to try to revive the economy, to move ahead on various measures including foreign investment in supermarkets and airlines, and de-regulation of fuel prices which continued into 2013.[33]

Manmohan's Over-stated Role

The role of Manmohan Singh in the early 1990s is often overstated. As has been seen in this chapter, he was certainly not the 'architect' of the 1991 reforms – an easy but inaccurate tag that is often used by foreign journalists and others. Nor was he even the primary implementer, though he did have a public role in pulling together and extolling the various reforms that emerged, and in painting a favourable picture internationally of a new and open India. He worked in particular with Chidambaram on the trade reforms and then had to sell them to colleagues and the country. The fourth person who played an essential and central role along with Rao, Singh and Chidambaram was A.N. Verma, Rao's principal secretary. An experienced senior bureaucrat, he understood what was required because he had been involved, as industry secretary, with Ajit Singh and Rakesh Mohan during the V.P. Singh government. He steered the implementation of the 1991 policy through the government with daily and weekly committee meetings on specific areas such as economic reforms and foreign investment, operating with the full authority of the prime minister.

Rao was an unlikely leader and reformer. A politician of considerable intellect but little charisma, he was Indira Gandhi's downtrodden foreign minister when I first saw him in the summer of 1983. He was being ignored by a bunch of braying Indian businessmen as they pressed forward around Gandhi, anxious to be seen bidding her goodbye as she left an investment conference in a Swiss alpine village. The businessmen were fleeing India's heat and had gone to the conference (some with girlfriends, at least two of whom had been flown in from London to the retreat) to be seen by Gandhi before moving on to weeks of leisure in the UK and the US. Rao was standing in the doorway of the chalet hotel, unnoticed and alone, when Gandhi left.

He was on the verge of retirement when Rajiv Gandhi was assassinated and the Congress won the general election in 1991, but was picked as a safe interim prime minister after Sonia Gandhi resisted sycophantic pressure to take the job. No one expected him to tackle the financial crisis or anything else with the focus and determination that he showed. Maybe, at his age and at the end of his career, he felt he had nothing to lose by challenging those who resisted change. He certainly had the intellect to recognize the depths of the crisis and to realize it could be a turning point in history. There is a nice story he told a colleague: that he had picked Singh as finance minister because he reckoned that he (Rao) would get the credit if the reforms succeeded, while ex-bureaucrat Singh could be blamed if they failed. As it turned out, Rao's calculation was wrong because the reforms were a success and Singh got the credit.[34]

Singh had learned how far India was lagging behind economically when, as secretary-general of the Geneva-based South Commission from 1987 to 1990, he saw the economic progress being made in south-east Asia. Before that, he had mainly been an advocate of trade reforms, and he was always worried about the effects that wider reforms would have on the poor, as he used to tell me in the 1980s during background conversations for the *FT* when he was the RBI governor. But there were other pressures in 1991 in addition to the financial collapse. The Soviet Union, which had always supported India economically and diplomatically for decades, was breaking up, and economic reforms had begun in China, so the immediate financial crisis made instant action both essential and sensible.

Singh only pushed reforms for as long as the prime minister authorized him to do so, and he backed off when Rao became nervous of a political backlash and put on the brakes in 1994–95 after unfavourable regional election results. Rao later told Gurcharan Das, author of *India Unbound*, that India had 'the right pace of reform and a faster pace might have led to chaos'.[35] He was also not in favour of wide-ranging privatisation, saying, 'You don't strangulate a child to whom you have given birth.' He favoured pro-poor and politically useful employment schemes. 'Growth was not enough. We had to attack poverty directly through employment schemes,' he said.

'Your Legacy Is at Risk'

Singh's overstated reputation as a liberalizer took a beating after he became prime minister for a second term in 2009 and mostly failed to win support for reforms from either Sonia Gandhi or coalition partners. As his reputation sank, his friends and colleagues gathered in Delhi one evening in April 2012 to launch a new edition of a book that updated what had been written in 1998 as a 'festschrift' or celebration of the 1991 reforms.[36] The event took place at a time when the government seemed to be losing control of events. International investors' views of India had been seriously upset by retrospective amendments to corporate taxation laws that hit foreign companies including Vodafone, the mobile telecom operator, and other factors such as project delays and corruption scandals.

Unfortunately, I could not be at the launch, but Adam Roberts, *The Economist*'s South Asia correspondent, was there and neatly caught the mood in a blog article. Headlined 'Manmohan Singh, India's prime minister, cut a lonely figure on the evening of April 14th', it said: 'The evening had the mood of an intervention: when friends and relations get together and, without warning, confront a loved one who has some sort of destructive habit that he won't admit to. In normal life, it might be an addiction to drugs or booze. In

India's political life, and the case of Mr Singh, it is a desperate failure to push on with reform.'[37]

I talked to some of the speakers and read their speeches that were more critical than anyone could have expected. The prime minister had sat silently while economists and others, far from lauding his recent achievements, told him, in the words of one of those present, 'your legacy is at risk'.[38] It was surprising and sad for Singh, then 79, to hear this from experts, colleagues and friends who had worked with him for decades. The approach was set by Isher Ahluwalia, head of ICRIER, a leading economic policy institute and joint-editor of the book, who made the important point that India had been taking strong economic growth for granted. She implied that the government had been sitting back and failing to take the steps needed to sustain that growth, which was 'under threat from a deteriorating macro-economic environment and a downturn in the investment climate'.

Developing this into a potent social issue, she pointed out that Indians born in 1991 were by then 21, and that half the population was below 25. 'This half of our population started life in India with 5.5 per cent growth which accelerated slowly and steadily to 8 per cent as they grew up. They are restive for more, not less.' Sharpening the criticism, she pointed to the 'unsustainability' of fiscal policies, incomplete financial sector reforms, infrastructure construction and regulatory frameworks, plus 'macro-economic management in an uncertain international economic environment' and 'challenges of overall governance'. By this point, the prime minister must have wondered why he had, reluctantly I was told, agreed to attend the event. Ahluwalia was not only a leading economist, but also a family friend along with her husband, Montek Singh Ahluwalia.

Raghuram Rajan went further. After saying how 1991 had changed India for the better, he warned of a 'paralysis in growth-enhancing reforms' that had been papered over by the high growth. This had made India 'dependent on short-term foreign inflows to a dangerously high extent, at a time that the international investor is increasingly sceptical about the India story'. By the early 2000s, he said, India had needed a second generation of reforms that included higher education, public sector industries, and allocation of resources such as land and telecoms spectrum. 'But powerful elements of the political class, which had never been fully convinced about giving up rents from the Licence Raj in the first place, had by then formed an unholy coalition with aggressive business people, whom I will refer to simply as the connected'. That led to 'coalition dharma – a coalition of the bad', which replaced the pre-1991 Licence Raj with a Resource Raj and led to 'massive fortunes generated by the connected and by politicians'.

Duvvuri Subbarao, then the governor of the RBI and previously economic adviser to the prime minister, warned that 1991's 'twin deficits' were back again. The fiscal deficit was 7 per cent in 1991 and was now rising at 5.9 per cent while the current account deficit at 3.6 per cent was higher than the 1991 figure and short-term debt at 23.3 per cent of GDP was now far above the 10.2 per cent it was in 1991. T.N. Ninan, who runs the *Business Standard*, then mocked (without naming them) the way that Manmohan Singh had allowed Sonia Gandhi to dominate policy, saying, 'We have copied the Communists, for whom the party is supreme and the government secondary.' The prime minister, he said, was also hampered by 'presidential-style chief ministers in the states' and coalition cabinet ministers who ran their own policies.

Through all this and much more, the prime minister sat silent for over an hour, speaking at the end only to say that he had agreed to come provided he did not have to speak. Many of those there found this stance not only inexplicable but worrying – had Singh really lost the wish to debate as well as the will to govern? The book's editors and contributors, the prime minister said, had 'thrown a new light on old problems' and had mentioned many challenges. 'There are difficulties. Life will not be worth living if there are no difficulties. I am confident, with great determination, we will overcome,' he said.

Privatisation – A New Word and Its Origins

Where, one wondered, was the 'great determination' to be found? What came to the fore that evening was a belated and unspoken realization that, despite his image, Singh had never been the sort of enthusiastic liberalizer that Chidambaram became from 1991. Neither he nor Rao provided the zeal and leadership that are essential to pursue a continuing programme of active reform against the political odds, such as Margaret Thatcher showed when she was prime minister of the UK ten years earlier,[39] nor the vision and strategy that Deng Xiaoping brought to China's opening up from 1979 as the country's supreme leader. Thatcher's approach was that of a bulldozer, pushing through opposition on the road map she knew she wanted to follow. Deng was more subtle and talked of 'crossing the river by feeling the stones under the feet'.[40]

Privatisation was not initially a priority for Thatcher though she became an enthusiast once she realized the potential, and it was not a target for Singh, who has never believed in changing India's economic base. In March 2009, he said: 'We are a mixed economy. We will remain a mixed economy. The public and private sector will continue to play a very important role.'[41] Just after he became prime minister in 2004, he said that no profit-making public sector unit (PSU) would 'normally' be privatised. To underline the change of policy from the former BJP-led NDA government, the Disinvestment Ministry, which aimed both to privatise (i.e., sell control) and divest (sell partial stakes) was scrapped and merged into the Ministry of Finance. That echoed the 'M' policy paper where Ahluwalia wrote that privatisation 'as a general strategy is ruled out'.

Privatisation became one of Thatcher's most significant legacies – not only because she introduced the policy itself, but also because she brought the word into the world's everyday vocabulary. I played a role is that when we launched the word on 28 July 1979 in *The Financial Times*.[42] The day before, I had telephoned Nigel Lawson (now Lord Lawson), a Conservative Party MP who had just become Financial Secretary at the Treasury, for a background briefing on denationalisation, as selling off government stakes in business had always been called.

During the conversation, he used the word 'privatisation', which I had never heard before. I put it in the first paragraph of an *FT* leader-page feature I was writing with an economics correspondent, Anatole Kaletski, saying: 'A new word has been circulating in Whitehall in recent weeks. It goes to the heart of the government's policy for reforming the ownership and bureaucracy of state-owned industries, but few ministers would admit to using it. The word is "privatisation" which, to those close to the centre of Tory thinking, means the government's well-known interest in selling public sector assets to private individuals, financial institutions, and anyone else [apart from foreign interests in some sensitive cases] who might want to buy them.' The *FT* features editor refused to put it in the article's headline, saying something like, 'no one will know what it means'. Instead, with vintage *FT* caution and precision, the headline read, 'Long and short term aims of denationalisation'.

People of course rapidly came to 'know what it means', and the word became used internationally. The Thatcher government's purpose was simply to put a positive and permanent private sector spin on the negative sounding policy of denationalisation, though some of its proponents wanted it to lead to wider public ownership by private individuals and interests, which did not happen. National businesses and services such as the railways, the steel industry, an airline, an aircraft manufacturer, gas supplies and a telecom provider were successfully sold off. But the policy went too far and broke up services such as water, electricity and airports (and, most recently, the post office) that were sold off to large corporations, including some based abroad, which were more interested in making profits than providing what the public needed.

The policy also developed into a worldwide craze for PPP (public–private partnership), which often blurs and confuses the conflicting priorities of providing adequate public services and making private sector profits. The private sector cannot be trusted to deliver public services in terms of quantity and quality, as has been seen in Britain with railways and hospitals, and in India with airports, where deals have been corrupted by land and other scams, and highways, where companies shirk responsibilities.

India has debated how far to go along the Thatcher path for over 20 years, but its lack of willingness to face major change has been demonstrated by more progress being made on divestment, which involves selling only minority stakes, than on privatising control. Manmohan Singh's reluctance to sell off profitable businesses reflects both India's old socialist approach, and maybe also justified scepticism about how far the Indian private sector could be trusted with the family jewels.

Lessons and Debate

Looking back, Ahluwalia has pointed to some lessons from the events of 1991 that are relevant today.[43] The main one is that ministers need to be prepared to give up discretionary powers in favour of 'transparent market driven processes', as Chidambaram and others had been in 1991. This is urgently needed now, not only nationally but even more so in the states – especially in infrastructure, mining rights and changes of land use, which lead to extensive corruption. Ahluwalia might have added that it is useful for the prime minister to be in charge of ministries where reform is planned, as Rao was in 1991 with industry.

Second, both Singh and Chidambaram were prepared to take risks over how a new trade policy would work in practice, even though finance ministry officials were not willing to do the same. 'They suffered from the fear of flying syndrome,' says Ahluwalia. Third, the events showed that, if political decision makers are 'clear about what they want', opposition from bureaucrats can be overcome. The other three points he listed were: it is easier to make changes when there is already some consensus among policy experts; individual reforms need to be part of a broad 'holistic' approach; and 'our much maligned system can deliver results very fast when necessary'.

The bigger lesson, not mentioned by Ahluwalia, is that the reform process since 1991 has been based on weak foundations, with little real substantive debate or popular acceptance. There has been a popular mantra mouthed by politicians and others from the mid-1990s that the 'reforms are irreversible'. That is broadly true, but it misses the point that this does not mean that new measures can be easily introduced. A parallel claim that there has been a consensus behind the reforms has never been true, as has been shown by resistance to the government's plans from vested interests and political opponents during 2009–2014.

There is now not even a consensus on the priority that should be given to economic growth, and how much it should be restrained in order to protect the environment and the livelihoods of people currently occupying land that is needed for mining and other development. There is an apparent consensus on the need for foreign investment, but that breaks down when vested interests try to protect their business prospects in, for example, the defence sector and in one or two other major areas such as insurance and retail trade and distribution.

There has been little debate on all this, and most policy changes after 1991 have been the result of pushes and pulls by vested interests (often, euphemistically, carrying suitcases). Many reforms that have (or have not) happened in industries ranging from telecoms and banks to airlines and retail stem far more from such pressures than from reasoned analysis and debate. Ratan Tata has said that he was told in 2000 that a government minister needed a Rs 15 crore bribe before he would approve a joint venture between Tata and Singapore Airlines. This would have opened up the aviation sector to foreign airlines but the move was successfully opposed by India's well-connected Jet Airways and others.[44] (Ratan Tata did not pay the bribe and the tie-up with SIA did not move ahead until 2013.)

This approach is a major weakness for an economic liberalization policy.[45] Foreign or domestic companies push for changes, supported by their governments, especially in the case of the US. That is then resisted by rival companies inside and outside India, supported by political parties that often reflect vested interests as much as their own policies. Ministers and bureaucrats are persuaded to tilt one way or another, sometimes nudged by various inducements and sometimes by legal action. Eventually someone wins and reforms are introduced – or aren't.

'Consensus for Weak Reforms'

Ahluwalia put it more gently in a 2002 paper,[46] revealing why there is so little cohesive policy, which applies even more today than it did then: 'Critics often blame the delays in implementation and failure to act in certain areas to the choice of gradualism as a strategy. However, gradualism implies a clear definition of the goal and a deliberate choice of extending the time taken to reach it, in order to ease the pain of transition. This is not what happened in all areas. The goals were often indicated only as a broad direction, with the precise end point and the pace of transition left unstated to minimize opposition – and possibly also to allow room to retreat if necessary. This reduced politically divisive controversy, and enabled a consensus of sorts to evolve, but it also meant that the consensus at each point represented a compromise, with many interested groups joining only because they believed that reforms would not go "too far". The result was a process of change that was not so much gradualist as fitful and opportunistic. Progress was made as and when politically feasible, but since the end point was not always clearly indicated, many participants were unclear about how much change would have to be accepted, and this may have led to less adjustment than was otherwise feasible.'

The alternative to that scenario would, of course, have been to have real debates so that everyone realized the full extent of what was needed and signed up to their implementation. However, that would probably have created a gridlock in the complex and corrupt democracy so, with a mixture of jugaad and chalta hai India has muddled on with political parties pushing reforms when they are in government and blatantly opposing them when in opposition. 'The process can be aptly described as creating a strong consensus for weak reforms!' says Ahluwalia.

What is required is political leadership. This need not necessarily be loud and vocal like that of Narendra Modi, the controversial chief minister of Gujarat who became the BJP's prime ministerial candidate with the backing of businessmen desperate for a strong government. The leadership could be quiet but firm, as Narasimha Rao's was in 1991, though he had the advantage of a financial crisis that gave him the reason to act. Manmohan Singh made the point in a speech in August 2013 when he said, 'reforms don't happen just because there is a professional consensus. They happen when the political leadership of the time decides to back these initiatives.'[47] He did not, of course, have that backing from the political leadership of Sonia Gandhi, though he was too restrained to say so explicitly.

Notes

1. Statement on Industrial Policy, Government of India, Ministry of Industry, New Delhi, 24 July 1991, http://dipp.nic.in/English/Policies/Industrial_policy_statement.pdf

2. 'An imbalance of liberalization: L.K. Jha talks to John Elliott, *Financial Times*, January 26 2003

3. Arvind Virmani, 'Policy Regimes, Growth and Poverty in India: Lessons of Government Failure and Entrepreneurial Success!', October 2005, Working Paper Series, Indian Council for Research on International Economic Relations (ICRIER); this paper traces and tabulates the history of India's economic restrictions and reforms from 1948 to 2004; http://icrier.org/pdf/WP170GrPov11.pdf He has a blog 'Dialogue with Virmani', http://dravirmani.blogspot.co.uk/

4. '30 Years of Change, and Status Quo', *Business & Economy*, 16

February 2012, http://www.businessandeconomy.org/16022012/storyd.asp?sid=6746&pageno=1

5. JE, 'Telephone Links for Commonwealth Talks', *Financial Times*, 8 September 1983

6. Robert Lloyd George, *North-South: An Emerging Markets Handbook*, Probus Publishing, Cambridge (UK), Chicago, 1994

7. Parts of these paragraphs appeared in a report I wrote in 1995: 'India and China – Asia's New Giants: Stepping Stones to Prosperity', Rajiv Gandhi Institute for Contemporary Studies, Delhi, 1995

8. Told to JE by the bureaucrat, July 2012, non-attributable

9. Montek Singh Ahluwalia in conversation with JE, June 2013; the article was headed 'Towards a restructuring of industrial, trade & fiscal policies', *Indian Express*, 11 July 1990, extracts courtesy of *The Financial Express* archives, 1990

10. Conversation with JE, December 2013 after the article was retrieved from *The Indian Express* archives

11. *Policy Making for Indian Planning: Essays on contemporary issues in honour of Montek S. Ahluwalia*, Foreword p. 17, Academic Foundation, New Delhi 2012, http://www.academicfoundation.com/n_detail/645.asp

12. Conversation with JE, December 2013

13. In conversation with JE, August 2013

14. In conversation with JE, June 2013

15. Shankkar Aiyar, *Accidental India, A History of the Nation's Passage Through Crisis and Change*, p. 69, Aleph, Delhi 2012; the first chapter, 'Bonfire of the Vanities', of this book goes into some more detail on the history and politics of the reforms; http://alephbookcompany.com/accidental-india

16. Trade Policy Reforms http://tradeportalofindia.com/contentmgmt/Desktops2.html?itemcode=I212&compid=itpo

17. Conversation with JE and also recounted in detail by Ahluwalia in an essay, 'Policies for Strong Inclusive Growth', in *An Agenda for India's Growth: Essays in Honour of P. Chidambaram*, Academic Foundation, Delhi, 2013, http://planningcommission.nic.in/aboutus/history/spe_strong1402.pdf

18. Manmohan Singh made a fulsome tribute to Chidambaram at the launch of the Festschrift in Delhi on 31 July 2013, http://pmindia.nic.in/speech-details.php?nodeid=1334

19. P. Chidambaram told the story at the launch of *Accidental India* (see footnote above), 23 October 2012; also see 'Statement on Industrial Policy', Government of India, Ministry of Industry, New Delhi, 24 July 1991, http://dipp.nic.in/English/Policies/Industrial_policy_statement.pdf

20. JE, 'India and China – Asia's New Giants: Stepping Stones to Prosperity', Rajiv Gandhi Institute for Contemporary Studies, Delhi, 1995

21. Arvind Virmani, 'Policy Regimes, Growth and Poverty in India: Lessons of Government Failure and Entrepreneurial Success!', October 2005, Working Paper Series, Indian Council for Research on International Economic Relations (ICRIER); this paper traces and tabulates the history of India's economic restrictions and reforms from 1948 to 2004; http://icrier.org/pdf/WP170GrPov11.pdf He has a blog 'Dialogue with Virmani', http://dravirmani.blogspot.co.uk/

22. 'The trouble with coalitions', *The Economist*, 22 November 2001, http://www.economist.com/node/875011

23. http://ridingtheelephant.wordpress.com/2011/12/01/wal-mart-co-fuel-indian-political-crisis/

24. Non-attributable conversation with JE, London, June 2012

25. http://ridingtheelephant.wordpress.com/2012/08/15/has-india-abandoned-economic-debate/

26. 'Licence raj has been replaced by land mafia raj', interview with Raghuram Rajan, *DNA*, 30 October 2010, http://www.dnaindia.com/opinion/1459666/interview-licence-raj-has-been-replaced-by-land-mafia-raj

27. 'Report no. 6 of 2013-Union Government (Ministry of Rural Development) – Report of the Comptroller and Auditor General of India on Performance Audit of Mahatma Gandhi National Rural Employment Guarantee Scheme; http://saiindia.gov.in/english/home/Our_Products/Audit_Report/Government_Wise/union_audit/recent_reports/union_performance/2013/Civil/Report_6/Report_6.html

28. Text of the legislation, http://www.prsindia.org/uploads/media/Food%20Security/Bill%20with%20Amendments.pdf

29. Minutes of the 24 July 2013 Meeting of the Technical Advisory Committee on Monetary Policy, http://rbidocs.rbi.org.in/rdocs/PressRelease/PDFs/IEPR370TAC0813.pdf

30. Surjit S. Bhalla, 'Manmonia's FSB: 3% of GDP', *Indian Express*, 6 July 2013, http://www.indianexpress.com/news/manmonias-fsb-3--of-gdp/1138195/0

31. http://ridingtheelephant.wordpress.com/2013/08/28/sonia-gandhis-2bn-bid-for-political-security/

32. 'India rejects WTO proposals on food security, trade facilitation', *The Times of India*, 4 December 2013; 'For India, food security is non-negotiable. Need of public stockholding of foodgrains to ensure food security must be respected. Dated WTO rules need to be corrected,' Anand Sharma, commerce minister, told a WTO meeting in Bali, http://timesofindia.indiatimes.com/business/india-business/India-rejects-WTO-proposals-on-food-security-trade-facilitation/articleshow/26829962.cms

33. This news report lists pending reforms: 'More reforms initiatives in next 2 to 4 months – P Chidambaram', PTI, 24 April 2013, http://articles.economictimes.indiatimes.com/2013-04-24/news/38790562_1_opposition-party-finance-minister-p-chidambaram-executive-actions

34. http://ridingtheelephant.wordpress.com/2009/04/01/manmohan-singh-marks-the-limits-of-liberalisation/

35. Gurcharan Das, *India Unbound*, p. 247, Penguin Viking, Delhi 2000

36. *India's Economic Reforms and Development: Essays for Manmohan Singh*, Edited by Isher Judge Ahluwalia and IMD Little, Second Edition updated as part of Oxford India Perennial Series, OUP Delhi, 2012. Texts and videos of the evening's event at http://icrier.org/page_book.asp?MenuId=25&SubCatID=1004

37. Adam Roberts, 'India's economic reforms: Now finish the job', *The Economist*, 15 April 2012, http://www.economist.com/blogs/banyan/2012/04/indias-economic-reforms?fsrc=gn_ep

38. http://ridingtheelephant.wordpress.com/2012/04/19/manmohan-singhs-friends-meet-him-and-say-your-legacy-is-at-risk/

39. http://ridingtheelephant.wordpress.com/2011/07/23/india-lost-for-words-20-years-after-its-1991-reforms/

40. JE, 'India and China – Asia's New Giants: Stepping Stones to Prosperity', Rajiv Gandhi Institute for Contemporary Studies, Delhi, 1995

41. The transcript of the 31 March 2009 *FT* interview is on http://www.ft.com/intl/cms/s/0/7f6fea0e-1bcc-11de-978e-00144feabdc0.html#axzz2XsryNahd; I wrote about it on my blog a day later, http://

ridingtheelephant.wordpress.com/2009/04/01/manmohan-singh-marks-the-limits-of-liberalisation/

42. http://ridingtheelephant.wordpress.com/2013/04/10/how-we-launched-thatchers-privatisation-word-in-the-ft-in-1979/

43. Conversation with JE and also recounted in detail by Ahluwalia in 'Policies for Strong Inclusive Growth', in *An Agenda for India's Growth: Essays in Honour of P. Chidambaram,* Academic Foundation, Delhi 2013, http://planningcommission.nic.in/aboutus/history/spe_strong1402.pdf

44. A television interview with Ratan Tata on NDTV, 20 December 2010, www.tata.in/media/reports/inside.aspx?artid=+3/rHRSGwIE=, and '"Tatas unlikely to do airline business again", says Ratan Tata', *The Hindu*, 9 December 2012, http://www.thehindu.com/business/companies/tatas-unlikely-to-do-airline-business-again-says-ratan-tata/article4181223.ece

45. http://ridingtheelephant.wordpress.com/2009/02/18/india%E2%80%99s-fdi-changes-reveal-weaknesses-in-industrial-policy-making/

46. Montek S. Ahluwalia, 'Economic Reforms in India since 1991: Has Gradualism Worked?', *Journal of Economic Perspective,* March 2002, http://planningcommission.nic.in/aboutus/speech/spemsa/msa008.pdf

47. Manmohan Singh at a P. Chidambaram Festschrift book launch in Delhi on 31 July 2013, http://pmindia.nic.in/speech-details.php?nodeid=1334

7

Unlocking Opportunities

The 1991 reforms had an enormous impact, opening up possibilities that had not existed for young Indians, and older ones too, to branch out into new lifestyles, entrepreneurial adventures and careers. Those already in the middle class, including women, were given job opportunities and mobility of employment that was unimaginable in the economically restricted and public sector-dominated India after independence. No longer was the security of lifetime jobs in various parts of government and the public sector the epitome of success. For many of those not yet in the middle class, there were opportunities for upward mobility to be grasped.

There are thousands of stories of children of poor parents who have suddenly done well in ways that would not have been possible earlier. Ram Lal, the son of a gardener who worked for my family and the *FT* office in the 1980s, is now a well-paid driver and his daughter is a qualified pharmacist in a government hospital. Dinesh Kumar, the 22-year-old son of a poor farmer on India's border with Nepal, earns Rs 12,000 a month as a trainee with Tarun Tahiliani, one of India's top fashion designers. He was a porter on Rs 2,500 a month in the INA market, one of Delhi's main retail food markets, when he began to go to a nearby night school run by Ritinjali, a voluntary organization. There he did a cutting and tailoring course that led him to study graphic design at Delhi University with funds provided by Ritinjali, and he graduated in 2010.

Slim, smart and smiling, with great yet modest self-confidence, Kumar told me that the best he could have expected at the market was maybe to become a shop assistant.[1] 'Now I'm designing Western clothes and I want to go abroad and become a big designer,' he said. He might move somewhere else in Delhi first, hoping to double his salary, but his target is Australia because that is where Amar Nath, another Ritanjili student from the same bazaar, is working as a management assistant for an electrical power company. I had interviewed Nath in July 2005, when he was 17, for *Fortune* magazine.[2] He had never been to a conventional school and had just begun to learn to read and write. He told me he had been inspired by 'meeting high-class people' in the bazaar and realized that 'speaking their English was a basic driving force'. He said he wanted to start his own hotel or restaurant and benefit from India's growing consumerism. His horizons changed to Australia and he is regarded as a role model by those now at Ritinjali.

Life Improves Near Panipat

I went back in October 2012 to Beejna, a village near the industrial city of Panipat, two hours north of Delhi in Haryana on a new highway to see what had changed since I first went there for an *FT* article in 1987. That visit was to see young women weaving cotton durries for their marriage dowries, and I wrote about Darshan, a slim 18-year-old bride-to-be who was working on a horizontal wooden loom in her family's small thatched mud-and-brick house.[3] She was weaving a light brown and green 3ft by 6ft durrie that was destined for a Habitat home-furnishing store in London, where it would sell for £25–30.

The *FT* business peg for this rural story was Britain's fashionable Habitat stores that were run by Terence Conran, a top furniture designer and retail entrepreneur. Conran had spotted the traditional brightly coloured dowry durries when he was taken to Panipat in 1969 by John and Bim Bissell, who ran Fabindia, a crafts-oriented shop (now a successful chain of stores) in Delhi. He thought it might become a trendy item in the UK and shipped over a container load, but in 1987 Habitat was facing a takeover bid that could end the trade and hit the Rs 45 (then £2) that Darshan and others received for three or four days' part-time weaving.

These young women had virtually no prospects apart from marriage. 'Between leaving school and getting married, they made the carpets because the Rajputs didn't like unmarried girls going out into the fields,' explained Satya Sharma, a local contractor. 'When they became married women, they had to stay fully indoors, so often they couldn't even do the carpets.' Taking durries as part of the dowry was an old tradition and it still continues, though it is now more symbolic because bridegrooms and their families prefer money, motorbikes and electrical goods like refrigerators and televisions.

It was clear when I returned that life had changed dramatically since the 1980s. A seven-kilometre flyover carried a highway through the centre of Panipat that had been clogged with traffic before. In Beejna, there were paved roads, though some were flooded because of a mishandled government project. There were many motorbikes, as well as several tractors that had just begun to appear when I first visited. In the fields, there were some combine harvesters that were unheard of in the 1980s. Cylinders of natural gas had replaced cow-dung patties as fuel in homes, which were now built of concrete and normal-sized bricks instead of more traditional stones, small bricks and mud. Several large ostentatious houses had been erected by the most successful families. Large controlled-humidity tents were beginning to appear on some farms for growing vegetables such as cucumber, brinjal and red pepper. Health care had also been transformed, though, as everywhere else in India, it did not always operate efficiently. Amateur midwives had been replaced by a local clinic that had opened ten years ago, and there was now a gynaecology section with ultrasound and other facilities that had been added recently.

Young women had opportunities to study and work outside the village, while their brothers and husbands could chase jobs and careers in the cities, many created as a result of the 1991 reforms. I met Krishna, a woman in her fifties, whose two sons had successful careers. One was a manager in a cardboard-box factory in the nearby town of Karnal, while the younger one, aged 32, was a manager in Delhi at an outlet of the Café Coffee Day chain, having earlier worked with KFC. His wife lived at the small Beejna family home and was training to become an air hostess in Karnal, while he earned enough for their five-year-old twin sons to be bussed 12 km daily to a Karnal school. 'We send the boys there so they can be educated in a more promising environment than the village,' said Krishna. 'It's where Kalpana Chawla went,' she added proudly, referring to a local hero and illustrating how aspirational Indians proudly latch on to accessible icons. (Chawla moved to America in the 1980s, became an American astronaut, and was killed in a NASA shuttle disaster in 2003.)

In a government-funded crèche attached to the village school, Krishna and two friends proudly produced mobile phones from their blouses and said everyone over the age of 16 had one. One of their husbands had a well-connected job as a court typist in Karnal, where their daughter studied in college and hoped to get a job in a bank. At the school, children were being taught under the shade of trees when we arrived. With 400 children of all ages, it was four times bigger than in the early 1980s. The pupils' horizons had expanded from the village to Karnal's call centres and shops, and beyond.

Clearly, prospects for the young had been transformed in these 25 years. Not everyone was successful, of course. I met a durrie weaver in Panipat who had set up his own factory but found it tough going, and both he and his wife wished he had stayed as a well-paid skilled employee. But they had consolations that would not have been possible in the 1980s – one son was running a 'tent house' business providing equipment for parties and the other one hoped to expand his father's factory one day.

Despite the enormous changes, old traditions remained. Krishna's daughter-in-law touched our feet as we walked into the house and when we left, but the daughter did not do so, showing the different status of the two young women in the husband's home. The daughter-in-law covered her head with her shawl as soon as a youngish man walked in, and removed it when he left.

Durries are now mostly made in factories, not in villages, though an elderly woman was weaving one with torn scraps of old material in Beejna, showing that the lifestyle of the very poor had changed little. Durries are also needed less because the charpoys on which they were used as thin mattresses are being replaced by plastic chairs. Bharat Carpet Manufacturers, the Panipat company that handled Darshan's durrie, has spun off another company, V-Weave, and has grown into a leading supplier to top American stores such as WestElm and Crate&Barrel. Madhukar Khera, who ran the firm in the 1980s, and his son Nikhil who is in charge now, have expanded traditional weaving skills to produce thick hand-spun wool rugs and other floor coverings. So, although the eventual takeover of Conran's shops did change the demand, and the brides-to-be no longer needed to weave them, the craft that started with the dowries is still thriving.

I found far less progress when I returned to a desperately poor tribal village adjacent to Kanha national park in the middle of India that I had last seen ten years earlier. Here, in this rural community, with the nearest city two-and-a-half hours away, the story was one of change but little progress. A 19-year-old son in the family I knew best had a modern-looking mobile phone, though he only used it for phone calls, and I was told almost everyone had mobiles in the more prosperous villages nearby. There were telecom towers in every large village (there had been two in Beejna). Many tribal people, particularly in the 1970s, had been crudely and insensitively shunted out of their traditional homes inside national parks. Later, when there was a formal resettlement process, they were cheated and harassed by forestry and banking officials on the preparation of their land and the handling of compensation. Most of the men had become heavy drinkers of the homemade 'mahua' liquor.

They and the women relied on casual labour for Rs 100 or so a day, working on repairing roads or in the mushrooming tourist resorts surrounding the national park. But few locals had the entrepreneurial drive, or the funds, to start small businesses such as roadside restaurants and shops. That was being done by people who had moved in from neighbouring towns. Many of the resorts catered to the brash new rich from the cities of Jabalpur and Nagpur, 160 and 260 km away, who had little care for the environment or the tribals. The local village market however had grown enormously in the past ten years, though it was still selling old-fashioned goods like plastic shoes, ancient-looking torches and religious posters. In other better-off farming villages, the young had dreams of venturing out to work in offices and call centres in distant towns, but not here.

The Maruti Revolution

One of the first signs that industry would change came at the beginning of the 1980s, at the same time that Indira Gandhi instigated the cement control reform mentioned in the previous chapter. This was when she initiated Maruti Udyog,[4] which became a successful joint venture with Suzuki of Japan. It will never be as famous as the Model 'T' Ford, or the Volkswagen Beetle, but the little Maruti Suzuki 800cc car that was first sold in 1983 is the most significant vehicle ever produced in India. The Ambassador car remains India's most famous saloon, but it is now a symbol of the manufacturing industry's limitations, whereas the Maruti has been the catalyst for India's modern and internationally competitive auto industry.

V. Krishnamurthy, a former top bureaucrat who became the founder-chairman, was told by Gandhi to revive the bankrupt Maruti car venture that had been started by her late son Sanjay Gandhi, who had been killed in 1980. She wanted a 'people's car', but instead the 800 became a car for the middle classes and was followed by larger models. I remember people in Delhi wondering how they would fit a driver into such a small car along with their families (they did!), and complaining (before they bought one) about how it nipped in and out of the traffic around larger, stodgier vehicles. Years earlier, there were similar complaints in Britain about the iconic Austin-Morris Mini.

The joint venture with Suzuki began to unlock India's hidden manufacturing strengths that had been bottled up by post-independence economic policies. I was at the opening of the factory in Gurgaon when Gandhi released the first cars to customers on 14 December 1983. I reported the next day in the *FT* that Osamu Suzuki, chairman of the Japanese company, had said to me that 'it is difficult to have a good operation in India'.[5] Demonstrating the Japanese determination to mark a new start for Indian industry, the imported management style decreed 'the recruitment of shop floor workers with an average age of 20 who have never worked anywhere before, wear grey overalls, do physical exercises every morning and prompt time-keeping'.

Few components could be made in India because there were virtually no suppliers producing to acceptable standards. Maruti Suzuki changed that with new concepts of quality, tight cost control and process engineering, sparking a revolution that spread across India's manufacturing industry. Not only were there no adequate component suppliers in 1983, but the idea of partnerships between a manufacturer and its suppliers was not understood. 'A supplier was treated almost like a servant,' says R.C. Bhargava, who was Maruti Suzuki's managing director in the 1980s and 1990s and is now the chairman.[6] Maruti changed that approach with a supplier development programme, taking 25 per cent equity stakes in some companies moving into India from Japan and elsewhere.

Now the roads are full of modern cars with Indian and international names, mostly manufactured in India, and Maruti is still the market leader. At the top end of the luxury range are imported names like Rolls Royce, Bentley, Lamborghini, in what has become their biggest market after China with foreign made models at prices up to Rs 4.5 crore, and some double that figure.

Business

The corporate scene has been transformed since 1991 – and it is for the better if one looks behind the crony capitalism that has drawn headlines in recent years and sees how companies of all sizes have grown, adapting to foreign competition and improving products. In the protected economy before 1991, the ambition of many big family business groups was to exploit links with government and prove their success by the size and visibility of their factories. They were less interested in efficiency and in operating profits. That changed when the economy opened up to international competition and foreign financing.

Information technology has played a special role because it brought a much-needed 'can do' confidence in the early 2000s to the business sector that had been bedevilled by India's image of poor-quality production. 'IT' has also provided direct employment for over 2.5m people, and maybe another 10m in spin-off work, with annual revenues of around $100 billion, 75 per cent exported. Call centres have become stepping stones to urban success for young people who may otherwise have been stuck in their villages for life.

Business families continue to dominate and are dynastically grooming younger generations to take over control though they now mostly have to earn their positions. They are supported by professional company directors and managers, with varying degrees of delegated authority, down the line. India's entrepreneurial potential has been demonstrated by companies such as the Tata and Reliance conglomerates straddling a range of industries, Bharti Airtel in mobile telephones (in Africa as well as India), Godrej in businesses from soaps to rockets, and Mahindra and Bajaj in autos. Some new businesses continue to excel at managing their relations with the government as entrepreneurially as their new ventures, with names like Adani in infrastructure, and various airlines, notably Jet Airways, emulating the success of the Ambanis. Many have formed pre-1991-style protectionist cliques, sometimes in league with the

Indian public sector, to restrict foreign investment in areas such as defence, airlines, insurance, supermarkets and retail food distribution until they are ready to cope with the competition.

In terms of caste and business communities, Marwaris, who were the most prominent among business families, have declined. This business clan comes from the deserts of Rajasthan and grew rich serving Mughal and British rulers, but its people are basically traders at heart so could not compete in a more open world. Names like Mafatlal, Dalmia, Scindia, Walchand, Shriram (DCM), Nanda (Escorts), and Modi have declined markedly and some have vanished. Just two branches of the once dominant Birla family empire remain significant: the Aditya Birla Group, which is run successfully by Kumar Mangalam Birla and is among the biggest in the country, and the *Hindustan Times* media group that is run by his cousin, Shobhana Bhartia.

Ratan Tata and Others

Ratan Tata, who headed the Tata conglomerate for 21 years till his 75th birthday in 2012, has been the most lauded businessman of the post-1991 era. He was a trailblazer, notably for spearheading foreign investments by Indian companies, spending about $20bn in just over a decade. It started rather unexcitingly with the purchase of Tetley Tea in the UK in 2000. More significant was the takeover of South Korea's Daewoo truck manufacturer in 2004, which showed that a company in India's largely unimpressive and uncompetitive manufacturing industry had the nerve and managerial ability to venture abroad and learn new skills. This marked what was becoming a turning point in Indian industry's self-confidence, which then grew rapidly in the mid to late 2000s, with many companies going abroad – and sometimes overextending themselves in terms of financial and managerial resources.

Tata Motors bought Britain's Jaguar Land Rover car business in 2007 from Ford Motor for $2.3bn, which became a winner because

Tata had the energy, finance and managerial strength to capitalize on design work started, but not carried through, by Ford. Less successful was a $11bn takeover of Europe's Corus steel business that left Tata Steel heavily indebted, but together the cars and steel acquisitions helped to turn Tata into Britain's biggest private sector employer with about 48,000 people on its payroll. By the time Ratan Tata retired, the group had become the first in India to record $100bn revenues (2011–12) and its interests ranged from tea to telecoms, software to hotels, wristwatches to defence rockets, and coffee (Starbucks) to power and steel with 450,000 employees worldwide.

No one has bestraddled Indian business in the way that Ratan Tata did. There has been no other Indian business figure of similar stature in the post-reform era, and no one near to being able to take his place as a symbol of managerial ethics and success despite the group's mixed reputation on environmental controls.[7]

Economics

The reforms had a surprisingly limited impact on sustained economic growth. In the 1960s and 1970s, the GDP growth rate had averaged only 3.5 per cent per year when other developing countries were growing much faster. The tentative reforms of the 1980s saw just under 5 per cent growth (5.6 per cent, if a 1988–91 boom is included), but that was largely based on a build-up of external debt that led to the 1991 crisis.[8] The 1991 reforms led to 6.7 per cent growth in 1994–95, but that slowed to 5.4 per cent in the second half of the 1990s, averaging 5.7 per cent over the decade – almost back to the 1980s' levels. India then entered what was billed as its shining years in the first decade of the 2000s, spurred as much by favourable global conditions as by the cumulative effect of the reforms, with growth nearing an unsustainable rate of 10 per cent. By 2013, however, it was back to not much more than 5 per cent as a result of adverse world economic conditions and insurmountable supply-side constraints within the country, ranging from bad infrastructure and skills shortages to weak and corrupt government institutions and blockages caused by environmental and other regulations.

Industry still only accounts for about 27 per cent of GDP, marginally more than 25 per cent in 1991. This is mainly because manufacturing has been stagnant at around 16 per cent since the 1980s (compared with 25–35 per cent in other Asian economies), employing only about 10 per cent of the workforce. Industry and government together have failed to capitalize on the potential generated by Maruti in the 1980s, and by the skills that enabled some leading companies to grow in later years. The services sector has grown to 60 per cent of GDP, but its labour force only accounts for 27 per cent of the total. There is a mismatch because manufacturing is not creating the jobs that India's so-called demographic dividend of young people will need in the next 20 years, while the services sector faces shortages.

The social record is disappointing. Poverty has been considerably reduced from 50 per cent of the population in 1990 to between 20 per cent and 30 per cent, according to (much debated) official figures, and there have been considerable improvements in areas such as access to drinking water and basic education, but it is more significant to say broadly that more than half of the 1.2bn population are poorly fed and with inadequate access to basic health care, clean water, sanitation facilities and adequate education. So slow has been the improvement of living standards that World Bank data shows only five countries outside Africa (Afghanistan, Bhutan, Pakistan, Papua New Guinea and Yemen) have a lower literacy rate for female youth, with similar low ratings for child mortality, underweight children and other social indicators.[9] 'There is probably no other example in the history of world development of an economy growing so fast for so long with such limited results in terms of broad-based social progress,' say Amartya Sen, economist and Nobel prize winner in 1998, and Jean Drèze, a development economist.[10]

This has led to a debate over how much policy priority should be given to pushing growth or to financing aid schemes that are inherently wasteful because of the weakness and corruption of public institutions responsible for distribution programmes, and because it is people who are not poor who often benefit from subsidies. The emphasis of the 2009 UPA government was more on distribution, with Sonia and Rahul Gandhi favouring handouts for the poor, while Manmohan Singh and his advisers wanted reforms and cuts in subsidies that would lead to growth. What is needed, of course, is a mixture of both, but what India needs most is basic changes in the way the governments in the states as well as in Delhi operate and implement policies that are already in place.

That said, the stories of Beejna, Maruti, Tata and others show that Narasimha Rao did indeed launch India on a new path in 1991, when he picked up the threads of reforms developed and debated in previous years, and turned them into policies that were then implemented. The gains that he set in motion are beyond doubt.

Notes

1. Conversation with JE, September 2013, along with others from Ritinjali, http://www.ritinjali.org/ – and Arun Kapur, who runs the night school and a second chance school – http://www.ritinjali.org/initiatives/second-chance-school as well as Vasant Valley School
2. JE, 'Great Expectations: Teenagers in India have big ambitions – and the confidence to match, *Fortune* magazine, 25 July 2005, http://money.cnn.com/magazines/fortune/fortune_archive/2005/07/25/8266604/
3. JE, 'Darshan weaves her way to a dowry', *Financial Times*, 14 November 1987
4. http://ridingtheelephant.wordpress.com/2008/12/14/today-is-the-25th-anniversary-of-the-maruti-suzuki-car-that-changed-india%E2%80%99s-motor-industry/
5. JE, 'India File', *Financial Times*, 15 December 1983
6. R.C. Bhargava and Seetha, *The Maruti Story: How a Public Sector Company put India on Wheels*, HarperCollins India, 2010, http://www.harpercollins.co.in/BookDetail.asp?Book_Code=3822

7. http://ridingtheelephant.wordpress.com/2012/12/29/ratan-tata-indias-sensitive-and-visionary-tycoon-steps-down/

8. Statistics and interpretation partly based on 'Prospects and Policy Challenges in the Twelfth Plan', a speech by Montek S. Ahluwalia, 21 May 2011, http://planningcommission.nic.in/aboutus/speech/spemsa/spe_21052011.pdf; also Arvind Panagariya, *India: the Emerging Giant*, Oxford, 2008

9. Jean Drèze and Amartya Sen, 'Growth in Its Place – It has to be but a means to development, not an end in itself', *Outlook* magazine, 14 November 2011, http://www.outlookindia.com/article.aspx?278843; also see Amartya Sen and Jean Drèze, *An Uncertain Glory: India and its Contradictions*, Allen Lane, London, and Princeton University Press, New Jersey. Reviewed in *The Economist, http://www.economist.com/news/books-and-arts/21580124-why-worlds-biggest-democracy-still-fails-too-many-its-people-beyond-bootstraps*

10. Ibid.

8

Losing the Environment

India's environment is at the centre of the debate over liberalization and the future of India's economic growth, and it is in a no-win situation. On the one hand, mountains and hills, forests and rivers have been plundered by mining that is often illegal, and by other industrial and commercial activities that have laid to waste much of India's natural heritage, causing social upheaval and irreparable damage. Sometimes there is loss of life, as was seen in the Himalayan state of Uttarakhand in 2013 when devastating floods led to more than 6,000 deaths.[1] On the other hand, environmentalists are blamed for challenging industrial, mining and highway projects and creating procedural blockages that slow down essential investment and development.

Environmentalists see the debate in terms of protecting forests, rivers and wildlife, and they worry that they are losing the battle, which indeed they are. Businessmen, almost without exception, see the environment as something that has to give way to allow investments and development to go ahead. They grumble that projects are being held up while those who are well connected bribe politicians and officials to let their projects through – though the environment ministry claims that the vast majority of proposals are sanctioned. Politicians usually back the growth story and are often involved at both the national and state level in trying to undermine the environmentalists, either by revising regulations, as Prime Minister Manmohan Singh has been trying to do since 2004, or by circumventing them and accepting bribes for doing so.

Tribal communities, who occupy potentially lucrative forests and mountains, complicate the issue. There are about 96m Adivasis in India, belonging to various 'scheduled tribes' that make up about 8 per cent of the population.[2] They are mostly forest dwellers who live in relatively remote regions that were inaccessible until the mid-1900s when they were penetrated by mining companies and others that did not have a good record of caring for the interests of those they displaced. Since then, huge sums have been spent in trying to bring these tribal communities into the mainstream, for the most part unsuccessfully. Tribals are also seen as a potential vote bank by politicians including Sonia Gandhi and her advisers. The threat to peace and security posed by Maoist Naxalite rebels is linked with this because they thrive in remote areas inhabited by tribal communities and where the environment is threatened by illicit mining and similar activities.

Put bluntly, the poor will remain poor and India will not meet its economic potential unless some forests are cut down, some mountains and rivers are mined, some tribal people lose their habitats, some coastlines are disrupted by ports, and agricultural land is used for industry. But that threatens precious natural resources and the livelihood of the poor, so the issue is how to ensure that development happens equitably, without devastating the environment and without adding to the already toxic air pollution, filthy rivers and health risks.

Tigers to China

The lack of public interest is demonstrated by the plight of wildlife, especially the tiger and the elephant. The tiger is India's national animal and one of India's greatest natural assets, yet there are only about 1,700 left in the country, according to a 2011 census that produced a range with a minimum figure of 1571 and a maximum of 1875.[3] That is better than the 1400 recorded in 2008, though new areas were added in the survey, including the important Sunderbans tidal mangrove forests in West Bengal. The increase was therefore probably not significant, and the numbers were dramatically down from an estimated 3,500 in 2002, though again it is difficult to compare the figures because a new counting method was used. If numbers continue to decline, eventual extinction of tigers in the wild would seem to be inevitable. And if the government cannot get to grips with the survival of this high-profile and iconic animal, it seems unlikely that it will be able to protect the rest of India's natural heritage.[4]

There is big money to be made by poaching tigers and smuggling their body parts out of India. Wildlife trafficking is the third or fourth largest illegal trade in the world after arms and narcotics, and is worth billions of dollars. 'India has a vast array of wildlife species that are highly valued in the illegal trade – from the spiny-tailed lizard of the desert to the musk deer of the Himalayan foothills to sea cucumbers from our coral reefs. And, of course, tigers. Unfortunately tigers are valued more than most other species because of their beauty, strength and power,' says Belinda Wright, one of India's leading wildlife conservationists, who runs the Wildlife Protection Society of India (WPSI).[5] 'Every part of the tiger – be it whiskers, eyeballs, penis or bones – has a use in traditional Chinese medicine,' she says. WPSI's wildlife crime database illustrates the scale of the trade – it has information on over 19,000 wildlife criminals and more than 22,000 wildlife cases involving some 400 species.[6] The Indian poacher makes an increasingly large profit and, on the international market, an animal can account for tens of thousands of dollars. Lowly officials grow rich on the kickbacks that they are paid to facilitate – or at least ignore – the poachers and traders as the parts travel by land across India, into and across Nepal, and then into China.

Sadly, the wild tiger does not attract the sort of widespread public admiration in India that it does abroad, even though it has a place in the Hindu religion with the goddess Durga being worshipped riding a tiger. So it is easy for the government to issue reports and then do little, and for senior bureaucrats in charge of protecting wildlife to be lauded internationally for what look like, but often are not, sound initiatives. What the government should be doing is revamping its grossly understaffed and unmotivated forest protection service – the state forest departments – and strengthening enforcement and prosecution of poachers and traders.

The problem however will never be solved just by tackling the supply in India's wildlife parks because this is a demand-driven trade. The only really effective way to protect tigers and other wildlife is to persuade China – the largest consumer of wildlife parts, such as tiger skin and bones, elephant ivory, bear bile and pangolin scales – to improve and implement their own wildlife protection laws, including a 1993 ban on the use of tiger bones in traditional Chinese medicine. 'If India wants to secure a future for wild tigers, it not only has to improve enforcement but stem the demand by talking forcefully to China to persuade it to ban all trade in tiger parts from all sources,' says Wright. India, however, seems scared of tackling China on this issue, as on so much else. Tiger farms in China have 7,000 or more captive breeding tigers which supply bone for traditional medicine, some allegedly with permits, despite the ban. The sad twist to the tale is that Chinese consumers want bones from wild, not captive, tigers.

The 'J Factor'

Much of the debate in recent years has centred on Jairam Ramesh, a highly intelligent, hard-working and extrovert economic-policy-adviser-turned-politician, who enjoys controversy and was a high-profile minister for environment and forests from May 2009 to July 2011. He then became minister of rural development. Though he has more critics than supporters stemming from his time handling the environment ministry, his ministerial journey illustrates the pressures and vested interests in the environment-versus-growth debate.

Ramesh, who qualified as a mechanical engineer and then studied public policy, has been at or near the centre of the government's economic policy-making since the 1980s. (I first met him around

1985–86 at the Planning Commission, then being run by Manmohan Singh). He has always been a committed reformer, and was India's first non-corrupt, policy-oriented and knowledgeable environment minister for at least a decade. When he was appointed, I wrote on my blog[7] that he was determined to clean up a ministry that had been allowing India's environment and wildlife to be plundered and to decay during the ten years that it had been headed by ministerial nominees from a regional Tamil Nadu-based party, the Dravida Munnettra Kazhagam (DMK). Ramesh was backed by Sonia Gandhi and Manmohan Singh and he said then that Singh had also asked him to moderate India's negative stance on climate change, saying, 'India has not caused the problem of global warming. But try and make sure that India is part of the solution. Be constructive; be proactive.'[8]

On the environment, Ramesh took on powerful corporate interests who fought back (with the help of parts of the media, especially *The Indian Express*) and accused him of being anti-growth and of blocking so many projects that investment was being driven abroad. The attacks sharpened after he halted construction for a year at Lavasa, a 25,000-acre rural city project in the undeveloped rolling hills of Maharashtra where there were allegations of illegal land acquisition and violation of environmental regulations. Built by Hindustan Construction, this project had backers with strong political links, including the family of Sharad Pawar, the state's most powerful politician and minister of agriculture in India's 2004–14 UPA governments.[9]

A few months after being appointed, Ramesh said he would not allow two coal mines linked to power projects planned by the Gujarat-based Adani Group near Maharashtra's Tadoba Andhari tiger reserve. Run by Gautam Adani, the group rivals Reliance's Ambani family for political punch in its chosen areas that include coal imports, which it dominates, as well as infrastructure projects. The government was split over what Ramesh was doing and his opponents included Praful Patel, a suave business-oriented politician close to Pawar and (at the time) a controversial aviation minister. The project was in

Patel's hometown of Gondia. 'We are not going to compromise ecological security in the name of development ... The ministry of environment and forests is going to be quite fundamentalist on these issues,' said Ramesh,[10] knowing that he had the backing of Sonia Gandhi, who had earlier opposed the mines.[11]

He gradually lost Manmohan Singh's support however, when he blocked other important developments including a $12bn steel project planned in Orissa by Posco of South Korea, which the prime minister was personally favouring. He halted more coal mines by introducing a 'no go' concept for just under half of the 600 areas involved, based on the density of their forest locations – 21 per cent of India's total land mass is covered by forests, including 2 per cent dense forest (which is thick with trees and a closed overhead canopy) and 10 per cent moderately dense. This sharpened an existing crisis in India's power sector by curbing the growth of urgently needed coal supplies. Also on Ramesh's list was an internationally controversial bauxite mining and alumina project being developed in a tribal-dominated area in Odisha by Vedanta, a London-based Indian metals and mining company. Others hit included a politically influential branch of the Jindal steel and mining family (later investigated for coal mining bribes) which was accused of ignoring environmental requirements on another Odisha steelworks.

Probably his most popular move was to ban the introduction of a genetically modified version of a popular vegetable, known as BT brinjal, which had been developed by Mahyco, a subsidiary of the multinational company Monsanto. Mass production of the modified aubergine had been approved by an environment ministry committee in October 2009, but Ramesh responded to an intensive campaign, partly led by Greenpeace, the environmental organization. He held public consultations in seven cities that were attended by about 8,000 people including farmers, scientists and activists, and in February 2010 announced an indefinite moratorium till studies established BT brinjal's safety and long-term impact on human health and the environment. He cited a lack of scientific consensus on its safety along with opposition from ten state governments and the lack of an independent biotechnology regulatory authority.

All this led to immense pressure from opponents who included, to varying degrees, the prime minister, Montek Singh Ahluwalia and other government ministers. Ramesh gradually had to give way on many of the coal mining 'no go' areas and other projects, though he usually often claimed – for example, on Lavasa – that he had ensured that regulations were followed or environmentally improved. He compromised with Patel on a new airport for Mumbai, claiming he had achieved 80 per cent of what he wanted. But he also admitted that he felt 'guilty' for succumbing to pressure to breach regulations in some cases. 'Unfortunately, many times I am forced to regularise. Because I have no option, because one refinery has been built … a steel plant has been built. So I am guilty in some cases of having actually condoned many environmental violations,' he said at a management conference in May 2011.[12]

Around the same time, despite knowing about inadequate relief and rehabilitation work, he gave conditional clearance to a 400MW hydroelectric project in Madhya Pradesh, at Maheshwar, which was part of a highly controversial engineering scheme on the Narmada, one of India's largest rivers. This followed intervention by the prime minister's office, which led Ramesh to say he had 'no option but to agree to lifting the stop-work order on the construction of the last five spillway gates'. He told the media that, even though he knew that regulations had been violated, he had to refuse to reverse clearances on various power projects and on a port being built by Tata Steel at Dhamra in Odisha.[13] Greenpeace and other environmental groups had earlier accused Tata, which was in a 50–50 joint venture with Larsen & Toubro (L&T), a large Indian construction company, of starting construction without obtaining adequate environmental clearances and without honouring commitments made by Ratan Tata, the company's chairman.[14]

Two months after making the remarks about being forced to approve projects, Ramesh was transferred in a ministerial reshuffle.[15] He left behind a very mixed reputation. There were the angry businessmen whose projects had been hit and who were not used to dealing with an environment minister who could not be bought. Experts had become bewildered and there was despair among environmentalists about his style and lack of consistency.[16] 'He was like the curate's egg,' says Bittu Sahgal, editor of *Sanctuary Asia*, India's leading wildlife magazine, using an English expression that means, depending on one's interpretation, 'bad, but I won't say so', or 'bad and good in parts'.[17]

Initially, the environmentalists had welcomed Ramesh, saying he was the most active and well-informed minister that India had ever had, and that he brought a positive focus to wildlife and other issues that had not been seen since Indira Gandhi was prime minister. Some felt let down because he had not honoured commitments, and many regarded his actions as capricious, publicity-seeking and sometimes politically motivated – for example, doing what he knew would be supported by Sonia and Rahul Gandhi for socially conscious vote-getting reasons on projects like Posco and Vedanta, while ignoring other, less sensationalist breaches of regulations. Ramesh denied this and said he divided projects into 'yes', 'yes but' and 'no' categories. That led to 95 per cent of applications being approved, 'down from 99.99 per cent earlier'. Perhaps his one-time environmental supporters were right to become disillusioned with such a small improvement after all the noise.

But Ramesh had put the environment firmly on India's political agenda and had begun to clean up a highly corrupt ministry, setting up new environmental and conservation regulations and institutions including coastal development guidelines and a National Green Tribunal to adjudicate on environmental issues. He also changed India's role in international climate change negotiations. In a speech to businesspeople three months before he was transferred, Ramesh appealed to them to 'take the environment far more seriously and not see it as a problem', adding: 'See the environment not as a cost or obligation or favour to someone else, but as something intrinsic to the growth process.'

His actions made it easier for his successor, Jayanthi Natarajan, to resist pressures from elsewhere in the government. She had previously been an able and sometimes tough Congress party spokesperson and was expected to be far less confrontational and more pragmatic than Ramesh. She scrapped the 'no go' coal mining areas and allowed some controversial power projects but, probably with Sonia Gandhi's backing, she challenged the prime minister's office and other government departments on various other issues. She successfully forced Singh to water down plans for a new National Investment Board that would reduce the impact of environmental and other regulations on new projects.[18] As a result, she pleased neither camp and was increasingly bracketed along with Ramesh by business interests and their supporters in the media. This was illustrated by an *India Today* article headlined 'Green Terror', which talked about the 'J factor' – Jairam Ramesh and Jayanthi Natarajan. It said they had made the ministry 'the single biggest stumbling block to India's growth story', which was scarcely fair.[19] Yet environmentalists complained that, between 2004 and 2013, the ministry had approved the destruction of 600,000 hectares of forestland, of which 250,000 hectares were for mining, and had rejected proposals to do with only 14,000 hectares.[20]

In December 2013, Natarajan was moved out of the ministry to the Congress party office and her job was taken over by Veerappa Moily, the petroleum minister and a leading critic of her ministry's decisions. On the same day, Rahul Gandhi told a business meeting that he understood their frustration over environmental clearances.

Ramesh continued to work in the same sort of areas when he moved to be minister for rural development, notably implementing long-delayed legislation on the use of land for industrial purposes and trying to develop areas previously held by Naxalite rebels. He used to say that the nature of the environment minister's job was 'to upset politicians, industry and environmentalists' and that he wanted to 'bring the environment into politics and public discourse'.[21] He certainly did all that but, sadly, he did not manage to change attitudes in the environment-versus-growth debate.

The bottom line is that the profits made by spoiling the environment are just too big and risky for a reasoned debate in India's present stage of development. In its rush for growth, there is little fundamental public interest in protecting the environment, scant respect for the rule of law, and widespread acceptance of corruption as a way of getting things done. This does not, of course, apply only to India. Growth versus the environment is a global conundrum, but it is more urgent in this country because of the need and pressure for growth, and because of the extent of the greed and corruption that has led to the environment being plundered.

Notes

1. 'Uttarakhand is paying the high price of anti-environmentalism', *First Post India*, 24 June 2013, http://www.firstpost.com/india/uttarakhand-is-paying-the-high-price-of-anti-environmentalism-900677.html

2. *World Directory of Minorities and Indigenous Peoples – India: Adivasis 2008*, UNHCR, http://www.unhcr.org/refworld/docid/49749d14c.html

3. Current Status of Tiger in India, WPSI website, http://www.wpsi-india.org/tiger/tiger_status.php

4. https://ridingtheelephant.wordpress.com/2008/02/13/demand-from-china-kills-indias-vanishing-tigers

5. 'Wild India's Grim Reapers: Interview with Belinda Wright', WPSI, *Conservation India*, 8 February 2011, http://www.conservationindia.org/articles/trends-in-wildlife-crime-interview-with-belinda-wright-wpsi

6. Database on Tiger Poaching, Trade & Wildlife Crimes, WPSI, http://www.wpsi-india.org/projects/poaching_database.php

7. http://ridingtheelephant.wordpress.com/2009/12/11/india-to-protect-the-environment-from-damaging-development-projects/

8. http://ridingtheelephant.wordpress.com/2009/12/09/jairam-ramesh-sets-the-pace-on-india%E2%80%99s-climate-change-and-environment-policies

9. 'Lavasa: slow motion city – Construction has picked up in the last year-and-a-half and tourist numbers are rising; still, Lavasa has not yet become the promised bustling city', *Business Standard*, 8 June 2013, http://www.business-standard.com/article/beyond-business/lavasa-slow-motion-city-113060700981_1.html

10. http://ridingtheelephant.wordpress.com/2009/12/11/india-to-protect-the-environment-from-damaging-development-projects/

11. 'Cong, NCP split over Adani mines', *The Times of India*, 3 August 2009, http://articles.timesofindia.indiatimes.com/2009-08-03/nagpur/ 28179621_1_adani-mines-coal-tiger-habitat

12. '"I have been forced to regularise illegality": Jairam Ramesh', *The Economic Times*, 6 May 2011, http://articles.economictimes.indiatimes.com/2011-05-06/news/29516925_1_regularise-constructions-environmental-violations

13. '"All go-aheads not green": Ramesh', *Hindustan Times*, 6 May 2011, http://www.hindustantimes.com/News-Feed/newdelhi/I-am-forced-to-regularise-compromise-on-green-norms-Jairam-Ramesh/Article1-694188.aspx

14. https://ridingtheelephant.wordpress.com/2008/05/29/greenpeace-targets-tata-over-rare-sea-turtles/

15. http://ridingtheelephant.wordpress.com/2011/07/12/jairam-ramesh-ousted-from-environment-in-india-reshuffle

16. Himanshu Thakkar, coordinator of the South Asia Network on Dams, Rivers & People, 'What Jairam did and didn't do as green minister', Rediff.com, 20 July 2011, http://www.rediff.com/news/column/what-jairam-ramesh-did-and-did-not-do-as-green-minister/20110720.htm

17. In conversation with JE, September 2013

18. 'Jayanthi Natarajan raises green objections to National Investment Board', PTI, 9 October 2012, http://indiatoday.intoday.in/story/jayanthi-natarajan-manmohan-singh-national-investment-board/1/224078.html

19. 'Green Terror: Outdated environmental laws and inflexible ministers strangle Indian economy', *India Today*, 8 October 2012, http://indiatoday.intoday.in/story/green-terror-jairam-jayanthi-regime-green-projects-vs-pmo/1/223589.html

20. 'Since 2004, 6 lakh hectares of forest cleared for mining', *The Times*

of India, 20 April 2013, http://articles.timesofindia.indiatimes.com/2013-04-20/developmental-issues/38692616_1_niyamgiri-hills-forest-rights-act-forest-clearance

21. Jairam Ramesh speaking at the Foreign Correspondents' Club, New Delhi, 14 February 2011

III

SOCIAL CHANGE

9

The Power of Protest

Just before Christmas Day 2012, I was standing on a Sunday evening with a thousand or more peaceful demonstrators near the ceremonial arch of India Gate – Delhi's equivalent of the Arc de Triomphe in Paris – when we were swept from the area by the force of a massive water cannon and by a horde of police and paramilitary wielding the lathis that they often use to beat the weak and vulnerable.[1] Till a few minutes earlier, the demonstrators, many of them young women, had been clustered in groups, some singing and some listening to speeches on the theme of 'Give us justice'. Others stood around television cameras, watching interviews. Sellers of chai, sweet potato and other snacks were doing a brisk business. No one expected that the security forces, who were attempting to clear serious troublemakers a few hundred yards to the west, would come round the monumental arch. 'Stay by our installation and you'll be okay,' joked Jehangir Pocha of the NewsX TV station who was broadcasting on the event.

When it became clear that NewsX's trestle table and equipment were not a safe haven, I turned and ran with the crowds till the police, lashing at anyone they could reach, caught up with me. It was then safer to turn and walk towards the charge, rather than to appear to be running away – which I did, with my hands half-raised, saying 'press, press'. The police dodged round me, swiping their sticks against those in their way. They continued irrationally to beat individuals, including women, who were leaving the surrounding area – a verbal instruction to go would have been enough. Tear gas shells could be heard going off nearby to deal with other demonstrators.

Brutal policing is commonplace in India, but that evening was significant because it was such an outrageously crude and vicious way to try to end the focal point of six days of countrywide mass protests that had been sparked by the gang rape and battering of a 23-year-old paramedical student. Driven around Delhi in a curtained bus, the student had been dumped with a male friend, virtually naked, on a dirt track beside a busy highway to the city's airport. This provoked a national outcry and intense international and local media attention that generated continuing coverage of atrocities against women for months. The student – called Nirbhaya (fearless) and Braveheart by the media before her name, Jyoti Singh Pandey, was revealed[2] – died on 29 December of multiple organ failure in a Singapore hospital. Three days earlier, she had been controversially flown there – a journey of 2,500 miles – after intelligence agencies apparently advised the government that there could be a massive public backlash if her seemingly inevitable death happened in India under the questionable care of Delhi doctors.

The day before I was caught in the police charge, thousands of demonstrators had staged unprecedented mass protests and had reached the gates of Rashtrapati Bhavan, the presidential palace on Raisina Hill that marks the other end of the grand processional Raj Path from India Gate. Tear gas shells were fired in the afternoon on the Sunday, and troublemakers in the crowd managed to advance a few yards along Rajpath, smashing police barricades, pelting stones and pushing back a paramilitary force several lines deep. Later the rioters lit bonfires with wooden media observation towers and fencing and smashed metal barricades. This enlarged the area engulfed with violence, but the incidents were isolated, and involved just a few dozen of the several thousand people there who were basically peaceful protestors and sympathetic spectators.

A Frightened Government

The unnecessary water cannon and lathi-charging – and sending Jyoti Pandey to die in Singapore – were the actions of a frightened government after three years of growing street protests and unrest. This came around the time that the Arab Spring uprisings were evicting regimes in Tunisia, Egypt and other Middle East (West Asia) countries. There was, of course, no risk of India's government being unseated, but ministers and officials were becoming aware that the complaints had a wider base than the immediate cases of rape and widespread, endemic male cruelty towards women.

The middle class was beginning to demand a voice that had not been heard before. There had been mass middle-class demonstrations against corruption in the previous 18 months, led by the veteran and publicity-savvy social activist, 74-year-old Kisan Baburao 'Anna' Hazare and Arvind Kejriwal, the politically ambitious anti-corruption campaigner who became the chief minister of Delhi in December 2013. These protests also carried a wider message that the tide was turning, particularly among young people in their 20s and 30s, against both rampant graft and poor governance. For decades, people had tolerated petty corruption in their daily lives, paying for minor government services. But in 2011, the protests erupted over delays in the creation of a Lok Pal, an anti-corruption ombudsman, at a time when the government was blatantly corrupt to an extent not seen before, condoned by an apparently 'clean' prime minister and Sonia Gandhi.

The motivation of the crowds was to target an indifferent and inactive government, a desperately slow legal system that failed to administer justice, and inhumanly violent police and security forces that mostly saw it as their job to beat, hurt and exploit the weak and defenceless, including women, instead of protecting them. The social media played a key role in the protests, providing unorganized angry middle-class people with the opportunity to air views that previously would not have been heard. Television channels escalated the protests with round-the-clock and overhyped coverage of seemingly endless discussion groups and on-the-spot interviews. I saw TV interviewers from leading channels virtually screaming into their cameras at India Gate as if they were in the middle of a war zone, whereas they were mostly surrounded by quiet, curious crowds. As with the Hazare anti-corruption movement, the women's rape protests would never have been so large were it not for television, plus the social media and, of course, mobile phone text messaging – a potent weapon in a country with nearly 900m mobile subscribers.

The government had certainly got the message from the women's demonstrations that some display of change was required. No doubt spurred by the imminence of a general election, due in just over a year (April–May 2014), it showed media-oriented and overhyped concern.[3] In a public relations splurge of insensitive symbolism, Sonia Gandhi and Manmohan Singh went to Delhi airport around 3.30 a.m. on a Sunday morning to meet Pandey's body with her family when she was flown back from Singapore. Two other political leaders went to the heavily guarded private cremation – one was Sheila Dikshit, the Delhi chief minister who, with assembly elections approaching, was trying to improve her image after playing politics over poor police handling of the issue. She had even been booed when she visited the protestors. Sonia Gandhi unusually led from the front, reflecting the nation's horror and grief, despite her own poor health.

Five weeks after the rape, Pranab Mukherjee, the country's president, said in his eve of Republic Day address: 'The brutal rape and murder of a young woman, a woman who was a symbol of all that new India strives to be, has left our hearts empty and our minds in turmoil. We lost more than a valuable life; we lost a dream. If today young Indians feel outraged, can we blame our youth?'[4] A week later, in early February, continuing what had become a rather crude media blitzkrieg, Sonia Gandhi again went to visit the family of the gang-rape victim and took Rahul Gandhi, who characteristically had been virtually invisible during the mass protests but was by then slightly more active because he had become the Congress vice-president.

Wave of Protests

These were the latest – and socially and politically the most significant – of a wave of protests that had swept India in recent years. They were historically important because they brought middle class and professional people out onto the streets, whereas earlier protests had mostly involved the rural poor opposing the conversion of agricultural and tribal land for industrial, mining and real estate development.

All the protesters – from the women at India Gate and the Hazare crowds to politicians and villagers who blocked industrial projects in West Bengal and Orissa – were demanding something better from modern India after more than two decades of economic development and six decades of post-independence democratic rule. The same message had been carried in November 2007 when 25,000 landless workers marched 320 km to Delhi to highlight their plight as real estate and other developments swept away their traditional agricultural jobs, often forcibly acquiring their land.[5] Members of the Gujjar pastoral tribe from Rajasthan, who had marched on Delhi a few months earlier, were asking for official tribal status and public sector job reservations because they felt left out of the growing riches around them. Such rural-based protests, however, rarely aroused more than passing interest in Delhi unless they involved massive violence and killings, or Naxalite activity.

The November 2007 march coincided with a big *Fortune* magazine Global Forum conference, in which a few hundred international businessmen were secluded in the old-style elegance of Delhi's Imperial Hotel. This prompted Jo Johnson, then the *FT*'s South Asia correspondent (later a Conservative member of parliament in the UK and policy adviser to David Cameron, the prime minister), to write about what the top executives would have seen if they had ventured out of their secluded surroundings: 'From the stunted and wasted frames of the landless, they would have observed how malnutrition rates, already higher than in parts of sub-Saharan Africa, are rising in many places, as wages lag behind soaring food prices. They would have learnt how the 120m families, who depend on the land for subsistence agriculture, generating no marketable surplus from one season to the next, live in terror of expropriation by state governments operating land scams in the name of development.'[6]

The common thread in all these protests related to the fact that, while life has been transformed in many ways for the elite and a growing middle class, many things have not changed. Villagers are being left behind as urbanization sweeps through their fields, making real estate profits for speculators, and tribals are losing out as mining companies dig in their remote forest and mountain habitats. Society is still male dominated, defying the economic and social changes of the past 20 years that have transformed many women's potential careers and lifestyles. Women are also frequently treated with disdain – especially by the police, as was evident with the gang rape and its aftermath.

In none of these instances had the government and other authorities performed adequately. There had been a failure both to transform the police into well-trained and socially responsible guardians of the law, and to revamp and speed up a legal system where cases can last for 20 years or more. It was a mark of official indifference that six years after the 2007 march, politicians were still squabbling about rewriting laws contained in a 1894 Act and curbing government powers to take over land compulsorily without adequate compensation for existing landholders.

Punishment

Even more frightening for the officials who sat huddled, wondering what to do, in the prime minister's office and ministry of home affairs on Raisina Hill that week in December 2012 was the realization that the anti-rape protests were entirely spontaneous and (despite the gradual involvement of some women's organizations) had no leader like Hazare, Kejriwal and their hangers-on to mobilize meetings and media hype. There was no one they could either pillory or engage in negotiations, as they had done with Hazare. Hosing and chasing the crowds away was therefore a quick and easy solution, followed by gesture politics that included a flood of sympathetic statements and public appearances from hitherto invisible, silent and often contemptuous politicians and police, plus a security clampdown in the centre of the capital that closed many roads.

The government set up what turned out to be one of the fastest ever committees of inquiry under a distinguished judge, J.S. Verma, a former Chief Justice of the Supreme Court, to recommend amendments to the criminal law that would lead to quicker trials and stiffer punishments for sexual assault against women. The Committee submitted its report on 23 January 2013,[7] and the government set up fast-track courts and introduced a temporary ordinance which introduced the death penalty for rape that led to death or left a victim in a coma. This was much tougher than the previous seven to ten years' imprisonment. The minimum sentence was doubled from ten to 20 years, with a maximum of life without parole, for rape of a minor as well as rape by policemen or others in authority, and gang rape. Public demands for the death penalty were met when the ordinance was replaced by new laws in April 2013 providing for execution of repeat offenders – with imprisonment for between 20 years and life before that.[8] That led to four of Jyoti Pandey's rapists being sentenced to death.

Stiffer penalties for police were also included in the new laws, which was significant because the police rarely helped victims, and were sometimes themselves involved in rapes. At the end of 2012, there were, for example, reports of a policeman and his nephew raping a young woman who wanted to be recruited into the force, and of a 17-year-old girl in Punjab committing suicide because she was being harassed after it had taken her 14 days to persuade police to accept her gang-rape accusation. A friend of mine wrote on Facebook[9] about how he and a woman lawyer living in west Delhi took an eight-year-old girl to the police with her semiliterate, frightened dhobi (laundryman) father, who lived nearby. The father kept repeating 'Meri beti ke saath kuch ladkon nein bura kiya' (some boys have done something bad to my daughter). The police at first were sympathetic, but after a day or two said: 'When both her parents are at work, she crosses two roads and the train tracks to move around with boys of another locality. She is a very bad character, and if any boy does anything to her, she totally deserves it'. The girl was only eight.

A Repressed Patriarchal Society

The women's protest movement, unlike the earlier corruption demonstrations, was genuinely spontaneous and was significant because women suddenly found that, for the first time in their lives, they could come out openly and talk about assaults that they had previously kept quiet about. An astonishing number of women have stories of being seriously harassed and attacked, often on buses where eve-teasing (men touching women provocatively) had turned into something more insistent and aggressive. Other stories are of rape nearer home. Statistics indicate that victims' relatives and neighbours are often the attackers. Police records show that in as many as 96 per cent of the cases men known to the victim were responsible for the rape.[10]

Bollywood films increasingly encourage frustrated men to assume their victims are available by depicting women provocatively, glorifying instant sex rather than relationships. The easy accessibility of pornographic material on the internet[11] and mobile phones is likely to have done even more than films to reduce respect for women and increase the desires and frustrations of young men who have been brought up in a basically repressed society.

India's patriarchal traditions, which have created a society where women have been dominated by men who show them little respect, were on display in reactions to the outcry over the gang rape. Illustrating the lack of concern about rape, political parties gave tickets in the 2009 general election to six candidates who had declared that they had been charged with rape, and 34 other candidates who declared that they had been charged with crimes against women.[12] In traditional male-dominated rural societies, and in the recently urbanized north Indian states of Haryana and Uttar Pradesh, local clan-based councils of male elders called khap panchayats rarely side with rape victims. When a spate of rapes happened in Haryana, a khap panchayat said the solution was for the young to get married, without any minimum age limit, so that their 'sexual desires find safe outlets'. Often young girls who belong to the Dalit community ('untouchables' in the caste system) are raped in a form of lower-caste oppression. Panchayats sometimes suggest a victim should marry the rapist because, so the argument goes, no other man in the locality will have her. Women are blamed for being provocative, or the intercourse is dubbed consensual – a line often taken by the police. Women can also be subjected to a humiliating and irrelevant 'fingers test'[13] to assess sexual activity, which defence lawyers then use to argue that rape has not occurred because such activity has been frequent and consensual. It was only in 2013 that the Supreme Court asked the government to change medical procedures.[14]

Patriarchal and macho attitudes have been exacerbated by rapid economic change. Women have in the past 20 years or so become free and able to develop professional and other careers where they progress rapidly, often outclassing men in their adaptability and lack of status-consciousness and other hang-ups. This, of course, has happened in many countries in the past 50 to 100 years, but in India it has been enormously faster and also more controversial because of traditional male attitudes that are evident across classes and castes, but are perhaps harshest in villages where these traditions are strong. Women are becoming economically equal with men, and are showing new independence in their careers, frequently outclassing male colleagues, and have more liberated private lives, especially in urban areas. Unemployment among poorly educated young men, who cannot find suitable semi-skilled jobs and have nothing to occupy their time, adds to the problem. There is a 'crisis of masculinity because women are doing well, and there is a vast pool of less educated and unemployed males who get little respect even at home,' says Ravinder Kaur, a sociologist at the Indian Institute of Technology in Delhi.[15]

Khap panchayats produce clan-based, chauvinistic and often violent reactions to social issues such as mixed-caste marriages, especially in Haryana and Uttar Pradesh, where the khap leaders are anxious to maintain their social importance in a rapidly modernizing environment. They cause 'honour killings' that are carried out by families or neighbours of young people who have broken what they see as binding codes of behaviour. Two widows who were said to be in a lesbian relationship were beaten to death in Haryana by a 23-year-old nephew of one of the women, who was a convicted rapist. There are stories of murder and of police not protecting eloping couples.[16] In 2011, family members of an 18-year-old girl who had married into a lower caste dragged her out of her in-laws' home and set her on fire in Andhra Pradesh. In 2010, an Indian man killed his step-daughter in Punjab because she was in love with a Belgium-based lower-caste boy. A couple were electrocuted to death in Delhi because the boy belonged to a different caste.[17] That 'such irrational diktats and barbaric decisions (like urging the murder of violators of marriage norms) are taken within less than 100 km of Delhi has only made for the worst publicity', says Bhupendra Yadav, a historian.[18]

The publicity, however, rarely moves beyond the shock and horror of discovering such attitudes exist within sight of the shiny office blocks of Delhi's satellite cities that house multinational companies. It fails to recognize the massive social changes that have taken place around cities such as Delhi, where social tensions and clashes created by a rapidly modernizing India are most stark.

Hazare's Movement

A groundswell of public opinion verging on anger against corrupt politicians and other officials led, in the spring of 2011, to mass protests across the country in support of a hunger strike by Hazare, who dressed evocatively with a pointed white cap, crisp white kurta and spectacles, reminiscent in some ways of Mahatma Gandhi. He was demanding legislation to create the Lok Pal, which had been on successive governments' legislative agendas since the late 1960s but had been continually delayed by objections from MPs and others who did not want their businesses and connections to be liable to investigations.

The government initially reacted dismissively and clumsily to the protests, but eventually caved in when it realized their strength and half-heartedly agreed to set up a joint drafting committee with the social activists to prepare fresh legislation.[19] Government and opposition politicians were scared of what might emerge and were anxious to undermine Hazare's authority and popularity. They assumed that, if they stalled for long enough during the summer months, they would eventually be able to ignore most of his demands. The assumption was that he would not be able to rebuild nationwide support five or six months later because, judging by previous experience, protestors' enthusiasm and energy would be dissipated and would not easily be revived. This seriously underestimated the strength of middle-class opinion driving the protests. This was not a frenetic rabble, brought onto the streets by vested interests but a young middle-class revolt that had a life of its own, separate from the ambitions of attention seekers who thronged around Hazare, including Baba Ramdev, a colourful black-bearded, saffron-robed and politically ambitious guru of dubious respectability.

The drafters failed to reach an agreement and Hazare revived his movement in June 2011, threatening a new hunger strike. In a panic, the government stupidly put him in jail when he failed to agree to terms for the length of his fast and accompanying mass protests. It then quickly reversed that decision and tried to release him, but he mocked the authorities by continuing to refuse food in jail until terms were agreed for a 15-day public fast. (Sonia Gandhi was ill in the US at this time, having had, it was widely assumed, an operation for cancer, and her absence contributed to the government's ineptitude).

The government was understandably resisting some of the demands that would have allowed the Lok Pal to cover the prime minister and the CBI and other investigative agencies. These powers would have been far stronger than was sensible in a parliamentary democracy, and there were also understandable public concerns that the Lok Pal could become another overstaffed and cumbersome part of a basically corrupt bureaucracy, thus preventing it from having any great impact on corruption. Ministerial and other spokesmen and negotiators, however, failed to capitalize on these reservations about the idea and infuriated public opinion through their arrogance, which strengthened the Lok Pal campaigners' voice.[20]

Eventually, a Lokpal and Lokayukta Bill covering both national and state-level ombudsmen was introduced in the Lok Sabha on 22 December 2011. It was quickly passed in five days, but remained stuck in the Rajya Sabha for more than 18 months.[21] The delay was initially caused by the creation of a select committee to suggest changes, which led to amendments to the bill being tabled in January 2013.[22] Then there appeared to be filibustering by the government, which did not have a majority in the upper house and feared defeat on key issues such as the prime minister being subject to investigation and the government losing control over the Central Bureau of Investigation (CBI). The session ended in uproar, without passing the bill, and it was not till December 2013 that the Bill was passed at a time when the government was desperate to show it was acting on corruption.

Hazare's campaign lost most of its momentum once the legislation was launched in parliament, but it led to an even more significant development when Arvind Kejriwal created the Aam Aadmi Party (AAP) to contest parliamentary and state assembly elections. Kejriwal had been involved in civic and social campaigns for about 12 years, initially with a voluntary organization called Parivartan that focused on local issues such as governance in a poorer part of Delhi, and on the right to information.

Kejriwal's first test came with an election for the Delhi state assembly in December 2013 when his party won an astonishing 28 of the 70 seats, and he himself defeated Sheila Dikshit, who had been the Congress chief minister for 15 years.[23] The Congress was decimated, winning just eight seats compared with 43 in the previous election in 2008 – a humiliating result that was far worse than had been expected. Although she had a comfortable 'aunty' public image, Dikshit's reputation had slipped because she had continuously tried to evade responsibility for Delhi's significant problems. She had deflected onto others criticism about both the appalling and corrupt preparations for the Commonwealth Games in 2010, and continuing problems with water and electricity supplies and high prices. She was also personally identified with the Gandhi family, so she epitomised much of what needed to be changed.

The Aam Admi Party's victory is significant because it underlined the desire for a break with the corruption and mismanagement of recent years. Kejriwal talked about a new sort of politics, and the party's election symbol was appropriately a broom. Focusing on local as well as state-level issues, the party produced individual manifestos for each of Delhi's 70 assembly constituencies as well as one for the state as a whole. Its success boosted its activities in other states, and it aimed to win enough seats in the 2014 general election to become a significant force in parliament.

RTI and CAG

The middle-class-driven surge of opinion against corruption was boosted by two factors – a Right to Information Act (generally known as the RTI) that came into force in 2005, and the appointment, in 2008, of Vinod Rai, a senior bureaucrat, as CAG. Rai turned this into a campaigning and interventionist role and his reports on issues such as the Commonwealth Games, coal mining and telecoms fuelled public anger and infuriated the government because they led to extensive media exposure and a series of official inquiries. The RTI

opened the doors to revelations of hitherto secret information at all
levels. Kejriwal used it to make dramatic headlines early in 2013 when
he revealed a series of corruption scandals that embarrassed companies
and top politicians. One of them challenged the Gandhi dynasty's
closely guarded privacy with an attack on Sonia Gandhi's businessman
son-in-law, Robert Vadra, who was a soft target.[24] Since she entered
politics at the end of the 1990s, Gandhi had drawn a much tighter
cloak of secrecy and silence around herself and her family than earlier
members of the dynasty ever managed, and Kejriwal's publicity broke
through that screen.

Gradually the government realized that the extensive corruption
during its time in office would become a major issue in the 2014
general election and it began to take more decisive action. There
was a flood of CBI inquiries into coal and telecom cases involving
some of India's best-known businessmen, and Rahul Gandhi used his
authority as Congress party vice-president to ensure that Lalu Yadav, a
convicted former chief minister of Bihar, lost his parliamentary seat[25]
when he was jailed for fraud in a case dating from the mid-1990s.

No one, however, was doing much about actually punishing
those most responsible for the endemic corruption. No significant
politicians or prominent businessmen, nor anyone the government
wanted to protect, was jailed. A few figureheads were arrested when
it suited the government to do so – usually to embarrass another
political party, or bring a partner into line, or create a diversion
from public demands for action. These were people whom the
government was prepared to sacrifice such as Suresh Kalmadi, who
presided over the CWG and was charged, with his henchmen, for
allegedly cheating and conspiring on a games contract as well as for
using forged documents and other offences.[26] A. Raja, the former
telecommunications minister who belongs to Tamil Nadu's DMK
and was dispensable, was charged, along with officials and company
executives, with offences that ranged from criminal conspiracy to
forgery and cheating.[27] Three of the executives belonged to a company
controlled by Anil Ambani, the less important and influential of the

two Reliance brothers. But little was done to speed up the handling of these and other cases.

On a broader front, the government passed the Lok Pal Bill through parliament and Rahul Gandhi took steps to show he realized action was needed. The government removed MPs' patronage powers to issue land, telephone lines and petrol station licences to favoured friends and supporters, though that too was only tinkering at the lowest and least important end of corruption. It also announced that prosecution of corrupt bureaucrats would be speeded up with stiffer penalties, but officials at all levels of government were so scared of facing corruption accusations that they became reluctant to take decisions.[28] This seriously delayed policy implementation at a time when the economy was beginning to slow down.

A 'Rosa Parks Moment'

At various times when the protests against rape and corruption were at their height, it seemed that life in India might never be quite the same again because the young and newly aspirational middle class had found its voice. Corruption had, of course, not stopped, and new rapes were being reported daily, but people had come out in protest, not pulled by organized campaigners, vested interests or political parties but by a demand from varied classes for India to change.

As someone said in one of the many television discussion programmes that ran for several weeks, 'the days when gradualism was acceptable are over.' To put it another way, the government could no longer rely on the quick fix of jugaad or the laid-back acceptance of the inevitable to avoid, or at least stem, social protest and unrest. The statement probably was over-optimistic but it did illustrate a growing belief that the economic and social changes that had begun in 1991 now needed to be reflected in government, the law, and the operations of the police – and that the domination of women by men needed to end.

Was this 'a Rosa Parks moment', wondered Nandan Nilekani. 'This is just like that moment in the US, when one woman's refusal to give up her seat in the bus sparked off the civil rights movement,' he suggested at the Jaipur Literature Festival at the end of January 2013. Rosa Parks was a black woman whose rebellion against oppression in Montgomery, Alabama, in December 1955[29] triggered, as Nilekani put it to me later, 'a whole set of events – the rise of Martin Luther King, Kennedy and his support for Civil Rights, MLK's famous speech "I have a dream" and, after Kennedy's assassination, LBJ [Lyndon B. Johnson] fulfilling his intent by passing the Civil Rights Act in 1965.'

Nilekani was suggesting that 'one seminal event that causes national outrage can have a string of positive consequences in terms of reforms'.[30] Tied with that, he believed that 'the aspiration of millions of young Indians would drive the change' in governance and other areas. He saw both Hazare and the outrage on the rape case as a demand for better 'public goods' such as safer cities, better women's rights and cleaner governance, and said this was 'very different from agitations that demand some quota or entitlements for some category of people'.

Rosa Parks' protest caught a potent moment in American history, when a spark was needed to generate change in race relations. That point may not have been reached in India. Unlike in the case of Egypt's Tahrir Square and the other Arab Spring uprisings that began late in 2010,[31] India's middle class is not yet ready to be a cohesive force, separate from political parties and other established organisations. A start was however made between 2011 and 2013 in Delhi and across the country. Middle-class opinion became a force that could not be ignored and the AAP's success in Delhi showed political parties that they could no longer take the voters for granted.

Notes

1. http://ridingtheelephant.wordpress.com/2012/12/23/police-fire-tear-gas-and-fire-water-cannon-at-peaceful-protestors-in-battleground-delhi/

2.   'India gang rape victim's father: I want the world to know my
      daughter's name is Jyoti Singh', *Sunday People* (UK), 5 January 2013,
      http://www.mirror.co.uk/news/world-news/india-gang-rape-victims-
      father-1521289,   http://www.mirror.co.uk/news/world-news/india-
      gang-rape-victims-father-1521289, and http://www.punjabnewsline.
      com/news/Jyoti-Singh-Pandey_-Delhi-braveheart_s-father-wants-
      world-to-know-this-name.html

3.   http://ridingtheelephant.wordpress.com/2013/01/03/gang-rape-
      reveals-the-real-india-and-the-glimmers-of-change/

4.   Address by the President of India, Pranab Mukherjee, on the eve of
      India's 64th Republic Day http://presidentofindia.nic.in/sp250113.
      html

5.   http://ridingtheelephant.wordpress.com/2007/11/01/the-plight-of-
      indias-landless-is-overlooked/

6.   Ibid, and Jo Johnson column in the *Financial Times*, http://www.
      ft.com/cms/s/0/dd8761a6-87b4-11dc-9464-0000779fd2ac,
      s01=1,stream=FTSynd.html?nclick_check=1

7.   Justice Verma Committee Report Summary, PRS research organisation,
      http://www.prsindia.org/parliamenttrack/report-summaries/justice-
      verma-committee-report-summary-2628/; Full report http://www.
      prsindia.org/uploads/media/Justice%20verma%20committee/js%20
      verma%20committe%20report.pdf

8.   'New anti-rape law comes into force', PTI, 3 April 2013, http://articles.
      timesofindia.indiatimes.com/2013-04-03/india/38247789_1_
      criminal-law-acid-attack-rigorous-imprisonment

9.   https://www.facebook.com/rvprasad/posts/10151345569564841

10.   Crime in Delhi 2012, http://www.delhipolice.nic.in

11.   'The Dark Side of Sunny Porn;, *India Today*, 18 February 2012,
      http://indiatoday.intoday.in/story/pornography-on-the-internet-hits-
      indian-society-sunny-leone/1/174081.html

12.   'Crimes against women including rape cases declared by MPs, MLAs
      and candidates', Association for Democratic Reforms press release, 20
      December 2012, http://adrindia.org/content/crimes-against-women-
      including-rape-cases-declared-mps-mlas-and-candidates

13.   'Prohibit Degrading "Test" for Rape – Forensic Exams Should Respect
      Survivors' Rights to Health, Human Rights Watch, 6 September 2010,

http://www.hrw.org/news/2010/09/06/india-prohibit-degrading-test-rape

14. '"Two-finger test violates rape survivor's right to privacy, traumatises her": Supreme Court', PTI, 19 May 2013, http://ibnlive.in.com/news/twofinger-test-violates-rape-survivors-right-to-privacy-sc/392604-3-244.html

15. In conversation with JE, January 2013

16. 'Fear of death envelops inter-caste couples', *The Times of India*, 25 January 2013, http://articles.timesofindia.indiatimes.com/2013-01-25/madurai/36547023_1_inter-caste-police-protection-parents

17. 'Honour killings: Supreme Court says those who kill for "honour" deserve death sentence', *Mail Today*, 10 May 2011, http://indiatoday.intoday.in/story/honour-killings-sc-for-death-sentence/1/137621.html; Bhupendra Yadav, 'Khap Panchayats: Stealing Freedom?', *Economic & Political Weekly*, 26 December 2009; http://www.epw.in/commentary/khap-panchayats-stealing-freedom.html

18. Bhupendra Yadav, 'Khap Panchayats: Stealing Freedom?', *Economic & Political Weekly*, 26 December, 2009, http://www.epw.in/commentary/khap-panchayats-stealing-freedom.html http://www.epw.in/system/files/pdf/2009_44/52/Khap_Panchayats_Stealing_Freedom.pdf

19. https://ridingtheelephant.wordpress.com/2011/04/20/india-is-at-a-turning-point-that-might-go-wrong/

20. https://ridingtheelephant.wordpress.com/2011/08/24/greed-breeds-social-unrest-in-india-and-the-uk

21. https://ridingtheelephant.wordpress.com/2011/12/28/are-the-lokpal-bill-and-the-ambanis-brotherly-love-for-real-or-just-for-the-numbers/

22. The Select Committee's accepted recommendations on the PRS Legislative Research website http://www.prsindia.org/theprsblog/?p=2448 and http://www.prsindia.org/uploads/media/Lok%20Pal%20Bill%202011/Lokpal%20Select%20Committee%20comparison%20with%20%20govt%20accepted%20amendments.pdf

23. http://ridingtheelephant.wordpress.com/2013/12/08/india-state-elections-demand-political-change-without-the-congress/

24. 'Robert Vadra's extraordinary jump to fame and power', 6 October 2012, http://www.rediff.com/news/slide-show/slide-show-1-robert-vadra-s-extraordinary-jump-to-fame-and-power/20121005.htm

25. http://ridingtheelephant.wordpress.com/2013/10/03/rahul-gandhi-stops-a-small-compromise-on-lalu-yadav-but-does-he-have-the-stamina-to-be-a-leader/

26. 'CWG scam: Delhi court frames charges against Suresh Kalmadi', PTI, 4 February 2013, http://articles.timesofindia.indiatimes.com/2013-02-04/india/36742391_1_promoters-of-two-construction-akr-constructions-p-d-arya

27. '2G scam: Charges against Raja, others', NDTV, 22 October 2011, http://www.ndtv.com/article/india/2g-scam-charges-against-raja-others-143384

28. https://ridingtheelephant.wordpress.com/2011/09/29/india-staggers-and-stumbles-along-a-long-corruption-trail/

29. 'Rosa Parks, 92, Founding Symbol of Civil Rights Movement, Dies', *New York Times*, 25 October 2005, http://www.nytimes.com/2005/10/25/us/25parks.html?pagewanted=all&_r=3&

30. In conversation with JE.

31. http://ridingtheelephant.wordpress.com/2011/02/11/india%E2%80%99s-protection-against-tahrir-square-style-rebellions/

10

The Plunder of Land

While it was corruption and rape that brought the middle class onto the streets in 2011 and 2012, it was land that caused unrest throughout the 2000s when it became the country's most sought after and controversial commodity. Land for real estate development and for mining was the biggest creator of greed, corruption, crime and wealth. Newly rich politicians, businessmen and bureaucrats cheated, bullied and swindled individuals and society of the country's riches, grabbing natural resources at low prices and reaping rich rewards.

Land should be the source of economic growth for a country, and of increased wealth and security for people both rich and poor. Instead, it became a symbol of much that is wrong with India. In some states, it has been causing a high proportion of killings and criminal cases – in Bihar, 50 per cent of murders and 70–75 per cent cases of criminal assault are due to land, according to police figures,[1] and the actual number could be higher.

Raghuram Rajan has noted that 'the predominant sources of mega wealth in India today are not the software billionaires who have made money the hard way'. Instead, he said in a 2010 newspaper interview,[2] 'It is the guys who have access to natural resources or to land or to particular infrastructure permits or licences. In other words, proximity to the government seems to be a big source of wealth. And that is worrisome because it means that those who can access the government and manage it are far more powerful than ordinary businessmen. In the long run, this leads to a decay in the image of businessmen and the whole free enterprise system. It doesn't show us in good light if we become a country of oligopolies and oligarchs. Eventually, this could even impinge on democratic rights'.[3]

In his book, *Fault Lines: How Hidden Fractures Still Threaten the World Economy*,[4] Rajan suggested that 'the licence-permit raj' of the pre-1991 decades, which had allowed well-connected manufacturing business houses to grab licences and squeeze out competitors, had given way to the 'raj of the land mafia'. He was pointing out that success now came not to the best real estate developers or the most socially and environmentally conscious mining companies, but to businessmen with contacts in government who could bribe politicians and bureaucrats to hand over access to land for real estate development and exploitation of coal, iron ore and other minerals. 'Earlier, you had to navigate the government for … licences and permits … Now you have to navigate the government for land, because in many situations land titles are murky, and acquiring land is difficult,' he wrote.

These scams were made easy because environmental laws and regulations had been breached on a massive scale, especially through the first decade of this century. The ministers of environment who were drawn from the DMK in Tamil Nadu facilitated illegal mining and real estate development across the country. What the minister allowed from his office in Delhi was echoed down through his ministry, agencies and state governments. Added to this, a lack of urban planning meant that there were few laws and regulations to control such activities, and those that did exist were bent or ignored.

Agricultural land in India has often been seized by state governments and their agencies, and by corporate friends and cronies, using legislation that stemmed from land acquisition laws passed in 1894, half a century before India's independence. These laws, which were only replaced in 2013, permitted compulsory government purchase of land for a 'public purpose', a provision that was intended to be used for developments such as highways, government buildings, airports, schools and slum clearance. It came to be used, instead, to acquire land for private sector projects including special economic zones[5] and the Tata Nano car factory that was aborted in West Bengal in 2008. It was also used to grab excessive amounts of land for real estate deals around projects such as airports and highways that were built and operated under suspect public-private partnership (PPP) arrangements. Sources have suggested to me that excessive land was also made available for commercial developments like information technology company campuses in order to boost market prices of stocks in which politicians had invested.

Capital Dislocation

In the states of Haryana and Uttar Pradesh that surround Delhi, rural areas and farmland have been bought up, speculated over and developed in the past three decades, and at a rapidly accelerating pace in the past ten years. This has created a vast National Capital Region (NCR) with a population of over 22m, including 16m in Delhi itself, covering nearly 13,000 sqm. It includes Gurgaon in Haryana, which stretches for miles of ribbon development to the south-west along the Jaipur highway, and Noida to the south-east in UP. There are also growing industrial centres at Ghaziabad and Faridabad along a highway that runs to the tourist centre and industrial city of Agra. Shiny blocks of offices, plus less grand factories and call centres have spread across farmland and around old villages, together with both plush and sleazy hotels, massive blocks of flats, shopping malls and golf courses. This has created instant wealth for a few lucky developers and landowners, but a loss of livelihood for the less fortunate landless and labourers.

Prices have rocketed. For example, the price of farmland a few kilometres from a highway in an area that has yet to be urbanized by the Gurgaon sprawl has risen 100 times over the last 16 years from Rs 2 lakh an acre in the late 1990s, when it was considered a remote rural location, to Rs 2 crore now that tower blocks of flats are appearing on the horizon, indicating that it will be part of an urban area in a few years. Another plot in a fashionable development of large houses on two- to five-acre plots, euphemistically called 'farm houses', near Delhi airport, has increased a thousand times over a longer period of 30–35 years from Rs 9,000–12,000 an acre to Rs 10 crore.

There is nothing remarkable about the location of either of these two examples.[6] Both are on land that, till the 1980s, was owned in small holdings by relatively poor farmers, and both have been swallowed up by rich owners and real estate speculators. Outside Gurgaon, where builders have been buying farmland speculatively at low prices for years, changes to a master plan proposed in 2012 meant that plots bought in 2003 for Rs 25 lakh an acre were worth Rs 6 to 7 crore, and more than twice that figure in some cases. 'Land dealers, on condition of anonymity, talk discreetly about how the master plan acts as a gold mine for the officials drafting it, the subject of strong lobbying by developers,' reported the *Business Standard* in 2012.[7]

Once land was commandeered, its value usually rose quickly, reaping profits for the public authorities and private sector companies involved, while the previous, usually poor, owners received relatively small amounts for what had been their livelihood for generations. That is often the main grievance, as has been shown in protests in Delhi and the states of West Bengal and Odisha. People's anger was directed not so much at having to part with their land, but having to do so under an ancient law that fixes compensation prices at current low levels and does not allow those involved to benefit from rapid increases in price once land use has been changed or developments started.

In 2009, using the 1894 law, the Greater Noida Industrial Development Authority in UP compulsorily acquired 5,000 acres of land from farmers in 16 villages at Rs 850 per sqm. A month later, having changed the land use from industrial to residential, it resold to private developers for about 13 times as much – Rs 10,000– 12,000 per sqm (the local high court later cancelled the orders for some of the land transfers after appeals). The development authority tried to stem criticism by saying that the higher price covered the cost of infrastructure work, such as roads, water supply, sewage and electricity, in addition to public facilities such as schools.[8] Two years earlier, the Yamuna Expressway Industrial Development Authority had notified 256 villages for development along the Greater Noida–Agra expressway and paid Rs 850 per sqm to the farmers. It sold at Rs 5,500 per sqm to private builders who planned to sell it at Rs 18,000 per sqm. 'Our problem is not with the sale. What is not acceptable are the exorbitant rates at which the private builders plan to sell our land,' explained one villager to *Tehelka* magazine at a time when violent demonstrations were breaking out against the land sales, halting some developments.[9]

This illustrates the scant regard that the wealth-generating rich and politically powerful – a relatively small minority – have had for the plight of the poor who make up two-thirds of the population. Often politicians and their friends use insider knowledge to buy up land cheaply in areas that they know will soon rise rapidly in value because of some big infrastructure project or because of a change in land use from agricultural to industrial or residential. Projects are sometimes intentionally delayed while politicians make profits by floating rumours about one site after another. While it is illegal to profit from insider trading in the stock markets, there is no law against profiting from insider trading in real estate!

Social Wasteland

Such upheaval and dislocation creates a social wasteland of urban sprawl, removing the stability of old rural communities and identities and providing instant wealth for those who sell their land well. 'When you can suddenly sell what you have for a crore an acre, the meaning of land changes,' says Ravinder Kaur, citing 2012 prices on a highway north of Delhi, in the state of Punjab. 'The sense of belonging somewhere goes, and people lose their roots.'[10]

That leads, she explains, to conflicting reactions of brash arrogance among the suddenly rich and anxiety among those who have not been so lucky.

People rarely know or seem to care about wise investing. All over India there are stories of money lost through extortion, squandered on quick purchases and later consumed in alcoholic despair. The *Tehelka* article told how One farmer sold his land for Rs 50 lakh and revelled in wealth he could never have dreamed of a few years earlier. He bought a small but smart Alto car, two motorbikes, a 12-room house, and married off his daughter. 'I am totally broke now. There is not a single paisa left. I was greedy for money at that time,' he said. 'Our situation was better when we were farmers. Nowadays, all we think about is survival.'[11]

The result of this social churn is a confusing melee of ambitions and frustrations with people falling back on violence as a way of expressing either their new sense of power and self-importance or the disenchantment of being left behind. This is especially evident in Haryana and UP where some areas, especially those on the outskirts of Delhi, have always been regarded as a gangland haven of lawlessness. It is here that labour unrest has broken out in new auto industry factories and it is also here that crude displays of new power have occurred.

Sons of regional politicians and others, suddenly rich with wealth from land deals and corruption, have typically shown scant respect for the law. In September 2011, a 22-year-old toll booth operator was shot dead on the Gurgaon highway by the driver of a sport utility vehicle (SUV) – regarded by India's new rich as a symbol of wealth – who refused to pay the toll of Rs 27. People from nearby villages were exempt from paying tolls if they could prove their identity, and an argument with the booth operator led to the shooting that was caught on closed circuit television.[12] In an earlier example of the arrogance of the newly affluent, a politically connected youth, the son of a Congress MP from Haryana, who later became a minister in the state's cabinet, shot a bar attendant in 1999 at a Delhi nightspot when she refused to serve him a drink. There were some 200 witnesses to what became known as the landmark 'Jessica Lal case',[13] but many 'turned hostile', refusing to give evidence. The youth was acquitted in 2006, but he was re-arrested after a public outcry and sentenced to life imprisonment.

The social dislocation and other problems caused by rapid urban development will continue for decades ahead, albeit maybe more slowly than during the millennial decade of high economic growth. The McKinsey report forecast in 2010 that 590m people would be living in Indian cities by 2030 – up from 340m in 2008 and 290m in 2001. It said there would then be 68 cities of more than a million people including 13 with more than four million and six with 10m. Delhi and Mumbai would be among the world's five largest cities. 'We will witness over the next 20 years an urban transformation the scale and speed of which has not happened anywhere in the world except in China,' said the report.[14]

Land Legislation

People who lose or voluntarily give up their land for industrial development have rarely been compensated adequately, and the laws and regulations have varied in different states (land is a 'concurrent' subject in India's Constitution, which means that both the central and state governments have powers). Records of landholding are often not available, or cannot be easily verified, which complicates acquisition. This has led companies to prefer that governments acquire land for them using the 1894 legislation's powers to acquire land compulsorily, often at low prices that do not reflect the real market price. In forest and tribal areas, it has meant that local people have not been properly consulted, as the stories in the next chapter show.

People giving up their land are often offered jobs in the new projects. This has commonly been one job per family, which can work well with unskilled jobs during construction work, but not so well when projects are completed and companies find local people unsuitable for skilled employment – for example, in a car factory. Some are given unspecialized jobs such as that of security guards, but many cannot even do those duties, so feel doubly shut out from their traditional occupations by both the real estate boom that they missed and the industrial boom that they cannot share. The poor also frequently lose out when compensation packages are being handed out. Land acquisition officers typically take a percentage cut to improve compensation amounts. In a relatively minor but illustrative example in Andhra Pradesh,[15] the government took over land for a highway project from a woman who had only recently bought it. She successfully won a court case for more compensation than the government had initially allocated, but the local land acquisition officer insisted on receiving a 10 per cent payment for releasing the money.

In its approach paper for India's 12th five-year plan, India's Planning Commission, which monitors the economy and proposes policy changes, said that independent estimates suggested only a third of the 60m people who had been displaced by development projects over 60 years had been resettled 'in a planned manner'.[16] Most of them were 'rural poor without any assets, marginal farmers, poor fisher-folk and quarry workers'. Around 40 per cent of those displaced were tribals and 20 per cent were Dalits. 'Given that 90 per cent of our coal, more than 50 per cent of most minerals and most prospective dam sites are in Adivasi regions, there is likely to be continuing contention over issues of land acquisition in these areas, inhabited by some of our most deprived people.'

The way forward, said the Planning Commission, was to 'move away from the colonial perspective of treating people as "subjects"', and instead treat them as citizens with rights guaranteed under the Constitution. That required a 'fair land acquisition law which resorts to compulsory acquisition only where it is unavoidable and provides fair competition'. The law should also mandate resettlement and rehabilitation provisions that were 'not reduced to what they have become, conditionalities without consequences'. Also required was an 'unequivocal commitment to imaginatively exploring ways of rebuilding the livelihoods of those adversely affected by development projects'.

This view underpinned government plans for new land legislation to replace the old 1894-based laws. Parliamentary Bills were first prepared in 2007, but lapsed because they were not passed by the time of the 2009 general election. A new Bill was tabled in 2011,[17] but it became the subject of controversy and amendments for over two years. It eventually became law in September 2013,[18] after being steered through parliament by Jairam Ramesh when he became minister for rural development.

The legislation provided for substantial land acquisition, rehabilitation and resettlement arrangements designed primarily to protect the poor who had previously lost out. Owners were to receive four times the market value of their land in rural areas, and twice the value in urban areas, so that they shared in future land values. Not less than 70 to 80 per cent of the owners would have to give their consent for sales to go ahead during complex consultation arrangements. Land that had not been developed after ten years would be returned to them. These provisions horrified industrialists who said that land costs would rise, and that there would be long project delays and cancellations because of resistance from communities. It also seemed likely that companies would not go for developments that covered large areas because of the problems involved in obtaining approval from numerous owners, and that they might look for sites in rural areas in order to cut costs.

The arguments were polarized around the Indian economy's basic dilemma – how to encourage industrial and other projects that are needed for growth while at the same time caring for the environment and for those whose lives are being uprooted. It is an argument that will continue, but it is important that the caring side of the argument is not lost in the clamour for growth.

Notes

1. 'Land row murders trigger concern', *The Telegraph*, 27 April 2012, http://www.telegraphindia.com/1120428/jsp/bihar/story_15425698. jsp#.UVbYlhcSaSo

2. 'Licence raj has been replaced by land mafia raj', *DNA*, 30 October 2010, http://www.dnaindia.com/opinion/interview_licence-raj-has-been-replaced-by-land-mafia-raj_1459666; interview with Raghuram Rajan when he was professor of finance at the University of Chicago's Booth School of Business and a part-time economic advisor to Manmohan Singh. A former chief economist at the IMF he became the chief economic adviser at India's Ministry of Finance in December 2012. His *Fault Lines: How Hidden Fractures Still Threaten the World Economy*, was named the FT-Goldman Business Book of the Year for 2010

3. Rajan based these remarks on an article written in 2008 for *Outlook* magazine by Jayant Sinha of the Omidyar Foundation, formerly a hedge fund manager and McKinsey partner. See also 'Has India's Gilded Age Lost Its Luster?', CNBC.com 5 November, 2012, http://mobile.cnbc.com/special_reports/5/content/49306639

4. Raghura Rajan, *Fault Lines: How Hidden Fractures Still Threaten the World Economy*, Princeton University Press 2010, http://press. princeton.edu/titles/9111.html

5. http://ridingtheelephant.wordpress.com/2007/05/01/special-economic-zones-are-about-people-not-just-development/

6. Information given to JE privately by owners.

7. 'Gurgaon master plan a gold mine for realtors', *Business Standard*, 5 November 2012, http://www.business-standard.com/article/companies/gurgaon-master-plan-a-gold-mine-for-realtors-112110500076_1.html

8. http://www.ide.go.jp/English/Research/Region/Asia/201108_sato.html

9. 'Blood on the road to Agra', *Tehelka*, 21 May 2009, http://archive.tehelka.com/story_main49.asp?filename=Ne210511BLOOD.asp

10. In conversation with JE, January 2013.

11. 'Blood on the road to Agra', *Tehelka*, 21 May 2009

12. 'Gurgaon toll plaza attendant killed, manhunt on', *Hindustan Times*, 24 September 2011, http://www.hindustantimes.com/India-news/

Haryana/Gurgaon-toll-plaza-attendant-killed-search-on-for-killers/Article1-749533.aspx

13. http://archive.tehelka.com/story_main48.asp?filename=hub 220111THE_INVESTIGATION.asp

14. 'India's Urban Awakening – building inclusive cities', McKinsey Global Institute, April 2010

15. Story told to JE by Andhra Pradesh contact

16. 'Faster, Sustainable and More Inclusive Growth – An Approach to the Twelfth Five Year Plan (2012-17)', paras 5.24-5.26, Government of India, Planning Commission, October 2011, http://planningcommission. nic.in/plans/planrel/12appdrft/appraoch_12plan.pdf

17. All About the Land Acquisition Debate, PRS Legislative Research http://www.prsindia.org/pages/land-acquisition-debate-139/

18. 'President gives nod to Land Acquisition Bill', *The Hindu*, 27 September 2013, http://www.thehindu.com/news/national/president-gives-nod-to-land-acquisition-bill/article5175768.ece

11

Protests and Blockages

India is rich in minerals but it has failed to capitalize on this potential wealth in a way that would enable three main interest groups to benefit – the national economy, the state where the minerals are found, and the farmers, tenants and tribals who lose their homes on land whose surface they own, though not the rights to mineral extraction. The same applies to industrial projects such as steelworks and special economic zones (SEZs). For years, companies have secured licences and environmental clearances – and the freedom to bypass them – by bribing politicians and officials in the central and state governments.

Large-scale projects became especially controversial in the 2000s, sometimes with violent clashes and deaths. Twelve tribals were killed in January 2006 during protests against a massive 3,400-acre Tata Steel project at Kalinganagar in Odisha. Other steel ventures planned by Arcelor Mittal – the world's biggest steel group, controlled by Lakshmi Mittal, a London-based Indian-born entrepreneur – also failed to move ahead in Odisha and Jharkhand, as has a $12bn steelworks in Odisha planned by Pohang Steel Company (POSCO) of South Korea. In West Bengal, politically backed opposition escalated to such an extent that 14 people were shot and killed by police during a demonstration in March 2007 over a proposed chemicals SEZ at Nandigram, and Tata Motors abandoned its proposed factory outside Kolkata for its Nano 'one lakh' car. A bauxite mine run by Vedanta Resources, a London-based group originally founded in India as Sterlite by Anil Agarwal, was hit because of dubious environmental clearances and other problems in Odisha's Niyamgiri Hills where tribals protected what they regarded as a sacred mountain. Vedanta had previously run into environmental problems and international controversy over cutting down forests and other work in the state.

Soon after it was elected in 2004, the Congress-led UPA coalition government tried to speed up such industrial and mining projects. It also started a new phase of SEZs, of which most floundered in controversy. Manmohan Singh gave prime ministerial support to the plans, but the edifice came tumbling down because it was built on weak social and economic policy foundations at a time when India's economy was booming, and there was a growing demand for the new wealth to be shared with those displaced by industry. Controversies over the use of land escalated from local protests to become national issues with the violent clashes, and Kalinganagar, Nandigram and Singur were seen internationally as symbols of what was wrong with the new India. At the same time, Jairam Ramesh, as the minister for environment and forests, was slowing down projects by rejecting or overturning environmental clearances in his attempt to clean up the ministry's operations.

The SEZs, Tata Motors and Posco stories, along with Odisha, show how development opportunities have been wasted in India's complex and often corrupt political and business environment. In all four examples, the losers have been the people living on the land because of the potential economic wealth that has not been realized, while India has lost out on growth.

SEZs

Kamal Nath, an energetic and engaging Congress politician famous for his handling of far-flung business and political connections since he worked with Sanjay Gandhi at the end of the 1970s, pushed the SEZ idea as minister for commerce and industry. He announced new tax breaks plus substantial investment, planning and labour law concessions. The idea was to emulate China's big and successful zones, such as Shenzhen adjacent to Hong Kong, which have become cities and have driven the country's growth. But he did nothing to ensure that the zones would be firmly based on manufacturing industry, which had provided the early Chinese zones with their foundations, as I saw when I lived in Hong Kong and visited Shenzhen and other areas in the late 1980s. He also did nothing to prepare for the social and human side of his SEZ dreams. His plans brought industrialists and real estate speculators rushing to his Delhi office, eager to demonstrate their enthusiasm and sign up for vast tracts of land. He built up the hype and encouraged international and domestic interest by unrealistically declaring that the zones would account for $5–6 billion foreign direct investment by the end of 2007.[1]

When the SEZ Act was passed in February 2005 and introduced with SEZ Rules in January 2006, there was a flood of applications for over 400 zones. Some 230 quickly received initial approval and over 60 were formally notified to go ahead, even though no plans had been drawn up to control acquisition and compensation for the land that would be needed. The applications eventually rose to just over 588,[2] but only a handful started successfully in the first couple of years and there are now only about 170, including 19 that existed before 2005. Businessmen paid low prices for agricultural land, whose values quickly rose, benefiting developers, politicians and bureaucrats who were often involved in land scams, but leaving behind the poor, frustrated previous owners. Companies frequently asked for far more land than they needed, so that they could hoard it and later sell or use it for other purposes at massive profits.

Some industry-oriented and comprehensively planned SEZs went ahead[3] and boosted inward foreign investment and exports, but there was concern about large projects that looked like rampant real estate speculation without a manufacturing base. This especially applied to two mammoth schemes of up to 20,000–25,000 acres each that were planned by Mukesh Ambani's Reliance Industries (RIL). One was to be a joint venture with the Haryana state government in a prime development area adjacent to Gurgaon and another nearby area on the Delhi-Jaipur highway, just 11 km from the capital's international airport. The plans included a cargo airport and a 2000 MW power plant.[4] The other zone was with the Maharashtra state government in the district of Raigad, adjacent to Mumbai.[5] Both schemes have since been abandoned.

The government's official aim was primarily to encourage manufacturing investment with good infrastructure, especially in areas where industry might not otherwise go. There was, however, no conceivable economic reason to give Reliance generous taxation and other concessions on the popular Jaipur highway which was already awash with investment, and it looked as if Ambani was more interested in broad-based real estate speculation and development. This typified the group's overconfident approach to business expansion following the death in 2002 of Dhirubhai Ambani, Mukesh's politically subtle and better-connected father. The SEZ experience showed that, while Mukesh had good enough contacts and clout to sign up with the state governments, he could not steer the projects through the political storm that was generated when his SEZs became one of the symbols of corporate greed.

Sonia Gandhi, in one of her early populist interventions as leader of the coalition government, sensed a looming crisis and, in September 2006, said that 'prime agricultural land should not normally be diverted to non-agricultural uses'. She added that 'resettlement and rehabilitation policies must be strengthened and implemented in an effective and credible manner which will inspire confidence in all the people who are displaced.'[6] Her statement 'had all the major leaders running for cover,' wrote a former government official in November 2006.[7] 'Mr Sharad Pawar, the Minister for Agriculture, himself interested in the SEZs in his political power base of Maharashtra, was quick to give a rejoinder that only marginal lands were being used. The Commerce Minister, Mr Kamal Nath, said that he had already written to all the chief ministers that there should be no acquisition of agricultural lands.' There was considerable confusion after these statements, until the prime minister, during a visit to the

UK in October, said that 'special economic zones have come to stay', even though there were 'certain aspects, such as the use of prime agricultural land, which must be addressed'.

Concessions were proposed, including limiting the maximum land area allowed for each zone to 5,000 hectares (12,500 acres), and requiring that at least half of an SEZ should be used for manufacturing and other core activities. This led Ambani to halve the size of both his schemes. In Mumbai, farmers confirmed their opposition in a 2008 referendum, and his scheme there was scrapped in 2011 after Reliance had managed to acquire only 13 per cent of the site. The Delhi–Gurgaon project became unviable because of investor concerns and potential social unrest, and was shelved in 2012 after Reliance's six-year approval period had expired. The company said it was facing problems linking up the land areas that it had been given by the Haryana government and those it had acquired on its own.[8] Haryana then asked for its 1,383 acres to be returned and farmers demanded the land be given back to them. They claimed that values had rocketed from the Rs 20 lakh per acre they had been paid by the Haryana government in 2006 (along with promises of jobs in the SEZ) to Rs 8 to 9 crore per acre.[9]

The finance ministry was never happy about Nath's schemes because it saw that excessive tax concessions were being offered for little return. Other critics said there would not be much additional investment because most companies would build factories already planned for other areas in order to reap the tax and other benefits. 'Of course, the government says that only new investment will benefit, but who is to judge what new investment is? The poorly paid tax inspector?' wrote Raghuram Rajan.[10] 'If you create perverse economic incentives and then rely on bureaucrats to stand in the way of businesses exploiting them, the outcome will be little more investment than would otherwise have happened and a lot less revenue, but much richer bureaucrats.' He might have added 'richer politicians too', but that would have been a tad too controversial and anyway did not need to be said.

'In India one has to weave one's way through the procedures. That's not just a legal process or a financial process – it's a social process,' Kamal Nath told me in September 2008. 'In a democracy, all the stake-holders have to have a voice – and in India they have a particularly loud voice.' He was referring to POSCO's problems and what he called its 'learning curve', but it was a lesson he should have also learned over the SEZ debacle.

Singur and Nandigram

'We have little choice but to move out of Bengal. We cannot run a factory with police around all the time,' exclaimed Ratan Tata,[11] then head of the Tata group and chairman of Tata Motors, when he announced in October 2008 that he was closing the almost complete Nano factory at Singur in West Bengal and moving elsewhere. With that memorable exit line, he marked Tata's departure after two years of often violent and politics-based opposition over two big industrial projects in the state – his factory, which was almost ready to start turning out 250,000 cars a year, and a 10,000-acre chemicals SEZ planned by the state government for Indonesia's Salim group at Nandigram, near the port of Haldia. Both disputes blew up in 2006 over the prospect of agricultural land being compulsorily acquired for industry, and together demonstrated growing social unrest that lay beneath the country's economic boom.

West Bengal had been run for over 30 years by a Left Front government led by the CPI-M, with Buddhadeb Bhattacharjee as the chief minister from 2000 (till he was defeated in 2011). A mild and somewhat scholarly looking white-haired man in his mid-sixties, Bhattacharjee had been feted internationally as a forward-looking economic reformer, who saw the need to modify leftist policies with private sector (including foreign) investment in order to revive his intellectually strong but industrially backward state. An interview with him was a must for visiting editors of foreign business magazines and newspapers who were bemused by his inherent contradictions.

But he misjudged people's growing exasperation with decades of harsh and increasingly corrupt and ruthless communist rule. Amazingly, he expected them to accept that the government, which had implemented admired land reforms earlier in its 30-year rule, was now giving agricultural land to rich private sector corporations such as Tata.[12]

The storm started at Nandigram, a poor rural area in East Midnapur district, 170 km from Calcutta. Nandigram had a history of opposition to its rulers, initially the British, which had helped it to become a leftist stronghold with relatively low literacy and little industrial activity.[13] Bhattacharjee negotiated with the Salim Group, Indonesia's biggest conglomerate whose interests range from noodles to real estate, to build a chemical complex there in a newly designated SEZ. The deal could ultimately have grown from 10,000 acres to 40,000 acres, but opposition to the transfer of land had been building up months before the deal was signed in mid-2006. By then, resistance was also growing against Tata's car factory at Singur, which had been announced in May. Bhattacharjee wrongly expected that his party's political clout and street-level muscle, especially in Nandigram, would push both deals through.

Violent demonstrations and clashes between villagers and police-supported CPI(M) cadres built up at Nandigram in 2007, generating some of the worst riots seen in the state's history. In January, after violence first erupted, thousands of local farmers blockaded the area against government officials. Then West Bengal opposition politicians moved in. Mamata Banerjee, a maverick and temperamental leader of the anti-communist All India Trinamool Congress (TMC) party, realised she could use the growing disputes to rebuild her faltering career as a regional politician. Having set up her Trinamool (grassroots) party in 1997 when she broke away from the national Congress party, Banerjee successfully used the land disputes to burnish her populist image. It led her to victory in the assembly elections in 2011 when she became the state's chief minister, ending 34 years of leftist rule. Other opponents of the CPI(M) united to fight the Nandigram plans, culminating in 14 people being killed in March 2007 when police clashed with villagers protesting against land acquisition.

A month after those killings, Salim abandoned the Nandigram project. (A local financial associate planned a replacement chemical complex on a largely uninhabited 13,000-acre island in the estuary of Koltata's Hooghly River, but this did not materialise during the time of communist rule and was cancelled by the Banerjee government.) Violence continued in the Nandigram area throughout 2007, when armed cadres of the CPI(M) tried to re-establish their control by ousting rival political groups and Naxalite extremists who had moved in during the troubles. Houses and shops were burned and ransacked, and fear was spread by patrolling motorbike convoys carrying red flags. Instead of trying to rein in his party's activists, Bhattacharjee endorsed what they had done, saying they were 'justified'. Referring to earlier violence by the opposing groups, he said that 'the opposition has been paid back in the same coin'.[14] Reports of the Left Front's ruthlessness with opponents had often been heard during the previous three decades, but no one expected such an open and top-level endorsement of lawlessness. (Bhattacharjee later publicly regretted having made the 'same coin' remark.)[15]

The dispute over Tata's Nano factory at Singur was not nearly as violent as the battleground at Nandigram, but it did far more economic and social damage because nothing has happened on the site since 2008 when Tata departed. Originally, the Nano was to have been made in Uttarakhand, a state northeast of Delhi, in the foothills of the Himalayas, where Tata Motors already had a plant. It was switched after Bhattacharjee invited Ratan Tata to Bengal and matched Uttarakhand's special hill-state investment incentives that included low-cost land, low interest financial loans and substantial tax waivers. At Tata's request, the 90-year agreement, comprising four pages of text and eleven pages of financial spreadsheets, was kept confidential, though the text briefly appeared on the government's website in response to a court order till Tata appealed for its removal. It is now back on the website following the change of government.[16]

Bhattacharjee's officials proposed six sites, including one at Kharagpur, a town famous for its Indian Institute of Technology (where Telcon, a Tata company manufacturing heavy earth-moving equipment, successfully became the anchor investor in 2010 in a 1,200-acre industrial park). Ratan Tata wanted the Nano plant to be more accessible for staff living in Kolkata than Kharagpur would be, 120 km from the capital. He chose Singur, just 45 km away, which also provided high visibility for the Nano brand name on the busy National Highway 2 from Kolkata to Delhi. He refused an offer from Bhattacharjee to move elsewhere when the opposition began and the site was hit by monsoon flooding.

The drawback, which Tata ignored or did not fully realize, was that the site, divided into 3,500 small plots, mostly less than an acre, was on well-irrigated agricultural land that produced two good rice crops a year plus potato and other vegetables. This was used by opponents as an argument against the project, though the site had already been designated as an industrial park. Three industrial buildings (a cold store and factories for glass bottles and condoms) were already being built and had to be closed and transferred when the state government commandeered the land for Tata.

The government based its land acquisition on the controversial 1894 land acquisition law's compulsory transfer provisions for 'public purposes', which triggered arguments about whether the law could be used for a private sector project. Political opposition, and national and international media coverage, focused on the loss of the agricultural land but the real issue – as elsewhere in India – was the level of compensation received by agricultural owners and tenants. Under the 1894 law's compulsory purchase rules, compensation was paid according to the market price at the time, which meant it did not reflect later price increases when the value of land escalated, as it did two or three times within six months to a year. There was also resentment that Ratan Tata had given the impression that he was

primarily trying to help West Bengal by building the Nano there –
'almost like a philanthropist' as one official put it – when in fact he
was insisting on the state providing heavy investment incentives.

Banerjee escalated the row in December 2006 when she went on a
hunger strike for 25 days, but Tata went ahead with construction work
in January 2007. This led to fresh demonstrations that continued
through the year and at least two farmers committed suicide. Tata
had been allocated 997 acres, but the Trinamool argued that it only
needed 600 acres, which provided a fresh basis for opposition. Tata
said the other 397 acres were needed for 55 component suppliers'
factories. Compromises were sought to exclude those acres and to
allow some 2,000 objectors and others not receiving compensation
to stay on their land, which Tata rejected.

Both the factory and the jobs could have been saved, had it not
been for the two stubborn and emotional people involved. One was
Banerjee, who was focused single-mindedly on political victory in
the 2011 assembly elections, with little care for the economic and
social damage she caused along the way. The other was Ratan Tata,
encouraged by his controversial public relations adviser, Nira Radia,
who was regularly in Kolkata liaising on the Singur negotiations.
A peace deal was eventually brokered by West Bengal's governor,
Gopalkrishna Gandhi,[17] on 8 September, and Banerjee called off her
protests. This did not, however, sufficiently guarantee the future of
the project for Ratan Tata, who had refused to attend the governor's
talks, saying they were political rather than industrial.

Both sides took irreconcilable positions. Banerjee probably felt
secure with the thought that Tata would not leave because it had
invested $350m in the factory's workshops and assembly lines that
were virtually complete, and the car launch was planned for a few
weeks later. She also probably assumed it could not quickly find
an alternative site. Both assumptions were wrong. Ratan Tata had
earlier accused industry rivals of encouraging the opposition[18] but
now he was exasperated by a series of thefts from the plant site, and
by intimidation and assaults on engineers including Japanese and

German experts who were installing machinery. He announced the withdrawal on 3 October and made an emotional departure after personally attacking Banerjee.[19] 'We have to shift because of Mamata Banerjee,' he declared.[20] He quickly chose a new site in Gujarat, where he was welcomed by Narendra Modi, the chief minister.

Of the 13,500 people (mostly landowners but including a few hundred others such as share-cropper tenants) on the 997-acre site, 11,000 had by this time accepted and received compensation while the other 2,500 (with 297 acres) had either refused the money because they were unwilling to hand over their land, or had their payments held up in ownership disputes. Some people had already been employed on or around the project – about 180 were working for Tata and its component suppliers, while about 650 were in supporting services and over 900 were receiving technical or semi-technical training.[21] Once the land transfer was fixed, none of the 13,500 had any rights to the land under the 1894 legislation so, when Tata departed, they lost both their old agricultural livelihoods and the one-job-per-family that Tata was offering. They also lost the prospect of other future employment – there would have been 1,500 jobs in the Tata factory, plus thousands more in consequential manufacturing and service activities. (The automotive industry estimates that total employment can amount to more than five times the basic figure).[22]

Banerjee promised during her election campaign that, when she became chief minister, she would provide nearly 400 acres of land to the 2,500 people who had not received compensation (though only 297 acres were available, of which 220 belonged to the unwilling category). One of her first moves when she was elected was therefore to pass the Singur Land Rehabilitation and Development Act cancelling Tata's ownership rights. The government then took possession of the land at night without giving adequate notice to Tata, and without offering the company compensation. Tata spotted flaws in the Act and started a case against the government, which included a compensation claim for its lost investment – estimated at

Rs 500 crore out of a total expenditure of Rs 1,500 crore. In mid-2013 the Supreme Court suggested Tata consider returning the land to the previous owners,[23] but it was no longer suitable for agriculture.

When I visited the site a few weeks after Tata had left, those without jobs were destitute. Biswanath, a 42-year-old, had given up his half-acre land and said he had been beaten up by Trinamool activists for doing so. Expecting a Tata job, he'd distributed the Rs 300,000 he had received in compensation among seven brothers and two sisters, and had spent his own share. 'Now I am consuming alcohol,' he said.

The main lesson to be drawn from both the Singur debacle and the Nandigram crisis is the need for a company to be closely involved in community affairs in order to build local trust and support among those being displaced. This has to happen even if the state government is purchasing the land because it is the company that can give assurances about the future, including the possibility of jobs. Tata stayed largely aloof and, though it had medical teams working in the area, did not try to secure community endorsement for the project by explaining how the 997 acres would be used and by spelling out the job and other benefits that the factory would bring.

This was odd because the group had faced more community opposition in different parts of India than many other companies. Tata Steel had learned the need for involvement at the Kalinganagar project in Odisha where 12 tribal people had been killed in 2006. Till then, Tata had left the Kalinganagar consultations with the state government, but it changed tack and took over the job of resettlement, realizing it needed to build trust with the local people. Hemant Nerurkar, a former managing director of Tata Steel, has said the company learned the hard way the necessity of consultation and communication with local people in proposed areas of development, particularly those at risk of displacement.[24] Speaking at the Jaipur Literature Festival in January 2013, he said, 'We went and communicated, communicated and communicated with the people ... most of us don't understand the local feelings.'[25]

Kalinganagar marked a turning point in attitudes over how to handle the transition of agricultural land for industry. National and regional politicians, along with companies, realized that a more cooperative stance had to be adopted, and that fed into the debate on new land legislation. Ratan Tata, however, did not apply that lesson at Singur and he underestimated the importance of harnessing local support – a few weeks after he had departed, there were still big signs saying 'Welcome Mr Tata' along the highway and many smaller posters on walls and telegraph poles calling for him to come back. The area had begun to prosper with small new eateries and services such as taxi firms opening up. Life could have been good, if only Ratan Tata and his people had been more involved in local affairs, and Mamata Banerjee less so.

POSCO

POSCO is the latest of a string of multinational mining companies that have tried unsuccessfully to start projects in the eastern coastal state of Odisha. Its plans involve what would be India's biggest ever inward foreign direct investment. Manmohan Singh personally gave his support, but the project was just too big, too foreign, and too high profile to have had an easy start almost anywhere in India. In Odisha, where there is a history of blighted projects, it had no chance. It is now many years behind schedule – the first four million tonnes per annum phase was to have been commissioned in 2010 but continuing protests and fear of riots makes it unclear when construction will begin.

The POSCO story is important because it shows how easy it is for a potentially large contributor to India's economic growth to be stalled, even when it is a well-meaning company. POSCO cannot itself be blamed for the delays because, aside from any possible dealings with individual politicians and bureaucrats, it does not appear to have tried to bend regulations or mishandle people living on the site. It seems to have been badly advised because it did not realize that it takes several years for such a project to progress, and it chose the wrong site. It wanted to be on the coast so that it could export iron ore – an ambition that set the company on the road to controversy in the early days.

POSCO came to India looking for iron ore reserves and downstream customers to bolster its position as the world's fourth largest steelmaker. It signed an MoU with the Odisha government in 2005 and expected to move ahead quickly with what would be the first-ever integrated steel project undertaken on a greenfield site by any steel company outside its home country. Other Korean companies – notably Hyundai Motor, LG and Samsung – had become market leaders in India for their autos and consumer electricals manufacturing and marketing businesses in the 2000s, so POSCO could never have envisaged more than a short delay when it arrived.

'We'll try to win the heart of the people, and believe we can achieve that,' Cho Soung-Sik, chairman and managing director of POSCO India told me, three years into the delays. The agreement with the Odisha government included a private port, an SEZ, and iron ore mining rights. POSCO planned to commission the first 4mtpa phase in 2010 but, three years later, it had obtained neither the steelworks land nor the port site, nor had it secured separate iron ore mining rights. Jairam Ramesh gave heavily qualified environmental clearances in 2011, but this was challenged by a petitioner at India's National Green Tribunal, which suspended the approval in March 2012.[26] Meanwhile, the state government began acquiring land for the first 2,700-acre phase of the project, and after large-scale protests and clashes with police over blocked access to the site,[27] this was completed by July 2013. The project, however, still faced continuing local resistance and bureaucratic hurdles.[28]

When I visited the site in September 2008,[29] my car bumped along a track beside a broad sweep of bright green and well-cultivated paddy fields. We stopped at a rough bamboo gate at the entrance to Dhinkia village, guarded by a group of villagers in order to block access by

POSCO, the government and police. This was the stronghold of Abhaya Sahu, a local official of the Communist Party of India (CPI), who rigidly controlled the resistance movement. Though the opposition was coming from a tiny fraction of the land area, it was crucial because it controlled access to the proposed new port. Sahu moved there in 2005, after the killings at Tata's Kalinganagar plant raised the profile of project demonstrations. He set up the POSCO Pratirodh Sangram Samiti (POSCO protest and resistance committee), hoping this would establish the CPI as a political force in the area. Members of POSCO staff were briefly kidnapped by Sahu's group in May and October 2007 when they visited the steelworks site, and one protestor was killed during a clash between villagers and labourers building an access road for POSCO in 2011. Sahu was temporarily imprisoned on various charges in 2008 and 2011 when the government was trying to reduce his power.

Sitting on a pink plastic chair and dressed – suitably for the hot, humid weather – in a white singlet and dhoti, he brusquely told me: 'We will never let POSCO build here.' Though it was a poor area, there was enough prosperity for people who wanted to stay. 'This is fertile land,' he said, referring to what the villagers called the local 'sweet sand' where they cultivated betel vines for labour-intensive crops of paan leaves. There were also cashew nut, fruit and rice crops as well as fishing. Most villagers lived in rough mud-plastered homes covered with straw roofs, but the betel-vine crop provided a good living for landless labourers of Rs 200 to Rs 250 a day, double the wages in other nearby areas, and Rs 20,000–30,000 a month for a family owning land. Sahu said he planned to start opposition later in POSCO's iron ore mining area, where a leading BJP politician and former central government minister was also involved.

POSCO was promising bigger plots of land and homes on a nearby site to those who moved, plus compensation for existing homes and land, which had been accepted by other villages. There was also one job per family on offer in the steelworks (both during construction and after commissioning), plus job training for a second family member. Those who wanted to continue fishing, the company said, would receive assistance including a boat and nets, and POSCO would build a new wooden jetty. There would also be help and advice on animal husbandry and other occupations. 'If people want more, we will negotiate,' said Gee-Woong Sung, then POSCO-India's project director, but this failed to break the deadlock.

The company's experience illustrates what can happen when executives step outside territories they know well and try to operate in a political and bureaucratic culture which, they gradually discover, is very different from what they had expected. 'POSCO can't understand officials who don't mean "yes" when they say "yes" and don't mean "no" when they say "no",' an influential Odisha official told me in 2008, insisting on anonymity. The company also seemed to believe that blunt speaking would help. According to the same source, a very senior and impatient POSCO executive unwisely thumbed the company's agreement in a government meeting and impatiently told officials they should 'act on the agreement and hand over the land' – not quite the way to win friends and influence people in India. In July 2013, POSCO abandoned a planned $5.3m steel project in Karnataka after three frustrating years of delays and protests over use of land, but it is not pulling out of Odisha, presumably because the state government has provisionally allocated rich iron ore mines that make it worth staying on for, indefinitely.

Odisha

Odisha is one of India's poorest states. though one of the richest in minerals, and its failure to realize its potential is far greater than most other states. Few big mining and metals projects involving bauxite for aluminium and iron ore for steel have been able to start for two decades or more, and large-scale successes are rare. Plans by groups such as Essar, Vedanta, Jindal and Bhushan have hit problems with environmental approvals, or have been involved in controversies over coal mine allocations, though Tata Steel is nearing completion at its once-troubled Kalinganagar site. In total, the state government has signed 93 memorandums of understanding (MoUs) with companies since 2000, mostly for the steel and power sector.[30] Out of 50 steel MoUs, only 30, mostly small and medium projects, had been partially or fully completed and they were producing just a tenth of the envisaged 83.66m tonnes per annum capacity by the middle of 2012. Out of 29 power projects, only about six had been completed.

The Odisha bureaucracy is notoriously corrupt and appears to operate with scant concern for the wishes of Naveen Patnaik, the chief minister for the past 13 years, who is consequently not able to fulfil project implementation promises he makes to big investors. 'In other states, if a company pays up at the top level, it usually gets delivery,' says Biswajit Mohanty, an environmental activist and freedom of information campaigner, who runs the Wildlife Society of Orissa. 'But in Odisha, the lower-level bureaucrats ensure that projects are blocked unless they too are rewarded.'

Illegal mining, together with poor environmental protection, is widespread among well-known companies as well as smaller concerns. Tata Steel was among 103 iron ore mining companies asked by the state government in November 2012 to 'show cause' why it was exceeding approved production.[31] In 2009, Jharkhand-based Rungta Mines, run by Siddharth Rungta, who was then the president of the nation-wide Federation of Mining Industries, was named as a serious violator in reports of illegal mining.[32] The CAG made more allegations of unlawful extraction of iron ore, manganese ore and coal in excess of approved limits and without prior environment clearances in March 2013.[33] A commission was set up by the central government in November 2010 to report on illegal mining across the country. M.B. Shah, a retired Supreme Court judge who headed the commission, said in March 2013 that the Odisha state government had 'taken some steps' to curb the activities after his commission started work.[34]

Foreign groups such as Norsk Hydro of Norway, Alcan of Canada and Continental Resources of the US became tired of costly and frustrating delays in the mid-1990s and left India. Resistance has frequently come from tribal and other communities protecting their homelands, often encouraged and organized by NGOs. It has sometimes been alleged that multinational companies finance these NGOs in order to stem the flow of bauxite into world markets from India and other rival countries. Some reports suggest that local opposition to bauxite mining in the state only began after India started exporting the mineral, thus triggering international interest and resistance.

The indigenous communities are mostly forest dwellers living in remote regions such as Odisha's mineral-rich central highland areas, which account for about a quarter of the country's tribal population. Threats to these communities attract social leaders and tribal welfare NGOs, as well as political activists such as Sahu at POSCO, who teach the tribals to speak up for their rights. But while protest movements have become more effective, the government has responded slowly and reluctantly, protecting old relationships and doing little to compensate those who lose their land.

Tribals regard some of the areas involved as sacred – for example, the Niyamgiri Hills where Vedanta Alumina was planning a $1.7 billion bauxite and aluminium project till Jairam Ramesh became environment minister. In August 2010, Ramesh refused to let Vedanta's joint venture partner, the state government's Orissa Mining Corporation, start mining. He withdrew the first stage of forest clearance approvals that had been granted in 2008, and also refused a second stage. He did this on the basis of reports by two committees he had set up which highlighted damage both to the area's biodiversity and also to the Dongriya Kondh tribal community that lived on the hills and claimed that their Niyam Raja deity lived on a hilltop just ten kilometres from the mining area.[35] His ministry also barred Vedanta's Lanjigarh refinery from buying bauxite from 11 mines in the state of Jharkhand where, Ramesh said, there were no mines with bauxite approvals. He accused the refinery itself of commandeering forest land and carrying out a six-fold expansion without permission.[36] After the rejection of the environmental clearances, the refinery shut down in December 2012 because of a shortage of bauxite.

In April 2013, the Supreme Court put the future of the project in the lap of the gods when, referring to the tribal forest dwellers, it said, 'If the bauxite mining project in any way affects their right to worship their deity, known as Niyam Raja, in the hilltop of the Niyamgiri range of hills, that right has to be protected.' It said that the local gram sabha (village council) should decide whether the tribals had religious rights in the area and whether 'the proposed mining area, Niyama Danger, 10 km away from the peak, would in any way affect the abode of Niyam Raja'.[37]

This was significant because it recognised the role of local opinion in determining the future of projects and led to all the gram sabhas voting against mining, which cast further doubt on the project's future.[38]

Notes

1. http://ridingtheelephant.wordpress.com/2007/05/01/special-economic-zones-are-about-people-not-just-development/

2. Government of India official SEZ website http://sezindia.nic.in/about-osi.asp

3. Sri City on the borders of Tamil Nadu and Andhra Pradesh is one of the best examples of a zone firmly based on business activity but including social and infrastructure township facilities http://www.sricity.in/

4. http://articles.economictimes.indiatimes.com/2006-06-20/news-by-company/27437256_1_reliance-haryana-reliance-signs-hsiidc

5. 'Mukesh's Great Gamble', *Business Standard*, 15 April 12006, http://www.business-standard.com/article/beyond-business/mukesh-s-great-gamble-106041501025_1.html

6. 'SEZs: "Farmers must get proper compensation for land", says Sonia', 23 September 2006, http://news.webindia123.com/news/articles/India/20060923/459929.html

7.   *Dr S.* Narayan, then Visiting Senior Research Fellow and Head of
     Research at the ISAS, National University of Singapore, and a former
     Finance Secretary and economic adviser to the Prime Minister of
     India, '*The Special Economic Zones in India: An Update*', Institute of
     South Asian Studies (ISAS), November 2006, by www.isn.ethz.ch/
     Digital-Library/Publications/Detail/?ots591=0c54e3b3-1e9c-be1e-
     2c24-a6a8c7060233&lng=en&id=26965

8.   'Reliance SEZ on way out, Haryana govt wants its 1,384 acres back',
     Indian Express, 18 January 2012, http://www.indianexpress.com/
     news/reliance-sez-on-way-out-haryana-govt-wants-its-1384-acres-
     back/900903/0

9.   http://www.thehindu.com/todays-paper/tp-national/tp-newdelhi/
     gurgaon-farmers-want-their-land-back/article4327284.ece

10. Raghuram Rajan, 'From Paternalistic to Enabling – India needs to
     adopt a style of government that unleashes the people's entrepreneurial
     zeal', *Finance and Development*, September 2006, Volume 43, Number
     3 IMF, http://www.imf.org/external/pubs/ft/fandd/2006/09/straight.
     htm

11. 'Tata abandons cheapest car plant', BBC, 3 October 2008, http://
     news.bbc.co.uk/2/hi/south_asia/7651119.stm

12. http://ridingtheelephant.wordpress.com/2011/05/09/west-bengal-
     hopes-for-a-communist-rout/

13. Asis Kumar Das, *A Timeline of Nandigram (22 August 2005 – 17
     June 2008)*, published by *Mazdoor Mukti* (Workers' Emancipation)
     on Scribd.com, http://www.scribd.com/doc/3604739/Nandigram-
     Timeline-22-August-2005-17-June-2008

14. http://ridingtheelephant.wordpress.com/2007/11/20/poor-
     governance-in-indian-states/

15. 'Amidst apologies, Buddha says all's well on home ground', http://
     content.ibnlive.in.com/article/04-Dec-2007politics/amidst-apologies-
     buddha-says-alls-well-on-home-ground-53581-37.html

16. Agreement between Tata Motors Ltd., Government of West Bengal and
     WBIDC,(undated),http://www.wbidc.com/images/pdf/Agreement%20
     between%20TML,%20WBIDC%20and%20Government%20of%20
     West%20Bengal.pdf

17. 'Singur row resolved, Mamata calls off stir: Drama Precedes Guv-
     Brokered Peace Deal', *The Times of India*, 8 September 2008, http://

epaper.timesofindia.com/Repository/getFiles.asp?Style=OliveXLib:Lo
wLevelEntityToPrint_TOI&Type=text/html&Locale=english-skin-c
ustom&Path=TOIBG/2008/09/08&ID=Ar00100

18. '"Clear evidence of rival hand in Singur": Ratan Tata', *Hindustan Times*,
6 February 2007, http://www.highbeam.com/doc/1P3-1211488401.
html

19. '"I hope there is a bad M and good M": Tata', PTI, 7 October 2008,
http://articles.economictimes.indiatimes.com/2008-10-07/news/
27720805_1_singur-ratan-tata-nano-small-car-project

20. 'Buddhadeb's Nano new Bengal dream is over', *Indian Express*, 4
October 2008, http://www.indianexpress.com/story_mobile.php?
storyid=369344

21. Information provided to JE by West Bengal sources.

22. Automotive Mission Plan 2006-2016, para 2.6.5, Department of Heavy
Industry, January 2007, http://www.dhi.nic.in/Final_AMP_Report.
pdf

23. 'SC asks Tata Motors to consider returning Singur Land', *Economic Times*,
11 July 2013, http://articles.economictimes.indiatimes.com/2013-07-
11/news/40515178_1_tata-motors-singur-land-tata-nano

24. Media release on 'Whose Land is it Anyway?' Jaipur Literature Festival
session moderated by JE, 27 January 2013, http://jaipurliteraturefestival.
wordpress.com/2013/01/28/whose-legacy-is-it-anyway-land-people-
and-development/

25. Audio on Jaipur festival website http://jaipurliteraturefestival.org/
program-2013/27-jan-2013-program/

26. 'Green panel suspends POSCO's environmental clearance', *Business
Standard*, 31 March, 2012, http://www.business-standard.com/article/
companies/green-panel-suspends-posco-s-environmental-clearance-
112033100038_1.html

27. http://www.newageweekly.com/2013/02/police-attack-villagers-to-
acquire-land.html

28. 'Orissa govt pre-empts land acquisition bill, completes land
acquisition for Posco', *Business Standard*, 4 July 2013, http://
www.business-standard.com/article/companies/orissa-govt-pre-
empts-land-acquisition-bill-completes-land-acquisition-for-posco-
113070400796_1.html

29. http://ridingtheelephant.wordpress.com/2008/09/17/posco-on-a-

learning-curve-about-india%E2%80%99s-%E2%80%9Csocial-process%E2%80%9D/

30. 'MoU signed projects to go under CAG scanner', 14 June 2012, http://www.visionofdate.com/2012/06/mou-signed-projects-to-go-under-cag.html

31. 'A Hotbed of Controversy', *Business World*, 10 November 2012, http://www.businessworld.in/en/storypage/-/bw/a-hotbed-of-controversy/607520.0/page/0

32. 'Mining scam unearthed in Orissa', CNN-IBN, 27 September 2011, http://ibnlive.in.com/news/ballerylike-mining-scam-unearthed-in-orissa/188072-3.html

33. 'CAG finds illegal mining in Orissa', *Asian Age*, 27 March 2013, http://www.asianage.com/india/cag-finds-illegal-mining-orissa-674

34. 'Justice M.B. Shah Commission probing illegal mining', Indo-Asian News Service, 4 March 2013, http://www.ndtv.com/article/india/justice-mb-shah-commission-probing-illegal-mining-to-miss-deadline-338228

35. 'It is "no" to Vedanta's mine project in Orissa', *The Hindu*, 24 August 2010, http://www.thehindu.com/news/national/it-is-no-to-vedantas-mine-project-in-orissa/article591546.ece

36. 'Centre rejects eco-clearance for $1.7bn Vedanta mine', *Hindustan Times* 24 August 2010, http://www.hindustantimes.com/India-news/NewDelhi/Centre-rejects-eco-clearance-for-1-7-bn-Vedanta-mine/Article1-591035.aspx

37. 'SC leaves Vedanta's fate in tribal deity's hands', *The Times of India*, 19 April 2013, http://articles.timesofindia.indiatimes.com/2013-04-19/india/ 38673085_1_gram-sabha-alumina-project-bauxite-mining-project

38. 'Last gram sabha opposes Niyamgiri bauxite mining', *Hindustan Times*, 19 August 2013, http://www.hindustantimes.com/India-news/Odisha/Last-gram-sabha-opposes-Niyamgiri-bauxite-mining/Article1-1109960.aspx?htsw0023

IV

DYNASTY

12

Families Galore

South Asia is swamped with dynasties that have rarely contributed much to their countries' well-being or development. They have played a dominant role in politics since before the countries gained independence from Britain, and they survive partly because of strong feudal, tribal and hierarchical traditions and hereditary social structures[1]. The poor and unsophisticated sections of the electorate look up to them as icons and achievers beyond their reach. Middle-class supporters respect their legacy and seem to subscribe to the principle of the 'devil you know is better than one you don't', while the elite cling to them in order to share their prestige and powers of patronage, which is especially important in status-conscious and influence-peddling societies.

In India, members of the Nehru-Gandhi family have resolutely clung to power at the top of the Congress party and India's government for most of the years since Jawaharlal Nehru became India's first prime minister, but the country would probably have been better off without them. In Pakistan, the Bhutto family has led the Pakistan People's Party (PPP) since the 1970s, but has done little for the good of the country. Bangladesh has been riven by battles between two dynasties, while a dictatorial family is now running Sri Lanka.

These dynasties have provided what should have been transitional leadership as their countries have developed political systems to replace colonial rule. Yet, while they have helped to build or restore democracy at some stage of their history, they have thwarted the

193

emergence of other leaders and new ideas. The Nehru-Gandhis have blocked the top jobs and internal democratic development of the Congress party, and have also imposed their views on policy. Rahul Gandhi has tried to introduce democratic grassroots elections that ultimately could transform the party and sideline his dynasty but, without his family in control, that would almost certainly have happened earlier. As Mark Tully, the veteran BBC correspondent, wrote in 1991 at the end of his best-known book *No Full Stops in India*[2], 'For all its great achievements, the Nehru dynasty has stood like a banyan tree overshadowing the people and the institutions of India, and all Indians know that nothing grows under the banyan tree.'

Greed and corruption lie behind many dynastic ambitions. A large number of sons, daughters and other relations of Indian politicians are now encouraged to enter politics by their families and by political parties. They frequently run family business interests, which is part of the reason for a surge of political dynasties in recent years. Their involvement broadens and protects the base of politicians' riches and powers of patronage, and it also helps with the management of illicit wealth passing from one generation to another.

That partly explains why politicians' relatives are often rumoured to be handling their parents' corrupt deals. They can help to protect the money involved and provide continuity in what might be called investment management. Massive amounts of money gained from bribes are often invested in real estate and other ventures through *benami* (Hindi for anonymous) names that are either false or belong to less visible people such as associates and servants. Sometimes the money is laundered through 'round tripping' via Mauritius and other tax havens and back into India as investments, with the politicians' identities hidden in the benami names and shell companies. The downside for the families is that the people whose names are being used sometimes refuse to hand back the wealth, for example after a politician dies, so the existence of a dynasty can help to manage such problems. On the other hand, relatives become ambitious and use their proximity to someone in power to further their own separate business interests, with or without a politician's knowledge.

Political parties gain from dynasties because, as with film stars and sports stars, family candidates are instantly recognisable, so they usually have less difficulty selling themselves in huge political arenas like India where there can be as many as 30 candidates and three million potential voters in one constituency. Most important of all, it is the family name that matters – Brand Gandhi generates instant recognition. It is not surprising therefore that, in the past decade, there have been increasing numbers of dynastic parliamentary candidates, in addition to the older political families who are led in terms of prominence by the Gandhi clan – Rahul and his Italian-born mother Sonia, plus Sonia's estranged sister-in-law Maneka and her son Varun who are BJP MPs. The brands may not always pull in the votes however, as Rahul Gandhi discovered humiliatingly when he campaigned in state elections in 2012 and 2013. The offspring's activities bring enhanced importance to a family brand and to its longevity in the public spotlight. This strengthens politicians' own positions because they will have people around them who can (usually but not always) be trusted.

This is not to argue that all dynasties are necessarily corrupt, nor that all the family members who go into politics do so merely for reasons of sustaining power and patronage down through the generations. And, of course, India is a democracy, so all dynastic aspirants have to win elections and confirm themselves as leaders, as the Nehru-Gandhis have done since the 1920s. Dynasties are also common in many other areas – from company promoters to film stars and lawyers. In all of them, as with politicians, individuals have to establish their own success to a greater or lesser degree.

In Western democracies, elected dynasties play a limited role. In America, the Bush family has not come to dominate the Republican Party and the charismatic Kennedys, though influential, only produced one president and have not controlled the Democratic Party. The Clintons so far have only had a husband and wife with top jobs, though their daughter Chelsea admitted in a *Vogue* magazine interview that she doesn't rule out entering politics, seeing it (in a way that is unusual in India) as 'part of being a good person ... part of helping to build a better world [and] ensuring that we have political leaders who are committed to that premise'.[3] In Britain, Winston Churchill's heirs were high profile but failed to carve out a political niche, while Margaret Thatcher's offspring did not try, though both the Churchills and Thatchers cashed in on their parent's name in their careers.

Dynasty has enabled women to become leaders in Asian societies[4] where it would otherwise have been difficult for them to attain high office (though this has not made a significant difference to the role of other women in these countries, apart from token appointments). More often than not, the women have, like Sonia Gandhi, been the widows or daughters of assassinated former leaders. In Pakistan, there was Benazir Bhutto, the daughter of Zulfikar Ali Bhutto who was executed in 1979. She herself was assassinated in 2007 (after which her husband Asif Ali Zardari became Pakistan's president and their son Bilawal Bhutto Zardari is now entering politics).

In Bangladesh, there are two warring families headed by Sheikh Hasina and Begum Khaleda Zia, who have both been prime ministers. Both entered politics after the assassination of close relatives. Hasina's father, Sheikh Mujibur Rahman, leader of Bangladesh's independence movement and its first prime minister, was killed in a 1975 army coup along with other family members. Zia's husband, General Ziaur Rahman, seized power after Mujib's assassination and was himself assassinated in an abortive 1981 coup. By destabilizing each other's governments when they are in opposition, the two women have allowed their feud to stymie the development of one of the world's poorest countries, and both have sons or other relatives lining up to succeed them. In Sri Lanka, there was the Bandaranaike dynasty and the country is now controlled by a new dynasty led by President Mahinda Rajapaksa. In Myanmar, there is the iconic opposition leader, Aung San Suu Kyi. The small Himalayan countries of Nepal and Bhutan used to keep it simple with hereditary monarchs, but Nepal's was ousted in 2008,[5] and Bhutan's has been partially replaced by a democratically elected government.

The Families

The acceptance of dynasties fits with the idea of making do with things as they are – if a dynasty works, why change it! But does it work? It has certainly been supremely important in India because of the Nehru-Gandhi leadership of both the Congress party and the central government, but the country's politics would have developed differently if the family had moved to the sidelines in the second half of the twentieth century. Despite persistent rumours – unproven and denied – that have continued to swirl around the Gandhis since the Bofors gun corruption scandal in the late 1980s, few people would suggest that the family is in politics primarily for financial or personal gain.

Positive committed motives can be ascribed to other dynastic rising stars of Rahul Gandhi's generation such as Jyotiraditya Scindia, Sachin Pilot and Jitin Prasada, who are all in their thirties or early forties. Scindia is the aristocratic heir to a maharajah's title in Madhya Pradesh and to the Gwalior parliamentary seat where his late father, Madhavrao Scindia, was an MP. From widely differing backgrounds, they are all sons of former senior Congress ministers and became ministers of state in the Congress government elected in 2009. Some were given further promotions. In the same age group, Omar Abdullah, National Conference chief minister of Jammu and Kashmir and the son and grandson of former chief ministers, is also in politics for constructive reasons, ignoring the advice passed down from his grandfather Sheikh Abdullah, Jammu and Kashmir's first chief minister, that 'politics is a dirty game and once you are in it, you'll never be able to get out'.[6]

Sachin Pilot, who is in his mid-thirties, is married to Omar Abdullah's sister, merging two dynasties. To test his commitment, one has to go no further than his official bungalow on Delhi's Safdarjang Road, close to the prime minister's enclave and opposite the exclusive Gymkhana Club. There, every morning, this tall, slim and at first glance rather stern-looking politician, holds a durbar for 100 or so of his constituents from Rajasthan and for the poor from Uttar Pradesh (his family's home state) and elsewhere. They are given chai, visit toilets (he's installed six to accommodate them), and wait to meet this grandson of a rural Gujjar dairy farmer who went to Wharton in the US. 'It gives them a sense of belonging,' he told me when I interrupted a morning session.[7] 'About 20 per cent get the work they want done, while the others are able to talk about what they need – work transfers, police problems, family feuds, buffaloes that have run away. This is a job a politician can do.' I wondered as I left how many other senior politicians had this dedication – probably not more than four or five.

Pilot says he had never thought of entering dynastic politics, but with hindsight it seems to have been inevitable. He told me that he made his first political speech when he was 12, at a village meeting held by his mother, who was standing for Rajasthan assembly seat. 'They called me to speak, so I did, for about one and a half minutes. So I got recognition and later an opportunity to run in elections.' His father, Rajesh Pilot, was a minister in the Congress governments of the 1980s and 1990s and had been considering challenging Sonia Gandhi for the party leadership not long before he was killed in a car crash in 2000. Sachin was in college in the US at the time, and his mother took over Rajesh's parliamentary seat while Sachin finished his studies. In 2004, it seemed natural for him to stand in her place, and since then he has campaigned for the poor and especially for the Gujjars, who want to enhance their official tribal status – he was briefly jailed in 2007 when he joined mass Gujjar protests that blocked a highway to Delhi.

In 2009, he became minister of state for communications and information technology and in 2012 was promoted to be minister of corporate affairs. At the age of 36, he successfully enacted the new companies legislation by first gaining support from coalition parties and then steering it through parliament. The bill, which repealed 57-year-old laws, had been pending for about a decade and, after receiving cabinet approval at the end of 2012, it needed someone with Pilot's energy and drive to make it become law.

In an older generation, there is Naveen Patnaik, the Biju Janata Dal (BJD) chief minister of Odisha, who is in his mid-sixties. He is a rare example of dynastic success rather late in life, and he might be the last of the line. Naveen was a dilettante international socialite, mixing with people such as Jacqueline Onassis and Mick Jagger, until he fell unexpectedly into politics and became an MP in the late 1990s on the death of his father, Biju Patnaik, a former chief minister of Odisha. Naveen's elder brother Prem, a Delhi-based businessman, was not interested in entering politics, nor was his sister Gita Mehta, a well-known author partly based in New York.

I remember Naveen talking emotionally at Delhi dinner parties about how ineffectual he felt (and was) in the face of the state's appalling rural poverty, which he was personally encountering for the first time. He later became the state's semi-reclusive chief minister and astounded both supporters and critics by being elected consecutively three times.[8] He has managed to maintain a clean image with his electorate by reducing their exposure to petty corruption, despite allegations that his government (and specific ministers) accept bribes on large mining and other projects. He has never married, so has no heirs to succeed him. Perhaps conscious that a rival Patnaik family had lost elections because voters had tired of their dynasty, he has played down his own family links, and his brother and sister are rarely seen in Odisha. So, unless one of them changes their mind and decide to cash in on the family legacy, Naveen might close the dynasty, at least for a time.

Few have the sense of service of Scindia through his royal lineage or Pilot through his rural background – both of whom are following on from their fathers, who were two of the most respected Congress MPs of their generation and set high standards for their sons to follow.

Dynastic Surge

There has been a surge of dynasties in India during the past decade, most of whom do not have the strong public service credentials that can be attributed to the Gandhis and other young politicians mentioned earlier. Defenders and apologists for what has been happening argue that dynastic politicians have to go through the hoop of being elected, and that their only advantage is the family brand, which eases their entry into politics.

The best survey was conducted by Patrick French, an author and historian, when he was writing a book, *India: a Portrait*[9], with the help of regional journalists and a young statistics cruncher, Arun Kaul. They found that, led by the Gandhis, more than a third of the Congress party's MPs elected in 2009 had come into politics through a family link.[10] Literally all the MPs (not just Congress) aged under 30, and more than two-thirds of those under 40, were from hereditary political families, whereas less than 10 per cent of MPs over the age of 70 were dynastic. He classified 27 MPs as 'hyper-hereditary', including 19 from the Congress, meaning those who had multiple family connections and several family members with political careers.

Regional state-based parties had a higher incidence of hereditary MPs than national parties. All five MPs from Uttar Pradesh's Rashtriya Lok Dal Party (National People's Party) had family links, including Ajit Singh, the party leader and son of Charan Singh, who was briefly (1979–80) prime minister. This was also true of six out of 14 MPs belonging to the Orissa-based Biju Janata Dal led by Naveen Patnaik and three MPs from Jammu and Kashmir's National Conference headed by Farooq and Omar Abdullah.

Seven out of nine MPs from the Maharashtra-based Nationalist Congress Party (NCP) – founded and led by Sharad Pawar, a

powerful national and regional politician who split from the main
Congress party in 1999 over Sonia Gandhi's emerging role – hailed
from political families. Only one MP from the NCP did not have
a politically significant family background. Pawar's acolyte, Praful
Patel, is one of the country's richest MPs.

Although it did not figure in French's research, the DMK in the
southern state of Tamil Nadu, has a complex web of family and
business relationships, rivalries and intrigues. The network is headed
by the state's veteran former chief minister M. Karunanidhi, one
of whose sons, M.K. Stalin, has been mayor of Chennai, a state
government minister, and then deputy chief minister between 1996
and 2011. Karunanidhi's nephew, the late Murasoli Maran, and one
of Maran's sons, Dayanidhi Maran, have both been MPs and central
government ministers in recent years. Murasoli had developed close
political links in Delhi over four decades,[11] and the family runs a
large media empire. Among the posts Dayanidhi held was that of
telecommunications minister, which he lost in 2007[12] because of a
family feud, and textiles minister, a post from which he resigned in
2011 over telecom corruption scandals.

Dayanidhi was succeeded in 2007 by A. Raja, a DMK MP who
was at the centre of the 2011 telecom scandal and was closely linked
with Karunanidhi's daughter, Kanimozhi, a member of the Rajya
Sabha. Both Raja and Kanimozhi were imprisoned in February 2011
(Raja for six months and Kanimozhi for 15 months). Tamil Nadu's
other main political party, the state-based All India Anna Dravida
Munnetra Kazhagam (AIADMK) has had a different sort of dynastic
succession based on the film industry's massive popularity – its leader
and chief minister, J. Jayalalitha, was the mistress of the late M.G.
Ramachandran, a former chief minister who broke away from the
DMK and set up his own party.

Rivalries spurred by the pursuit of riches and power have
disrupted many dynasties like the DMK family in Tamil Nadu. This
was spectacularly evident during the 2012 state assembly elections
in Punjab, where politics have been controlled by six landed families

since Partition. The best known are the current two rival party leaders – Captain Amarinder Singh, 69, of the Patiala Royal family and leader of the Congress party, and Parkash Singh Badal, 84, of the Shiromani Akali Dal, who in 2012 unexpectedly defeated the Congress and became the chief minister for the fifth time since the 1970s. Amarinder Singh's wife Praneet Kaur is a Congress MP from the family's home constituency of Patiala and became a minister of state for external affairs in 2009. Amarinder Singh liked to show he was born to rule – I once saw him browsing in a bookshop in Delhi's Khan Market while his fleet of about ten Ambassador cars and Maruti jeeps, packed with gun-toting security guards, arrogantly blocked traffic at the entrance to the market.

One of the most famous – and infamous – examples of self-serving dynastic greed, aggrandisement and infighting is provided by Lalu Prasad Yadav and his wife Rabri.[13] An MP at 29, Lalu Yadav became Bihar's chief minister in 1990 and was forced to resign in 1997 when he was facing jail over a series of corruption allegations, notably a 'fodder scam'. He was accused (and later convicted) of being involved in syphoning off Rs 950 crore from the state government's animal husbandry department. He then planted his uneducated wife, Rabri Devi, in the chief minister's chair, and their relatives fought for prestige and wealth across the state. Between them, the husband and wife dominated Bihar's politics for 15 years till 2005 when they were swept from power in state assembly elections (and again rejected in 2010)[14] by a desperately poor electorate who realized that this backward-caste champion was doing nothing for them in terms of development. Yadav had come to power on a wave that should have led to a new deal for the poor. Instead, he showed little interest in the job of government and concentrated on building up his own image and only helped his family and Yadav caste to improve their lot.[15]

French surmised that, since the tendency to turn politics into a family business was being emulated across northern India at the state level, with legislators nominating relatives, there was no reason to believe it was not spreading to districts. Other sources suggest that in Mumbai's 2012 municipal elections, where for the first time 50 per cent of the seats were reserved for women, many of the women candidates were 'stooges for their politically ensconced kin', representing men in their families 'who are the back room boys'.[16]

Evidence found later by French supports my theory that wealth and greed are linked with the growth of dynasties.[17] Aaditya Dar, one of his postgraduate researchers, merged their survey findings with a report on the 2009 financial and criminal records of Lok Sabha MPs prepared by the Delhi-based Association for Democratic Reforms.[18] Based on MPs' official (though not always complete) declarations of wealth, this showed that hereditary MPs were four-and-a-half times wealthier than those with no significant political background. Hyper-hereditary MPs (those with multiple family connections, such as Praneet Kaur from the Patiala dynasty mentioned above) were the wealthiest of all. Their average total assets were roughly double those of the hereditary MPs, and they exceeded even MPs with a business background. Of the 20 richest MPs, 15 were hereditary politicians and 10 were in the Congress.

India's dynastic surge may well be the effect as well as the on-going cause of a sharp decline in the quality and effectiveness of Indian politics and governance that began in Indira Gandhi's time as prime minister. Standards of public life have worsened even faster in recent years as personal greed has replaced many politicians' concern for the country – especially among regional parties, whose role has expanded dramatically since the 1980s.

Notes

1.   JE, 'In Asia, the dynasties still rule', *New Statesman*, 8 November 1999, http://www.newstatesman.com/node/136052
2.   Mark Tully, *No Full Stops in India*, Viking-Penguin, 1991
3.   'Waiting in the Wings: An Exclusive Interview with Chelsea Clinton', *Vogue*, September 2012 http://www.vogue.com/magazine/article/waiting-in-the-wings-an-exclusive-interview-with-chelsea-clinton/#8

4. JE, 'In Asia, the dynasties still rule', *New Statesman*, 8 November 1999, http://www.newstatesman.com/node/136052

5. 'Yesterday the palace, today the suburbs for deposed king of Nepal', *The Independent*, 12 June 2008, http://www.independent.co.uk/news/world/asia/yesterday-the-palace-today-the-suburbs-for-deposed-king-of-nepal-845055.html

6. NDTV – Full transcript: 'Your Call with Farooq Abdullah', 18 March 2012, http://www.ndtv.com/article/india/full-transcript-your-call-with-farooq-abdullah-186907

7. Conversations with JE, May 2012 and September 2013

8. http://ridingtheelephant.wordpress.com/2009/04/23/orissa%E2%80%99s-reclusive-enigma-looks-set-for-an-election-victory/

9. Patrick French, *India, A Portrait – An intimate biography of 1.2 billion people*, Penguin Books

10. Patrick French's news website that he launched when *India, A Portrait* was published http://www.theindiasite.com/family-politics/family-politics-how-nepotistic- is-the-indian-parliament/

11. Gopu Mohan, 'Maran & Bros', *The Sunday Express*, 12 Oct 2011, http://www.indianexpress.com/news/maran-&-bros/860364/0

12. http://ridingtheelephant.wordpress.com/2007/05/15/dynasties-rule-ok/

13. Sankarshan Thakur, *The Making of Laloo Yadav – the Unmaking of Bihar*, HarperCollins India, 2000

14. http://ridingtheelephant.wordpress.com/2010/11/25/bihar-election-shows-a-better-future-as-evidence-of-india%E2%80%99s-corruption-spreads/

15. JE, 'Feudal Failings', book review, *Biblio*, January 2001 – http://www.biblio-india.org/showart.asp?inv=16&mp=JF01

16. http://www.ndtv.com/article/cities/mumbai-civic-polls-only-8-percent-of-women-candidates-are-graduates-175835

17. Patrick French, *Father, son and unholy politics*, *The Week*, 4 May 2012, http://week.manoramaonline.com/cgi-bin/MMOnline.dll/portal/ep/theWeekContent.do?tabId=13&programId=1073755417&categoryId=-1073908161&contentId=11528955

18. Aaditya Dar, 'The business of family politics in India', 2 April 2012 http://theopendata.com/site/2012/04/the-business-of-family-politics-in-india/

13

Nehru and the Gandhis

'We are distraught – what can we do but vote for her son?'[1] That was the cry I heard in the run-up to the December 1984 general election that gave a landslide victory to Rajiv Gandhi and the Congress party. A few weeks earlier, on 31 October, I had been in the Himalayan hill station of Mussoorie listening, along with British diplomats and other journalists, to Tibetan refugee children singing at lunchtime for Princess Anne, who was visiting from the UK as president of the Save the Children Fund. The drivers turned on their car radios and heard the news – on Pakistan Radio – that Indira Gandhi, India's prime minister, had been shot. We wondered if it was true, or did Pakistan Radio put such disinformation out every day! Mark Tully overheard two policemen talking about the shooting, so drove back to Delhi where his BBC colleague, Satish Jacob, had been the first person to broadcast news of her death over the airwaves. There were no easily available telephone links, so the rest of us, including Michael Thomas of *The Times*, decided it must be true rather more slowly, and started a seven-hour drive back to Delhi. Our cars were plastered with news sheets mourning Gandhi's death as we passed through towns on the way south.

I was back in my Delhi office that evening in time to write the lead story for the front page of the next morning's *FT*, reporting that Indira Gandhi's son, Rajiv, had been sworn in as prime minister, and that violence was spreading.[2] The next day, I was among the crowds thronging around the steps of Teen Murthi House, a museum that had been the home of Jawaharlal Nehru, India's first prime minister and Indira's father, where her body, face uncovered, lay in state on a gun carriage. 'Tears and Tear Gas, Fighting and Flowers' was the headline the *FT* put on my story reporting how thousands of young people had fought and jostled for a view of the body. They were beaten back by police with vicious lathis and eventually tear gas when the teeming crowds threatened to overwhelm the body.

An era ended that day and another began. One of India's most notable politicians and strongest leaders was dead, shot by her Sikh security guards, leaving behind a controversial legacy that is still debated.[3] Indira Gandhi was gone but in the spirit of 'the king (or queen) is dead, long live the king', Rajiv Gandhi had quickly been made the Congress leader and prime minister so as to ward off potential rivals. That succession established the Nehru-Gandhi family far more firmly as a political dynasty than it had been before, leading to the rise later of Rajiv's widow, Sonia, and their children Rahul and Priyanka.

While leaders of India's other parties have changed, with a flood of dynasties only appearing relatively recently, the Nehru-Gandhis have resolutely stayed at the top of the Congress and of politics. The party has been out of power for only about thirteen years since the country's independence in 1947. Members of the dynasty have headed the party for all but nine years and have provided three prime ministers – Jawaharlal Nehru, Indira and Rajiv Gandhi – plus Sonia Gandhi, who is the undisputed chairperson of the United Progressive Alliance (UPA) coalition elected in 2004 and 2009.

This raises various questions:

- Have successive members of the Gandhi family sought to perpetuate the dynasty, or has its survival been dictated more by events?
- Has the family been good, or not, for India since it began to wield influence in India's struggle for freedom from British rule nearly a century ago, and has it slowed down the country's development?
- Can such a dynasty continue to perpetuate itself at a time

when people's instinctive loyalties to long-established icons are changing and they become more aspirational and better educated, demanding economic development, not sops?

• Are the Nehru-Gandhis the only people who can hold the Congress party together and enable it to win general elections?

The Dynasty Begins

Jawaharlal Nehru's father, Motilal, a patrician Hindu Pandit and prominent lawyer whose family came from Kashmir, was active in India's freedom movement and in the Indian National Congress in the 1910s. He linked up with Mohandas Karamchand (Mahatma) Gandhi, India's leading independence campaigner, and also brought Jawaharlal into politics. Gandhi spotted Jawaharlal Nehru as a budding young political leader around 1918–1920 and ensured that he became India's first prime minister in 1947. (None of Mahatma Gandhi's descendents have claimed a stake in politics, though a civil servant grandson, Gopalkrishna Gandhi, became High Commissioner in Sri Lanka and later Governor of West Bengal from 2004 to 2009.)

A later coincidence helped promote the name of the modern dynasty. Indira Nehru married Feroze Gandhi, a young Parsi political activist, whose family name was spelt Gandhy (though some members of the family deny this).

Sunil Khilnani, a historian who has been working on a biography of Nehru, has written that the change of spelling was done at Nehru's suggestion to hide Feroze's Parsi origin.[4] Whatever the reason, it gave the family an association with the stronger brand name that still causes helpful confusion today. No one knows how many of the poor, who have instinctively voted Congress in past general elections, believe that the Gandhis are descendants of the nation's founding father, but there must be many. (Foreigners who do not know India well also assume that there are direct family links.)

It seems that Nehru did not consciously set out to found a

dynasty, which contrasts sharply with the family's later, more overt, ambitions. While he was prepared for Indira to be involved in politics and have a chance of becoming prime minister after him, he did not want to trigger an automatic succession. As it happened, she did not become prime minister until 20 months after her father's death when his immediate successor, Lal Bahadur Shastri, died during a visit to Tashkent in the then Soviet Union. Kuldip Nayar,[5] a veteran journalist who was Shastri's information officer, writes that Shastri was convinced he was 'not uppermost in Nehru's mind' as the successor and says that when asked directly who he thought Nehru had in mind, Shastri replied: *'Unke dil main unki saputri hai* – 'In his heart is his daughter'.[6] (The circumstances of Shastri's death are a mystery.[7] Suggestions that he was poisoned have most recently been raised by Kuldip Nayar,[8] who was with Shastri in Tashkent at the time.)

Other writers disagree about Nehru's intentions. Various historians and biographers have argued, as Frank Moraes did in 1960, that Nehru did 'not want to create a dynasty of his own'.[9] Katherine Frank, in the most detailed biography of Indira Gandhi, writes that Nehru 'had always gone to great lengths to avoid any behaviour that could be interpreted as nepotism'.[10] She quotes an earlier biographer and Nehru family member saying that he was 'not grooming her [Indira] for anything' and that he had said he did not want to 'appear to encourage some sort of dynastic arrangement'.[11] Nehru was not keen on Indira being made a member of the Congress party's central working committee (CWC), but did not stop her becoming a somewhat reluctant party president in 1959. Some Congress leaders undoubtedly had ulterior motives in promoting her, assuming that she would be malleable and would act as a conduit to Nehru at a time when there was rivalry between Shastri and others to become Nehru's eventual successor.

Indira's own views are not clear and it seems that insecurity and a wish for privacy made her at times something of a reluctant heir apparent – she initially resisted taking the party presidency in

1959 and refused a second term. When she was questioned about becoming prime minister by journalists on a visit to New York in April 1964 (just a month before Nehru died), she said she 'would not' like the job. The journalists pressed her, and eventually asked, 'But are you going to say that you would refuse to serve?' To which she answered: 'Well, shall I say that 90 per cent I would refuse.'[12] She did avoid the job a month later, but took it in 1966, having served in Shastri's government as information minister. She had strong personal ambitions to exercise power, and these were initially more concerned with her own authority than with dynastic perpetuity. Later she wanted to be succeeded by her younger son Sanjay, whom she had brought into politics to help her in the 1970s. Sanjay revelled in the brutal exercise of crude political power and, according to P.N. Dhar, one of her closest officials, 'was impatient for the driver's seat' by 1976.[13] He played a leading role in enforcing Indira Gandhi's controversial State of Emergency (1975–77).

With a career as an Indian Airlines pilot, Rajiv Gandhi never wanted to enter politics, and only did so reluctantly to help his mother after Sanjay was killed when a light plane he was piloting over Delhi crashed in June 1980. I met Rajiv in January 1984 and asked him whether he would one day succeed his mother. He was an MP and a Congress general secretary at the time and had made a success of organising preparations for the 1982 Asian Games in Delhi.[14] 'That's a very long way off,' he said.[15] But if something were to happen to his mother, was he ready for the top post, I asked, echoing the question asked of his mother 20 years earlier. 'That's a very difficult question because I've only been in this game for a couple of years. Yes, I think I'm in it for life, but I do think I need more experience,' he replied. In it for life indeed – and his widow after he was assassinated in 1991, and their children too.

Sonia Gandhi had no political ambitions for years after she entered the family, but eventually became active a few years after Rajiv's death when she was encouraged by a coterie of eager courtiers to do her dynastic duty. She has said that she felt 'cowardly to just sit and watch things deteriorate in the Congress for which my mother-in-law and the whole family lived and died',[16] though that may not have been the complete story. Some private sources have suggested to me that she feared legal action over a 1987 Swedish Bofors gun contract that had dogged her husband's later years, and needed to get into politics so that she would have the power to deflect official investigations and legal cases. Others say she wanted to rebuild the power and influence of the family in various ways so as to secure them an elite, stable future.

Basically, however, she felt she had to act as a bridge for the dynasty so that the succession would pass via her from Rajiv to their son Rahul (or, as a second option, if Rahul failed, their daughter Priyanka). That has made her the family's most single-mindedly dynasty-driven member, determined to secure the top slot in the Congress and thus access to prime ministership. Perhaps her determination to ensure the succession stems partly from the insecurity of being foreign-born and not a blood relation of the Gandhis, plus an Italian mama's concern to ensure her family's station in life. Rahul and Priyanka, says their tutor, were 'taught of sacrifices and patriotism from the cradle to adulthood'.[17]

Sonia cleverly sustained her ambitions when the Congress unexpectedly won a general election in 2004 by making Manmohan Singh the prime minister, while she stayed in overall charge. She then pushed Rahul, who was reluctant to take on a major role. When he was a teenager, Rahul once told his father that he wished they could go back to happier days when Rajiv had been an Indian Airlines pilot with no political aspirations. 'I can't now, because now I have a belief in my people. There is no going back,' was Rajiv's reply, according to Mani Shankar Aiyar, a leading Congress politician and Rajiv confidante.[18] Aiyar said that was 'the ethos of these kids growing up'. Rahul tried to buck that trend and not live up to the ethos, preferring to spend long and unaccounted-for time abroad and it took a long time for his mother and others to rein him in. Eventually, in July 2012, making a rare public appearance at an official function in Delhi, he announced: 'I will play a more proactive role in the party and the government,'[19] which he eventually did six months later when he became vice president of the Congress and official number two to Sonia.[20]

Other members of the Nehru-Gandhi family could have bid for an active political life, but none has done so, apart from Maneka Gandhi, Sanjay's widow, and her son, Feroze Varun Gandhi. Maneka and Sanjay had a stormy six-year marriage before his death. She did not get on with her mother-in-law, who preferred the quieter and more cooperative Sonia, and eventually Indira threw her out of the family home in March 1982.[21] A year later, I interviewed Maneka for the *FT* on the first anniversary of her eviction. She had just founded her own political party, the Rashtriya Sanjay Manch, and I asked the inevitable question about her prime ministerial ambitions. She said it was 'a bit early to say "yes" at the age of 26', but when I tempted her further, she said (with hindsight, somewhat unrealistically), 'If I've gone into something, I might as well make a success of it.'[22]

She eventually became an MP in 1989, having merged her party with the then Janata Dal, and held various ministerial posts, moving on after a spell as an independent to the Bharatiya Janata Party (BJP). She remains an MP but is no threat to the mainstream dynasty, though she hopes that her son Varun, who became a BJP MP in 2009, will emerge as a national figure. Feroze has adopted his father's hard-line approach to politics and transformed himself during the 2009 election campaign from a soft-spoken young man to a ranting Hindu nationalist speaker, delivering widely condemned tirades against Muslims.[23] This was said at the time to be a carefully planned and orchestrated strategy aimed at developing a distinct dynastic brand but, although he was elected to parliament, the BJP has been slow in encouraging him to develop into a national figure.

To return to my initial question, the efforts of successive members of the family to perpetuate the dynasty have been far more important to its survival than the course of events – and that has become increasingly true with successive generations. Nehru seems not to have been wholly committed to the idea of his daughter succeeding him, whereas Indira saw first Sanjay and then Rajiv as her helpers and likely successors. Rajiv did not have time to consider such things before his death, and would probably have said that Sonia was a most unlikely successor because of her foreign and non-political background. Sonia then saw it as her maternal and dynastic duty to bridge the gap and establish Rahul as the born-to-rule successor, and pushed this far more overtly than earlier generations had.

Tragedy, Death and Acceptance

The family's history has been laced with tragedy and the premonition of death. Sanjay Gandhi was killed in a plane crash. Indira Gandhi then unwittingly sowed the seeds for more catastrophes when she encouraged a militant Sikh leader to become a political activist in Punjab in the late 1970s, and condoned separatist Tamil activity in Sri Lanka in the early 1980s. That led to her assassination by her Sikh guards in 1984, and indirectly to her son Rajiv's killing by a Tamil suicide bomber in 1991. Indira had a premonition of her own death, and Sonia has said the family feared for Rajiv's life: 'After my mother-in-law (Indira) was killed, I knew that he too would be killed … all of us, my children and me, knew that it was just a question of when,' she said in a television interview in 2004.[24] She pleaded with her husband not to become prime minister but he held her hands, hugged her, and said he 'had no choice', adding, 'he would be killed anyway'.[25] Indira Gandhi said earlier that Sonia had threatened to leave him if he entered politics.[26]

Rahul Gandhi spelt out the trauma of assassination – and how it lives on in the minds of his family – when he accepted his appointment as vice president of the Congress in January 2013. In an unexpectedly emotional speech, he referred to Indira Gandhi's killing by her Sikh security guards: 'When I was a little boy I loved to play badminton. I loved it because it gave me balance in a complicated world. I was taught how to play, in my grandmother's house, by two of the policemen who protected my grandmother. They were my friends. Then one day they killed my grandmother and took away the balance in my life. I felt pain like I had never felt before. My father was in Bengal and he came back. The hospital was dark, green and dirty. There was a huge screaming crowd outside as I entered. It was the first time in my life that I saw my father crying. He was the bravest person I knew and yet I saw him cry. I could see that he too was broken.'[27]

Later in 2013, explaining the sacrifices made by his family, he said during a political campaign speech, 'Communal forces killed my grandmother, my father and will probably kill me too. But I don't care.' He went on to expand what he had said earlier, explaining how Beant Singh (one of his grandmother's assassins) had asked him where his grandmother slept and if her security was adequate. 'He told me how to lie down if somebody throws a grenade at me. At that time, I did not understand what he meant. Years later, I understood that Satwant Singh and Beant Singh were planning to throw a grenade at her during Diwali … I saw my grandmother's blood. I also saw the blood of her killers Beant Singh and Satwant Singh. I used to play with those who killed her. I was angry with them for a long time … It took me 15 years to control my anger against them. I understand the pain of losing someone very close. I lost both my grandmother and my father to acts of terror.'[28]

Members of the family have not usually been accepted by many of their peers at the start of their political dominance, and have had to fight to keep their positions. Indira Gandhi had to face down powerful regional leaders, which led her to split the Congress and win support with socialist economic programmes and with a 1971 war that turned East Pakistan into independent Bangladesh. Rajiv was accepted as the leader after his mother's death, though he faced extensive opposition on policies from within the party. Sonia Gandhi played it more cannily and waited until 1998 when the party was desperate for her to become its saviour.

There was, however, a party revolt against her as a foreigner a year later. This led to a split and the creation of the breakaway Nationalist Congress Party in May 1999 by, among others, Sharad Pawar, the powerful politician from Maharashtra who became its leader, and P.A. Sangma, a politician from Meghalaya in the north-east of India, who was later speaker of the Lok Sabha and stood unsuccessfully as a candidate to be president of India. The BJP had been playing up the foreigner angle in 1999 and Sonia had called a meeting of the party's central working committee to plan a rebuttal. Sangma electrified the meeting by saying the feeling was shared by some in the Congress. 'We know nothing about you or your parents,' he said. 'How do we defend you?'[29] Pawar added that perhaps the party should declare that only an Indian born on Indian soil could head the government. Sonia faced down the revolt, but the event seems to have coloured her tactics since then.

From Nehru to Rajiv

Nehru's first contribution was leading India into independence with Mahatma Gandhi. He celebrated the moment in 1947 with a memorable speech that still echoes today, marking India's 'tryst with destiny' awakening 'to life and freedom' at 'the stroke of the midnight hour'. Many of his foreign and domestic policies, however, now appear to have been unwise, even destructive, though some may have been appropriate for their time. His controversial economic centralism and cooperative approach to China are now generally regarded as well-meaning but misguided. One biographer has described Nehru, who died a broken man in May 1964 just 18 months after the China defeat, as 'greater than his deeds'.[30] That seems an apt epitaph. A different first prime minister might have had fewer dreams and made fewer mistakes, but he might not have matched the strong secular and democratic course that Nehru and his fellow leaders set for India in 1947.

Following that 'greater than his deeds' thought, Indira Gandhi was not as great as she should have been, and her deeds were more damaging than she probably intended.[31] Her mistakes are generally seen as the actions of an insecure woman, desperate to build power and relying too much on her malevolent, power-hungry younger son, Sanjay, who encouraged her to declare and sustain the 1975–77 State of Emergency. She increased her father's socialist economic controls, though she did begin to unravel them in the early 1980s.[32] This paved the way for the beginnings of economic liberalization.

Most damagingly, she also opened the doors to widespread corruption, which has eaten devastatingly into politics, business and everyday life. This began the undermining of institutions such as the civil service and the judiciary, leading to the politicization of the civil service and crony capitalism. She also mishandled the Sikhs' Khalistan independence movement in the Punjab, allowing it to escalate until she ordered the army into the Golden Temple, the Sikhs' holiest shrine in Amritsar. In foreign relations, she understandably saw the old Soviet Union as a friend that had never let the country down. She practised damaging hegemony in South Asia, though she won massive popularity with the 1971 Bangladesh war.

Strangely, Indira is seen more favourably abroad as a great though flawed leader who did her best to manage a massive poverty-stricken and fractured country. But there was more to her than that. She tried more than any government before or since to protect India's environment that has been progressively plundered since independence in 1947.[33] She is also remembered for strengthening the confidence of Indian women, and for her ability to reach out to people and to care. Rescuing a disastrous and corrupt business escapade in vehicle manufacturing that had been started by Sanjay Gandhi, she initiated Maruti Udyog,[34] which became a successful small car joint venture with Suzuki of Japan and triggered a gradual modernization of India's engineering industry.

Rajiv Gandhi tried to modernize a highly resistant country and curb corruption. Fascinated by technology, he encouraged developments in electronics and telecommunications, and began to computerize government departments and election campaigns. He inspired India's youth with a vision of a modern India. For eighteen months, he could do virtually no wrong. J.R.D. Tata, the veteran head of Tata, praised him by comparing his methods with those of his mother: 'You paid money to the Congress and you were in. You got everything you wanted – (industrial) licences, growth, the support of the party. That was the policy. Now Rajiv Gandhi has changed all that,' Tata said in a magazine interview.[35] Gandhi was even praised after his first year by Atal Bihari Vajpayee, the BJP's president and later prime minister, who told me, somewhat mischievously: 'He has made a good beginning. India is moving. As opposed to Mrs Gandhi, he is good.'[36]

But India was not ready for Rajiv's vision of the future, and he was quickly dragged down by vested interests that preferred things as they were and blocked his reforms. Initially he tried to clean up the government and disbanded some of the networks of his mother's regime, dismissing Pranab Mukherjee, who had been Indira's finance and commerce minister, and R.K. Dhawan, who had wielded immense power running her office. (Both later worked their way back to the centre of Congress politics. Mukherjee became a minister in the 2004 and 2009 governments and president of India in 2012.) But Gandhi was hit by the debilitating Bofors corruption scandal in 1987, which wounded him politically and continued to haunt the Gandhis. In April 2012, the Swedish police chief who had been in charge of the investigations 25 years earlier, said that Gandhi 'watched the massive cover-up in India and Sweden and did nothing'.[37]

In foreign and regional affairs, Rajiv began to mend fences with the US, and also with China. He went to Beijing (with Sonia) in December 1988 on what was the first visit by an Indian prime minister after the 1962 war, and was welcomed by Deng Xiaoping, China's supreme leader.[38] He tried (disastrously) to force peace in Sri Lanka where, in 1987, he became involved in an ill-advised and thankless posting of Indian troops to the country's troubled Jaffna peninsula. He also came (maybe unwittingly) close to war with Pakistan at the end of 1986 when escalating army exercises almost triggered a conflict.

At home, he launched an unsuccessful peace initiative on the Sikh leaders' demands for some form of autonomy in the state of Punjab. His policies on Muslim rights and Hindu nationalism – including a highly controversial Hindu temple at Ayodhya and an equally controversial ruling on Muslim women's rights – encouraged communalism and contributed to Hindu-Muslim riots. Overall, his political popularity slipped rapidly from 1986 onwards. Constant reshuffles of ministers (more than twelve in four years), plus defections of some trusted colleagues and changes of senior bureaucrats, made matters worse. Eventually, accused of arrogance and insensitivity – and blighted by the Bofors scandal – he lost the 1989 general election, five years after his landslide victory. He was assassinated in 1991 during the next general election campaign, before he had a chance to show if he could put into practice what he had learned in the mid-1980s.

But Rajiv Gandhi's legacy should not be dismissed, as it often is by India's elite, as being of little or no importance. If Nehru was greater than his deeds and Indira was not as great as she should have been, Rajiv's hopes and dreams were greater than his ability in the 1980s to achieve them. His most important legacy was his vision of a new, young India, and the work he did that led to India's economic development in the following 20 years. Whether he would have won the 1991 election had he lived, is an open question – results from polling that took place before his death made it appear less than certain. But his death sparked a sympathy wave that returned a Congress government, just as Indira Gandhi's assassination had done for him in 1984.

Some observers thought that the dynasty's political dominance was finished. Rajiv Gandhi had not been seen as a successful prime minister, and he had no obvious and immediate family successor. Sonia Gandhi, then 45, was shy and inexperienced, and Rahul and Priyanka were still young (aged 21 and 19). Furthermore, the immediate emergence and acceptance of Narasimha Rao seemed to indicate that the Congress could rule without a Gandhi in charge, even though Rao was chosen only because he was assumed (wrongly) to be too old and unambitious to be significant.

It is never wise to write off dynasties however, because admirers and advisers continue to cling to a family, even if it fades for a time, imbuing it with an aura of importance in the hope that it will gradually regain influence and eventually return to power. That is what happened during the 1990s. Sonia Gandhi gradually emerged from the mourning and seclusion of a widow and eventually became the Congress party's leader, fulfilling her unexpected legacy as head of the family and re-establishing the dynasty with unexpected skill and patient determination. At the same time, her two children, Rahul and Priyanka, grew into potential future heirs, enhancing the dynasty's image of perpetuity.

Notes

1. JE, 'What can we do but vote for her son?' *Financial Times*, 21 December 1984
2. JE, 'Rajiv Plea to Shun Violence – Son named Prime Minister after assassination of Indira Gandhi', *Financial Times*, 1 November 1984
3. http://ridingtheelephant.wordpress.com/2009/10/31/indira-gandhi-%E2%80%93-a-flawed-legacy-25-years-after-her-death/
4. Sunil Khilnani, 'States of Emergency', *The New Republic*, 17 December 2001, http://www.newrepublic.com/article/states-emergency
5. Kuldip Nayar, *Beyond the Lines*, p.169, Roli Books 2012, http://www.amazon.com/Beyond-Lines-Autobiography-Kuldip-Nayar/dp/8174369104
6. Ibid., p. 131.
7. http://www.dnaindia.com/india/report_43-years-on-mystery-shrouds-post-mortem-of-lal-bahadur-shastri_1279124
8. Kuldip Nayar, *Beyond the Lines*, p.169, Roli Books 2012

9. Frank Moraes, *India Today*, p. 232, Macmillan, 1960: 'There is no question of Nehru's attempting to create a dynasty of his own; it would be inconsistent with his character and career', http://www.amazon. co.uk/India-Today-Frank-Moraes/dp/B0007ITK9M

10. Katherine Frank, *Indira – The Life of Indira Nehru Gandhi*, p. 250–251, HarperCollins, London 2001, http://www. harpercollins.com.au/books/Indira-Life-Nehru-Gandhi-Katherine-Frank/?isbn=9780007372508

11. Krishna Nehru Hutheesing, *Dear to behold; an intimate portrait of Indira Gandhi*, p. 149, Macmillan 1969, http://books.google.ae/ books/about/Dear_to_behold.html?id=mY8BAAAAMAAJ&redir_esc=y

12. Katherine Frank, *Indira*, p. 273.

13. P.N. Dhar, *Indira Gandhi, the Emergency and Indian Democracy*, p. 329, OUP 2000, http://books.google.ae/books/about/Indira_Gandhi_ the_emergency_and_Indian_d.html?id=EzRuAAAAMAAJ&redir_esc=y

14. Nicholas Nugent, *Rajiv Gandhi Son of a Dynasty*, p. 47, BBC Books 1990, UBS Delhi 1991, http://books.google.ae/books/about/Rajiv_ Gandhi.html?id=gxxuAAAAMAAJ&redir_esc=y

15. JE, 'The only man for the job', *Financial Times*, 3 November 1984

16. NDTV, *Walk the Talk*, *Indian Express*, 7 March 2004, http://www. indianexpress.com/oldStory/42528/

17. 'Her class of '84', *The Times of India*, 9 June 2004, http://timesofindia. indiatimes.com/city/Her-class-of-84/articleshow/727253.cms?

18. 'A Dynasty at Crossroads', Reuters, 11 September 2011, http:// graphics.thomsonreuters.com/AS/pdf/Gandhis_2709mv.pdf

19. http://indiatoday.intoday.in/story/rahul-gandhi-ready-for-prominent-role-in-government/1/209257.html

20. https://ridingtheelephant.wordpress.com/2013/01/20/rahul-gandhis-inevitable-and-incredible-appointment-as-congress-no-2/

21. Katherine Frank, *Indira*, p. 459

22. 'Maneka challenges a dynasty – John Elliott meets the Indian Premier's ambitious daughter-in-law', *Financial Times*, 29 March 1983

23. http://ibnlive.in.com/news/varun-gandhis-speech-marks-a-new-low-in-indian-politics/87851-37.html

24. A rare television interview with Sonia Gandhi – by Shekhar Gupta, editor of the *Indian Express* on *Walk the Talk*, NDTV, partial video on http://www.ndtv.com/video/player/walk-the-talk/walk-the-talk-sonia-gandhi-aired-february-2004/290097 and also in the *Indian Express*. Excerpts of the two-part televised interview are on the Congress Party website http://www.aicc.org.in/new/walk-the-talk.php

25. Sonia Gandhi, *Rajiv*, p. 9, Penguin Viking 1992, http://libibm.iucaa.ernet.in/wslxRSLT.php?A1=27994

26. As told to Kushwant Singh and reported in Mark Tully and Zareer Masani, *From Raj to Rajiv – 40 years of India's Independence,* p. 131, BBC Books 1988, http://books.google.ae/books/about/From_Raj_to_Rajiv.html?id=clVuAAAAMAAJ&redir_esc=y

27. Speech by Rahul Gandhi, All India Congress Committee session, Jaipur, 20 January 2013, text on http://www.aicc.org.in/new/RG_Speech.pdf, and video http://www.youtube.com/watch?v=KLRKuBJgLgo

28. 'Communal forces killed grandmother, my father. Will probably kill me too', *Indian Express*, 24 October 2013, http://www.indianexpress.com/news/-communal-forces-killed-grandmother-my-father.-will-probably-kill-me-too-/1186526/0

29. Vir Sanghvi and Namita Bhandare, *Madhavrao Scindia: A Life*, p. 304, Penguin Viking 2009

30. M.J. Akbar, *Nehru – The Making of India*, p. 582, quoting words used in another context by Rabindranath Tagore, Viking London, 1988, http://books.google.ae/books/about/Indira_Gandhi.html?id=gbEBAAAAMAAJ&redir_esc=y

31. http://ridingtheelephant.wordpress.com/2009/10/31/indira-gandhi-%E2%80%93-a-flawed-legacy-25-years-after-her-death/

32. 'An imbalance of liberalisation – L.K. Jha talks to John Elliott', *Financial Times*, 26 January 2003

33. *Indira Gandhi on Environment & Forests*, Ministry of Environment & Forests, Delhi, 2009

34. http://ridingtheelephant.wordpress.com/2008/12/14/today-is-the-25th-anniversary-of-the-maruti-suzuki-car-that-changed-india%E2%80%99s-motor-industry/

35. JE, 'See it in perspective', *Financial Times*, 31 October 1986, quoting (undated) *Illustrated Weekly of India*.

36. JE, 'One year on, Rajiv Gandhi's India is still edging forward', *Financial Times*, 31 October 1985

37. http://ridingtheelephant.wordpress.com/2012/04/25/indias-slide-leads-to-an-international-down-grade/ and http://www.indianexpress.com/news/no-one-from-india-met-real-investigators-of-bofors-gun-deal/940978/

38. Nicholas Nugent, *Rajiv Gandhi*

14

The Sonia Years

The Italian daughter of a builder from Orbassano near Turin in northern Italy, Sonia Maino was born on 9 December 1946. After school in Italy, she went to Cambridge in Britain to learn English in a city language school. Friends who were at Cambridge University at the time have told me they remember her as 'nice and unassuming' – part of a 'temporary students' social circle in the city that understandably tried to break into the university crowd and meet boys'. She succeeded, meeting her future husband in a Greek restaurant in January 1965, soon after she arrived. They married in 1968, with no thought that either of them would end up in politics.

From such a background, it is scarcely surprising that she stayed mostly in the shadows immediately after Rajiv's death in 1991. It soon became clear, however, that she and her advisers were dabbling in politics from behind the high walls of her central Delhi home at 10 Janpath, and she became increasingly available to be feted by important visitors from home and abroad, though she spoke little when she met them. She slowly shed her image of a shy widow and her gradual emergence was encouraged and used by various Congress factions to undermine Narasimha Rao's prime ministerial authority, despite his successful economic reforms.

In 1996, Rao lost a general election, and the Congress floundered in opposition with weak leadership. Gradually, Sonia Gandhi was sucked further into the party's maelstrom and, late in 1997, consulted friends about whether or not she should get fully into politics. She was reminded by one of them about a letter that Nehru had written to Indira, telling his daughter that she should either get into politics fully or get totally out because being half in and half out was ineffective and blocked others rising up in the party.[1] Sonia's decision to get in came quickly after that conversation.

Her aim, she said when she made the move at the end of December 1997, was to save the party from collapse, which of course was necessary to ensure that her late husband's dynastic legacy at the head of the party was protected till it could be passed on to their son, Rahul. She became a member of parliament and then party president in March 1998, ousting Sitaram Kesri, an ineffectual but wily elderly politician, at a time when the party needed a fresh image for an imminent general election. Kesri knew his time was up but clung to his post till Sonia's courtiers engineered a coup. This rescued the directionless and badly led party – and possibly the Nehru-Gandhi dynasty – from collapse. In the general election, she campaigned energetically, addressing large crowds at nearly 100 meetings, often accompanied by Rahul and Priyanka. This transformed the campaign into a real contest and revived the Congress's morale, but it was not enough to stop a BJP-led coalition from winning the election.

To begin with, Sonia was far from effective as a politician, though she had sufficient personality and dynastic charisma to pull political crowds and maybe votes across India.[2] She was a poor speaker in both Hindi and English. Years later, she still delivers her English-language speeches and statements as if each carefully enunciated word and phrase is a hurdle to be jumped. Her biggest misjudgement came in April 1999 when the BJP-led coalition government lost a confidence vote in parliament. Support had been withdrawn by one of its allies, the AIADMK from Tamil Nadu, whose leader, Jayalalitha, had grown close to Sonia. Within days, Sonia met President K.R. Narayanan and, standing in the forecourt of Rashtrapati Bhavan, proudly proclaimed to massed television cameras, 'We have 272' (the number of MPs needed for a majority in parliament).[3] The television sound byte acted as a catalyst for growing criticism, sharpened by the media and the BJP, that this foreign-born member of the Gandhi clan who had not proved herself in any way as a politician or party leader, was trying to vault into the prime minister's post. A backlash in urban areas, encouraged by the BJP, ridiculed the idea of India, as a country of one billion people, turning to a foreigner.[4] Possible allies refused to line up behind her in a confidence vote, and the power bid failed, leading to a general election later in 1999, which the BJP won.

After the election, with the BJP-led coalition back in power with a larger majority, Gandhi remained a remote figure. She was shielded by advisers, who seemed nervous to expose her to public scrutiny lest her limited mastery of language and public affairs, and lack of experience, were again revealed as they had been with the '272' claim. Slowly, however, she grew in stature and, haltingly and falteringly, began to lead the Congress in parliament and develop some charisma.

Sonia might have faced continuing challenges of the sort mounted by Pawar and Sangma in May 1999 when they broke away and formed a new party, if three leading Congress politicians of her own generation had not died within 15 months of each other while she was growing into the Congress leadership. Rajesh Pilot, who was considering standing against her in the party presidential elections that were to be held in November 2000,[5] was killed in a car crash five months earlier, aged 55. Madhavrao Scindia (56) died in a plane crash in September 2001 and Jitendra Prasada (62) did not recover in January 2001 from a brain haemorrhage. Their deaths robbed the Congress of its next generation of leaders, leaving no one near the top of the party who could challenge the dynasty.

Pilot told David Loyn, a BBC correspondent who was then based in Delhi and knew him well, that he had asked Narasimha Rao towards the end of 1999 whether he should stand against Sonia. Rao had replied, 'not yet'. Pilot was, however, likely to stand a year later, as Loyn revealed in an obituary in *The Independent*.[6] 'He believed that Congress would never be electable under its present leader, Rajiv Gandhi's Italian-born widow Sonia,' wrote Loyn. 'The party gives huge powers of patronage to the leader, encouraging sycophancy, and making opposition risky. But in London last month [May 2000] Pilot told me that he was close to declaring that he would stand against Sonia Gandhi as party president later this year. He had the encouragement of several senior figures, and he thought he might unseat Gandhi if she did not stand aside first.' After Pilot's death, Prasada, who had been Rao's private secretary and had been marginalized by Sonia,[7] did stand but was humiliatingly defeated[8] in what was to become the only contested presidential election of Sonia's political career. He died soon after.

Sonia rarely allowed herself to be questioned closely in public (even in later years) but became secure as party leader because she seemed to many to be growing into a potential election winner. She gained enough confidence to woo other potential parties nationally and to do an arduous 60,000-km countrywide tour in the run-up to the May 2004 general election. Her tour marked a re-launch of the Gandhi dynasty, at a time when its future looked shaky[9] and the Congress was not expected to win.

Rahul Gandhi, then 33, made his political debut in the 2004 campaign after spending most of his twenties abroad. His emergence gave supporters confidence that the dynasty would continue into the future, and he was the star turn. Elected for the first time as a Congress MP from Amethi in Uttar Pradesh, his father's old constituency, he was seen as the heir to the family dynasty and the reincarnation of his father. 'I come as a son and as a brother – and as a friend – elections come and go but I'll stay,' he shyly told Amethi villagers on a day when I followed him on the election trail.[10] He had a candour that defied allegations of spin, and his audiences were impressed, not just because he was young and seemed honest and sincere, but because he looked and sounded like his father. For them, Rajiv had returned, 13 years after he was assassinated, and life might be good again.

He said his agenda was to 'tackle the bigotry that divides caste and class against each other'. Friends of the family likened that to his father's (unsuccessful) ambition in the 1980s to steer India away from increasingly corrupt and self-serving governance. Rahul said his 32-year-old sister Priyanka was his 'best friend – supportive, good-hearted and sensitive', and she said he was 'a good sincere human being who cares for people and their problems'. Priyanka showed how she could mix more naturally with crowds than Rahul. She did not stand as a candidate, but helped with her mother's successful campaign in Rae Bareli, the constituency next to Amethi. She looked set for wider political involvement in the future.

There was, however, still considerable disenchantment with Sonia Gandhi's leadership, despite her visibly improved performance. During the election campaign, several leading Congress politicians were privately saying that Sonia Gandhi should step aside so that the party could mount a more effective opposition to the BJP.[11] They speculated that a serious defeat in the general election could lead to her being challenged for the leadership, or that dissidents would split the party, as had happened before. This was because no one – not even the Gandhis – expected the Congress to win, so the debate was about how to react to different levels of defeat. Leaders loyal to the dynasty said it was a 'semi-final' for the next election that they could win, perhaps as early as 2006 if the new government did not last its full term.

Such speculation was instantly swept aside when it became clear that the Congress and its allies were winning. The party was euphoric, but the result was not primarily an endorsement of the Congress, nor of the Gandhi dynasty. Sonia Gandhi had undoubtedly prepared the ground by uniting and galvanizing her party, but the outgoing BJP government had over-sold its election slogan of 'India Shining' and, with its regional allies also doing badly, lost the election more than the Congress and the Gandhis won it. The result was a stunning example of how India's electorate throws out national and state leaders when it thinks that things are not as they should be – as it had done when it rejected Indira Gandhi in 1977 after the Emergency.

By the time the result was announced on 13 May, it looked as if
the dynasty's future was assured – maybe even with Sonia Gandhi
as prime minister because she had built enough credibility since
the 1999 debacle. The political significance of her Italian origin
had dogged her from the time she entered active politics, but the
BJP had failed to capitalize during the election campaign on the
possibility of India having a foreign-born prime minister. With the
Congress about to form a government, however, the BJP stepped
up its campaign. Two BJP leaders threatened to resign from their
political positions in protest, and the party decided to boycott the
presidential swearing in of a Sonia Gandhi-led government.

In the subsequent turmoil, Gandhi announced at an emotional
meeting of her MPs that she would not be prime minister, and she
confirmed this a day later. Before the election, she had dodged the
question and said that, if they won, Congress MPs and coalition allies
would together choose a prime minister after the polls. Her decision,
which brought tears to the eyes of some MPs, was flagged as an act of
tyaag or renunciation in keeping with the highest traditions of India's
culture, and she was seen to be combining this with wisdom when
she named Manmohan Singh as the prime minister.

However, praise for what she had done was tempered when those
who watched politics closely realized that she had not renounced
political power at all. She had merely renounced accountability
by passing the difficult and accountable prime minister's job to
someone who would not challenge the dynasty. She had changed
the party's constitution so that, as the president of the Congress and
its leader in the Lok Sabha, she would choose the prime minister.
She remained chairperson of the coalition, and headed a new
National Advisory Council (NAC) that was created to give her the
status of a minister of state with an office staffed and paid for by the
government to monitor the implementation of the UPA's Common
Minimum Programme manifesto and, as it turned out later, push
pro-poor policies.

The dynasty was back where it had been in the days of Nehru and his daughter and grandson – with a member of the family in charge of the government, and with a new generation in the wings.

The Good Years

The 2004–09 UPA coalition government was stable and worked because there was empathy between the Congress and a communist-led Left Front that gave parliamentary support from outside the coalition. There was also an effective coalition coordination committee. Sonia Gandhi found it easy to deal with some of the Left leaders, as the American Embassy in New Delhi noted in a 2005 cable to the State Department in Washington that WikiLeaks publicized in 2011, accurately noting that she seemed 'more comfortable working with the often high-caste and well-educated Communists than with regional satraps'.[12] This was despite the fact that the Left blocked many economic reforms and other policies. The chemistry between Sonia and Manmohan Singh also worked well, with her running the party and politics and him the government, despite efforts by some ministers to undermine Singh by reporting primarily to Sonia. Singh had frequent frustrations with the Left, especially over opposition to a civil nuclear deal with the US. 'How can I run the government like this?' he asked rhetorically in 2007, hinting, some thought (wrongly, as it turned out), that he might resign.[13]

Sonia made her mark mostly by insisting on the government introducing policies that would help the poor and by using a virtual power of veto on policies she considered bad – usually on economic reforms and development. This often displayed her empathy with the Left and the liberal economists and social activists she appointed to her National Advisory Council.

The extent of her interventions were revealed in 2012, when *The Economic Times* successfully filed a right to information application with the National Advisory Council secretariat and found she had written 25 letters to Manmohan Singh and 17 to various cabinet ministers from the time the council was constituted for a second time in 2010.[14] These mostly pushed her social reforms agenda on issues – some major and some minor – such as a rural employment guarantee scheme, legislation on food security and tribals' forest rights and enforcement of environmental regulations on controversial mining and other projects. Between 2010 and 2012, she ensured that domestic workers were included in legislation on protecting women against sexual harassment at work. In January 2011, when there was a controversy over tribal people in the Andaman and Nicobar islands being exposed to tourism, she told the then home minister, Chidambaram, that 'the Ministry of Home Affairs may coordinate with them (Tribal Affairs Ministry) so that all issues related to the Jarawa tribe are comprehensively addressed'.

She stopped petrol price rises in 2006 and also dramatically slowed down the use of agricultural land for industry by saying such land should not be used for special economic zones that were then being pushed unwisely fast by Kamal Nath, the commerce and industry minister, who had strong equations with the business sector. She also tried to slow down talks on free trade agreements with Asean countries because she feared they could hurt India's farmers. Some of these and other initiatives originated with her council, but not all. After she had personally vetoed the oil price rise, a well-connected Indian businessman dubbed it, in a conversation with me, as a display of 'amazing democratic autocracy'.

In 2009, the Congress won an unexpectedly strong victory, with Manmohan Singh playing an important vote-pulling role alongside a public relations offensive to raise the profile of Rahul Gandhi and the more charismatic and astute Priyanka.[15] There were hopes that the government would do better than it had in the previous five years because it was supported by various regional parties and not the communist-led Left.[16] The Congress, it seemed, would be able to lead a much more stable government with fewer corrupt cabinet ministers from regional parties, especially in lucrative infrastructure and transport ministries. There were hopes of economic reforms being implemented without being held back by the Left, which would pull in foreign and domestic investment which had been lacking.

The Stars Fade

The predictions and hopes turned out to be totally misplaced. The coalition was constantly disrupted by its partners and lacked any cohesion. The cabinet was not of a better quality, and economic policy making and implementation came to a virtual standstill. Sonia Gandhi and Singh knowingly allowed a welter of corruption scandals to develop, and failed to handle them effectively when they became crises because the Congress was more interested in keeping the coalition intact and appeasing corrupt regional partners. The Gandhi-Singh chemistry was also far less effective than it had been.

The dynasty suffered in 2011 from Sonia Gandhi developing unexplained health problems, while Rahul continued to fail to acknowledge that he was her successor. In short, the government lacked visible leadership. Singh and Sonia Gandhi rarely spoke in public on major issues and Rahul, the heir apparent to both of them, was even more silent. Because of Sonia's position as the Congress 'High Command', no one dared challenge her as the party leader or Singh as the prime minister.

By mid-2012, the Nehru-Gandhis were providing a prime example of the problems that dynasties can cause. Their determination to stay in control, whatever the cost to India, was preventing the Congress from developing and electing new leaders and it was depriving the country of the quality of government it desperately needed. Absolute loyalty to the dynasty, namely Sonia and Rahul, had become a primary qualification for most top, and sensitive, posts. This led to key government posts being given to those who were seen as loyal rather than capable. A prime example was A.K. Antony, the defence minister, who was kept in his post even though he failed to reform the defence industry and ensure adequate preparedness of the forces.[17] Shivraj Patil was home minister from 2004, even though he was clearly inadequate at a time of increasing security concerns – Sonia Gandhi only agreed to move him after a devastating terrorist attack in Mumbai in November 2008.[18] The president of India from 2007 to 2012, Pratibha Devisingh Patil, was chosen by Sonia to be India's first woman president because of her loyalty to the Gandhis, but she turned out to be one of the most undistinguished and self-serving in the country's history.[19]

Singh had been appointed prime minister in 2004 because Gandhi knew that, as well as being a distinguished and respected veteran public servant and economist, he would not challenge her authority and would keep the prime minister's seat warm for her son. He constantly pushed aside advice from close advisers to assert himself more and build a power base as head of government alongside Sonia Gandhi's party and coalition leadership.[20] And he said several times that he would hand over when Rahul Gandhi was ready to succeed him.[21] It seemed that, approaching 80, he was no longer up to the job but did not want to resign for having failed, preferring to hang on till he could gave way to the heir apparent, who was little more than half his age at 41 and showed no sign of wanting to take over.[22] With no other acceptably loyal candidate, Singh was kept in the job instead of being allowed to retire, and was boxed in by the dynasty and its coterie so that he was less than effective in most areas, apart from foreign relations with the US and Pakistan.

It had become clear by now that the dynasty was becoming a drag on India's economic development because both Sonia and Rahul believed that the way to keep the Congress in power was to channel subsidies and funds to the poor, irrespective of how wasteful that could be, while discouraging growth-oriented economic reforms that might do short-term harm to the Congress's pro-poor image.[23] The worry was that they were not interested in striking a balance between pro-poor and growth initiatives, but focused solely on the first as the route to election success.[24] This contrasted with the constructive economic growth policies that Rajiv Gandhi had initiated in the 1980s.

The image of a government adrift, constrained by the inadequacies of dynasty and a coalition, was magnified by reports of extensive graft and extortion, especially corruption scandals in the coal and telecom industries that Singh appeared to have condoned for years. Foreign investors were worried by the growing evidence of corruption, and how far and deep its tentacles reached into India's institutions and the country's overall performance. A London-based banker friend, in a superb British understatement, emailed me that 'India is looking sticky'. I replied: 'Sticky indeed, but nothing much that we didn't know about, just woodwork crumbling a bit and everything crawling out!'[25]

The reputations of top politicians and others were publicly undermined by revelations from Arvind Kejriwal, the founder of the Aam Aadmi Party.[26] One of Kejriwal's hottest targets was Robert Vadra, a brass ornaments trader who 15 years earlier had married Priyanka, Rahul's sister.[27] A stocky fitness enthusiast, Vadra had accumulated surprising wealth through land deals in Haryana and elsewhere after his marriage. Many of the deals were with DLF, the leading and well-connected real estate developer, though it was not clear whether the investments were on his own account or were linked to the Gandhis' money. Leading Congress ministers including Chidambaram publicly defended Vadra when the accusations were first made, presumably thinking that was what Sonia Gandhi would want, but they quickly backed off as details of the land and property deals emerged and indicated close links with DLF and regional politicians.

During this period, there was also the national furore over rape and violence against women and about police brutality. Economic growth and the value of the rupee were both declining and there were loud complaints from businessmen about inadequate government, a lack of economic reforms, growing power shortages and blockages on new investment projects, and other problems. Parliament was failing to function because of disruption by opposition parties, and key legislations on issues such as land allocation, mining, foreign investment in insurance, food security and banking reform were stalled. In an attempt to reboot India's international image, Pranab Mukherjee was replaced in the middle of 2012 as finance minister by Chidambaram, who brought fresh energy to the ministry and persuaded Sonia and Rahul Gandhi to speak in favour of reforms that would generate economic growth. But none of this succeeded in halting the general decline.

It seemed to be too late. Sonia Gandhi's experiment of being in command as the dynastic head of the coalition without any constitutional accountability while a captive prime minister met her wishes, was not working. She was successfully keeping the Congress party and her dynasty in business, but India was being badly governed.

Notes

1. Private conversation with source
2. JE, 'At last, India's imperial phase draws to a close', *New Statesman*, 10 May 1999, http://www.newstatesman.com/node/134728
3. Rasheed Kidwai, *Sonia – A biography*, p. 125, Penguin Books India 2003, updated and revised 2012, http://penguinbooksindia.com/hi/book-category/biography?page=1
4. JE, 'At last, India's imperial phase draws to a close', *New Statesman*, 10 May 1999, http://www.newstatesman.com/node/134728 5. *Sonia a Biography,* pp. 75–77 as above ee.
6. David Lyon, 'Obituary: Rajesh Pilot', *The Independent* (UK), 14 June 2000, http://www.highbeam.com/doc/1P2-5070727.html
7. Vir Sanghvi and Namita Bhandare, *A Life of Madhavrao Scindia*, p. 303, Penguin Viking India 2009
8. 'A victory of sorts – Sonia Gandhi trounces Jitendra Prasada … but not in an election that was completely free and fair', *Frontline,* 25 November 2000, http://www.frontline.in/static/html/fl1724/17240280.htm
9. 'The unlikely heiress, Can Sonia Gandhi lead Congress to victory?', *The Economist*, 22 January 2004, http://www.economist.com/node/2370836

10. 'In the Name of the Father – The new Gandhi generation', *The Economist*, 24 April 2004, *http://www.economist.com/node/2618146*

11. Ibid.

12. 'Sonia more comfortable with Left than with regional allies', *The Hindu*, 27 March 2011, www.thehindu.com/news/the-india-cables/article1574328.ece

13. http://ridingtheelephant.wordpress.com/2007/10/23/indias-unhappy-pm-faces-unclear-future/ and http://business-standard.com/india/news/pm-talks-toughallies-over-nuclear-deal/302065/n

14. 'Sonia Gandhi's letters guiding Prime Minister & cabinet ministers', *Economic Times*, 13 August 2012, http://articles.economictimes.india times. com/2012-08-13/news/33182673_1_domestic-workers-sonia-gandhi-law-minister

15. http://ridingtheelephant.wordpress.com/2009/05/12/india%E2%80%99s-voting-ends-%E2%80%93-after-four-weeks-of-hot-air/

16. http://ridingtheelephant.wordpress.com/2009/05/16/congress-wins-%E2%80%93-communists-lose-%E2%80%93-orissa-stable/

17. http://ridingtheelephant.wordpress.com/2012/04/04/army-intrigue-and-graft-hits-indias-defences/

18. http://ridingtheelephant.wordpress.com/2008/11/30/chidambaram-is-a-good-choice-as-india%E2%80%99s-home-minister/

19. 'Dogged by Controversy', *Outlook* magazine, 30 April 2012, http://www.outlookindia.com/article.aspx?280623

20. Sources in his office told JE.

21. 'Manmohan Singh says open to Rahul Gandhi succeeding him', *Economic Times*, 29 June 2011, http://articles.economictimes.indiatimes.com/2011-06-29/news/29717287_1_lokpal-bill-congress-high-command-prime-minister

22. http://ridingtheelephant.wordpress.com/2012/02/06/government-in-blundering-retreat-on-corruption-crisis/

23. http://ridingtheelephant.wordpress.com/2012/07/09/time-mag-misses-the-target-in-dubbing-manmohan-singh-an-under-achiever/

24. http://ridingtheelephant.wordpress.com/2012/08/15/has-india-abandoned-economic-debate/

25. http://ridingtheelephant.wordpress.com/2012/09/11/india-is-looking-sticky-as-the-system-crumbles/

26. 'Popular war on corruption ignites India – A former tax man is taking his campaign to the streets', *The Independent*, 14 October 2012, http://www.independent.co.uk/news/world/asia/popular-war-on-corruption-ignites-india-8210445.html

27. 'Robert Vadra and DLF accused of illicit links by Arvind Kejriwal', NDTV, 5 October 2012 http://www.ndtv.com/article/india/robert-vadra-and-dlf-accused-of-illicit-links-by-arvind-kejriwal-276051

15

Waiting for Rahul

Sonia Gandhi has managed to build around herself such an exclusive and untouchable aura of personal privacy and secrecy, combined with ultimate authority, that few people have dared publicly to question her role or criticize her supremacy despite the government's growing failings. Apart from election campaigns, she has rarely appeared in public and never made herself available for the sort of public questioning routinely faced by most national leaders elsewhere.[1] She has done this with a style of modest elegance, her demeanour refined, and the effect much more persuasive than that of many other politicians.

Before she entered active politics in the late-1990s, Gandhi seemed unassailable, protected by a charismatic protective halo. Believers say that once someone steps outside a chakra's psychic circle of protectiveness, it shatters and cannot be repaired.[2] Gandhi however managed to retain her psychic chakra when she ventured into the real world of politics and even extended its reach so that the whole family became virtually unassailable, growing aloof with an understated but pervasive arrogance. The acceptance of this preeminent position would be envied by many less democratic rulers, as would Sonia Gandhi's ability to rule with a minimum of public utterances.

Remote, Aloof – and Ill

This, of course, is the secret of her success. By rarely commenting on, or becoming associated with day-to-day policies and other such issues, she rarely exposed herself to criticism and thus avoided the risk of arousing controversy and generating political attacks that could undermine her authority and upset the future of the dynasty. She intervened on pro-poor subjects such as fuel prices and the industrial use of agricultural land and, later, on legislation providing food aid, but she mostly stayed away from major controversies such as India's 2008 nuclear deal with the US and foreign direct investment regulations (though both she and Rahul Gandhi made one or two references in favour of foreign involvement in supermarkets). Neither she nor Rahul showed any interest in foreign policy, which they left to Manmohan Singh. 'Rahul won't pontificate on things that might go against him,' said a friend.[3]

Among the mysteries is the question of who advises Sonia Gandhi and the family, and manages so successfully to modulate their appearances and utterances. 'The Gandhis don't give their very closest loyalists top posts, preferring to keep them close,' a contact with links to the family's coterie told me, citing, as an example, Suman Dubey, a former journalist and newspaper editor who advises Sonia as a friend on media and other matters and plays down his proximity and insider knowledge. 'Suman is the closest outside the family and he doesn't want anything anyway,' said my source. Ahmed Patel, her political secretary, is her closest full-time adviser, running her office and acting as her gatekeeper, high-powered political manager, and guardian of the status quo. Then there are various Congress politicians and others who have fluctuating roles.

At a *Hindustan Times* Leadership Summit conference in October 2007 that I attended, Sonia was asked who her advisers were and she said (twice) that she consulted 'my son, my daughter and my son-in-law' when making key decisions. Sources wonder whether there is someone else in addition to Patel, maybe outside India, who provides Rahul with an elder's advice. Lee Kuan Yew, Singapore's veteran political leader, for example, met Rahul when he was on a week-long visit to the city state in 2006, learning about politics and development[4].

In 2005, the American Embassy reported (in the cable[5] that discussed Sonia's affinity with the Left) that the party had evolved an elaborate protective culture. 'Mrs Gandhi's inner circle carefully controls her access to information, and inoculates her from criticism, while her carefully scripted public appearances protect her from making gaffes or missteps. This has the advantage of preserving the "sanctity" of Mrs Gandhi and the dynasty, but can also complicate her efforts to wield power.' Gandhi, the embassy report continued, deliberately attempted to preserve the image of being above the fray politically, 'taking maximum advantage of Congress culture, which prescribes that the party figurehead be surrounded by an "inner coterie" to provide advice, and shield the leader from criticism and dissent'.

That protection, however, went too far on 4 August 2011 when a Congress party spokesperson announced that Gandhi, then 64, had been diagnosed 'with a medical condition'. On the advice of her doctors, she had travelled abroad and was likely to be away for 'two-three weeks', said the spokesperson, adding that the surgery had been successful and her condition was 'satisfactory'.[6] Beyond that, her health was a 'personal matter' and the people of India should respect her family's request for privacy.

She had appointed four people to look after the party's affairs in her absence – Rahul Gandhi, A.K. Antony, Ahmed Patel and Janardhan Dwivedi, the party spokesperson. The naming of this group indicated that the illness was serious, as did the fact that Rahul and Priyanka had left the country with her (even though Rahul was one of those left in charge). Yet there was no official announcement on the nature of the illness, nor of where she had gone, though she was widely reported to have had a cancer operation in New York's Sloan-Kettering Cancer Center where she had apparently already been treated for several months.[7] (A year earlier, she had left Delhi at short notice, cancelling meetings with David Cameron, the British prime minister, who was visiting.[8] She flew with Rahul, and it was thought Priyanka, to the US, reportedly because her mother was ill there, though later it was suspected that she was tested or treated for her own illness.)

It arguably borders on arrogance and disdain – and a lack of responsibility – for the leader of a ruling coalition and its main party to go abroad without explanation. The reasons have remained officially a secret, as have the nature of her illness and whether the suspected cancer has been successfully removed. She returned to Delhi after just over a month away, and appeared to recover and stabilise from the operation in the following months though she never looked completely well. She gradually returned to political work, but occasionally cancelled appointments because of 'ill health' and made regular return visits to the US for tests, and maybe treatment.

Tamed Media

The media's response to her disappearance was relatively limited after the BBC and AFP broke the news internationally. There were prominent reports in India, but only two newspapers – curiously, both business titles – ran critical editorials within a few days of the announcement. 'Such lack of clarity on the well-being and whereabouts of someone who, right now, is the most important political leader of the country is just not acceptable,' said *The Economic Times* on 6 August. Normally pro-establishment, its headline was explicit: 'Sonia Gandhi a national leader and her health not just a private matter.'[9]

The *Business Standard* (then edited by Sanjaya Baru, an economist and journalist, who had been Manmohan Singh's trusted spokesperson and speech-writer from 2004 to 2009) ran an editorial on 7 August under the headline 'Right to information – Ms Sonia Gandhi's health is a matter of public concern'. 'In a democracy the people have a right to know detailed information about the health of their leaders,' it said. 'This is neither a "private matter" nor can the family of the concerned public personality have the last word on the matter.'[10] There was a good television panel debate (including Baru) on some of these issues a few days later,[11] but there was little more comment for several weeks. Congress party spokespeople stated that only information the family wished to share would be publicized. In another formulation, they said the government could only issue information that it received – suggesting that the government itself did not know about its leader's health.

The only thorough reporting of the illness came much later in the *India Today* weekly news magazine, which ran a cover story in its 16 October issue headlined 'How ill is Mrs Gandhi?'[12] Challenging the family's insistence on secrecy, the story broke new (but not necessarily accurate) ground on the illness by reporting an (anonymous) New York doctor saying it probably wasn't cancer but 'was most likely an unusual disorder, pancreatic tuberculosis' whose symptoms can be very similar to cancer.

Politicians around the world enjoy varying degrees of privacy, as *The Hindu* discussed on 22 September 2012 when, some weeks after Gandhi's return, it ran an editorial headlined 'The omertà on Sonia Gandhi's illness' – mischievously, given her origins, using the Italian word *omertà*, which means code of silence[13]. Such scattered coverage scarcely amounted to a real attempt to discover – either through an official spokesperson or other sources – the nature and seriousness of the illness. This sort of disregard by the media of its proper role in guarding the public interest is surely not healthy for a democracy. Even if one recognizes that politicians like Gandhi will guard their privacy as much as they can, this still leaves the question of the Indian media's largely hands-off response – a reaction that enabled the family to ignore the limited criticisms.

Reports on the private lives and personal liaisons of politicians are rare, but that is surely different from failing to explore why the country's top leader had gone abroad for a possibly life-threatening operation. Presidents in the US are accustomed to public exposure and even the illnesses of Cuba's former ruler, Fidel Castro, have been publicly discussed. In India, a heart bypass operation on Manmohan Singh in 2009 was announced, though the illnesses of former prime minister Atal Bihari Vajpayee, 87, have been largely kept private.

The family's wish for secrecy has also blocked information on frequent private visits abroad by Rahul Gandhi. A right to information request in 2012 failed to produce any answers.[14] Rahul's private life has been a mystery. Everyone, of course, has a right to privacy, but that surely reduces with increased public importance and responsibility. So little is known that Delhi buzzes with gossip about where he regularly vanishes – is it abroad as is often rumoured (Dubai, Bangkok, London?), or just to the homes of friends near his central Delhi home? Does he have a girlfriend?[15] The only one ever seen publicly was Colombian (or Spanish, as he reportedly said in 2004), but she is rumoured to have married in Colombia and he was said to have moved on to an Afghan girlfriend or someone in a south Delhi colony, among others. The most visible side of his private life has been regular evening exercise sessions at the gym in central Delhi's Lodhi Hotel (previously the Aman), which is owned by DLF.

The illness saga also underlined how the Gandhis expect favourable treatment in the media without briefing journalists and editors, and without making many public appearances or any effort to generate good reporting. In October 2005, I wrote a piece in *The Economist*[16] which, I discovered later, the family did not like. I had asked for an interview with Rahul Gandhi and, if not with him, with someone he nominated, but nothing had been forthcoming. In the piece I wrote that 'Rahul Gandhi, whose weekend hobby is racing motorbikes with friends on a private dirt track near Delhi, has refused to emerge as an iconic figure'. He had 'not made much of a mark as an MP, having spoken only once in parliament' since he was elected in 2004. And he was 'prone to political gaffes'.

The previous month, I wrote, he had reportedly told *Tehelka*,[17] a weekly newspaper, that there was 'no governance' in the state of Bihar, which was embarrassing since the state had been under direct rule by the Congress-led central government since earlier in the year. He had also said that he did what he liked, despite his mother's views, and appeared to boast (probably flippantly) that he could have been prime minister when he was 25. The *Tehelka* story revealed, I wrote, 'a straight-talking, sometimes naive, young man, with firm views and ambitions'. He had said his idea of politics was 'very different from what is being done now'. In the 2004 election campaign his advisers had kept him as quiet and out of the public eye as possible, fearing, as he put it, that 'every time I want to do something ... it may go wrong'. The Congress insisted the Tehelka story was based on an un-taped 'background chat'.

A few weeks later, I was introduced to Sonia Gandhi at a *Hindustan Times* conference dinner and mentioned I had written an *Economist* piece on Rahul Gandhi, and that I wished I had been able to talk to him. 'Not a very good piece,' came her instant reply, which was remarkable because she'd had no idea that she would meet the (anonymous) author. She said she was unhappy that I had failed to state that the *Tehelka* article was not based on an interview (which I had in fact indicated). She showed more interest in that negative point than in taking the conversation further or suggesting a meeting.

What the family does encourage – or at least makes no effort to stop – are vast spreads of large advertisements placed in newspapers by government ministries at taxpayers' expense to mark various family anniversaries. On Rajiv Gandhi's 69th birth anniversary on 20 August 2013, there were nine half-page advertisements and three full pages just in the Delhi edition of *The Indian Express* celebrating his birth, two of them also marking the launch for a Sonia Gandhi promoted food security programme that day. The previous year, on 21 May, named Anti Terrorism Day to mark Rajiv Gandhi's assassination in 1991, advertisements remembering and praising him included 5¾ pages in the *Hindustan Times*, 5¼ in *The Times of India*, 4 in *The Hindu* and 3½ in *The Indian Express*. Analysis on a media blog, *Sans Serif*, showed that Jawaharlal Nehru's birth anniversary in November 2011 was marked by 58 government advertisements covering 26¼ pages in 12 English newspapers.[18]

Reluctant Rahul

Sonia Gandhi's central political importance was demonstrated by the UPA government's erratic behaviour while she was away ill, especially on two key issues – the Anna Hazare anti-corruption movement and an on-going telecom scandal. Manmohan Singh failed to seize the opportunity to exert the authority that should have gone with his job, and Rahul Gandhi equally failed to rise to the challenge as heir apparent. Other key politicians such as home minister P. Chidambaram and telecom minister Kapil Sibal fumbled their briefs, while the four leading Congress party figures Sonia Gandhi named as being in charge (including Rahul) made no public impression. She was clearly missed and it gradually began to be apparent that this Italian-born non-political mother and housewife had developed what some would see as her psychic chakra so that it not only protected her but also gave her a position of command.

That, of course, begs some questions. Did the disarray while she was away develop because the government was missing her and her advisers' sure touch, and had she developed a little-known sense of what needed to be done politically? Or were ministers and officials scared to make decisions that might arouse her (or Rahul's) wrath later? Or was it because the Gandhi dynasty dominated government channels of authority and decision-making to such an extent that the cabinet and administration could not function without her? Whatever the answer – and maybe it was a mixture of all three – it certainly demonstrated how lost the government was without her.

Rahul played little part in this dynastic dominance. In the previous couple of years, he'd had flashes of success – for example, in February 2010, when he made a dramatic foray into Mumbai and challenged the street power of Maharashtra's chauvinist political party, the Shiv Sena. I wrote on my blog – over-optimistically, as it turned out later – that this 'was a significant step forward in his emergence as a national figure'. By using local trains instead of a planned helicopter to cross the city, he had showed 'more courage than most of India's prestige-oriented politicians would contemplate'.[19] He spent some years laboriously touring the poorest parts of India, meeting people and hearing their problems, and trying to regenerate the Congress party's youth organization – preparing himself, he often said, for his political future. He garnered widespread though not always favourable publicity for visiting and chatting with poor villagers, and staying with them – even taking David Miliband, then Britain's foreign secretary, to a high-profile village sleepover early in 2009.[20] These were the sort of flying visits that might be made by a paternalistic monarch, and were easily mocked by his critics, especially when it emerged that there was none of the follow-through action expected from a practising politician.

His appearances in parliament were rare, and he made only three important speeches and interventions in his ten years as an MP. The first was in July 2007 on energy security and the benefits of nuclear power, soon after he had been appointed a general secretary of the Congress. The second was in August 2011, on anti-corruption measures in a Lok Pal Bill – that was the only time he took part in a debate in the first four years of the 2009 government, when the average count for other MPs was 33 times.[21] (Sonia Gandhi's record was no better). The third came in December 2013, again on the Lok Pal Bill.

Marketing experts were commenting late in 2011 that Rahul needed to develop himself as a brand because not enough was known about him and what he stood for.[22] As general secretary in charge of the Youth Congress, he had reorganized structures and local party elections, and contributed to other organizational matters. But he had shown absolutely no grip or interest in policy. More importantly, he had shown no continuity of purpose, often vanishing without trace from the public scene.[23] He rarely spoke out on major issues or crises, such as the country-wide mass protests about corruption, gang rape and the treatment of women in 2011 and 2012. He made adequate election-style speeches to crowds of thousands but rarely engaged in public debate or gave media interviews. This matched his mother's reclusive approach, but he seemed far more detached than her.

Rahul continually resisted public invitations from Manmohan Singh to join the government as a minister, and also resisted suggestions that he should play a larger role in the party. Eventually, however, he put his political reputation on the line when he energetically led the Congress party's campaign in Uttar Pradesh's 2012 state assembly elections, and developed during 200 meetings as a powerful (though inconsequential) speaker.[24] The Congress, however, was routed in what in effect was a rejection of him and his election campaign.[25] The party won only 27 seats in the 403-seat assembly, up from 22 in 2007, and its share of the votes went from 8.61 per cent to just 11.63 per cent. It even lost heavily in three parliamentary constituencies (Amethi, Rae Bareli and Sultanpur) that were regarded as the family's fiefdoms where Rahul and Sonia Gandhi and another loyalist had been MPs.

The results showed that Gandhi had little impact in many constituencies that he had visited during the campaign (and in places where he had gone in the previous couple of years). The family had projected their dynastic credentials with aplomb – some reports suggested arrogance – but Rahul was not identified personally with the state's future. He was not standing as the potential Uttar Pradesh chief minister (that would have been an extraordinarily difficult job, which he scarcely needed to tackle when the prime minister's post was within his grasp), and he had not developed any brand image. He spent most of his election speeches telling his poor audiences about what they did not have and how awful the incumbent government had been, instead of producing concrete proposals about how he would boost their livelihoods. The result was a serious blow because it underlined his failure to emerge as a capable politician in the years since he became a member of parliament in 2004.

I noticed his lack of presence in an informal atmosphere one afternoon in August 2012 at Delhi's Visual Arts gallery where he and Sonia Gandhi had gone (with impressively minimal security) to see works by Devangana Kumar, daughter of the Lok Sabha Speaker, Meira Kumar. Although she looked tired and unwell, Sonia had a presence, but what struck me most was how unimpressive Rahul looked on an occasion when he was not performing publicly. He dutifully followed his mother around the exhibition but he showed scant curiosity while she asked questions about the socially significant works (photographs of servants of the British Raj reproduced as large prints on velvet). He did not have any of the presence and charisma that one would expect from a 42-year-old leader.

This reticence made me wonder whether he could ever grow into the top role. A friend suggested that maybe we should genuinely sympathize with his plight. He has a family legacy that he is unable to escape – an assassinated grandmother and father, both revered leaders, a mother who had defied conventions to be similarly recognized, and a country that put him on a pedestal he would rather avoid. All his adult life he has been in the shadow of his mother, as he was that afternoon. He has a sense of duty and genuinely wants to bring real democracy to the Congress, but he knows he is not a natural heir to his larger-than-life family. It is a strange mix, and begs the question whether he would change if and when he took the top role. Would he then grow into his destiny? That Saturday afternoon, he looked as if he just wanted to fade away.

Priyanka, his sister, would have been so much more personable in the art gallery, as she always shows when appearing in public. She has an easy, approachable style and is able and willing to talk informally with people she meets (including foreign journalists). That is something that Rahul shies away from. There has been speculation about whether she will – and should – take over the lead role from her brother, but Sonia has decided that her son should be her heir. Priyanka has always said she does not want to enter politics, though she has been playing an increasingly supportive role in Amethi, her mother's constituency, which might lead to her becoming its member of parliament.

Rahul Emerges

Eventually, in January 2013, Rahul took the big step that he had shirked for so long and was made the party's vice president, which confirmed him as his mother's number two and heir apparent to the party leadership. It was an 'inevitable and incredible appointment'.[26] It was inevitable because, despite his reluctance, he had been seen for years as having the dynastic right to rule India. Yet, it was incredible that a person who had shown little ability or interest in fulfilling that destiny should be chosen in a vibrant democracy of over a billion people – and that this should be accepted without question by senior and able Congress ministers and other party leaders. Some of those leaders would have made a better job in the future of being the party president and prime minister, but they and others saw a Gandhi – and Rahul was the one to hand – as the best bet to hold the party together and provide the sort of iconic image for it to win elections and keep them in their posts of power and patronage.

The announcement came at a large party conference and Rahul made an acceptance speech that was strong on emotion and on what was wrong with the corrupt and power hungry in India.[27] It reflected a famous speech made by his father Rajiv Gandhi as prime minister in 1985, attacking Congress power brokers who, he said, had handicapped ordinary party workers. Rajiv failed to change the system and his son offered nothing more, apart from a pledge that he would work for the party and the country. He generated a rousing standing ovation from the audience and tears from some leaders. In the months that followed, he challenged established systems and worked hard at trying to reform the party's constituency and state-level organization, picking new local leaders and candidates who might revive the badly run party. This showed the power he could wield when he chose to do so – for example, in the choice of young ministers and regional political leaders, though it upset many existing power brokers.

Rahul made remarks that seemed to suggest he might renounce the prime minister's job, as Sonia had done in 2004. His plan to reorganize the Congress with grassroots elections would also logically and significantly reduce the chances of the Nehru-Gandhi dynasty continuing into another generation after him. It was beginning to look as if that might be what he ideally wanted with democratically elected grassroots party members rising up through the ranks.[28] When he was asked by journalists and Congress MPs in the Central Hall of Parliament in March 2013 whether he wanted to be prime minister, he was reported to have said that was the wrong question. 'Today, I see how MPs feel without power and it is the same story in all the parties, be it the Congress or the BJP. I want to empower the 720-odd MPs in Parliament. I want to give voice to the middle tier, empower the middle-level leaders. There are some parties in India which are run by one leader, two leaders, five to six leaders and 15 to 20 leaders. My priority is that I want to empower the MPs as also the 5,000-odd legislators in various states.' He was also reported to have said that he regretted that political parties prevented youth from acquiring key positions at a time when the young were seeking a greater say in political affairs. 'At one point, the pressure from the youth will be such that there will be an explosion'.[29]

These remarks chimed with criticism he had frequently voiced about the Congress party's 'high command' culture (even though that was his mother's role), and seemed to suggest that new people would rise up. But it was not clear whether Rahul was envisaging these new leaders being ready to take over the top job in 20 years' or so when he might retire, maybe leaving nothing for the next generation of the Nehru-Gandhi dynasty to do. Moreover, he only talked about giving power to MPs and 'voice to the middle tier, empower the middle-level leaders'. Did it mean that he envisaged a dynastically defended glass ceiling above that level? He was similarly vague about what he intended to do when he spoke for the first time to a business audience in April 2013. His theme was that India's future lay in taking politics down to pradhans (village headmen) to give 'a billion people the power to solve the problems' and facilitate development.[30] At that meeting he showed he had developed an easy style of impromptu public speaking, but he presented no policies and had no answers to specific questions that he was asked about how to solve clashes between the central government and the states, and what to do about inadequate water supplies.

He needed, however, to do much more than simply talk about grassroots power to restore the dynasty's image that was steadily declining. This had been demonstrated the previous October with Kejriwal's allegations about Robert Vadra's business dealings. The family, it seemed, was becoming vulnerable to personal attacks, albeit only against someone who had married into the family rather than a member of the dynasty. It raised questions about whether Sonia's protective chakra was becoming vulnerable.[31] Dipankar Gupta, a sociologist, suggested that the Vadra attack indicated the collapse of a 'taboo' in Indian politics about exposing and naming members of the dynasty, though he followed taboo traditions and only wrote 'R for Robert' to indicate who he was writing about and did not use the words Vadra, Priyanka, Sonia, or the Gandhi dynasty, choosing instead to refer to a 'particular family'.[32] Yogendra Yadav, a political pollster and pundit who became a member of Kejriwal's political party, praised the revelations because they had 'violated a code of silence observed in Delhi's corridors of power'.

Different Priorities

During this time, it gradually emerged that Sonia and Rahul Gandhi had different priorities. Sonia wanted to maintain the old Congress systems of dynasty and patronage that had allowed her to emerge and reign supreme, along with economic policies based on aid schemes designed to help the poor while doing little or nothing to lift them out of their lot. Rahul shared that economic vision for short-term electoral benefits, believing that the poor would then vote for the Congress. But he was mainly focused on reforming the way the party was run and empowering people both in the party and outside to develop their futures. That vision is not

based on conventional economic reforms favoured by the trio of
Manmohan Singh, Chidambaram and Montek Singh Ahluwalia,
but on empowering local villages to run their own affairs and
by developing grassroots voluntary organizations and self-help
groups.

Sonia's determination was illustrated in August 2013 when she
made a rare speech in the Lok Sabha to introduce a Food Security
Bill against the wishes and advice of senior ministers and economic
advisers. Politicians in India usually give bangles, saris, electrical
goods and even laptops away at election time in order to woo voters,
but Gandhi raised the bar with the handouts that increased the
government's food aid bill to $20bn a year.[33] 'There are people who
ask whether we have the means to implement this scheme. I would
like to say that we have to figure out the means. The question is
not whether we can do it or not. We have to do it,' she said in
parliament[34] in a speech that hit the value of the rupee and upset
Chidambaram's efforts to halt the slide in the country's economy. A
few days earlier, she had launched the Bill as part of the Congress
party's platform for imminent assembly elections in the state of Delhi
(which the Congress lost badly). She chose to do this on the birth
anniversary of Rajiv Gandhi, who however might not have approved
because he believed in constructive economic growth policies, not
well-meaning but wasteful handouts. (Sonia Gandhi's ill health was
also evident on the day she introduced the Bill in the Lok Sabha
because she had to leave parliament and be taken to hospital for tests
before the legislation was voted on and passed.)

Rahul Gandhi Wakes Up

Rahul Gandhi's impatience with old-style politics was best
demonstrated a few weeks later when he burst unexpectedly into a
Congress party press conference in Delhi and denounced a government
plan to pass legalisation that would have nullified a Supreme Court
order issued two months earlier[35] and allowed politicians convicted

of crimes to remain members of parliament while their cases were appealed.[36] The plan was to introduce a quick temporary ordinance, pending permanent legislation, so that Lalu Yadav, the regional leader from Bihar, could stay in parliament while he appealed conviction and an imminent sentence on a massive fraud case dating from the 1990s. Gandhi described the ordinance as 'complete nonsense' and declared that it should 'be torn up and thrown out' – which it was, a few days later, when the cabinet reversed its decision to introduce the measure. Sonia Gandhi was clearly not pleased with her son's political guerrilla warfare, and Rahul said she had told him 'that the words that I used were strong'. With hindsight, he added, he felt 'maybe my words were wrong ... but the sentiment I felt was not wrong'.

The most significant remark that Rahul made when he invaded the press conference was that 'if we want to fight corruption in this country, whether it's us the Congress party, or the BJP, we cannot continue making these small compromises because, when we make these small compromises, we compromise everything'. In other words, he considered his mother, her advisers and the cabinet had gone too far with such compromises when they decided to protect Yadav by introducing the ordinance quickly, before his jail sentence was announced a few days later.

For decades, maintenance of political power has provided an excuse and a cover for the gradual criminalization of governance. Gandhi seemed to understand that this had crippled the power of institutions and wanted to change course. It was an implicit criticism of both Manmohan Singh and his mother, who had presided over a highly corrupt government and party and had made 'small compromises' such as keeping corrupt politicians in the cabinet so that their parties would continue to support the coalition government.

Rahul Gandhi was clearly emerging as a potential reformer, if only he could be more consistently convincing and if he followed up his occasional forays into current events with focused moves to clean up the country's politics and governance. His behaviour, however, was still too erratic to be effective and he showed no understanding of the intricacies of policy making. His efforts to galvanize voters failed again with the assembly elections in December 2013, as they had earlier. The Congress was routed in Delhi by the BJP and the new Aam Aadmi Party founded by Kejriwal, the anti-corruption campaigner, as well as losing in three other states.

The AAP's victory and the Congress defeats spurred Gandhi into action and he forced the government to revive the Lok Pal Bill that would set up an anti-corruption ombudsman. The main parties had resisted the legislation for decades and the government had only agreed to produce the Bill two years earlier under intense pressure from Anna Hazare, who was then working with Kejriwal. The BJP amazingly co-operated with the government and the Bill was passed through both houses of parliament and enacted within a few days.[37] Gandhi hoped this would show that the Congress was serious about tackling corruption and he made a powerful speech in parliament – only his third in ten years – calling for six other anti-corruption bills to be implemented covering subjects such as public procurement, foreign bribery, judicial standards and whistleblowers. He also forced the Congress-led Maharashtra state government to re-open a corruption case on an army-linked real estate scandal.

It seemed that the assembly election results had at last made the Gandhis realise that the country wanted a change, not just between the Congress and the BJP, but with the election of new figures like Kejriwal, who did not carry the baggage of established politicians. For the first time in his political career, Rahul Gandhi took command of a policy. He was clearly in charge, replacing his mother and sidestepping Ahmed Patel, her trusted aide, who was said to have been blocking many of his earlier initiatives. But he had woken up too late. Defeat loomed for the Congress in the 2014 elections. Rahul Gandhi's best hope was that he would build up enough personal credibility to be able to reform the party for a later election, maybe working with his sister Priyanka, who was becoming more active politically.

Crisis of Confidence

The dynasty was by now having its worst crisis of confidence for two decades, which raised the question of whether the family has or has not been good for India. The country would certainly have benefited from a wider choice of prime ministers. Nehru initially set India on a sound footing in 1947 but Shastri could, historians suggest, have been a better leader of the country than Indira Gandhi if he had lived – and that might have thwarted the dynasty's survival.

Sonia Gandhi's main contribution has been to the Congress party, not to the country, Offsetting that has been her determination that Rahul should succeed her. She stymied the Congress's development by not encouraging democratic elections for party leaders either nationally or around the country, thus playing into the hands of those who wanted to resist change. For years she held back the promotion of new, young leaders while Rahul dithered about what to do. By contrast, when Rajiv Gandhi was prime minister in the 1980s, young politicians such as P. Chidambaram, Madhavrao Scindia and Rajesh Pilot were given key responsibilities as ministers of state – Chidambaram handled national security when he was 40.

One can argue, of course, that Sonia has benefited the country because her revival of the Congress enabled it to be a viable alternative to the Hindu-nationalist BJP. However, her lack of vision beyond soft-liberal populist policies was a reminder that India's main reforms have happened when the dynasty has not been in power – the early years of the Narasimha Rao 1991–96 government and the BJP's 1998–2004 period.

The conclusion has to be that India would be better off if the dynasty lost its automatic top role. The Gandhis' supporters argue that it is essential they continue as leaders in order to hold the Congress party together because, without them, it would splinter and there would not be any nationally viable party apart from the BJP. Coalition governments would then be weaker without the Congress as a focal point around which other parties could gather.

That, however, is a negative argument for keeping a dynasty which is so out of tune at a time when there are growing demands for significant changes in the way that India is governed.

Notes

1. http://ridingtheelephant.wordpress.com/2013/12/18/anti-america-and-anti-corruption-are-key-issues-as-india-general-election-looms

2. http://ridingtheelephant.wordpress.com/2011/10/03/dynastic-secrecy-protected-by-india%E2%80%99s-tame-media/

3. JE, 'In Asia, the dynasties still rule', *New Statesman*, 8 November 1999, http://www.newstatesman.com/node/136052

4. Conversation with JE

5. Aarthi Ramachandran, *Decoding Rahul Gandhi*, pp 81-83, Tranquebar Press/Westland, Delhi 2012, http://www.westlandbooks.in/book_details.php?cat_id=5&book_id=348

6. 'Sonia more comfortable with Left than with regional allies', *The Hindu* March 27, 2011 www.thehindu.com/news/the-india-cables/article1574328.ece

7. 'Sonia Gandhi undergoes surgery', *Indian Express*, 4 August 2011 http://www.indianexpress.com/news/sonia-gandhi-undergoes-surgery/827112/

8. http://www.firstpost.com/politics/sonia-was-being-treated-for-cancer-for-8-months-reports-54551.html

9. 'Her mother ill, Sonia flies to US with Rahul', 30 July 2010 http://www.expressindia.com/latest-news/her-mother-ill-sonia-flies-to-us-with-rahul/653776/

10. 'Sonia Gandhi a national leader and her health not just a private matter', *Economic Times*, http://articles.economictimes.indiatimes.com/2011-08-06/news/29858915_1_rahul-gandhi-active-politics-sonia-gandhi Aug 6 2011

11. 'Right to Information – Mrs Sonia Gandhi's health is a matter of public concern', *Business Standard*, 7 August 2011

12. http://ibnlive.in.com/videos/175244/the-last-word-sonia-gandhis-illness.html

13. 'How ill is Mrs Gandhi?', *India Today*, 16 October 2012, http://india today.intoday.in/story/sonia-gandhi-cancer-surgery-in-us-upa-2g-

scam-manmohan-and-rahul-gandhi-lurch-into-crisis/1/153246.html
and http://ridingtheelephant.wordpress.com/2011/10/03/dynastic-
secrecy- protected-by-india%E2%80%99s-tame-media/

14. 'The omertà on Sonia Gandhi's illness', *The Hindu*, 22 September
    2012, http://www.thehindu.com/opinion/lead/article2473752.ece

15. 'Government denies information on Rahul's foreign trips, *The Times
    of India*, 7 October 2012, http://articles.timesofindia.indiatimes.com/
    2012-10-07/india/34305718_1_rti-applications-rahul-gandhi-foreign-
    trips

16. http://ridingtheelephant.wordpress.com/2013/01/20/rahul-gandhis-
    inevitable-and-incredible-appointment-as-congress-no-2/

17. 'The fifth monarch – Will Rahul sit on his great-grandfather's (and
    grandmother's and father's) throne?', http://www.economist.com/
    node/4494143

18. Rahul Gandhi speaks with *Tehelka* magazine, 24 September 2005
    – later claimed not 'an interview', http://www.tehelka.com/story_
    main14.asp?filename=Ne092405_I_could_CS.asp

19. Ritam Sengupta, '323 ads, nearly 160 pages to mark 5 anniversaries',
    Sans Serif, 14 November 2011, http://wearethebest.wordpress.com/
    2011/11/14/323-ads-nearly-160-pages-to-mark-5-anniversaries/

20. http://ridingtheelephant.wordpress.com/2010/02/08/rahul-gandhi-
    shows-the-nehru-gandhi-dynasty-is-firmly-embedded%E2%80%A6
    %E2%80%A6%E2%80%A6/

21. http://ridingtheelephant.wordpress.com/2009/01/27/india-raised-
    ulster-when-rebuking-miliband-on-kashmir/

22. Parliamentary Performance, research by PRS –http://www.prsindia.
    org/mptrack/rahulgandhi and http://www.prsindia.org/mptrack/
    SoniaGandhi

23. 'As a brand, Rahul Gandhi hasn't taken off', *The Times of India*, 20
    November 2011, http://articles.timesofindia.indiatimes.com/2011-
    11-20/special-report/30421925_1_rahul-gandhi-brand-prahlad-
    kakkar

24. http://ridingtheelephant.wordpress.com/2013/01/20/rahul-gandhis-
    inevitable-and-incredible-appointment-as-congress-no-2/

25. 'Rahul Gandhi emerges as Manmohan Singh declines', http://
    ridingtheelephant.wordpress.com/2012/02/06/government-in-
    blundering-retreat-on-corruption-crisis/

26. http://ridingtheelephant.wordpress.com/2012/03/06/crony-capitalists-line-up-changes-in-up-as-rahul-gandhi-stumbles/

27. http://ridingtheelephant.wordpress.com/2013/01/20/rahul-gandhis-inevitable-and-incredible-appointment-as-congress-no-2/

28. Transcript of Rahul Gandhi's speech at AICC Session, Jaipur, http://www.sify.com/news/full-text-of-rahul-s-first-speech-as-congress-vp-news-national-nbvk60ffaei.html and video http://www.ndtv.com/video/player/news/congress-will-support-every-indian-says-rahul-gandhi/262506

29. http://ridingtheelephant.wordpress.com/2013/03/13/would-rahul-gandhi-like-to-close-his-family-dynasty/

30. 'Rahul Gandhi says no to marriage and prime ministership', *Indian Express*, 6 March 2013, http://www.indianexpress.com/news/rahul-wrong-to-ask-me-if-i-want-to-be-pm/1083780/0

31. http://ridingtheelephant.wordpress.com/2013/04/04/rahul-gandhi-dreams-with-a-beehive-of-buzzing-thoughts/

32. http://ridingtheelephant.wordpress.com/2012/10/23/corruption-tamashas-and-gossip-flood-india-but-change-will-be-very-slow/

33. Dipankar Gupta, 'Our political parties are throttling democracy by declaring certain issues and debates out of bounds', *The Times of India*, 13 October 2012, http://articles.timesofindia.indiatimes.com/2012-10-13/edit-page/34414269_1_taboos-caste-system-scandals-pile

34. http://ridingtheelephant.wordpress.com/2013/08/28/sonia-gandhis-2bn-bid-for-political-security/

35. 'Sonia's ambitious food bill wins LS vote; UPA gets its "game-changer"', *Hindustan Times*, 26 August 2013, http://www.hindustantimes.com/india-news/newdelhi/sonia-s-ambitious-food-bill-wins-ls-vote-upa-gets-its-game-changer/article1-1113348.aspx

36. 'Cabinet overrules Supreme Court, clears ordinance to protect convicted MPs', PTI, 25 September 2013, http://www.indianexpress.com/news/cabinet-overrules-supreme-court-clears-ordinance-to-protect-convicted-mps/1173585/

37. http://ridingtheelephant.wordpress.com/2013/10/03/rahul-gandhi-stops-a-small-compromise-on-lalu-yadav-but-does-he-have-the-stamina-to-be-a-leader/

V

GOVERNANCE

16

Illicit India

Corruption is ruining India. It pervades Indian society and government at all levels, undermining the authority of those responsible for running the country, crippling institutions, and frequently leading to bad decisions. The individual whims and wishes of politicians and bureaucrats, often corrupt and maybe also vindictive or vengeful, override laws and regulations. Distrust in public life has developed to such an extent that officials are often assumed to be guilty until proved innocent, which now impedes decision-making and ultimately, slows economic growth. The international image of India is suffering because what used to be regarded as relatively harmless 'baksheesh' is now seen as criminal fraud, deception and extortion, fed by personal greed and a lack of respect for the law.

Bribes, fraud and deception have become accepted as a way of public life, with the rewards far exceeding the minimal risk of detection and even rarer risk of punishment. People at all levels of society feel they have to fall in with much of it, whether or not they are actually motivated to do so. But it leads to bad decisions, increased costs, poor-quality work, project delays, and plundering of national assets. It is practised at all levels of society, particularly among politicians who, once their caste or social group moves into the mainstream of the country's political and economic life, begin to emulate those who arrived earlier. For them, corruption has become a get-rich-quick option that suddenly generates enormous and irresistible wealth while they are in power and the going is good.

This is demonstrated by the massive unaccountable wealth declared at election time by established politicians, though there must be much that remains hidden.

'Corruption rules over the country with its stranglehold in every aspect of the state and consequently in all aspects of the life of citizens,' says Bibek Debroy, an economist, in the best recent book on the subject. With co-author Laveesh Bhandari, he points out that corruption and bribery have become 'a universally recognised medium of interaction and transaction between the citizens and the government'.[1] It happened across all areas and levels of politics and bureaucracy, the judiciary, and publicly owned enterprises. 'The parasite has eaten into the edifice of the state. Lower level bureaucracy and police thrive on bribes and baksheesh, higher level on grease money and scams.' Such criticism, of course, also extends to financial services, where India has had major stock market and other scandals, the corporate world and sport.

Debroy and Bhandari stress the role of administrative problems that are caused by 'improper allocation of discretion not backed up by adequate monitoring, poor enforcement of laws, and lack of punishments'. This 'creates an environment where corrupt behaviour has become more a norm rather than an exception'. Discretion, they say, is 'the power to judge what is to receive priority', which can involve the power to veto or delay, or to approve and sanction, or maybe both.[2]

'On big ticket corruption, the problem is that whatever you do, you will never be able to eliminate discretion and discretion opens up avenues for abuse,' says Debroy.[3] He differentiates 'big ticket' corruption with large-scale bribes and projects from 'small ticket', which is due to shortages in many services that include health, education and electricity and water supplies and even banking services and access to aid schemes, especially for the poor.

Corruption stories fill the headlines of newspapers almost every day, tumbling out one after another, with each story edging earlier ones out of the public gaze. In the few weeks that I wrote the first draft of this chapter, the news was dominated by a surge of scandals that illustrated the range and frequency of scams. The minister for railways resigned over bribe allegations. There were long-running stories on coal mining and telecommunication scams that stretched to the prime minister's desk. There were more developments in a dramatic cricket match-fixing scandal in the glitzy IPL with political, business and other links that included a leading family-controlled company based in Tamil Nadu. A $500m penalty was levied by US authorities on a top pharmaceutical business for falsifying drug research results and other malpractices. The Bharatiya Janata Party's state government in Karnataka was voted out of power after five corruption-riddled years, and a former Uttar Pradesh state government was accused of large-scale draining of funds allocated for construction of a chief minister's egotistical monuments. The son of a former chief minister in Andhra Pradesh was refused bail after a year in jail during investigations of massive graft and extortion led by him and his late father.

The coal and telecom scandals involved a nexus of politicians and companies that fixed and fiddled contracts and licences, and were especially shocking because the government tolerated them, even when they were being widely talked about. The cricket and pharmaceutical scandals were significant because they pulled down icons of what were unwisely dubbed the 'India Shining' years of the 2000s when the country was riding high on strong economic growth. Corruption in the states of Karnataka and Andhra Pradesh had dragged down the international reputation of their capital cities, Bengaluru and Hyderabad, which led India's information technology boom in the 2000s. All the unfolding sagas illustrated the malpractices that lay behind much of that growth in the mining, communications and manufacturing industries, showing how weak the foundations of modern India were.

Corruption happens in all types of societies; India is not alone in this. Its impact varies according to market forces and political systems. In some countries – China, for example – it has eaten into the structure of government, but it does boost economic development because bribes paid to a minister or a city mayor usually generate official approvals and economic activity such as construction of infrastructure projects. In India, it slows growth because of the pushes and pulls of a hyperactive democracy, and the greed of politicians and other vested interests. Extensive and complex government rules and regulations within an overdeveloped state apparatus provide politicians and officials with endless opportunities for exercising discretionary powers, and businessmen with consequential opportunities to gain illicit advantages over competitors. This is corruption at its most destructive. In India, it is damaging the heart of the society, pushing dishonesty down to the lowest levels so that even members of tribal communities and other poor suffer when they take their first steps into India's mainstream economy.

Permissive Religion

One of India's many curious contradictions is the way widely publicized acquisition of obviously illicit wealth is not only practised but is tolerated in an open society when two-thirds of the population struggle to make a living. 'The only surprising fact about most corruption stories is that anyone in authority gets surprised. Everyone in charge knew that the Commonwealth Games Organising Committee was buying toilet paper at art paper prices, and turf at the rate of platinum. This was not considered unusual, let alone criminal, because the price of cream is built into public expenditure,' says M.J. Akbar, a newspaper editor and author,[4] in a colourful reference to problems that dogged preparations for the Commonwealth Games in Delhi in 2010.

'The biggest culprit is society itself,' says Nitte Santosh Hegde,[5] a leading anti-corruption campaigner who was the Lokayukta (state corruption ombudsman) for the state of Karnataka from 2006 to 2011, having earlier been India's solicitor general and a Supreme

Court judge. 'Wealth is regarded as a sign of success – you are felicitated. Society has lost the sense of differentiating between legitimacy and illegitimacy. When I was young, people didn't respect the corrupt – you never invited people perceived to be corrupt to a function,' adds Hegde, who was born in 1940. 'Now hordes of people welcome them when they are let out of jail.'

That this should happen and be tolerated leads to the suggestion that India's religious and cultural base encourages, or at least tolerates, such crimes and bending of rules. In the Bhagavadgita, Lord Krishna advocates doing one's duty detachedly without caring about personal consequences, but he breaks the rules of warfare – one could say cheats – to win a battle in the larger epic of the Mahabharata. 'In Hinduism, there is no binding or universal code of conduct that gives unequivocal primacy to the moral dimension,' says Pavan Varma, a diplomat-turned-politician and a prolific author. Ethics do 'not have an absolute or unalterable definition,' he suggests in his book, *Chanakya's New Manifesto*.[6]

'Our understanding of right and wrong appears to be related far more to achieving whatever result is desired than to absolute notions of morality. To pay something to an official to lubricate the movement of a file is right if it smoothens the way to the desired goal. The payment of bribe is routinely looked upon as a matter of judicious investment, not morality. No invocation to Lakshmi, the goddess of wealth, emphasises the importance of making money only by conventional legitimate ways. The goddess represents wealth and prosperity; she is worshipped for these, not for how that prosperity is arrived at … In fact, for all the condemnation that corruption publicly provokes, Indians are ambivalent about the practice. They consider it bad when they have to bribe when they don't want to; they consider it good if a bribe gets them what they want. In this sense, corruption is like litmus paper; it takes on the colour of the specific experience.'

This is echoed by Namita Gokhale,[7] who says that the Hindu concept of an 'individual view of destiny' leads to a disregard of the greater common good. 'A society segmented by caste and community is often narrowly focused on the advancement of the immediate family and kin. Although there may be enormous public outrage about corruption, moral ambiguity sets in and justifications come into play when it becomes convenient to do so. Presented with a choice of transforming their family's prospects, by bending the rules or taking a bribe, large or small as the situation may merit, they will rationalize it into an ethical or pragmatic framework.' Although Gokhale is talking here about Hindu culture, it applies across India and in other developing countries where improving the lot of oneself and family is a primary aim, especially at a time of economic expansion and rapidly rising expectations.

Fifteen years ago, I wrote:[8] 'Politicians have little alternative but to take bribes because there is no other way that they can finance their political party activities, while officials' salaries are so low that they are easily tempted. Even the most honest officials say they will take bribes, or at least not object to others doing so, providing decision-making is not upset.' At the most petty level, officials have always charged the public for doing ordinary work like issuing government forms, keeping telephones working or even delivering post. In rural areas, local officials persuade members of remote tribal and other communities to accept cash in place of subsidized goods, such as seeds or fertiliser, but then pay them only a fraction of what the goods are worth. Road builders bribe officials to award them contracts and to ignore inferior materials and poor workmanship, making extra profits for the builder and guaranteeing him more work (and the official more bribes) when the road breaks up.

'At a higher level, in the pre-1991 days of India's investment controls, companies bribed officials to obtain business licences and block competitors. Go even higher, and government ministers and officials took and still take multi-million-dollar bribes on large projects and contracts, frequently leading to shoddy work – often paid through consultants or partners so that the companies (especially American, because of US laws) can deny they paid anything. Such bribery and extortion is not confined to the public sector: executives in private sector corporations take bribes for giving business to suppliers and contractors.'

Since I wrote that, the scale and extent of corruption has escalated dramatically. Economists often argue that it should decline a few years after a country liberalizes its economy and removes restrictive regulations that had previously created openings for graft. That has not happened in India, as it theoretically should have done from the mid-1990s, partly because the government still wields extensive basic powers that give politicians and bureaucrats in the central and state governments the freedom to interpret laws and regulations as they wish and to generate massive riches for themselves and their cronies.

Large-scale illicit wealth now comes largely from manipulating the allocation and regulation of licences for natural resources such as the development of land, mining rights, oil exploration, mobile telecommunications, airlines and aircraft landing and maintenance slots at airports, and permissions to import new aircraft. Illegal mining is widespread across the country, ranging from sand in river beds to marble, coal and other minerals, often carried out in defiance of Supreme Court orders and closely protected by well-rewarded state-level politicians. There are associated environmental and other approvals that govern when and where such resources can be used, plus approvals for construction and completion of buildings and other items. Then there are large-scale contracts for building and operating highways, ports, and airports that are fixed. As Raghuram Rajan said in 2010, 'the predominant sources of mega wealth in India today [are] the guys who have access to natural resources or to land or to particular infrastructure permits or licences. In other words, proximity to the government seems to be a big source of wealth.'

Most of India's fastest-growing companies, aside from those in information technology, operate in these sorts of areas – the Ambani brothers' two Reliance businesses (oil and gas exploration, telecommunications and infrastructure), Naresh Goyal's Jet Airways, the Adani group of Gujarat (coal imports and trading, ports and energy), K.P. Singh's DLF (Delhi land and real estate), and the GMR, GVK and Lanco infrastructure companies from Hyderabad and Bengaluru. The families and their executives in charge of such companies are closely connected to central and state-level politicians and bureaucrats. Politicians also invest in companies that they are helping. Often (without pointing specifically at any of these names), a company's unusually rapid expansion raises suspicions that financial investment is coming from politicians' bribe money, maybe through proxy names. The funds are often kept abroad and are funnelled back through private equity and other investment companies located in the African island nation of Mauritius, India's officially recognized tax haven, or elsewhere.

Talking about links between companies and bureaucrats, a source told me that 'they buy people's souls, offering senior officers, with five years' career to go, double their salary'. He was referring to defence industry agents and armed service officers and said that the agents would have 'twenty-five generals still in service on call at any time'. This happens far more widely than armament deals and is another example of how tolerant India is of potentially corrupt relationships. The boardrooms and top echelons of many fast-growing companies are littered with retired bureaucrats and officers, often people who spent much of their career in industries such as power and telecommunications where the companies operate. 'Some of the large business groups also fund politicians in the Opposition as a hedge to ensure that any decision that may be given in their favour is not opposed by them. They also treat such funding as a long-term investment,' says B.V. Kumar, a former head of the government's economic intelligence bureau. Most business houses, he says, 'maintain' MPs to influence government policies or decision-making.[9]

Corrupt Democracy

The roots of corruption are to be found in elections, starting with would-be candidates paying parties to be allocated a constituency.

Candidates then bribe voters with liquor, cash and other inducements ranging from saris to laptop computers (though people frequently accept the gifts from opposing parties and then make their own decisions). Payouts continue during the formation of governments when massive amounts of money are paid in 'horse trading'. This happens in local and state assembly elections and, in various forms, in both houses of parliament. A Congress MP has claimed that he was once told that a candidate for the Rajya Sabha had budgeted Rs 100 crore to secure a seat, but only had to spend Rs 80 crore.[10] Later the MP withdrew the allegation, but I have been given (confidentially by a reliable source) the name of a businessman who paid Rs 35 crore to a national political party and Rs 40 crore to a regional party to ensure election in the Rajya Sabha's preferential vote system.

Leaders of potential coalitions use an array of political and other contacts to cajole small parties and individual members to join them with a mixture of money, ministerial posts and other favours. Lakhs of rupees change hands, as they do sometimes when a government faces a confidence or other threatening vote in parliament. In what is famously known as the JMM case, a small party in the state of Jharkhand was bribed in 1993 with Rs 2.8 crore to vote in parliament against a motion of no-confidence in Narasimha Rao's Congress government.

Politics have become criminalized and elections have become the 'biggest source of corruption in the country', says former chief election commissioner S.Y. Quraishi, explaining that candidates spend vast amounts of money they cannot afford and need to recover after they are elected. 'Political power is strong and competition bitter and involvement of criminals is a challenge,' he says.[11] As many as 162 of the 543 members of the 2009–14 Lok Sabha had criminal charges pending against them, compared with 124 in the previous parliament.[12] Criminals began by influencing politicians and then decided to get into politics themselves, he adds. According to data collected by two Delhi-based political monitoring organizations, about 30 per cent of members of parliament and of state assemblies

had declared criminal cases pending against them in their own
election affidavits.[13] Quraishi's solution is to ban candidates facing
charges that had been lodged in a court for six months (which would
give potential candidates time to counter false charges trumped up
by opponents). Moves along these lines have begun in the courts.

Politicians amass huge funds while they are in power, both in state
and central governments, which they use for organizing elections,
buying votes, horse trading and other party activities, as well as
building up enormous and ostentatious personal wealth. More than
a third of the 4,013 candidates who contested in six state elections
during the twelve months to May 2013 declared assets of over one
crore rupees, far in excess of what they could have earned legitimately
and well beyond the dreams of most people in India.

Real estate and construction companies are especially useful
for laundering and storing funds because their accounts are easily
fudged, which encourages close relationships between politicians
and the companies. At the time of elections, builders send funds
to help finance campaigns. An academic study that looked at the
cement industry found that demand decreased when builders had to
slow down their projects after sending money to the politicians.[14] In
another example, a chief minister in north India was said to ensure
there was continuing income by telling builders to pay their dues to
her over a period of 15–20 years. 'The relationship between land,
builders and politicians is symbiotic because the builder can't get
land without the politician's help, and then gets locked into the
financial exchanges,' says a member of parliament.[15]

Kumari Mayawati, who has been chief minister of Uttar Pradesh
four times, is a notable example. The daughter of a post-office worker,
she is a leader of the Dalits, the desperately poor 'untouchables' at
the bottom of the Indian caste system. She built up such extensive
wealth – and declared at least some of it – that she ranked with famous
film stars and cricketers as one of India's top 20 taxpayers in 2007–08
when she paid Rs 26.26 crore. Affidavits she filed at election time
showed that her assets had inexplicably doubled during her last term

as chief minister (2007–12) to Rs 111.64 crore. The income was euphemistically declared as admirers' gifts and, apart from sporadic court cases on specific projects, no one has seriously pursued the reasons or sources of such unaccounted wealth. Mayawati's personal extravagances included sending her private jet empty to Mumbai to get her preferred brand of sandals at a cost to the state exchequer of Rs10 lakh, according to US diplomatic cables written in 2008 and published by WikiLeaks.[16] The cables said she was paranoid about her security and 'fears assassination', employing 'food tasters' to guard against poisoning and maintains a 'vice-like grip on all levels of power'.

Known locally as Behen-ji (sister), she ostentatiously ordered the state government to build massive pink sandstone and bronze monuments, stupas and domes in large parks in Lucknow, the capital of Uttar Pradesh, and in Noida on the edge of Delhi, at a reported cost of Rs 4,500 crore[17] during her last stint as chief minister. They were designed to glorify her and Kanshi Ram, her mentor, who founded her political party, the Bahujan Samaj Party (BSP), as well as Bhim Rao Ambedkar, a revered Dalit leader at the time of India's independence. She wanted them to be seen as symbols of empowerment for the Dalits, comparable with the palaces and forts of India's powerful Mughal rulers.

She did little during four terms as chief minister to develop the state, especially in rural areas, although, with widespread and plausible allegations of massive corruption, she licensed impressive highway and other projects, including a race track for a successful grand prix.[18] She lost the last state assembly election in 2012, but she still garners adulation from the millions of poor Dalits who know they will never have even a tiny fraction of the fortunes she has amassed. Since then, the UP Lokayukta has alleged that Rs 1,410 crore was siphoned off by 199 named politicians and government officials during the purchase and erection of the sandstone monuments[19] and the state government's mining department has said that the sandstone was mined illegally.[20]

The Power to Say 'No'

Often regulations are designed to increase the discretionary system's ability to disrupt progress lucratively, rather than achieving the purpose for which the regulations are intended. There is, for example, regular harassment of companies starting new businesses with state governments' labour and other departments demanding payoffs during construction and fire departments withholding protection approvals – often with officials inventing problems to help the extortion.

A source in the private sector says this about serving with bureaucrats on a government committee:[21] 'Never once did I feel that they were proposing things for the good of the nation or for the basic purpose we were there. They were fighting for their own turf and for what they could gain personally from it. Ironically, they might well have moved on to other jobs or retired by the time the policies were implemented, so they might not gain themselves, which presumably means they are instinctively guarding a corrupt system rather than trying to introduce new positive policies.'

Amitabha Pande, a retired senior civil servant who writes a blog, 'Notes from a Subversive Bureaucrat', explained the system in one of his articles: 'First, decentralise and devolve the power to say "no" right down the line, and centralise the power to say "yes" in a way that obtaining a "yes" decision will mean having to go through many hands, all of whom can say "no" at each stage before you get anywhere near the final decision-maker'.[22] The headline on the article was 'The Power to Say Yes', but it should surely have been called 'The Power to Say No'. I asked him to explain how it works – the blog was written in relation to the defence ministry, where Pande once worked, but he says it 'applies to most situations where government has to approve a proposal, make a purchase, grant a licence, give an environmental clearance, whatever'. His explanation below is based on a hypothetical internal matter within the bureaucracy, but it would equally apply to a company or individual trying to obtain approval for something. The power of junior officials to block the wishes of his superiors should never be under-estimated, as his example shows:

'Let us say, I want approval to take up a post retirement job with a private firm. Under the Rules, such permission can be given only if I can satisfactorily show that in my official career I did not have any dealings with the company. Most approvals are given on a "case by case basis". My application or proposal made out to the Secretary Personnel will go from him to the Section concerned and to the lowest functionary – the "dealing hand" – generally called the "assistant". The assistant has no power to give this permission, but he is the first level in the hierarchy who "examines" the case and 'puts up' on file to the next higher level of the section officer. In his examination of my career profile, he may discover that the firm I intend to take up a job with has at some stage handled the food business, with which I too was concerned at one stage of my life and therefore there could have been a connection. He can, therefore, reject my application or object that I have not made a full disclosure. No one can question his authority to say "no" because it is his job to do due diligence on my application, and he is only doing his job in raising a very valid objection.

'I will now need to gratify him to have the file sent to the next level. That person can find yet another flaw in my application and this process can go on and on until I have satisfied each level and have had my file reach the secretary personnel or the minister or the PM as the case may be. Even if I reach that level, I may well be told that as there have been so many objections raised on my file, it will be inappropriate to overrule the objections raised through the passage of the file. So either I pay a sum large enough (having already paid all the levels of hierarchy to bring it this far) for that person to overrule his subordinates, or he gets them to change the file and put up a fresh case which is now clean and free of all objections so that subsequent scrutiny does not show any deliberate mishandling of the case. This price may be too much for me, so I have the option of either spending through my nose to get the approval or I give up.'

A friend told me about how his housekeeper had applied for a pension from a bank where her late husband had worked and was told to obtain a certificate from a tehshildar (local tax official) with details of her dependent children. 'Someone at the bank introduced her to a tout who first wanted Rs 3,500, then Rs 7,000, which she eventually paid, declining my offer of help because she did not want justice, only the piece of paper,' says Surendra Rao, a former head of an economic think tank.[23] After many visits, the certificate was procured. She had clearly known that it was not worth trying to fight the system, and the bank official saw an opening to create work for a tout, and possibly also receive a reward. 'Such procedures are one cause for low-level corruption,' says Rao. 'It seems that the bureaucracy in government and the public sector has created procedures that require intermediaries to get the bureaucrat to exercise his discretion on whether to sign the form or not. Such discretionary powers exist at all levels and they invariably are sources of additional income for the bureaucrat. Even to do the job he is employed for, the bureaucrat expects additional payment. When he is violating a rule to favour an applicant, the fee is higher.'

Wealth Equals Success

Hegde's view that 'the biggest culprit is society itself' has been well illustrated by Sonia Gandhi and Manmohan Singh who condoned corruption in many areas of their government – not least by having Lalu Prasad Yadav, the leader of the Rashtriya Janata Dal (RJD), a regional political party in Bihar, in the cabinet as the railway minister from 2004 to 2009. Yadav, a short stocky man with a proud gait and cropped white hair brushed forward, had been jailed on remand (and released on bail) five times for alleged involvement in a mid-1990s corruption scandal when he was Bihar's chief minister.[24] Aid money for fodder and other animal husbandry totalling Rs 900 to 1,500 crore (estimates vary) were siphoned off from government funds.

The CBI filed a charge sheet in 1997 and formal charges were framed against Lalu and 44 others in 2000.[25] In a move that illustrated how corruption charges have little impact on political careers, Yadav installed his wife as chief minister when he was forced to give up the post because of the charges and between them they ruled for a total of 15 years. He then became an MP and was the railway minister in the 2004–09 Congress-led government when he became popular with Sonia Gandhi. He was eventually convicted in October 2013 along with 44 others and sentenced to five years in jail, which threatened to upset his plans to rebuild his run-down party for Bihar's state elections in 2015 and secure prominent roles for his two sons.[26] He was later released on bail but had to leave the Lok Sabha because of a new Supreme Court ruling that convicted MPs could not retain their seats, even if they appealed.[27] (A Congress government plan to legislate against the court ruling was abandoned after the dramatic intervention by Rahul Gandhi.)[28]

Yadav's case illustrates how, till very recently, people have rarely been punished, except occasionally with shortish jail sentences during investigations. Many cases are eventually closed or drag on indefinitely without convictions, and that is what Lalu had been anticipating, hoping that a change in his political fortunes would continue to keep him out of jail. Even though many of those involved have been named publicly, investigating agencies (often conveniently) say they find it impossible to gather sufficient and precise evidence. That makes it easier for the guilty to buy their way out of trouble, and no one is ever forced to pay back the illegal funds in modern India where greed is a bigger driver of attitudes than morals.

The Lalu conviction and jail sentence came at a time when attitudes were hardening, and the Congress-led government knew that it had to take action to try to reduce the impact of corruption on voting in the coming 2014 general election. RTI legislation was leading to the exposure of fraud and extortion, but not enough was being done to prosecute and convict offenders. Whistleblowers who exposed corrupt deals were themselves being punished (in the past they been killed)[29] instead of people they were naming.

Ashok Khemka, a senior bureaucrat in the state of Haryana, was transferred from his job three days after he cancelled a land deal involving Robert Vadra, Sonia Gandhi's son-in-law.[30] He was then officially charged with exceeding his powers on the Vadra case, and of failing in his duties when he briefly ran the state's seeds corporation and reported widespread corruption. A year after the Vadra action, court proceedings alleging administrative misconduct were started by the Haryana government with the approval of Bhupinder Singh Hooda, the chief minister who has close ties with Sonia Gandhi.[31]

It is ironical that Gandhi should allow such action against an apparently honest official at a time when Congress leaders were responding to popular demand for a tough line against the corrupt. In what must have been the quickest punishment in the history of corruption, Pawan Bansal, the minister for railways, had been forced by the government to resign a few months earlier, in May 2013, just a week after allegations emerged linking his family to bribes. It was alleged that Bansal's nephew was to be paid Rs 10 crore (about $2m) for arranging that a senior railway engineer was made the 'member electrical' of the Railways Board, which runs the railways within the ministry. The bribe was to be paid through a contractor, having been raised from a group of businessmen dealing with railways signalling and other equipment. During that week, CBI inquiries and a stream of media reports revealed links involving Bansal, his family, and businessmen in a network of deals, plus the rapid growth of family companies. When he resigned, Bansal asserted he had 'nothing to do with all this'.[32] Arguments about his involvement continued as the legal process slowly evolved.[33]

The scandal itself was scarcely a surprise – paying for public sector jobs happens in many developing countries, and maybe in more developed ones as well. Such appointments are often financed with money from companies that are promised contracts, as was allegedly planned in this case. Nearly 20 years ago, I was told about a public sector corporation chairman's job that was available in return for a payment of two crore rupees.[34] A prominent private sector company was offering to make the payment, and the candidate knew it would expect to be given every contract or other services that it demanded while he was the chairman. The fact that the company itself was delivering the payment would, of course, increase its hold over him. Many public servants have to pay such bribes to get their jobs. They range sometimes all the way from top ministry bureaucrats to the public sector corporations' board directors and on to income-tax officials and traffic police. The top people need to cover their costs by making money on policy decisions and contracts they handle, as well as by helping their sponsors. Tax officials take bribes to clear files, and police charge drivers a few hundred rupees for speeding or jumping traffic lights instead of formally booking them. The more lucrative the job, the higher the price.

Corruption has also spread across the judiciary and the defence forces, notably the army, which shows how graft has become embedded even in areas that are regarded as the bedrock of a society. As far back as 2007, Transparency International, the corruption monitoring organization, noted that while the upper judiciary could usually (but not always) be regarded as relatively clean, there were many points at which court clerks, prosecutors and police investigators could misuse their powers with a high level of discretion, especially in the processing of paperwork.[35] 'This erosion of confidence has deleterious consequences that neutralise the deterrent impact of law,' said the report. People 'sought shortcuts' unlawfully through bribery, favours, hospitality or gifts. A prime example was unauthorized building in Indian cities where construction and safety laws were flouted in connivance with persons in authority. J.S. Anand, then the chief justice, said in 2005: 'Delay erodes the rule of law and promotes resort to extra-judicial remedies with criminalisation of society ... Speedy justice alone is the remedy for the malaise.'[36]

Many of the bribe-generating ruses used in government and the public sector are also prevalent in the Indian private sector where there is extensive corruption within and between companies that goes far beyond giving and accepting minor favours. It is especially so in procurement departments where managers take bribes for placing contracts and even for approving invoices when work is done. A partner in an international auditing firm says that staff in recruitment departments demand regular payments of 10 per cent or more of salaries from newly recruited employees, while clerks in accounts departments require 'facilitation' payments for writing cheques to suppliers and contractors.[37] A foreign finance director working in India told me how the company's taxation staff created annoying complications in their work that later vanished – he assumed after bribes had been extorted and paid to tax officials by clients, presumably with a percentage being taken or retained by his staff. There are also cases of accountants allowing clients improper favours and ignoring non-compliances and deviations in expectation of future rewards.

The Congress Role

Corruption was especially prevalent before India's independence in the police and in revenue and public works departments (as it is today). Most British colonial officials saw what they called 'customary' arrangements as an intrinsic part of Indian society, and they relied on them to underpin their authority. 'Powerful landowners might control the local police constable, or compel free labour among the landless poor. The Raj needed them to help maintain law and order, and pay revenue,' says William Gould, a British academic.[38] 'A local revenue official might take a commission (or dasturi – customary payment) to allow cultivators access to land records, or a railway official might accept a "gift" (daalii) to arrange faster carriage for consignments of goods'. Gould notes that the first officially coordinated predecessors of anti-corruption drives, which have become an important part of the Indian political scene in the past few years, were run by provincial Congress governments in the late 1930s to contrast their democratic principles against the corrupted colonials.

Given that history, it is ironic that the Congress party, especially over the past 30 years, has encouraged corruption and protected its perpetrators. There were scandals in independent India's first government when the prime minister, Jawaharlal Nehru, seems to have been reluctant to institute inquiries and take action. Among the most famous cases was a foreign contract for army jeeps and the allocation of a quota for cycle imports.

Indira Gandhi, when she was prime minister, encouraged the collection of bribes both within India and on international deals, partly in order to enable her party to have to rely less on funds raised by powerful regional party bosses, known as the Syndicate, which she was trying to downsize. The system of licences she introduced for industrial production, restrictive trade practices and foreign exchange regulations opened the way for extensive graft that increased during her controversial 1975–77 State of Emergency. Institutionalizing corruption, she put L.N. Mishra, minister of state for commerce, in charge and he 'attached a price tag to every licence, permit or clearance that he issued', writes S.S. Gill, a senior bureaucrat in the late 1970s and early 1980s.[39] Mishra 'disbursed money like a king', with sealed envelopes dispatched 'to a variety of beneficiaries who included not only politicians but also journalists and all sorts of touts'. Unlike today's politicians, however, Indira Gandhi was not generally perceived to be making her family enormously rich, though there have always been rumours about the avariciousness of other members of her household.

There were scandals involving Sanjay Gandhi,[40] but the tag of corruption came more specifically closer to the family after Rajiv Gandhi succeeded his mother as prime minister in 1984. Despite a basically clean personal image, there was (and still is) a widespread suspicion that his family and (or) his friends benefited from a Bofors howitzer gun contract. Ever since, there has been frequent (unsubstantiated) gossip in Delhi about the family, now headed by Sonia Gandhi. These rumours have been sharpened by controversial business dealings, especially Robert Vadra's. Relatives frequently use their proximity to a politician to further their own separate business and other interests, cashing in on perceptions of their apparent proximity to power by taking favours and peddling their apparent (but not always real) ability to influence decisions, with or without the politician's knowledge. For example, it is not clear how much Priyanka and the other Gandhis knew or were linked to Vadra's deals. Their scarcely credible response was that, since he had been a businessman before his marriage, he was legitimately pursuing his career.

Such cases rarely stay in the headlines for long because leaders of the main political parties, usually follow a code that they do not attack each others' top leaders and their families over personal affairs, including corruption.[41] This has generally been followed by both the leading parties, though the BJP did attack the Gandhis over the Vadra allegations. 'There are ethics in politics. Never attack family. The Congress never attacked Atal Bihari Vajpayee's son-in-law Ranjan Bhattacharya ... Have we ever said a word against them? They have a private life of their own,' said Digvijaya Singh, a seasoned politician and general secretary of the Congress, after Arvind Kejriwal publicized Vadra's business deals.[42] 'We had enough evidence, but we never attacked them. Don't make me open my mouth about Ranjan Bhattacharya,' he added. Bhattacharya, a popular figure on Delhi's inner political social circuit, is married to the daughter of a close woman friend of Atal Bihari Vajpayee, the former BJP prime minister, and is recognized as Vajpayee's foster son-in-law.[43] He was given an official position in Vajpayee's prime ministerial office and grew from working as a hotel manager to an owner of hotels and other real estate between 1998 and 2004 when the BJP was in power.

Jail, Bail and Lucrative Jobs

Politicians have rarely been jailed. In the rare instance it has happened, like in the Lalu Yadav case, the politicians involved have usually, like him, been freed on bail. The Sukh Ram telecom case dating from the early 1990s illustrates how India's colossally slow legal system and its seemingly endless avenues for appeals delays judgements for many years. This was one of the first examples of major graft linked to the allocation of natural resources in the newly liberalized years after 1991.[44] The allocation of licences for 21 telecom regional 'circles' became highly controversial because of the tender terms and quotations, notably bids made by Himachal Futuristic Communications (HFCL), a company that had links with Sukh Ram, the telecommunications minister, and was based in his home state of Himachal Pradesh. Ram also had links through another company with the son of the then prime minister, Narasimha Rao, whose political base was in the Andhra Pradesh state capital of Hyderabad. Money totalling Rs 3.6 crore was found concealed in bags and suitcases when Sukh Ram's residence was raided in August 1996. He was eventually convicted in 2002 on a 1997 charge for various degrees of involvement in the award of two telecom contracts. In one of them, Advanced Radio Masts (ARM) of Hyderabad supplied overpriced and poor quality telecom equipment that caused an estimated loss of Rs 1.6 crore to the government. In 2002, Ram was sentenced with two others to three years in jail on the ARM case, but this was suspended, pending appeals. In November 2011, Ram, by then 86, was ordered to serve his sentence,[45] but the Supreme Court soon granted him bail.

In January 2013, Om Prakash Chautala, the veteran head of a regional party and a former chief minister of Haryana, was sentenced to ten years' imprisonment along with 55 other people, including his son Ajay, for various crimes including conspiracy and forgery during the selection of over 3,000 junior teachers in 1999.[46] The original selection list had been replaced with fake lists during a recruitment process aimed at ending an acute shortage of teachers in 18 districts of the state. This was exposed in 2003 when an official (who was among those convicted) approached the Supreme Court as a whistleblower, saying he was pressured to replace the original lists. Chautala was sent to jail in January 2013 when he was 78, and four months later was granted interim bail for six weeks to undergo heart surgery. Lacking political clout with Hooda's Congress party, he then returned to jail. In another case, Bangaru Laxman, a former BJP president, was sentenced to four years in jail in 2012 at the age of 72, having been caught in a sting operation in 2001, receiving a bribe in a defence contract, but was released on bail.

When regional parties join national coalition governments, they push for their MPs to be given what are known as 'lucrative' ministerial posts, as M. Karunanidhi, the septuagenarian leader of the DMK, did successfully after a general election in 2009. He forced Manmohan Singh to keep Andimuthu Raja, a DMK MP, as the telecom minister despite corruption allegations that had been building up for a year or so before the election.[47] Praful Patel of the Maharashtra-based NCP was similarly retained as aviation minister against, it was believed, Manmohan Singh's wishes. Both the DMK and NCP were important members of Singh's coalition government, so it was expedient to keep them happy.

Patel was aviation minister from 2004 to 2010 and then heavy industries minister. His time dealing with aviation ministry was especially controversial because of deals for airport projects and the decline of Air India, the national carrier, while private airlines bloomed. I once described him on my blog as the 'government's top Teflon Man' because of the way that suggestions of wrongdoings slipped off his back.[48] Jitender Bhargava, a former Air India executive director, mentions some of them in his book *The Descent of Air India*.[49] He writes about what he describes euphemistically as Patel's political interference in the working of the airline. Decisions were taken, he says, without any consideration for the airline's future. Foreign airlines were given far greater access to India's airports than was justified by customer demand, which damaged Air India's ability to generate revenues.[50]

Once an MP receives a post, he is expected to deliver funds to his party and can expect trouble if he does not do so, as Suresh Prabhu of the Maharashtra-based Shiv Sena discovered when he was forced by his party leader to resign from a BJP coalition government in 2002 for not cashing in on his job as power minister. As a result, the government lost an able, honest minister, and the crisis-ridden power sector lost a committed reformer that it desperately needed. 'Even cynics were shaken when Shiv Sena supremo Bal Thackeray ordered power minister Suresh Prabhu to resign on the ground that he was too honest,' wrote Swaminathan Aiyar, a leading columnist. 'Never before has a Minister been sacked on the ground that he did not make money at all, and so was unfit for high office.'[51]

2G Telecom

The most explosive corruption cases to hit Manmohan Singh's 2004–2014 government involved the use of discretionary powers to avoid inviting competitive tenders for the allocation of telecommunications and coal licences. The biggest and longest-running case (dubbed the '2G scam' because it involved second-generation wireless telephone technology) involved the allocation of licences, together with reported kickbacks of at least $40m. This was widely known about, and even reported, for two years before it turned into a political crisis at the end of 2010. I ran an article on my blog in November 2008 headed 'India's telecom minister "should be fired" for a company's 700 per cent profits'.[52] I was repeating a comment in *Mint*, a leading Indian business daily that said, 'Raja should be fired',[53] referring to A. Raja, the telecom minister. A few days earlier, the *Business Standard* had an editorial headed *Licensed to make a killing*. Telecom spectrum needed for mobile phones had been 'handed over' by Raja to a few 'select' companies. *Mint* said that his 'mistake' (a kind euphemism) was that he did not auction the spectrum: instead, he allocated it to companies that applied on a first-come-first-served basis for fees that were far below what should have been charged.

Two of the companies, Swan Telecom (owned by DB Realty) and Unitech, were real estate and infrastructure businesses with no telecom experience or assets. When the awards had been made some months earlier, I had asked a contact why these companies were entering telecom. It was pointed out to me that Raja's previous post as environment minister brought him into contact with such real estate companies that wanted to obtain land allocations and permission, so what could be more natural than to see such friendly companies following him to the telecoms ministry! Unitech paid Rs 1,651 crore for its spectrum allocation and then sold a 60 per cent stake to Telenor of Norway for Rs 6,200 crore, putting a valuation of $2.1bn on the company. That was a profit of about 700 per cent in less than a year – just for owning the spectrum, without any customers or experience. Swan similarly paid about $340m and sold 45 per cent of its equity for $900m to Etisalat of Abu Dhabi, giving the company a valuation of $2bn – a six-fold increase. In both cases, the extra funds more than filled coffers depleted by a dramatic downturn in the real estate market.

The alarming point about this story was not just that a cabinet minister had conducted these deals, but that he was not stopped for more than two years, despite the wide and critical publicity, and was reappointed after the 2009 election. It emerged later that reservations had been voiced by the PMO and the finance ministry about the allocation method, though the fact that neither Manmohan Singh nor Chidambaram stopped the licences brought allegations later that they had wilfully condoned the corruption. Arun Shourie, who was the telecommunications minister in the previous BJP government, was given documents by a ministry official that proved Raja's dealings with the companies involved. Shourie told me that he personally offered the documents to Manmohan Singh in October 2009 and warned him that it was a 'massive corruption scandal that would explode'. Shourie says that the prime minister touched his turban in apparent despair and exclaimed, 'What can be done!' The prime minister's office failed to follow up on Shourie's offer of a briefing.[54]

Police and other inquires began in 2009, and the story blew up into a major scandal when the CAG estimated in a report in November 2010 that there had been a notional loss to the government of Rs 176,000 crore.[55] That was an inflated figure based on notional assumptions of lost government income, and it was reduced later to Rs 69,626 crore and then to Rs 57,666 crore. Raja was quickly dismissed and the Supreme Court criticized Manmohan Singh for the government's 'inaction and silence'.[56] In its report, the CAG found that as many as 85 out of 122 new licenses issued to 13 companies in 2008 did not satisfy eligibility conditions.[57]

Raja was arrested along with a senior bureaucrat and others, including Shahid Balwa, the promoter of DB Realty, who was charged with others of channelling Raja's bribe money into real estate – a money trail showed that payments of Rs 200 crore had been made by DB Realty to Kalaignar TV, a company in which the family of the Tamil Nadu chief minister had stakes.[58] Investigations involved other companies, but all the 13 people who were arrested, including Raja, were released on bail in 2012.

Spin-off ramifications from this scandal reached across the Indian establishment with the publication of private taped mobile phone conversations centred on Nira Radia, a lobbyist and public relations consultant. They revealed networks of politicians, officials, fixers and a few excited journalists discussing 2009 cabinet formation during its 'horse-trading' phase as well as other policy issues. Ratan Tata, who was then the head of the Tata group, was embarrassed because he had personally made Radia the group's main public relations consultant and his trusted adviser, and was heard speaking with her on the tapes. Other contacts and associates caught (some apparently innocently gossiping) in the conversations included N.K. Singh, a wealthy former top finance ministry and PMO bureaucrat; Tarun Das, creator and ex-head of the Confederation of Indian Industry; and Pradip Baijal, a retired senior bureaucrat who worked for Radia's firm.[59]

Coalgate

The coal scandal – dubbed Coalgate by the media – began with a leaked draft report in March 2012 from the CAG that alleged the government had lost Rs 10.6 lakh crores ($210bn) by allocating mining licences to around 100 private and public sector companies without competitive tendering. This focused on the years 2004–2009, when Manmohan Singh held the coal minister's portfolio. Licences had been allocated since coal mining was opened to the private sector in 1993. Competitive bidding was first proposed in 2004, but was not implemented till 2010. Five months after its first report, the CAG cut the figure to Rs 1.86 lakh crore ($37bn), based on an assessment of the gains that could have been made by private sector companies that were allotted 57 coal blocks, including nationally significant names such as Tata, Reliance (Anil Ambani's group), and the Jindal family-controlled mining and steel group.[60] The more important loss, at a time when coal was urgently needed to boost serious power shortages, was that many of the companies had failed to start mining and instead sat on the assets, waiting for their value to rise. Some companies had filed inaccurate information and were not even eligible to be awarded captive mines or capable of doing so.[61]

The CAG said that a screening committee of officials that allotted coal blocks was responsible for the decisions, but the BJP blamed Singh and demanded his resignation.[62] The Congress fought back by arguing that states ruled by the BJP such as Rajasthan, Jharkhand and Madhya Pradesh had opposed competitive bidding. The coal ministry cancelled many of the allocations, but the controversy expanded. The CBI investigated the claims and began by registering charges against relatively small companies. In May 2013, there were allegations of a cover-up by the law minister (who had to resign), and by officials in the prime minister's office, who were apparently trying to protect the prime minister's reputation by influencing the drafting of CBI documents to be presented to the Supreme Court.[63] In June

2013, Naveen Jindal, head of one of his family's businesses and a Congress member of parliament, was accused, along with a former minister of state for coal, of fraud and corruption in the allocation of a coal licence for Jindal Steel & Power.

This illustrated how, once investigations begin into a sector of Indian business, all sorts of potentially dubious and allegedly corrupt links emerge. Jindal, a Delhi socialite and polo player, was well connected with Congress leaders, so it was significant that the CBI felt free to investigate him. The CBI later filed a case suggesting that Kumar Mangalam Birla, chairman of the respected Aditya Birla group, had met a top coal ministry official and wrongfully persuaded him, after seeing the prime minister, to allocate a coal block in Orissa that had been reserved for the public sector.[64] This created a furore because Birla had been regarded as beyond reproach, and the lobbying he appeared to have been doing was normal business practice in any country. This led Manmohan Singh to break his customary silence and his office issued a statement saying he considered the allocation of the block to Birla as 'entirely appropriate'.[65]

The prime minister did indeed have a reasonably sound case, which he had spelt out in parliament in August 2012,[66] but his words did not resonate for long in the furore and clamour generated by a parliamentary opposition bent on undermining the government and by an over-excited media. Singh's line was that coal was urgently needed for power projects and the quickest way to mine it was to award licences and contracts on a select basis with favourable terms for private sector companies that would quickly generate electricity. As Singh said in parliament, the allocations were not regarded as 'revenue-generating activity' but a way of boosting electricity supplies – according to that argument, the CAG's calculations of losses were wrongly based.

There was, of course, nothing wrong with allocating licences, provided the policy was clear, and provided strict and fair rules and conditions were set and monitored so that they allowed no favouritism. Unfortunately, in India, corruption and discretionary powers are so deep-rooted that such arrangements are unlikely to be operated ethically and are understandably (and usually correctly) regarded with suspicion. In the 2G case, it was clear from the start that licences were being awarded to unqualified and undeserving companies and, in the coal case, the rules were so loosely drawn and administered that undeserving companies received projects. The responsibility for both cases rested with Manmohan Singh because on 2G he knew what Raja was doing and failed to stop it. On coal, he himself had been the coal minister and therefore presided over the malpractices and resisted moves to switch to competitive bidding. Coal blocks were allocated to undeserving companies and reputable companies were unwilling or unable to complete projects and generate power because of bureaucratic and other delays.

Paid Media

India's media is often lauded as one of the most free in the world. It is not, however, really free because of widespread corruption which leads to distorted, biased stories and editorial lines. Journalists and editors are also richly rewarded by companies and politicians, and a considerable amount of what appears in the media is 'planted' by vested interests. In a *British Journalism Review* article in 2001,[67] I wrote that, with some notable exceptions, editors and reporters were not so irreverent towards authority as their counterparts in many other countries, and they were far more flattered by the attention of people in important positions. This made them more vulnerable to accepting planted information favourable to their contacts, and to being persuaded not to run controversial stories. Many journalists welcomed favours offered by politicians and businessmen, often with 'brown paper envelopes' and other gifts. One company, which is known to be the most adept at managing political and public opinion, is widely believed to have journalists (as well as politicians and civil servants) on its payroll.

I also told this story: 'When I was first in India for the *Financial*

Times in the 1980s, S.P. Hinduja, the elder of the infamous Hinduja brothers, failed to persuade me to ghost-write articles for him, hinting at fat fees. When I returned in 1995, he and his brothers tried, again unsuccessfully, to get me to ghost-write a book on governments that they had dealt with around the world. Together with other journalists, I was later given a small TV set after a press conference [held in Mumbai's Taj Hotel where I was staying] by the Hindujas' cable TV company. I returned the set so fast [once I had got back to my room and saw what I had been given] that I forgot to note down what model it was, so could not put a value on the implied bribe.'[68]

Such cameos are not in themselves very dramatic; but they illustrate one aspect of the sharp decline that has taken place in the standards of Indian journalism. The quality of the media has worsened, and the opportunity for companies to influence it has increased, with the growth of what is called 'paid news' where politicians and businessmen pay for favourable coverage. It surfaced as a scandal in 2008–09, with many reports of politicians paying for favourable stories in a general election, with newspapers and TV stations taking the initiative and offering such coverage in return for substantial payments.

This was especially prevalent with Hindi-language local and regional newspapers and television channels.[69] The chief minister of Haryana even admitted it. 'When I noticed the leading paper of my state printing baseless reports on its front page day after day, I called them up and offered money to print the right picture. The paper in question apologized. They even returned the money taken from my rival to publish news items against me,' said Hooda.[70] The Bennett Coleman group started paid news in its titles that include the *Times of India*, and was followed by others including the *Hindustan Times* and the Bhaskar group, India's largest local-language newspaper publisher. This was taken a stage further with a system called Private Treaties, where Bennett Coleman accepts smallish equity stakes in companies in lieu of payment for its advertisements. It allegedly gives those companies favourable editorial coverage, though it denies the allegation.

The lines of ethics and professional standards have therefore become blurred in the media, as they have throughout India's public life with the spread of extortion, fraud and other forms of corruption. There is considerable public discussion about how this should be changed, but little sign of much significant happening.

Revolution 2020

The young are being influenced and harmed by this corrupt world around them in the same way that generations of children in conflict zones such as Kabul or Kashmir grow up assuming that bombs and stone throwing are a normal way of life. Nowhere is this better described than in a novel, *Revolution 2020*,[71] written by Chetan Bhagat, a bestselling author and popular youth icon in his late thirties, whose stories about ambitious young Indians in places like call centres and technology institutes sell 500,000 copies a year.[72]

In *Revolution 2020*, subtitled *Love, Corruption, Ambition*, Bhagat exposes rampant corruption, not in the more obvious crony capitalist centres of Delhi and Mumbai, nor in the activities of chief ministers like Mayawati and Yadav, but in the politics and businesses of smaller cities and towns. His story is about India's tertiary education system that turns out under-educated youth who are ill-equipped for careers. It is also about corruption in provincial politics and local land deals. Gopal, the main character, comes from a poor family in Varanasi, the sacred Hindu city on the River Ganga. He adores his childhood friend, the beautiful Aarti, whose family is better off, but he has a rival in their more self-confident middle-class friend, Raghav. Gopal sets out on a path followed by millions of India's youth, traipsing round ill-qualified cramming schools and phoney colleges. He fails his degree exams while Raghav succeeds with his studies and makes Aarti his girlfriend. Eventually, Gopal falls into the clutches of a local politician who persuades him to build and run a college (even though he has no degree) on family land that he has unexpectedly inherited. That draws him into a life of deception and corruption with the politician whom Raghav, by now a campaigning journalist, seeks to expose.

The novel graphically illustrates how India is wasting its demographic dividend with about half of its population below the age of 25. Instead of equipping the youth for jobs that would contribute both to their future and India's development, an inadequate education system is turning out many potential failures who find it easier, as Gopal does, to fall in with the corruption they see around them.

Corruption is a deeper and more dangerous problem in India than it is in many other countries. It is not just a case of people in power taking bribes, or even creaming off government funds. The foundations of democracy and social stability are being eaten away, and the effectiveness of institutions, already weakened by jugaad, are further destroyed.

Notes

1. Bibek Debroy and Laveesh Bhandari, *Corruption in India – the DNA and the RNA*, p. 7, Konark Publishers, New Delhi, 2012, http://www.konarkpublishers.com/books/851

2. Bibek Debroy and Laveesh Bhandari, 'Corruption in India', *World Financial Review* http://www.worldfinancialreview.com/?p=1575

3. Bibek Debroy in email conversation with JE

4. 'Silence of the vultures', *Sunday Guardian*, 18 May 2013 http://www.sunday-guardian.com/analysis/silence-of-the-vultures

5. In conversation with JE, December 2012

6. Pavan K. Varma in conversation with JE – and quoted from *Chanakya's New Manifesto – To Resolve the Crisis within India*, pp, 126-7, Aleph Book Company, Delhi, 2013, http://alephbookcompany.com/chanakyas-new-manifesto

7. Namita Gokhale in conversation with JE, March 2013; she has examined the understanding of Hindu mythology and religion

in two of her books *In Search of Sita* and *The Book of Shiva* http://namitagokhale.com/books.html

8. JE article in December 1999 for a private circulation publication in the UK.

9. B.V. Kumar, *The Darker Side of Black Money*, Konark Publishers, Delhi, 2013 https://ridingtheelephant.wordpress.com/2011/04/20/india-is-at-a-turning-point-that-might-go-wrong/

10. 'Rajya Sabha seats available for Rs 100 crore: Congress MP', Zee TV News, 29 July 2013, http://zeenews.india.com/news/nation/rajya-sabha-seats-available-for-rs-100-crore-congress-mp_865209.html

11. Lecture at the British Council, Delhi, 16 March 2013, attended by JE – also reported at http://www.firstpost.com/india/polls-biggest-source-of-corruption-former-cec-quraishi-794605.html

12. Full Details of Pending Criminal Cases of MPs (Lok Sabha 2009 Election), http://adrindia.org/research-and-reports/lok-sabha/2009/full-details-pending-criminal-cases-mps-lok-sabha-2009-election

13. National Election Watch and the Association for Democratic Research, http://adrindia.org

14. Devesh Kapur and Milan Vaishnav, 'Quid Pro Quo: Builders, Politicians, and Election Finance in India', Working Paper 276, December 2011, http://casi.sas.upenn.edu/system/files/Quid+Pro+Quo+-+DK.pdf , Center for Global Development, 1800 Massachusetts Ave., NW Washington, DC 20036 www.cgdev.org

15. Conversations with JE, non-attributable

16. 'Mayawati obsessed with grooming, fashion: WikiLeaks', *India Today*, 6 September 2011, http://indiatoday.intoday.in/story/mayawati-wikileaks-bsp/1/150243.html

17. http://ridingtheelephant.wordpress.com/2012/01/17/these-elephants-are-not-for-riding/

18. http://ridingtheelephant.wordpress.com/2011/10/30/india-shows-what-it-can-do-with-a-winning-formula

19. 'Maya memorials: Lokayukta indicts 199 for graft', *Indian Express*, 21 May 2013, http://www.indianexpress.com/news/maya-memorials-lokayukta-indicts-199-for-graft/1118340/

20. 'Mayawati memorials caused huge losses of royalty, says probe', *The Times of India*, 22 May 2013, http://articles.timesofindia.

indiatimes.com/2013-05-22/lucknow/39445008_1_several-mining-leaseholders-memorials-large-scale-illegal-mining

21. Told non-attributably to JE

22. Amitabha Pande, 'The power to say yes', *Indian Express*, 2 November 2012, http://www.indianexpress.com/news/the-power-to-say-yes; former secretary to the government who handled army procurement in the 1990s and describes himself as 'an iconoclastic former IAS officer who never fitted into the mould', Pande runs his blog at http://notesfromasubversivebureaucrat.blogspot.in/

23. In conversation with JE; Surendra Rao, formerly a senior business executive, director general of NCAER, and first chairman of the Central Electricity Regulatory Commission

24. 'Fodder scam: Lalu preparing for worst as verdict looms?', *Mail Today*, 9 May 2012, http://indiatoday.intoday.in/story/fodder-scam-lalu-yadav-rabri-devi-bihar-rjd-leader/1/188050.html

25. 'Blow for Lalu in fodder scam trial', *Business Standard*, 14 August 2013, http://www.business-standard.com/article/current-affairs/fodder-scam-lalu-s-plea-rejected-sc-for-quick-end-to-trial-113081300997_1.html

26. 'Sons Lite – Lalu Prasad has inducted his sons into the party,' *Business Standard*, 25 May 2013, http://www.business-standard.com/article/beyond-business/sons-lite-113052401029_1.html

27. 'Lalu Yadav jailed for five years as India finally gets tough on graft', Reuters, 3 October 2013, http://in.reuters.com/article/2013/10/03/india-lalu-yadav-jailed-fodder-idINDEE99206O20131003

28. http://ridingtheelephant.wordpress.com/2013/10/03/rahul-gandhi-stops-a-small-compromise-on-lalu-yadav-but-does-he-have-the-stamina-to-be-a-leader/

29. 'Corruption – In India, Whistle-Blowers Pay with Their Lives', *Bloomberg Business Week*, 20 October 2011, http://www.businessweek.com/magazine/in-india-whistleblowers-pay-with-their-lives-10202011.html

30. 'The Mother Of All Sweetheart Deals', *Outlook* blogs, 18 March 2011, http://blogs.outlookindia.com/default.aspx?ddm=10&pid=2457&eid=31

31. 'Haryana govt chargesheets Ashok Khemka for nixing Robert Vadra-DLF land deal', *The Times of India*, 6 December 2013 http://timesofindia.indiatimes.com/2013-12-06/india/44863011_1_robert-vadra-dlf-ashok-khemka-skylight-hospitality

32. 'Bansal defends his decision to resign, says he has done nothing wrong', CNN-IBN, 12 May 2013 http://ibnlive.in.com/news/bansal-defends-his-decision-to-resign-says-he-has-done-nothing-wrong/391117-37-64.html

33. 'Railway bribery: More transcripts point to Pawan Bansal's role', CNN-IBN, 9 August 2013, http://ibnlive.in.com/news/railway-bribery-more-transcripts-point-to-pawan-bansals-role/413013-37-64.html

34. Information given to JE, not attributable

35. 'Indolence in India's Judiciary', Global Corruption Report 2007, Transparency International, http://www.transparency.org/whatwedo/pub/global_corruption_report_2007_corruption_and_judicial_systems

36. Letter to the Prime Minister of India on 7 April 2005, reproduced in *South Asia Politics*, vol. 5, no. 1 (2006)

37. Conversation with JE, not attributable

38. 'A Brief History of Corruption in India', an article by Dr William Gould, Senior Lecturer in Indian History, University of Leeds, on 'The India Site', http://www.theindiasite.com/a-brief-history-of-corruption-in-india/ . His book is *Bureaucracy, Community and Influence: Society and the State in India, 1930-1960s,* Routledge, London, 2011

39. S.S. Gill, *The Pathology of Corruption*, pp 50-61, 63-69, HarperCollins *Publishers* India, Delhi, 1998-99

40. Ibid., p. 65

41. http://ridingtheelephant.wordpress.com/2012/10/23/corruption-tamashas-and-gossip-flood-india-but-change-will-be-very-slow/

42. 'Never attack family: Digvijaya Singh's lesson on political ethics', NDTV, 16 October 2012 http://www.ndtv.com/article/india/never-attack-family-digvijaya-singh-s-lesson-on-political-ethics-to-arvind-kejriwal-280101

43. 'The Son in Law also rises', a gossip column account of Ranjan Bhattacharya's life, Rediff.com, 25 July 1998, http://www.rediff.com/news/1998/jul/25abv.htm

44. This magazine article shows the wheeler-dealing in the early-1990s' opening up of telecommunications: 'The Great Telecom Scam – The record Rs 3.66 crore seizure at Sukh Ram's residence raises questions

about Narasimha Rao's credibility and his reforms regime', 4 September 1996, http://www.outlookindia.com/article.aspx?202038

45. Sukh Ram was bailed in January 2012. This report traces the course of the cases: '1996 Telecom scam: HC orders ex-minister Sukhram to serve sentence', 21 December 2011, http://www.indianexpress.com/news/1996-telecom-scam-hc-orders-exminister-sukhram-to-serve-sentence/890402/0

46. 'Chautala, son held guilty in teachers job scam', *The Hindu*, 16 January 2013, http://www.thehindu.com/news/national/other-states/chautala-son-held-guilty-in-teachers-job-scam/article4312083.ece

47. https://ridingtheelephant.wordpress.com/2009/05/22/regional-party-ambitions-cloud-india%E2%80%99s-new-cabinet/ and https://ridingtheelephant.wordpress.com/2009/05/28/india%E2%80%99s-cabinet-problems-show-it-needs-a-house-of-lords-for-ruffled-egos/

48. http://ridingtheelephant.wordpress.com/2008/11/23/%E2%80%9Cbed-and-bhai%E2%80%9D-rules-india%E2%80%99s-aviation/

49. Jitender Bhargava, *The Descent of Air India*, pp. 115, 157, Bloomsbury Publishing India, 2013, http://www.amazon.in/The-Descent-India-Jitender-Bhargava/dp/938295113X

50. Ibid pp. 120, 151

51. 'Suresh Prabhu and Simple Simon', Swaminathan S. Anklesaria Aiyar's 'Swaminomics' column includes a useful summary of the power sector's losses and problems at the time, 25 August 2002, http://swaminomics.org/suresh-prabhu-and-simple-simon/

52. http://ridingtheelephant.wordpress.com/2008/11/11/india%E2%80%99s-telecom-minister-%E2%80%9Cshould-be-fired%E2%80%9D-for-allowing-a-company-700-profit/

53. 'Raja should be fired', *Mint*, 11 November 2008, http://www.livemint.com/2008/11/10212808/Raja-should-be-fired.html?atype=tp

54. Arun Shourie talking to JE, September 2013, said he met Manmohan Singh in October 2009 in the gallery of the Rajya Sabha. He also explained the events in August 2013 in a television interview – video here: http://ibnlive.in.com/news/narendra-modi-has-the-best-poll-agent-in-manmohan-singh-arun-shourie/417441-37-64.html

55. 'Here's how CAG report on 2G scam blasts Raja', Rediff.com, 16 November 2010, http://www.rediff.com/business/slide-show/slide-show-1-tech-what-the-cag-report-on-2g-scam-says/20101116.htm

56. http://ridingtheelephant.wordpress.com/2010/11/15/another-corrupt-indian-politician-sacked-but-can-anything-ever-change/

57. 'Underbelly of the Great Indian Telecom Revolution', *Economic and Political Weekly*, December 2010, http://www.epw.in/insight/underbelly-great-indian-telecom-revolution.html

58. 'Lawmaker Kanimozhi Arrested in Telecom Case', *Wall St Journal* on line, 20 May 2011, http://online.wsj.com/article/SB10001424052748704904604576334762982058284.html

59. http://ridingtheelephant.wordpress.com/2010/12/03/radia-tapes-highlight-media-flaws-that-fit-with-modern-india/ and http://ridingtheelephant.wordpress.com/2011/01/04/jairam-ramesh-wins-in-2010-for-tackling-india%E2%80%99s-corrupted-environment/

60. http://www.thehindu.com/multimedia/archive/01181/Coal_Block_Questio_1181374a.pdf

61. http://www.hindustantimes.com/India-news/NewDelhi/Coal-scam-Firms-in-Chhattisgarh-and-Jharkhand-benefited-most/Article1-917932.aspx

62. http://indiatoday.intoday.in/story/coal-scam-bjp-demands-pm-resignation/1/213587.html

63. *CBI 'made to' share Coalgate report with government*, *Times of India*, 27 April, 2013 http://articles.timesofindia.indiatimes.com/2013-04-27/india/38861258_1_status-report-coal-scam-probe-coal-ministry

64. *Coal block allocation scam: K M Birla named in CBI's report*, *Business Standard*, 16 October 2013, http://www.business-standard.com/article/current-affairs/coal-block-allocation-scam-k-m-birla-named-in-cbi-s-report-113101500114_1.html

65. Prime minister's office press release, 19 October 2013, http://pmindia.gov.in/press-details.php?nodeid=1720

66. 'PM's statement in Parliament on the Performance Audit Report on Allocation of Coal Blocks and Augmentation of Coal Production', Prime Minister's Office press release, 27 August 2012 http://pmindia.gov.in/pmsinparliament.php?nodeid=62

67. http://www.bjr.org.uk/

68. http://ridingtheelephant.wordpress.com/2010/12/03/radia-tapes-highlight-media-flaws-that-fit-with-modern-india/

69. 'Paid news in the Hindi press', *The Hoot*, 12 May 2010, http://

thehoot.org/web/home/story.php?storyid=4545&mod=1&pg=1&sec
tionId=4&valid=true

70. 'Paid-for news – News You Can Abuse', *Outlook*, 21 December 2009
    http://www.outlookindia.com/article.aspx?263242

71. *Revolution 2020: Love, Corruption, Ambition*, Rupa Publications India,
    2011, http://www.chetanbhagat.com/books/revolution-2020/

72. 'Chetan Bhagat, India's Charles Dickens', Rediff.com, 27 December
    2012, http://www.rediff.com/getahead/report/chetan-bhagat-indias-
    charles-dickens/20121227.htm

17

Indefensible Defence

Poor governance and extensive corruption have such a strong and negative impact on the way that India's defence establishment operates that it is reasonable to wonder what the Ministry of Defence and the armed forces, with their annual budget of approaching $40bn and a vast defence establishment of over four million people, see as their primary role. It should be to protect India by building up the defence capability with the latest technologies and efficient well-trained manpower, utilizing the best available domestic manufacturing industry to produce world-class aircraft, tanks, guns and ships. Instead, it seems to be to protect jobs for bureaucrats, armed forces officers and other public sector employees, giving prestige and powers of patronage to those at the top of the establishment, and maintaining India's position as the world's biggest arms importer, while sustaining extortion and bribes at every level of government from ministers and top bureaucrats down through the defence ministry and the armed forces to poorly performing public sector corporations and ordnance factories.

Exempted from the economic liberalization measures of 1991, the defence establishment has resolutely resisted attempts to open up the sector, apart from rare exceptions. This has ensured that it can continue on its jugaad path of mixing expensive imported equipment with the worst practices and outdated systems, relying on chalta hai to cover its tracks. As a result, India's defence preparedness for possible conflicts is declining, despite occasional advances such as the launching, in 2012 and 2013, of the first nuclear-propelled submarine and aircraft carrier built in India, and a partially successful Russia-assisted missile programme.

With a capital expenditure budget of some $16bn (2013–14), India has been the world's largest buyer of foreign defence equipment since 2006, accounting for 10 per cent of global arms sales.[1] It spends at least 70 per cent of the budget on importing aircraft, tanks, guns and other weapons and equipment that it should be fully capable of making itself. Of the remaining 30 per cent, two-thirds is spent on equipment produced, mostly inefficiently, by the public sector, which leaves only about 10 per cent for Indian private sector companies. In the mid-1990s, a committee headed by A.P.J. Abdul Kalam, a senior defence bureaucrat and scientist and later India's President, said that the indigenous content of India's weapons should rise from 30 per cent to 70 per cent by 2005, but nothing happened.

China was the world's biggest weapons importer till 2006–2007, mostly buying old Soviet-era technology from Russia,[2] but it has dramatically modernized its defence manufacturing industry in recent years. This has not only cut its need for foreign equipment, but has also turned it into the world's fifth-largest arms exporter with $11bn orders between 2011 and 2012.[3] (Pakistan, its close ally, takes 55 per cent of the sales,)[4] This sort of transformation is something that India has singularly failed even to try to do despite its success in other areas such as space technology (in November 2013, it launched a ten-month spacecraft mission to Mars).

Manmohan Singh's national security advisor, Shivshankar Menon, has warned that talk of India's strategic autonomy and of increasing degrees of independence has little meaning unless there is 'a quantum improvement' in India's defence production and innovation capabilities.[5] 'A country that does not develop and produce its own major weapons platforms has a major strategic weakness, and cannot claim true strategic autonomy. This is a real challenge for us all,' he said.

A chief of army staff, General V.K. Singh, highlighted inefficiencies (during a public row over his retirement age), in a letter he sent to the prime minister that was leaked to the media.[6] He said that 80 per cent of India's armoured tanks were night blind, and listed tank ammunition and air defence problems. The infantry had 'deficiencies of crew-served weapons' and lacked night-fighting capabilities. Elite special forces were 'woefully short' of 'essential weapons', and there were 'large-scale voids' in critical surveillance capabilities. 'Like the medieval times you fight morning to evening and take rest at night – Pakistan has 80 per cent of tanks capable to fight at night,' said Rahul Bedi, a defence journalist.[7] 'Planning and strategic thinking of the Indian Army's procurement programme is in complete shambles. Bureaucrats and politicians are throttling the procurement process'.

The high level of foreign purchase has been needed because India's generally inefficient defence research and its defence public sector undertakings (DPSUs) could not meet demand – not even, till recently, for high-technology equipment like modern helmets and night-vision goggles, let alone the latest fighter aircraft, submarines and guns. This is primarily because the private sector has generally been kept out of doing more than supplying minor components, while the defence establishment enjoyed the combined benefits of protected jobs, patronage, prestige and foreign kickbacks. Yet private sector companies in the field of automobiles, engineering systems and information technology have proved themselves in the past decade to be internationally competitive and have the potential to become significant defence manufacturers.

Tatra Tangle

A scandal that dominated Indian newspaper headlines for weeks in 2012 brought together all the corruption, poor public sector production, lack of technological development and defence establishment intrigue that has been allowed to develop since India's independence, especially in the army. This was coupled with disarray at top levels, exposing intense personal and caste-based rivalries among generals, especially those in line to become the chief of army staff.[8] The scandal emerged during General Singh's humiliating public row with the government over his birth date, which dictated when he would have to retire. In addition to criticizing poor army equipment, he also alleged that he had been offered a Rs 14 crore ($2.8m) bribe by another general in the army to continue to buy nearly 1,700 all-terrain Tatra army trucks that he claimed were faulty (not to be confused with India's Tata Motors, which also makes army trucks).

The vehicles, which are widely admired for their flexible-axle agility on rough ground, are made (complete or as components) in the Czech Republic by Tatra Trucks, which is controlled by an Indian-owned UK-based company called Vectra. They are assembled in India by Bharat Earth Movers (BEML), a PSU, under a deal that was struck in 1986 when Rajiv Gandhi's Congress government was in power. Technological know-how was to be gradually transferred to BEML so that 85 per cent of the trucks would be made in India by 1991, but only 50–60 per cent Indian content had been achieved 21 years after that date. The left-hand drive had not even been changed to India's right-hand drive, yet some 7,000 trucks had been delivered to the army. BEML also incredibly waived its rights to the axle technology, which was the trucks' key asset. The business was investigated by the CBI with allegations that the army was charged as much as 100 per cent, and maybe more, for the trucks above their ex-factory cost and that spares were also overcharged, but little progress was made on the case.

Manoj Joshi, a journalist and defence specialist who was a member of a government security taskforce in 2013, says the army chief of staff in 1987 told him that he had wanted to import the trucks direct from what was then Czechoslovakia, but had been persuaded to allow BEML to handle them and indigenize the production. 'Over the years, BEML has merely taken kits and put them together and passed them on to the army after marking up their prices. As the army chief forecast, the trucks would have been cheaper to import,' wrote Joshi.[9]

A Trail of Inadequacy

To see the problems in perspective, follow this trail. The inefficient, heavily protected public sector's involvement with new weapons starts with a massive spread of defence research organizations under a vast Defence Research and Development Organisation (DRDO) that has had a monopoly on design and development. Then there is an equally massive spread of nine DPSUs, and 39 government ordnance factories run by an Ordnance Factory Board. Together employing some 1.8m people,[10] these organizations have had first rights to virtually all orders unless a prior decision has been made to buy abroad. They are supposed to secure India's defences by producing the best that the country can obtain, but instead they are self-sustaining monoliths that have blocked the entry of the increasingly capable and more entrepreneurial private sector which, they claim, cannot be trusted to handle India's defence secrets. Yet they themselves share secrets with foreign private sector suppliers, as do the armed forces.

Equipment specifications frequently aim at a level of technological perfection and precision that slow down heavily bureaucratic tendering processes, and are often designed to favour either a specific Indian public sector producer and/or a specific foreign supplier. Decision making is so cumbersome and lethargic that expensively produced equipment is often years out of date by the time it is delivered – some projects are never completed such as a Trishul SAM missile that was abandoned after 17 years. Public sector maintenance is inadequate and undermines reliability. Foreign orders often involve large bribes of perhaps five per cent or more of the contract value, and the use of agents who have been officially but unsuccessfully banned since the 1980s, which companies expose to trip up rivals.

The government has no illusions about the damage that is being done. Pallam Raju, minister of state for defence from 2006 to 2012, warned at an army seminar in February 2010 about the risks, implicitly ceding potential victory to China which has, for example, better field and rocket artillery and conventional battlefield ballistic missiles. 'History is a testimony that no nation has been able to prevail in a conflict with lower threshold of technology in the defence sector,' he said. 'Countries or the armies with lower technologies would have won a battle here and there, but you will find hardly any example, wherein a higher technology military power has been overwhelmed by lower technology power in the long run'.[11]

A background paper prepared for the seminar revealed what General Singh talked about later, saying that 'most of India's ground-based air defences are obsolete'. Upgrades of basic artillery equipment were 'ten years behind schedule'.[12] An array of generals attending the event, which was being held at India's biennial national defence exhibition, did not blink at such unpatriotic statements – they knew only too well they were true. Three months later, in a discussion document arguing for more foreign direct equity investment in defence companies, the commerce ministry said that 'only 15 per cent of equipment can be described as 'state-of-the-art' and nearly 50 per cent is suffering from obsolescence'.

The armed forces have been warning the Ministry of Defence for years to accelerate orders for urgently needed new equipment. In a September 2012 policy brief for the National Bureau of Asian Research, Gurmeet Kanwal, a retired army officer and former director of the Delhi's Centre for Land Warfare Studies, wrote: 'The army's mechanized forces are still mostly "night blind". Its artillery lacks towed and self-propelled 155-mm howitzers for the plains and the mountains and has little capability by way of multi-barrel rocket launchers and surface-to-surface missiles. Infantry battalions urgently need to acquire modern weapons and equipment for counterinsurgency and counterterrorism operations to increase operational effectiveness and lower casualties'.[13] A year later, *Jane's Defence Weekly* reported that it had been told by a senior army artillery officer that the range of some field guns on the Chinese and Pakistani frontiers 'barely crosses India's borders, rendering them ineffectual'.[14] Yet the defence ministry failed to finalize a contract to buy 145 M777 lightweight howitzers from the US arm of the UK-based BAE Systems in October 2013, even though the company was saying it would have to close down its production line.[15]

In the Indian Air Force, the problem is different. Orders for new aircraft can be excessively slow – it took India 20 years to order Hawk trainers from the UK in 2004 – but they do happen. There is, however, a high rate of crashes. Out of 872 Russian (originally Soviet) MiG fighters bought, or partially made in India by the government-owned Hindustan Aeronautics (HAL), between 1966 and 1980, as many as 482 had crashed by mid-2012, killing 171 pilots. Reporting the figures to parliament in May 2012, Minister of Defence A.K. Antony said that the causes of accidents were both human error and technical defects[16] – inadequate pilot training, poor-quality manufacture and maintenance by HAL, cannibalization of aircraft for spares, and tough conditions.[17]

Ajay Shukla, a journalist and former army officer who specializes in defence issues, wrote in March 2013 that over the previous five years, a total of 50 aircraft had crashed, including 37 fighters and 13 helicopters, causing the death of 17 pilots, 18 service personnel and six civilians.[18] Quoting figures released by the defence ministry in parliament, he said that the air force lost the equivalent of one fighter squadron (16–18 fighters) in crashes every two years. Consequently, it had only 32 or 33 operational squadrons compared with a minimum requirement of 42. 'With each [Russian] Sukhoi-30, the cheapest aircraft being currently inducted, costing close to Rs 350 crore, the loss of eight fighters per year to crashes amounts to an annual loss of over Rs 2,800 crore,' he added. Costs would rise if and when the Rafale, a French fighter produced by Dassault of France which was then being considered, was purchased at perhaps Rs 450–500 crore per aircraft. That was also the anticipated price for an Indo-Russian fifth-generation fighter aircraft scheduled to become operational towards 2020.

The Indian Navy has a better record than the other armed services. It has been developing a capacity to design and build most of its warships in India,[19] which the army and air force do not have for their equipment. It also goes for gradual improvements in its equipment, whereas the army and air force tend to look for dramatic new prestige weapons that slow down purchases.

India initially learned its shipbuilding skills from British Leander-class frigates that it built in the 1970s, and from Kashin-class destroyers sourced from Russia in the 1980s. The Delhi class destroyer was built in the 1990s followed by successfully designed frigates and corvettes and, more recently, an aircraft carrier that benefited, along with other navy ships, from the development in India of warship-grade steel at half the cost of imports.[20] 'The navy's import content is noticeably lower than the other services,' says Shukla.[21] 'In the current crop of warships being built, there is 90–95 per cent indigenisation in the "float" section such as the hull, about 60 per cent in the "move" section (engine, transmission), and 40–45 per cent on weapons and sensors.' The DRDO's few successes include the development of this special steel with the Indian public and private sector, and the design of a sonar radar. The navy's weapons systems are still imported, the DRDO having failed with the Trishul missile.

But the navy's fleet is ageing, and the introduction of new warships is years behind schedule. This is mainly because of inefficient and overmanned public sector naval dockyards that produce ships slowly – by international standards – and have prevented the private sector from establishing a significant role. The CAG estimated in 2008 that the ageing and mostly Russian submarine fleet had only a 48 per cent operational availability,[22] and it has not improved since then. A 30-year submarine-building plan was approved by the government in 1999 but none of the planned 24 submarine vessels has gone into service. The country's underwater capability took a hit in August 2013 when the navy's most modern submarine, which had recently had an $80m refit in Russia, was destroyed in an explosion.

There is a lack of expertise in submarine design, which could have been met by collaboration with HDW of Germany if a 1980s deal had not been scrapped, after four vessels had been delivered, because of allegations of bribes. Progress on building six Scorpene submarines in India under a 2005 contract with France has been slow and the first is not expected till 2016–17, over four years late.

Foreign Suppliers

India's foreign suppliers have traditionally been led by Russia, which inherited the overwhelming dominance of the old Soviet Union and still has around 80 per cent of the orders, according to the Stockholm International Peace Research Institute.[23] Between 1950 and 2012, the Soviet Union and Russia (excluding other former Soviet bloc countries) had 69 per cent of the sales, rising to 77 per cent between 2000 and 2012 (83 per cent in 2012 alone). In the same period, the UK slipped from the number two spot with 15 per cent to 4.3 per cent in 2000–12 (6 per cent in 2012). Israel rose from 1.5 per cent to number two with around 4.8 per cent (5.3 per cent in 2012), while France fell from 3.8 per cent to 1.4 per cent. In two years of negotiations from 2011, two European groups were short listed, led by Dassault of France's Rafale fighter, on an $11bn-plus contract for 126 multi-role combat aircraft, defeating both American and Russian contenders and boosting France's role.

The total US order book of concluded or pending deals by mid-2013 amounted to nearly $11bn,[24] which will probably make it the third-biggest supplier. It delivered virtually nothing between 1964 and 1986 and then only tiny amounts till 2006, because it was boycotting India for the supply of lethal and technologically sensitive items. It is now picking up from just over one per cent between 1950 and 2012 to around two per cent to three per cent in the last two or three years following a New Framework for India–US Defence Relationship that was agreed in 2005. India is, however, still wary of buying essential equipment from America because of the risk that supplies would be stopped if Washington disapproved of something India had done, for example in the development of nuclear arms. This may have affected decisions in 2011 on the big fighter contract, where Boeing and Lockheed Martin's aircraft were rejected, much to America's amazement and annoyance (though its Boeing and Lockheed fighters were said by experts to be inferior to the short listed European jets).[25] The 2005 agreement led, in 2009, to a $2.1bn contract for eight Boeing P-81 maritime surveillance aircraft and a $1bn deal for six Lockheed Martin C-130J Hercules military transport aircraft[26] – neither of them seen as being essential as fighters and hence not so sensitive in terms of availability of spares – and ten Boeing C-17 Globemaster heavy lift transport aircraft for $4bn.

The public sector has become increasingly dependent on imports for its supposedly India-based manufacturing and assembly projects. Many DPSUs and ordnance factories order components quietly from abroad and cloak them in apparently Indian-made defence equipment – as was illustrated by the Tatra truck story. That enables them to avoid having to develop their own technologies and opens the door for them to accept foreign bribes. 'We are manufacturing high-end products like SU 30 MKI, Brahmos and Scorpene subs, but these are licensed productions of foreign-designed weapons, and even here we know that key assemblies will be imported till the very end of the programme,' says Manoj Joshi, referring to Russian Sukhoi aircraft, Indo-Russian Brahmos missiles and French Scorpene submarines.[27] The DPSUs then charge the defence forces much higher prices than they have to pay their foreign suppliers, thus increasing their profits. 'There is evidence which seems to suggest that the DPSU managers were actually going out of the way to serve the interests of the foreign company, rather than the company they headed,' wrote Joshi.[28] 'Insiders will tell you that this is not as uncommon a phenomenon in our DPSUs and ordnance factories as it may seem.' Another expert describes many DPSUs as 'traders not manufacturers'.

This poses the question, why such a situation has been allowed to continue for so long. The immediate answer is that the characteristics of jugaad and chalta hai provide the cover for the powerful defence establishment's vested interests to maintain the status quo and enjoy the consequential hefty bribes and other favours. Foreign suppliers support this because they prefer to manufacture and assemble expensively abroad, and pay the bribes (usually indirectly to obscure the sources), while relying on India's low-cost manufacturers for relatively minor components. Such an approach prevents Indian companies growing into competitors as final assemblers of complex weaponry.

Everyone, with some exceptions of course, from public sector chairmen down to office peons and manual labourers, thrives on a system that, despite the patriotism and loyalty of many of those involved, sees the protection of employment as its primary aim, with technical, commercial and financial issues as subsidiary considerations. Along with the DPSUs, the defence ministry does not want change, and nor do the mass of the armed forces, despite considerable unhappiness with what is available from the public sector. There are also politically powerful trade union federations in the industry that thrive in the present set-up and resist change.

Senior retired officials, who have spent large parts of their careers in the defence establishment, are amazingly critical of how they had to work, citing misguided procedures, excessive secrecy, and a lack of planning, communication and transparency.[29] I have heard them talk about how procedures are aimed more at spending budgeted funds than building defence capability, and that procurement of weaponry is 'not seen as an issue of national security' but as a bureaucratic exercise.

Antony and Other Blockages

In recent years, the failure to introduce reforms has been led by the defence minister, A.K. Antony, a mild veteran Congress politician from the southern state of Kerala, where he was earlier chief minister. He is proud of his uncorruptable reputation, and is regarded as one of the politicians most trusted by Sonia and Rahul Gandhi. This has made him secure in the post, despite increasing criticism of his lack of drive and effectiveness. Appointed in 2006, he shied away from as many reforms as he could, and slowed down plans that were being backed by his predecessor, Pranab Mukherjee, now India's President. Antony's Kerala base is significant because the Congress there is pulled leftwards by a communist-led coalition that is its main rival for power in the state assembly. This strengthens his support for public sector trade unions that resist change to protect their members' jobs. Uday Bhaskar, a defence and security policy expert and former navy officer,[30] wrote Antony an open letter in May 2012, saying his track-record was 'disappointing'. Bhaskar taunted him by suggesting that the defence forces were so ill-prepared that India could 'inadvertently repeat the 1962 experience' – a reference to its defeat that year by China. The Cabinet Committee on Security and Political Affairs, Bhaskar added, suffered from 'perceived abdication in decision-making' and there was 'stasis in higher defence management'.[31]

Even though Antony's stance accounts for policy blockages from 2006 to 2013, there is a larger question of why earlier governments did not try to improve domestic performance and reduce India's reliance on foreign suppliers. Structurally, the problem lies in the make-up of the Ministry of Defence where, under the defence secretary, who is the top bureaucrat, there are two secretaries separately responsible for production and procurement. The defence production secretary has line management responsibility for the performance of DPSUs and the ordnance factories, so is in effect required by his remit to support the public sector and not the private sector, which therefore has no top official in the ministry whose job it is to argue its case.

'Arming without Aiming'

More broadly, it has been suggested that tolerance of the current system stems both from a deep post-colonial ambivalence about the use of force, and from the country's avoidance of foreign entanglements, which together limit its desire for foreign clout. This lack of a broad-based strategic foreign and defence culture means it is only necessary for India to equip its army and air force, and to a lesser extent the navy, to defend the country against its neighbours, notably on the long and disputed Himalayan borders with China, where it lost in 1962, and with Pakistan, against which it has fought and won three wars and one undeclared near-war. Based on that argument, guns, tanks, missiles and aircraft can be bought haphazardly or developed domestically, even more haphazardly and unreliably, to fight across mountains and deserts, plus ships that are required more now that China is muscling in on nearby oceans and seas. For this limited canvas, defence and arms equipment do not need to be planned at the strategic policy level that happens, for example, in the US, the UK and China.

Stephen P. Cohen and Sunil Dasgupta of America's Brookings Institution described this as 'the puzzle of enduring shortcoming in Indian defense policymaking', in *Arming without Aiming*, a book that was originally published in 2010. They looked at 'the enduring nature of these weaknesses', and why the Indian political system had allowed them to persist for so many years. 'Previously, others have argued that culture and identity, caste and class divisions, poverty, the absence of political will, and the threat environment, explain Indian defense policy choices,' they wrote in a new preface to a paperback edition.[32] 'But we noted that India's defense policy was rooted in a doctrine of military-strategic restraint that was, at its outset, an ideological rejection of the use of armed force as the tool of colonizers. In rejecting colonization, India also rejected the instruments used by the colonizers. After independence, the cold war's neo-colonial hue solidified Indian preferences for restraint. Since then, the bureaucracy has institutionalized restraint in so thorough a manner that a breakout is hard to imagine in the absence of a major crisis.'

Cohen and Dasgupta acknowledge that not everyone agreed with their interpretation when it first appeared (and became a surprising best-seller in India). They note in the paperback edition – optimistically from their viewpoint – that 'many Indians do not see their country as being bound by strategic restraint', and instead 'want India to behave like a great power in the mold of the United States, Britain, and China – assertive powers willing and able to defend their interests with military forces when necessary'. Arguably, however, they are seriously underestimating the strength of policy opinion that does not want India to play a big international role beyond its regional interests, irrespective of how much that might annoy policy hawks both in Delhi and in Washington DC (including experts at the Brookings Institution).

One needs therefore to look to other catalysts for change on arms purchasing. One is technological because software and electronics are playing a growing role in defence equipment and are making it easy for foreign suppliers and countries, including seemingly friendly ones such as the US, to undermine the effectiveness of guns, helicopters or aircraft that they supply by withholding sensitive and sophisticated refinements. 'This is no longer just a question of strategic autonomy; today it is also a military-technical issue, in an era when the capabilities of defence equipment depend more on software than on hardware and when it is increasingly easy to compromise weaponry sold to another country through the introduction of malware and kill switches,' says Shukla.[33]

Public Failings

Output per employee in the DPSUs and ordnance factories is less than half the average level in India's general manufacturing industry in the public as well as the private sector, according to a Boston Consulting Group report.[34] The report put the defence public sector figure at Rs 15 lakh per year compared with Rs 20–40 lakh in industry generally,[35] and suggested that the defence figure should be double its present level at around Rs 30 lakh. Despite the navy's relative successes, Indian warships are being built way over cost and time estimates – frigates of the Godavari class took 72 months to build and Delhi class destroyers 114 months, while more recent Shivalik class frigates are taking 112 months compared with a 60-month target, says Manoj Joshi.[36]

A basic problem with both the defence research and production corporations is that they focus on developing and manufacturing a specific gun, aircraft or ship, instead of building the sort of general engineering capabilities that private sector companies such as L&T, Godrej and Tata Power have done with finely tuned metals and engineering systems, according to Naresh Chandra, a veteran civil servant who headed a government taskforce on national security in 2012. 'Don't beat your brains out over developing a gun or a tank, but find your overall strengths, buy in what you need with a well-developed supply chain and assemble your platforms,' he says.

The DRDO has a hefty budget – Rs 10,610 crore for 2013–14 – and 52 laboratories. It employs some 5,000 scientists and about 25,000 support staff who are involved in projects ranging from combat vehicles and armaments to submarines and aircraft. But instead of being a centre of excellence, it has frequently failed in both technical and financial terms to meet the needs of the military, which then buys abroad. According to a report by the ministry's Controller General of Defence Accounts (CGDA) in 2012, only 29 per cent per cent of the products it developed in the previous 17 years were being used by the armed forces.[37] That is mainly because of DRDO failings, but it is also the result of the defence forces enjoying buying abroad and consequently resisting, or at least not welcoming, some DRDO developments.[38]

The CAG report noted that, in several cases, the DRDO bought equipment after spending large amounts of money on its own unsuccessful research and development, or offered equipment that was more expensive than was available on the open market. It spent Rs 6.85 crore developing explosive detectors, which it offered to the army for Rs 30 lakh each at a time when foreign versions were available for Rs 9.8 lakh each, including the cost of repairs and maintenance.[39]

The main DRDO successes have been surface-to-surface missiles called Agni and Prithvi, but it has failed to produce smaller missiles for the army and navy, which bought instead from Israel. The army resisted buying its Akash surface-to-air missile for a decade but now recognizes that it is a success. After 30 years of work, the DRDO's Aeronautical Development Agency (ADA) has also failed (initially hampered by US sanctions that blocked component deliveries) to produce an acceptable version of a light combat aircraft called the Tejas to replace Russian MiG 21s.[40] HAL, which should be focusing on developing the technological and manufacturing capability to produce aircraft of Indian design, prefers to focus instead on building foreign fighters and other aircraft under licence where it has had a monopoly for decades. Russia's Sukhoi-30MKI, 'which was initially bought fully-built from Russia for Rs 30 crore per fighter, is now made by HAL (substantially from Russian systems and sub-systems) for well over 10 times that figure,' Shukla wrote in a report in December 2012 that went unchallenged.[41] 'Building expensively suits HAL well; since its profits are a percentage of production costs, higher costs mean higher profit.'

The development of the army's Arjun battle tank is a story of almost 40 years of delays, performance controversies, specification changes, increasing use of foreign components, and indecision about how many tanks to order or whether to abandon it.[42] The DRDO began work in 1974 and continued for 35 years till the tank entered service with an armoured regiment in 2009, during which time popular Russian tanks were used. Foreign component purchases still account for nearly 60 per cent of Arjun's production cost, and there is a strong lobby in the army which prefers Russia's old T-72s and more recent T-90s, even though the Arjun has done well in comparative desert trials against the T-90. Shukla argues that it is poor production facilities at the ordnance factories for the Arjun, and for the Tejas at HAL, that deter the army and air force from favouring Indian tanks and jets. 'The Tejas and the Arjun have a common problem: they are excellent indigenous designs that are undermined by poor production quality,' he wrote.[43]

The DRDO is now beginning to change under a new director general, Avinash Chander, who was appointed in June 2013. Previously in charge of the successful Agni missile programme, Chander has introduced top-line management responsibility for equipment development and production programmes by placing each of the DRDO's seven technology clusters under executive directors who have been moved from the organization's palatial Delhi headquarters to work in laboratories in Bengaluru, Hyderabad, Pune and elsewhere. They will no longer be advisers and co-coordinators, working separately from project managers, but will be responsible for projects developed by their laboratories. There is also a plan to build up India's export of equipment and partnerships with foreign manufacturers – the US is discussing jointly manufacturing anti-tank missiles in India and arranging for the DRDO to work with Lockheed Martin and Raytheon on future missile developments.

Private Sector

The public sector's dominant role was introduced when defence production was included in the Industrial Development Regulation Act of 1951. This was not changed by the 1991 reforms, but it was relaxed in 2001 when private ownership was formally allowed into defence manufacturing. Non-lethal items were opened up on a general basis, and lethal products were also released subject to licences issued case-by-case by the commerce ministry's Department of Industrial Policy and Promotion, with the approval of the defence ministry's Department of Defence Production. Foreign direct investment was also permitted up to 26 per cent of a company's equity. More than 26 per cent was allowed in 2006, but most applications were rejected (26 per cent is a significant figure in Indian company law because it gives an investor blocking rights on decisions since it can call emergency general meetings).

Little of significance happened in the following years because of opposition from the defence establishment. In 2005, a committee headed by Vijay Kelkar, a leading economist and government official and adviser, recommended, along with other reforms,[44] that the best private sector firms be given the status of Raksha Udyog Ratnas (defence industry jewels or champions). These companies would be treated by the government on an equal footing with DPSUs when allocating projects. In 2007, the ministry examined 40 companies and found 15 eligible including Larsen & Toubro (L&T), Godrej & Boyce, Tata Power SED (Strategic Engineering Division), the Mahindra group, and Tata Motors, together with information technology companies such as Tata Consultancy Services (TCS), Wipro, Infosys and HCL, and various public sector corporations that do not come under the DPSU classification.[45]

The private sector had been demonstrating its ability to produce the necessary sophisticated engineering as early as the 1950s and 1960s. That was when Godrej & Boyce, one of India's oldest family groups, built aluminium shells and research equipment for India's first nuclear reactor at Trombay. By the mid-1980s, it was making rocket parts for the country's space programme, along with L&T, a leading engineering construction company. These two firms had skilled welders, fabricators and engineers who enabled them also to become competitive internationally on pressure vessels and process equipment for the oil and petrochemical industries, which led to work on rockets and similar projects. 'We had skilled workmen who could do anything, fabricating sheet metal with precision machining and high-tech welding,' Jamshyd Godrej, chairman of the family-controlled company told me in 2007.[46] (Godrej's metal bashing and welding skills have produced thousands of more mundane office safes, filing cabinets and other metal products, and even made the world's last manual typewriters.)[47]

These two companies, and others such as Tata Power SED, developed similar skills and could therefore have been the basis, decades ago, of a flourishing international defence manufacturing industry, along with shipbuilders and others. This was stymied however, primarily by the defence establishment's opposition and its appetite for readily available imports. Significantly, India's development and production have thrived in areas such as nuclear science and rockets – as the Mars launch showed – where imports were not possible because of international bans on high-technology co-operation that continued till the 2009 deal with the US.

Indian companies had not been welcome in the West to participate in strategic programmes because of international worries over leakage of dual-use technologies, and America's space agency, NASA, would not consider working with them, explained Godrej. That boycott was strengthened by bans imposed after India's two nuclear tests in 1974 and 1998, and so 'we were isolated', he said. Illustrating the private sector's potential, the company is now contributing to building the Indo-Russian Brahmos missiles and supplying space and defence customers in the US, Europe, UK and Israel, in addition to India.

There was an early breakthrough for companies in 2006, when the army awarded two $20m contracts for rocket launchers to be used in its Pinaka missile system to Tata Power SED and L&T. This was the first time that private-sector Indian companies had been appointed as prime contractors on a defence project, however small, with overall responsibility for system integration. Tata and L&T had begun design work on the launchers for the DRDO 17 years earlier, in 1989, but had to wait till policy changes began to catch up with the army's needs for rapidly advancing technology. 'Like Israel, India has the right skills and low-cost design and testing capabilities to compete internationally,' Rahul Chaudhry, chief executive of the Tata company told me at the time.[48]

These and other companies, however, needed assurance of a flow of orders before they would commit investment and resources to product development, and they also needed help with research costs, none of which was forthcoming till recently. Government officials sometimes suggest that the private sector should have bid for contracts abroad to offset uncertainty at home, but companies were loath to shoulder the risks in highly competitive and complex export markets when they had not already developed expertise and sales in India. Some now admit that they should probably have acquired foreign defence manufacturers to gain access to technology and new markets, as the Indian auto industry has done, for example, most notably with Tata Motors buying Britain's Jaguar-Land Rover business from Ford of the US, but these groups had other priorities.

The Raksha Udyog Ratnas proposal would have given the companies the confidence to build capability in India and maybe abroad but, faced with strident opposition, A.K. Antony shelved the proposal in 2010 after he took over from Mukherjee, who had appeared to be in favour. Antony did so partly in response to complaints from the DPSUs, but there was also pressure from smaller private sector defence equipment companies, which argued that they would lose out. The crucial opposition, however, came from three trade union federations linked to Congress, the BJP and the CPI(M), which most unusually united to argue against the Kelkar proposals and especially the one on Raksha Udyog Ratnas.[49] Antony found these complaints irresistible, thus halting the most quickly implementable of reforms. The only proposal that went ahead was to introduce 'offset clauses' in projects that require foreign suppliers to buy 30 per cent of a contract in India, but Antony bowed to foreign pressure and watered down the plans that could have forced foreign suppliers to transfer significant technology.

Private sector progress has also been hampered by a lack of lobbying pressure in Delhi, where the heads of groups such as Tata, L&T and Mahindra have other, higher priority battles to fight. That could change if Mukesh Ambani, who runs Reliance Industries and has more influential muscle than the current private sector line up, succeeds in his ambitions to enter defence and become India's biggest private sector aerospace manufacturer. As a former defence ministry official said at a private meeting attended by a Reliance executive, 'We do expect things to change now you are here!'

He was referring to Reliance being chosen by Dassault of France as its Indian manufacturing partner on a $10–15bn contract for the 126 medium multi-role combat aircraft that Boeing and Lockheed lost.[50] Reliance's ambition to become a leader in a market where it has no experience by manufacturing Dassault's Rafale jets took the industry by surprise in 2012, but it was typical of the Ambani style and it could be a success because Reliance has ample cash reserves for

investment. Mukesh Ambani also has proven strengths in government
lobbying, though they are not as all-enveloping as they used to be.
The group is strong in engineering, albeit in building oil refineries
and petrochemical plants, not advanced mechanical engineering
products like aircraft. The proposed deal inevitably upset Hindustan
Aeronautics, which had assumed it would automatically be the main
manufacturing partner, as it has always been in the past for foreign
aircraft. That Dassault thought otherwise – the company said it was
not prepared to be responsible for the quality of HAL's work – was
an indication of HAL's declining reputation and of problems that
other foreign manufacturers have had with its poor performance.

Foreign Equity

It became evident during these years that big foreign defence
companies were not willing to commit advanced designs, management
time and money in joint ventures when they could only have a 26
per cent equity stake. There have been many link-ups between major
international companies from the US, UK, Israel and elsewhere with
Indian defence, engineering and software companies, but these are
more concerned with meeting requirements on the 'offset clauses',
and laying the foundations for later possible developments, than for
any significant current technology and manufacturing transfers.

In June 2010 and again in 2013, the commerce ministry proposed
a much higher foreign equity level of up to 100 per cent. Many
Indian companies and industry federations wanted 49 per cent
so that they could attract foreign investors and know-how, while
maintaining control of their companies and avoiding the risk of new
partners dominating boardrooms and changing management styles
and cultures. Against this, there were understandable concerns that,
even with the high equity levels, foreign governments could block
technology transfers on an item-by-item basis. That would have
meant that foreign companies had the benefit of higher equity stakes
without having to hand over technology. On balance, the industry

mood was for the 26 per cent to be raised to 49 per cent on a case-by-case basis, with safeguards against some countries, presumably China, together with other security-related restrictions including an ability to block takeovers.[51] This was resisted by Antony and the defence establishment, but the government eventually announced in July 2013 that the existing case-by-case rule for more than 26 per cent limit would be relaxed up to 49 per cent for what was called 'state-of-the-art' technology.[52] This looked significant at first glance, but it was so unspecific that it gave the defence establishment ample opportunity to block most applications and was unlikely to attract any significant foreign response.

Another whiff of reforms had come in 2011 with a revised defence purchasing procedure (known as DPP-2011). This picked up an idea broached in 2006 for a range of 'buy and make' categories that would enable the Indian private sector to become more involved, transferring technology from abroad that would then be used and developed in India with the help of government finance. Uncharacteristically, Antony implemented this in July 2012 when, after long delays, the Indian Army invited the private sector to compete against DPSUs for the design and development of a $2bn (Rs10,000 crore) internet-based project called the tactical battlefield communication system. The government would cover 80 per cent of development costs and the remaining 20 per cent would come from the private and public sector companies.[53] The US and other countries use the same sort of 'make' procedure, but the Indian defence establishment had lobbied strenuously against it, especially on this project. Bharat Electronics, a DPSU, wanted exclusive rights so that it could prove itself on advanced internet technology, though it would have almost certainly merely imported a massive amount of technology and components without India gaining any real know-how. The companies involved were L&T, Tata Power SED and HCL, competing against Bharat Electronics. The battle was far from over, however. Progress on awarding the contract has been slow, as have similar plans for a 'futuristic infantry combat vehicle' (FICV).

Antony began to acknowledge that the private sector should have a greater role from February 2013, when he came under pressure over the latest of a string of corruption cases on foreign defence contracts that eventually upset a planned $750m order with Finmeccanica of Italy for 12 British-made Augusta-Westland 'VVIP' helicopters. This case, which began with corruption investigations in Italy, drew Indian media attention to the 70 per cent import figure and led Antony to promise changes.[54]

The outlines of what might happen were announced in April 2013,[55] when the defence ministry admitted at last that 'the only way forward for the country is rapid indigenization of defence products, with both the public and the private sectors playing pivotal roles in this endeavour'. Preference would be given 'for indigenous procurement' with 'global cases being a choice of last resort'. It was not clear how much change this would generate, mainly because Indian-made aircraft, ships, tanks and guns would not be available unless foreign defence manufacturers and technology were attracted into the country with relaxed equity investment regulations. That was followed by a new defence purchasing procedure (DPP-2013) that aimed to boost private sector involvement by sharpening the definition of 'indigenous content' so that foreign components were not used by the DPSUs in supposedly Indian-made equipment.[56] There were also proposals for the defence establishment to share advance information on armed forces' requirement with industry, and to identify procedural entry points where companies could be involved in purchasing decisions.

It seemed, therefore, that reforms were on the way that would begin to correct some of the failings that have seriously impeded India's defence preparedness. But, once again, the momentum was swiftly dissipated and little more was done by Antony. The new defence minister appointed after the 2014 general election should make a difference, and Narendra Modi, the BJP's prime ministerial candidate, has talked about strengthening India's defences and opening up manufacturing to the private sector, especially in Gujarat.

But whoever has the next stab at reforms will find that the defence establishment is adept at stymieing changes.

Defence Graft

Corruption on India's defence deals is as old as the country's independence. Historians point to the army jeep scandal in 1948 as the first example. It involved V.K. Krishna Menon, India's high commissioner in London, who later became ambassador to the United Nations and Nehru's powerful defence minister. While he was the high commissioner, he organised a Rs 80 lakh contract with a UK company for 2,000 reconditioned jeeps, but only 155 were delivered. Menon was also involved in similar failed contracts for rifles and American B25 Mitchell bombers.[57] Official inquiries on the jeeps criticized the contract, which became highly controversial, but the government unilaterally closed the case in 1955 and Menon became a cabinet minister the following year.

The payment of bribes was dramatically revealed in 2001 when *Tehelka* (then a news website) ran a sting that filmed Bangaru Laxman, who was the BJP president, accepting Rs 1 lakh in cash as a kickback.[58] Others, including senior army officers, were also caught on film in the sting, which was called Operation West End after the name of a fictitious London-based company seeking sales for its thermal imaging binoculars. Laxman was jailed for four years in 2012 when he was 72, but was released on bail.[59] This was a rare case of a conviction for defence corruption – it has been the only one successfully achieved by the CBI out of 22 defence cases in eight years.[60]

Bribes and extortion are now an integral part of a self-serving and highly corrupt system where money is paid at all levels from a few hundred rupees to defence ministry clerks for moving files (or delaying those of competitors) to millions of dollars paid to politicians and officials responsible for placing large defence orders. There are various points in the purchasing procedure at which corruption kicks in.

When specifications are being drawn up, companies try to influence the choice of technologies and the wording of requirements so as to better their prospects and eliminate competitors. The next points are when companies are being selected for inclusion in formal requests for information, proposals and tenders, and then the conduct and reporting on field trials. That is followed by final shortlists and examination of technical and financial bids and the eventual award of the contract.

The largest, well-established companies do not usually have to pay bribes at the initial stages, though newcomers and smaller businesses do often need to persuade officers around the rank of a lieutenant colonel in the army to be included. Substantial payments are often needed for smaller and medium-size firms to be put on component-supplier lists by DPSUs and research organisations. This is especially significant if officials are to be persuaded not to go out to tender and only deal with a single supplier, which accounts for about 70–80 per cent of public sector orders.[61]

This happens in many countries, of course, and is probably worse in some, not least in Russia where officials expect to be paid bribes for supplying products as well as placing contracts. In India, the system has become so embedded that it is dragging down both the ethos and the military effectiveness of the armed services.

Bofors and Others

When I first came to India in the early 1980s and Indira Gandhi was the prime minister, there was gossip over who might have been involved, in Paris as well as Delhi, during the handling of alleged large-scale bribes on a big contract with Dassault of France for Mirage fighters, and on a 1981 order for four $150m submarines with HDW of Germany. The assumption, which seemed to be acceptable publicly, was that bribes were collected for Congress party funds, but that Gandhi did not personally benefit. She was believed to have a very small group of three or four people including a top minister, an official in her office, and a businessman located abroad who handled the money discretely and secretly in Delhi, London and maybe Switzerland. Sanjay Gandhi was also sometimes rumoured to be involved. In May 1987, I wrote in the *Financial Times* that Congress had 'increasingly relied on large kick-backs from defence and other international contracts for party funds', and that Sanjay Gandhi 'was believed to have orchestrated this for his mother before he died in a light aircraft crash a few days before the submarine deal was finalised in 1981'.[62]

Kickbacks ranging from 5 per cent to 10 per cent, I wrote, were assumed to have been paid to the Congress, irrespective of 'whether they were paid in India, into Swiss bank accounts, or were laundered in some way'. Having gained specific information from defence companies, I added, 'virtually every big contract was assumed to include such arrangements, and companies often knew whom to expect as the collector ... often the middlemen were assumed to be creaming off some cash for themselves, while individual ministers and top bureaucrats also made their own demands'. On one deal I heard directly about, the London collector said to the company chairman, 'do involve me from the beginning of your negotiations next time'.

The Mirage and HDW deals were eclipsed in 1987 by India's longest running and politically most significant defence scandal that arose while Rajiv Gandhi was prime minister, after India placed a $1.4bn contract in 1986 for 400 155mm howitzer guns with Bofors of Sweden.[63] This led to allegations of Rs 64 crore (then about $50m) bribes, which was a tiny amount compared with today's massive billion-dollar corruption, but the case has reverberated ever since through India's political system and the courts. It contributed to the defeat of Gandhi's government in 1989 because of suspicions (denied and unproven) that those close to him may have benefited, and it has embarrassed the Nehru-Gandhi dynasty for years.

When he came to power in 1984, Sanjay having died three years earlier, Rajiv disbanded the group of three or four people that had been handling his mother's arrangements. This may have helped the Bofors scandal to become so significant – possibly because the new arrangements were not so secure, or because someone who had been involved encouraged leaks. Statements made in recent years by retired government officials in India and Sweden who were involved at the time suggest that, even if he was innocent himself, Rajiv knew who had received Bofors' bribes and that he did nothing to stop it. MPs gleefully pointed out in the 1980s that the code name for one of the Swiss bank accounts used for the bribes was Lotus, which in Sanskrit means Rajiv.[64]

No one claimed that the wrong guns had been chosen – indeed, they have served India well, especially in the 1999 Kargil border war with Pakistan in Kashmir. The alleged crime was that money had been paid to middlemen to facilitate the deal. The accusations were first made by Swedish Radio and became a scandal in that country, which helped to keep the story alive in India where it was led by two campaigning newspaper editors, Arun Shourie of *The Indian Express* and N. Ram of *The Hindu*. It was alleged that Ottavio Quattrocchi, an Italian executive then based in Delhi for Snamprogetti, who with his wife was close to Rajiv and Sonia Gandhi, acted as a middleman in the deal and received kickbacks. Quattrocchi denied this but was behaving at the time as though he had an inside track on fertiliser plant, gas pipeline and other contracts, where Snamprogetti did controversially well. After long legal battles, including attempts to bring him back to India, the inquiries were closed and cases against him were dismissed in 2011. He died in 2013, underlining the closure.[65]

Unbanned Agents

The specific point on which the Bofors saga blew up was that Rajiv Gandhi, in an attempt to clean up corruption, had banned the use of agents and the payment of commissions on defence deals (though this did not rule out employment of consultants to fix appointments).[66]

That was, as it turned out, one of his most well-meant but useless moves. Many agents are well-known and are so visible that it makes a mockery of the government's official line since then that they do not – or should not – exist. Prime Minister Manmohan Singh said in 2006 that, since agents could not be eliminated, they should perhaps be recognized. As increasingly became the case with his remarks, however, no one did anything.[67] General V.P. Malik, a former chief of army staff, said that foreign firms in particular 'needed someone they can authorize and say is their agent'. But the present muddle suits the vested interests, who seem not to want to register and formalize their work. It also benefits other players in the defence establishment – and enables successive governments to embarrass their predecessors with allegations of corruption.

The main agent named in the Bofors case was Win Chaddha and his Delhi-based company Anatronic. Admiral S.M. Nanda, a high-profile and controversial chief of naval staff from 1970 to 1973, who led the bombing of the Pakistani city of Karachi in the 1971 India-Pakistan war,[68] was named (though he denied involvement) in the HDW scandal that arose after German officials told India a seven per cent commission had been paid to agents.[69] When he left the navy, Nanda headed the state-owned Shipping Corporation of India and then, after retirement, he founded a firm that initially dealt with offshore oil drilling and engineering deals, and later broadened into defence. His companies were called GlobalTech, Crown Corporation and Eureka and he was joined by his son Suresh, also a former Indian navy officer. In 2003, the family bought Claridges, a medium-sized up-market colonial-style hotel in central Delhi for Rs 930 crore (then about $25m) and three other hotels.

Also well known is Sudhir 'Bunny' Choudhrie, whose family originally worked with the Nandas and who figured in the *Tehelka* sting. London-based, he has close links with Israeli defence companies and with Russia's Sukhoi aircraft manufacturer,[70] and was named in 2013 in Italian courts as an agent for Finmeccanica on the VVIP helicopter corruption scandal involving Finmeccanica's Augusta

Westland company.[71] He was one of the early investors in Air Deccan,[72] a short-lived budget airline, and in Alpha Technologies, a Bengaluru-based defence equipment manufacturer with Israeli and other joint ventures. His C&C Alpha Group has real estate and hotel businesses.[73] He hit UK news headlines (including a BBC television programme)[74] in 2010 for having donated £750,000 to the Liberal-Democratic Party.

Others involved in defence deals include the London-based India-born (originally Iran-based), Hinduja family, whose name was linked to the Bofors and HDW deals, though they denied involvement. In Delhi, prominent names include Chetan Seth, a garrulous Delhi partygoer who is best known as India's only Cuban cigar importer and runs the Chemon Group that combines a foreign agent's work with production of defence equipment. They also include Vipin Khanna and Abhishek Verma, who was jailed for two years over leaks from the Indian navy. Verma has since then figured in various defence deals with German, Israeli and other companies and has been charged for revealing secret information.[75]

In October 2006, the government-controlled CBI raided 35 agents' premises in Delhi and other cities over a $269m contract placed with Israeli Aircraft Industries for Barak missile systems during the previous BJP-led coalition government. It subsequently registered cases against George Fernandes, the coalition's defence minister and leader of the small north Indian Samata Party. Also charged were Jaya Jaitley, a close friend of Fernandes and a former Samata president, and Admiral Sushil Kumar, a retired chief of naval staff. The CBI alleged that payments included Rs 20m had been given to Jaitley, and that the admiral had 'colluded' by favouring the Barak in preference to the Trishul missile system that was then being developed by the DRDO. The Indian navy was content with the Israeli missiles, and in January 2006 a $350m deal was struck for the DRDO and Israel jointly to develop a long-range Barak air defence system for use by the two countries' navies.[76]

'In addition to long-existing networks with names like Khanna,

Nanda and Choudhrie, foreign agents have flourished for decades, fattening on the capital city's cocktail circuit in apparent disregard of visa regulations or immigration controls,' says Ajai Shukla, a former army officer and defence specialist.[77] 'Although these agents (and others too numerous to be named) operate quite openly in India, it could legitimately be asked why the government has never taken action against them. The answer, according to a top government official, is that "MoD officials, and even political parties, do not want to stop the flow of funds that comes from these people. This is a gravy train and the money is distributed widely… to individuals as well as to political parties across the spectrum".'

Shukla also mentioned 'two expatriates, Swiss-American citizen, Guido Haschke, and British citizen, Christian Michel' who had been 'named by Italian prosecutors as key players in bribing Indian officials on the Augusta-Westland helicopter deal. 'Christian Michel, who runs Panama-registered Keyser Incorporated, has never bothered to hide his profession,' wrote Shukla. 'In 2004, he actually sued French aviation company, Dassault, for failing to pay him commission in New Delhi's Euro 350m purchase of ten Mirage-2000 fighters in the year 2000. The French court threw out his lawsuit, ruling that his agreement with Dassault had expired two years before the deal was concluded'.

Blacklisting

Corruption allegations have led to long lists of foreign companies being blacklisted, sometimes in the middle of contracts, which has seriously undermined the modernization of the armed forces for many years. Manufacture of Germany's HDW submarines and delivery of Sweden's Bofors' howitzer guns and ammunition were hit after corruption scandals in the 1980s. South Africa's Denel company was blacklisted in 2005 when it was supplying technology for howitzer ammunition after it was discovered it had paid UK-based agents on an earlier rifles order. In 2006, the defence ministry issued a list of 118 defence suppliers in India and abroad that had been banned, including some named by DPSUs.[78]

In March 2012, A.K. Antony, the defence minister, put a ten-year ban on six defence firms originally blacklisted in 2009 after the head of India's ordnance factories was accused of accepting bribes. The firms included Singapore Technologies Kinetic (STK) which was involved with supplies of howitzer guns and small arms, Israeli Military Industries with ammunition for Bofors guns, Germany's Rheinmetall Air Defence with land systems, and a Russian corporation with military systems. The most serious effect of these bans and other delays is that India has not had new artillery guns since the 1980s, that there have been shortages of ammunition and spare parts, and that ordnance factories delayed manufacturing Bofors guns in a factory at Jabalpur in central India for over 20 years.

Antony used these bans to protect his reputation of not being corrupt, and ignored the seriously negative impact it was having on supplies of military equipment. Eventually he was heavily criticized in 2013 when he reacted to the Finmeccanica helicopters' corruption allegations by warning that the Augusta-Westland contract might be cancelled, even though he had been ignoring public rumours of the alleged bribes for nearly a year till the news of the case in Italy built up in India. Only three of the urgently needed 12 VVIP helicopters had been delivered when payments to Augusta Westland stopped, as were deliveries of further helicopters, and the company began arbitration proceedings.[79] The contract was then terminated by Antony. Tenders for 197 military helicopters on a $1.5bn potential order, which had been stuck by a series of controversies for many years, also looked vulnerable because of allegations that an army brigadier in charge of field trials had asked for a $5m bribe from the company though, by the time this was publicized, Augusta-Westland had been ruled out of the competition on other grounds.[80] This led to calls for Antony to rethink the government's policy, with suggestions that the defence ministry should impose penalties on a foreign company while continuing to accept delivery of orders.

In addition to Antony's sensitivities, the continuing stream of corruption allegations has slowed down the award of contracts because officials became wary of signing off on large sensitive orders, fearing similar (true or false) bribe scandals that might erupt, maybe many years later. That fear reached crisis proportions under Antony, who proverbially tilted at windmills every time there was a hint of corruption. One solution would be for more contracts to be placed on a government-to-government basis without competitive tendering. That is sometimes done with Russian orders (though it does not eliminate bribes), and it has been done for a large proportion of the $11bn defence orders placed in recent years for US equipment.

Pakistan and China must surely enjoy watching India imposing all this self-inflicted damage on its war readiness and relish the thought that they themselves could not do much more harm in a border war. Indeed, an arch conspiracy theorist would suggest that agents working for these two countries might be engineering some of the setbacks – and maybe they are.

Notes

1. 'Rise in international arms transfers is driven by Asian demand', Stockholm International Peace Research Institute (SIPRI), 19 March 2012, http://www.sipri.org/media/pressreleases/2012/rise-in-international-arms-transfers-is-driven-by-asian-demand-says-sipri

2. 'Why China Snubs Russia Arms', *The Diplomat*, 5 April 2010, http://thediplomat.com/2010/04/05/why-china-snubs-russian-arms/?all=true . In April 2013, an article on the same website suggested China might be about to re-start buying Russian arms http://thediplomat.com/2013/04/12/a-russia-china-alliance-brewing/2/

3. Annual Report to Congress: Military and Security Developments Involving the People's Republic of China 2013, Office of the Secretary of Defense, http://www.defense.gov/pubs/2013_China_Report_FINAL.pdf – with a summary here: DOD Report on China Details Military Modernization, American Forces Press Service, 6 May 2013 *http://www.defense.gov/news/newsarticle.aspx?id=119943*

328 IMPLOSION

4. SIPRIasaboveand'ChinareplacesBritaininworld'stopfivearmsexporters', Reuters, 18 March 2013, http://www.reuters.com/article/2013/03/18/us-china-arms-exports-idUSBRE92G0L120130318

5. Shivshankar Menon, National Security Adviser, 'Our ability to change India in a globalised world', The Prem Bhatia Memorial Lecture, IIC, New Delhi 11 August 2011, Full text on http://www.prembhatiatrust.com/ click on Lecture 16.

6. 'India army chief says nation's defences obsolete', BBC, 28 March 2012, http://www.bbc.co.uk/news/world-asia-india-17532836

7. 'India will depend on US for military hardware', Rediff.com, 6 February 2010, http://news.rediff.com/slide-show/2010/feb/06/slide-show-1-india-will-have-to-depend-on-us-for-military-hardware.htm

8. http://ridingtheelephant.wordpress.com/2012/04/04/army-intrigue-and-graft-hits-indias-defences/

9. Manoj Joshi, 'Wheels Within Wheels', *Mail Today*, 28 March 2012

10. Arindam Bhattacharya and Navneet Vasishth, 'Creating a Vibrant Domestic Defence Manufacturing Sector', BCG-CII, March 2012, http://www.ciidefence.com/pdf/Creating%20a%20Vibrant%20Domestic%20Defence%20Manufacturing%20Sector%20V5.pdf

11. 'Defence imports affects National Security, Foreign Policy', speech by Minister of State for Defence M.M. Pallam Raju at seminar on 'The Indian Army: Next Generation Systems, An Evolution', 16 February 2010, http://pib.nic.in/newsite/erelease.aspx?relid=57904

12. https://ridingtheelephant.wordpress.com/2010/02/23/the-gun-that-has-crippled-the-equipping-of-india%E2%80%99s-armed-forces-is-%E2%80%9Cinnocent%E2%80%9D/

13. Gurmeet Kanwal, *India's Military Modernization: Plans And Strategic Underpinnings,* The National Bureau of Asian Research, Washington DC, September 2012, http://www.nbr.org/downloads/pdfs/Outreach/NBR_IndiaCaucus_September2012.pdf

14. James Hardy, 'India's Defense Procurement Bungles', *The Diplomat*, 27 October 2013, http://thediplomat.com/2013/10/27/indias-defense-procurement-bungles-2/

15. 'With no Indian orders, BAE Systems starts shutdown of M777 gun factory', *Business Standard*, 18 October 2013, http://www.business-standard.com/article/economy-policy/with-no-indian-orders-bae-systems-starts-shutdown-of-m777-gun-factory-113101800028_1.html

16. Government media release on http://pib.nic.in/newsite/erelease. aspx?relid=82906. This news website report also has more information on pending orders and production http://www.rediff.com/news/ report/one-hundred-seventy-one-pilots-39-civilians-killed-so-far-in-482-mig-crashes/20120502.htm

17. 'MiG-21 not widow-maker but trusted flying companion', *The Times of India*, 5 May 2013 http://articles.timesofindia.indiatimes. com/2013-05-05/india/39042282_1_pilot-error-aircraft-mig-21s

18. Ajai Shukla, 'IAF crashes lose one fighter squadron every 2 yrs', *Broadsword*, 21 March 2013 http://ajaishukla.blogspot.in/2013/03/ iaf-crashes-lose-one-fighter-squadron.html

19. Ajai Shukla, INS Vikrant's first victory: being built from Indian steel, *Broadsword,* 8 August 2013, http://ajaishukla.blogspot.in/2013/08/ ins-vikrants-first-victory-being-built.html and http://ajaishukla. blogspot.in/2013/08/an-eagle-in-borrowed-feathers.html

20. Ajai Shukla, 'The voyage of the Vikrant – The aircraft carrier is a result of the Indian Navy's quest for an affordable but potent vessel', *Business Standard*, 16 August 2013, http://www.business-standard.com/article/ beyond-business/the-voyage-of-the-vikrant-113081601151_1.html

21. In conversation with JE, August 2013

22. Report no. PA 5 of 2008, Union Government, Defence Services, Air Force and Navy Performance Audit, CAG of India, http://www.agap. cag.gov.in/GSSA/PDF_Files/brochure_on_CAG_Audit_Reports.pdf

23. SIPRI (www.sipri.org) produces the SIPRI Arms Transfers Database http://www.sipri.org/databases/armstransfers of international defence trade figures with Trend Indicator Values (TIVs) for country-by-country imports and exports based on deliveries at constant 1990 prices – http://armstrade.sipri.org/armstrade/html/export_values. php – with an explanation on http://www.sipri.org/databases/ armstransfers/background

24. US-India Business Council estimate, April 2013

25. https://ridingtheelephant.wordpress.com/2011/04/28/india-takes-a-nam-route-on-11bn-fighter-contract/

26. 'India investment in the US 2008-2010', FICCI-Ernest & Young, June 2010, http://203.200.89.92/invindia/indian_investment_studies.pdf

27. In conversation with JE March 2013

28. Manoj Joshi, 'The record of our arms industry remains one of

failure and disappointment', *Mail Today*, 30 April 2013, http://www.dailymail.co.uk/indiahome/indianews/article-2307125/THE-BIGGER-PICTURE-The-record-Indias-arms-industry-remains-failure-disappointment.html#ixzz2Rwjv4hIR

29. Discussions on 'Chatham House rules' at the Observer Research Foundation, Delhi, April 2013

30. Commodore C. Uday Bhaskar is former officiating Director of Institute for Defence Studies and Analyses, New Delhi (IDSA)

31. 'Three Years Of UPA II – An Open letter to Defence Minister', C. Uday Bhaskar, 20 May 2012, https://groups.google.com/forum/?fromgroups=#!topic/progressive-interactions/92OPy5fxRgY

32. Stephen P. Cohen and Sunil Dasgupta, *Arming Without Aiming: India's Military Modernization*, hardback, August 2010, paperback with new preface, pp ix-x, February 2013, Brookings Institution Press, Washington DC: 2013, http://www.barnesandnoble.com/w/arming-without-aiming-stephen-p-cohen/1101141747. Penguin India edition planned

33. 'Indigenising defence production: The necessary goal is', *Business Standard* and *Blogspot,* 8 March 2013 http://ajaishukla.blogspot.in/

34. 'Creating a Vibrant Domestic Defence Manufacturing Sector', as above

35. Annual Survey of Industries, Ministry of Finance, New Delhi

36. Manoj Joseph, 'The record of our arms industry remains one of failure and disappointment', *Mail Today*, 10 April 2013, http://www.dailymail.co.uk/indiahome/indianews/article-2307125/THE-BIGGER-PICTURE-The-record-Indias-arms-industry-remains-failure-disappointment.html

37. 'The secret world of DRDO', *New Indian Express*, 2 September 2012, http://newindianexpress.com/magazine/article598145.ece

38. Ajai Shukla, 'India's Defence Industrial Base is Changing with the Times', published November 2013 by the Royal United Services Institute for Defence and Security Studies (RUSI), London, http://www.rusi.org/publications/newsbrief/

39. Ibid

40. 'Tejas will not be ready for war before end-2015', *The Times of India*, 4 June 2013, http://articles.timesofindia.indiatimes.com/2013-06-04/india/39739543_1_tejas-lca-20-tejas-tejas-mark-ii

41. Ajai Shukla, 'Making the Tejas fly', *Business Standard*, 11 December 2012, http://www.business-standard.com/article/opinion/ajai-shukla-making-the-tejas-fly-112121100124_1.html

42. 'India Reverses Gear, Puts Arjun Tank Back in Production', *Defense Industry Daily*, 28 January 2013 http://www.defenseindustrydaily.com/india-plans-to-cap-arjun-tank-production-04984/

43. Ajai Shukla, 'Making the Tejas fly', as above

44. 'Kelkar Committee submits report on defence acquisition', MoD press release, 5 April 2005, http://pib.nic.in/newsite/erelease.aspx?relid=8386

45. http://ridingtheelephant.wordpress.com/2007/06/07/doors-to-open-for-india%E2%80%99s-defense-industry-jewels/

46. JE, 'Manufacturing takes off in India', *Fortune* magazine, 19 October 2007, http://money.cnn.com/2007/10/18/news/international/India_manufacturing.fortune/

47. 'Typewriters about to become a page in history', *Business Standard*, 17 April 2011 http://www.business-standard.com/article/beyond-business/typewriters-about-to-become-a-page-in-history-111041700035_1.html

48. 'India's defence industry, The private sector to the rescue, Technology outguns bureaucracy', *The Economist*, 6 April 2006, http://www.economist.com/node/6775113

49. 'TU Leaders Meet Defence Minister And Demand "Review Kelkar Committee Recommendations"', *People's Democracy*, CPI(M), 3 June 2007, http://pd.cpim.org/2007/0603/06102007_kelkar.htm

50. 'Rafale Partners with Reliance', Indian Defence.com, 2 December 2012, http://www.indiandefence.com/forums/indian-air-force/14774-rafale-partners-reliance.html and *Will Mukesh Ambani's defence aerospace gambit pay off for RIL?*, *Economic Times*, 12 May 2013, http://articles.economictimes.indiatimes.com/2013-05-12/news/39187189_1_indian-aerospace-reliance-industries-ltd-boeing-india

51. http://ridingtheelephant.wordpress.com/2010/08/16/indian-industry-sensibly-wants-curbs-on-big-fdi-in-defence-manufacturing/

52. 'More than 26% FDI in defence was allowed since 2006', *Economic Times*, 18 July 2013, http://articles.economictimes.indiatimes.com/2013-07-18/news/40657308_1_fdi-policy-defence-procurement-policy-defence-equipment

53. http://ridingtheelephant.wordpress.com/2012/07/02/indian-private-sector-gets-first-big-defence-industry-opportunity/

54. 'Why government has failed to encourage private sector in defence production', *Economic Times*, 19 March 2013 http://economictimes.indiatimes.com/news/news-by-company/corporate-trends/why-government-has-failed-to-encourage-private-sector-in-defence-production/articleshow/19052685.cms

55. 'DAC Approves Major Changes in DPP to Encourage Indian Defence Industry', Ministry of Defence media statement, 20 April 2013, http://pib.nic.in/newsite/erelease.aspx?relid=94799

56. 'Salient Features of Defence Procurement Procedure 2013', MoD media statement, 1 June 2013 http://pib.nic.in/newsite/erelease.aspx?relid=96361

57. S.S. Gill, *The Pathology of Corruption*, p. 48-49, HarperCollins Publishers India, Delhi, 1998-9

58. 'Operation West End: A story of how the suitcase people are compromising Indian defence' *Tehelka's* transcripts, http://archive.tehelka.com/channels/Investigation/investigation1.htm

59. http://www.thehindu.com/news/national/hc-grants-bail-to-bangaru-laxman-in-fake-defence-deal-case/article3987524.ece

60. 'CBI secures one conviction among 22 defence cases since 2004', *The Times of India*, 23 February 2013, http://timesofindia.indiatimes.com/india/CBI-secures-one-conviction-among-22-defence-cases-since-2004/articleshow/18636470.cms

61. Information gathered in many interviews by JE

62. Ibid

63. 'Bofors: The Complete Timeline', tracking events from 1985 to 2012, *NewsLaundry* blog, http://www.newslaundry.com/2012/06/bofors-the-complete-timeline/

64. JE, Gandhi's new broom fails to sweep clean, *Financial Times*, 6 May 1987

65. 'Ottavio Quattrocchi dies in Milan, Bofors buried', *Hindustan Times*, 13 July 2013, http://www.hindustantimes.com/world-news/Europe/Ottavio-Quattrocchi-dies-in-Milan-Bofors-buried/Article1-1092062.aspx

66. Ibid

67. 'Arms sales in India, Scandalous procurement, Round up the usual suspects', *The Economist*, 19 October 2006, http://www.economist.com/node/8058443

68. Admiral S.M. Nanda, *The Man who Bombed Karachi*, HarperCollins India, 2005

69. 'The Man In The Middle – The Nandas' links with the establishment helped them get around the ban on arms brokers', *Outlook* magazine, 28 March 2001, http://m.outlookindia.com/story.aspx?sid=4&aid=211156

70. 'Key missile deal agent has stake in Sukhoi', *DNA*, 7 April 2009, http://www.dnaindia.com/india/1245901/report-key-missile-deal-agent-has-stake-in-sukhoi

71. 'Arms dealer Bunny linked to Finmeccanica, *The Times of India*, 16 February 2013, http://articles.timesofindia.indiatimes.com/2013-02-16/india/ 37133043_1_defence-industry-vvip-helicopter-sudhir-choudhrie

72. Deccan Aviation Prospectus, 31 May 2006, http://www.sebi.gov.in/dp/deccandrhp.pdf

73. Group website http://www.ccalphagroup.co.uk/about_us.html

74. 'Liberal Democrat donor "was in arms deal probe"', BBC, 17 September 2010, http://news.bbc.co.uk/2/hi/programmes/newsnight/9010172.stm

75. 'CBI chargesheets arms dealer Abhishek Verma, wife, firm & ex-IAF man in OS Act case', PTI, 30 November 2012 http://articles.timesofindia.indiatimes.com/2012-11-30/india/35484012_1_c-edmond-allen-anca-maria-neacsu-verma-and-anca , and *Tehelka* magazine, 3 March 2013, http://www.tehelka.com/abhishek-verma-the-dealers-deceit/

76. 'India & Israel's Barak SAM Development Project(s)', *Defense Industry Daily*, 24 January 2013, http://www.defenseindustrydaily.com/india-israel-introducing-mr-sam-03461/

77. 'AgustaWestland AW-101: A choppy deal', *Business Standard*, 16 February 2013, and on Ajai Shukla's blog http://ajaishukla.blogspot.in/2013/02/agustawestland-aw-101-choppy-deal.html

78. 'Govt issues blacklist of 118 defence suppliers', *Indian Express*, 8 June 2006, http://www.indianexpress.com/news/govt-issues-blacklist-of-118-defence-suppliers/6000/0#sthash.xA4I0TVC.dpuf

79. 'Reports of violating VVIP copter contract premature: AgustaWestland

– Says legal processes looking into this matter have not been completed, after reports that Antony called the chopper maker guilty', *Business Standard*, 1 November 2013 http://www.business-standard.com/article/current-affairs/agustawestland-bares-fangs-to-mod-in-vvip-helicopter-cancellation-113103101005_1.html

80. 'Bribe charges in another copter deal', *The Times of India*, 3 April 2013, http://articles.timesofindia.indiatimes.com/2013-04-03/india/38247493_ 1_vvip-helicopter-deal-agustawestland-guido-haschke

18

Scam Andhra

Jawaharlal Nehru once described Hyderabad as a microcosm of Indian culture. He was praising it for its blending of culture and religion. Today it can still be seen as a microcosm of the country's culture – for the negative reason that the good India's first prime minister saw at the time of independence has been squandered by the corruption and illicit links between companies and government that are now part of India's political and business landscape.

A decade or so ago, Hyderabad – and the state of Andhra Pradesh whose capital it is – was a focal point in southern India of a booming information technology industry. It had become an international symbol of a country that saw itself growing into a world superpower alongside China. Bill Clinton visited it in 2000 when he was US President, marking Hyderabad's emergence as India's second high-technology centre after Bengaluru. Bill Gates of Microsoft, which set up its main India research facility in a new software zone along with Google, was not far behind, plus many others.

Now the city has become a symbol of what is wrong with India. It embraces dynastic political ambitions based on personal greed and the lauding of companies that have grown fat on fraudulent land and other deals, literally plundering the state's wealth. The trend first became widely noticed in 2009, when the Hyderabad-based Satyam, India's fourth largest software company, collapsed in a fraud scandal involving local politicians and a prominent business family[1]. The Indian government rallied round with top businessmen to rescue Satyam (it is now part of the Mumbai-based Mahindra Group) so

335

as to prevent it harming the country's then buoyant image, but they could not save Hyderabad's deteriorating reputation.

Indian and international investors had until then paid little attention to the political-business linkages and scams. That was no longer possible from 2009 because it soon became clear that Satyam and its allied infrastructure company, Maytas (Satyam spelt in reverse), were just the tip of a vast iceberg that gradually became exposed after the state's Congress chief minister, Y.S. Rajasekhara Reddy (YSR), was killed in a helicopter crash in September 2009.[2] YSR's death, just a few months after being re-elected for a second term, triggered a series of events that led to widespread police inquiries, court cases, and the jailing of businessmen and politicians.

A frantic campaign was launched within hours of the crash for Jagan (YSJ or Jagan as he was known to differentiate him from his father, YSR) to succeed him as chief minister.[3] This was despite the fact that Y.S. Jagan had virtually no political experience – he had become a member of parliament just five months earlier. Jagan's supporters were not, however, trying to ensure that Andhra had a strong and reputable leader in charge: in fact, rather the opposite. They wanted the dynastic succession to continue so that they and their business contacts could continue with the contracts, deals and favours that YSR and Jagan had set up during the father's five years in office. So avaricious was their greed that they openly campaigned and shouted slogans during the memorial and other functions that followed YSR's death, turning what should have been respectful and sombre occasions into a political jamboree. Sonia Gandhi received Jagan's claim when she arrived with Manmohan Singh for YSR's funeral, but she resisted the proposal, understandably thinking that Jagan, aged 36, was not the right candidate so early in his political career.

Businessmen involved in the state's companies form a new entrepreneurial community[4] that is significant in the same way as clans such as the Marwaris or the Chettiars. The Marwaris moved from their desert home state of Rajasthan to serve and make money, first with Mughal rulers in Delhi and then with the British in Calcutta.

The Chettiars, based in Tamil Nadu, migrated as traders and bankers to nearby countries. With easily identifiable names like Reddy, Raju and Rao, the Andhra businessmen travelled much smaller distances within Andhra, bearing farming wealth from the state's flourishing coastal regions to Hyderabad, especially when the city began to grow in the 1990s with the growth of information technology. There they worked with politicians, and together grew rich in real estate, land deals and infrastructure projects – and then became involved in politics themselves. Some have now expanded their businesses across India and abroad with power ventures, highways and airports. The most ambitious, however have become over-extended and faced financial problems.

The growth of Hyderabad's wealth has exacerbated a decades-old claim for the creation of a separate state of Telangana, centred on the city – one of several demands across India for the creation of new states. The claim has varied in intensity since 1956, when Hyderabad was merged into the newly formed state of Andhra Pradesh, and has frequently been mishandled by the central government, especially since 2009. It is only now being implemented.

Andhra Pradesh is rich in farmlands along its coastal regions, with a port and industrial city at Visakhapatnam (Vizag), and with a capital city, Hyderabad, that is built on a spectacular landscape of ancient rock formations, hills and lakes. It became prosperous and important because of its software and allied IT businesses. Now those advantages have been damaged by greed and corruption. This is not unique, of course. Corruption cases linking government, political dynasties, ministers, bureaucrats and business have emerged on a massive scale in many states, notably Maharashtra with irrigation and other scandals, Karnataka (mining and land), Tamil Nadu (national telecoms), Jharkhand (mining), Orissa (mining), Uttar Pradesh (land and infrastructure), and Delhi (Commonwealth Games).

Andhra Pradesh, however, is worth special study because, as a microcosm, it shows how a city and a region have been corrupted by a newly rich community impatient to boost its wealth and power.

People who have known Hyderabad for decades talk about how old traditions and attitudes have been swept aside in the rush for instant riches. 'I find today's new Hyderabad vulgar, obsessed with money and without any social conscience,' says Anvar Alikhan, a senior advertising/business executive, who lives there.[5] 'The amount of money sloshing around is astonishing. At a business meeting where we were discussing socio-economic segments, a client told me, quite straight-facedly, "Upper Income Group means someone with a net asset value of Rs 100 crore. Anything less than that is just middle class." A banker said that his wealth management department in the city was being shut down because of a lack of business opportunities. "Sure, there's lots of money, it's just that none of it is available for investment in things like shares, bonds and mutual funds, because it's all in cash".'

Irrigation in the 1800s

The story begins long before India's independence, with a British irrigation engineer, Sir Arthur Thomas Cotton, who wrote himself into the region's history in 1844 so memorably that there is a Cottonreddypalem village, plus many statues, and a Cotton Museum that was opened as recently as 1988 by the then Andhra chief minister, N.T. Rama Rao. Cotton's contribution was to produce a report in 1844 that led to giant barrages being built across the state's massive Godavari and Krishna rivers, plus other irrigation works. Together these projects turned the coastal delta region into the grain bowl of Andhra, which it remains today.

The main beneficiaries, as Harish Damodaran, a journalist, recounts in a well-researched book *India's New Capitalists*,[6] were the local Kamma peasantry, who later became the leading businessmen in Hyderabad. The Kammas, writes Damodaran, had a 'pronounced commercial bent' and cashed in not only as farmers but became canny traders, hoarding stock and watching market prices to decide when to sell, moving on later to run small rice and oil mills and rural money-lending. 'By the early decades of the twentieth century a stratum of agriculturalists had emerged who were looking at new avenues for investing savings accumulated from intensive farming of paddy and high value cash crops such as Virginia tobacco, turmeric and chilli.'

This created considerable wealth and also bred a generation of contractors who became accustomed to doing deals with politicians and government officials – a skill that would later yield fortunes in the days of YSR. They started with small irrigation projects and gradually evolved as large-scale civil engineering and construction contractors.

Telangana

While the coastal regions boomed, the Telangana region, with Hyderabad as the capital of one of India's 500 'princely states', lagged behind for over 200 years under the thumb of the hereditary ruler, the all-powerful Nizam of Hyderabad. Nehru wrote in 1946 that it was 'a typical feudal regime supported by an almost complete denial of civil liberties'.[7] The Nizam was eventually ejected from his throne by the Nehru government in September 1948 in what may have been the bloodiest of all India's mass killings, with reports of 50,000 Muslims killed and maybe many more[8].

The Telangana people's demand for some sort of constitutional identity began in 1956 when the coastal regions were merged with the Nizam's old Hyderabad state to form a Telugu-speaking Andhra Pradesh. A few years later, in the 1960s, the Telangana movement developed into a bid to resist domination by bureaucrats and others from the coast who, through hard work and long hours that contrasted with the typical Hyderabadi's laid-back approach, had aggressively cornered high government positions. The demand for a Telangana identity was then fudged and rebuffed by successive Indian governments.

When Hyderabad started to grow rapidly in the 1990s, the wealthy from the coastal regions helped to finance the state's politicians, grabbing land for construction projects together with licences and contracts in the city and the rest of the state. The new wealth was displayed in the shiny office blocks and shopping malls that came up across the city, along with palatial houses that have gradually destroyed the city's Deccan Plateau rock landscape. Geologists say these rocks are 2,500 million years old, making them among the oldest – and hardest – in the world. 'Uncontrolled quarrying and destruction for the sake of building material and more building space threatens to make these rocks a thing of the past,' says a local conservation organisation.[9]

By the time YSR died, the wealth and development of the city and its surroundings far surpassed the coastal regions.[10] The inflow of wealth and power gave fresh impetus to the Telangana cause in the 2000s because of local resentment at what was widely seen as a takeover of the city,[11] with local people suffering discrimination when it came to jobs, government services and education.

Unlike most other state bifurcation claims, the Telangana cause had by this time become primarily focused on wealth and business interests, not the more usual motivations of language and ethnic divisions (although there are cultural and dialectic differences – Urdu was the official language under the Nizam). The Telangana activists wanted to keep Hyderabad as their capital (the first time such a claim had been proposed by a potential breakaway state), which led to strong opposition from the powerful and rich newcomers from the coastal regions, who feared that their investments and prospects in the city would be hit. They feared a crash in real estate values, together with a cutback on infrastructure projects and other deals, and even thought they might be driven out by the new Telangana rulers. This led many of them to favour a compromise, with the city becoming a self-contained Union Territory – a sort of mini city-state – independent of both Andhra and the new Telangana.

Among the most powerful and vocal anti-Telangana politicians have been Lagadapati Rajagopal, founder of the once rapidly-growing but now heavily-indebted Lanco Infratech infrastructure, power and construction group. A Congress MP, he was one of the financiers of a padayatra in 2003 by YSR that helped to bring him to power. Rajagopal's development plans in and around Hyderabad could be hit hard if the state is split. Another Congress MP with powerful Delhi connections is T. Subbarami Reddy, whose Gayatri group has many infrastructure projects. Also facing possible losses from a split would be Andhra-born G. Mallikarjuna Rao, founder-chairman of the Bengaluru-based GMR group that built Hyderabad airport and controversially has a massive 5,400 acres of land around the site, with the right to develop it. National and local politicians are widely believed to have invested anonymously in similar companies through proxy names and other routes though that may never be proved.

In December 2009, the Congress-led central government was faced with a long fast by a leading local politician, K. Chandrasekhar Rao, leader of the Telangana Rashtra Samithi. He appeared to be endangering his life to revive his crumbling political image as the head of the Telangana movement. The government gave way and agreed to create a new state,[12] but that impulsive and humane decision led to violent demonstrations, as well as resignation threats by about half the members of the state's legislative assembly, and a revolt by businessmen who felt threatened. This paralyzed the state government (and sparked follow-on bifurcation claims from other states), though it did succeed in enabling KCR to end his fast. Predictably, once the fast was over, the central government backed off and hoped to indefinitely stall the Telangana claim.

The Congress had traditionally had strong support in the Telangana region since Nehru's government ousted the Nizam, but that was dissipated by the way the party's national leadership mishandled both the separate state issue and Jagan Reddy's claim to his father's mantle. It broke the party's hold on the state, which is politically important because Andhra is often a key player in national coalition politics. The state-based Telugu Desam Party, led by Chandrababu Naidu, who was chief minister from 1995 to 2004, had such a big stake in the

1998–2004 BJP-led government that Naidu was the coalition's chief co-ordinator in Delhi. The state also contributed 30-odd MPs to the two Congress-led national coalitions in 2004 and 2009. After Jagan (and his mother, YSR's widow) broke from the Congress and formed the YSR Congress in 2011,[13] the Congress was badly defeated in state assembly by-elections with Jagan's YSR party winning 15 seats.

Eventually, in August 2013, the government started the constitutional procedure to set up a separate Telangana state, probably with Hyderabad as its joint capital for ten years. It did this not through a well developed strategy based on sound principles of regional government but simply because the Congress hoped that the decision would strengthen its support base in the 2014 general election. The plan backfired, however and led to political, industrial and social unrest as Jagan Reddy and others encouraged strikes that shut down power supplies, closed schools and took buses off the roads in various parts of the state.

Business

The main business communities involved in the flow of investment into what became a booming metropolis are the Reddys, Rajus and Raos, besides the Kammas, Komatis and Kapus. They all come from coastal Andhra or Rayalaseema, an adjacent under-developed region. Some of these communities have also settled in nearby states – Reddys in particular have gone to both Tamil Nadu and Karnataka. Several invested in the now famous Telugu film industry that originated in Madras, now Chennai, the state capital of Tamil Nadu.

Hyderabad's urban growth took off when Chandrababu Naidu successfully turned it into an international information technology centre. Naidu had become chief minister in 1995 after staging a party coup that ousted his father-in-law, N.T. Rama Rao, a famous and colourful film-star-turned-politician. One of India's most focused younger state leaders, Naidu picked on software development to be Andhra's growth engine because it involved relatively low capital investment and had short lead times that enabled start-ups to begin operations quickly. It also had a faster multiplier effect than other industries because it raised the state's international profile by attracting big names such as Microsoft, followed later by Google, Facebook and many others to the new high-tech city.

'Here you can hire 50 good people in two or three months instead of a minimum of six months in the US,' Srini Koppulu, an Indian-born executive from the US told me in 2000 when I interviewed him for a *Fortune* magazine article.[14] Microsoft had sent Koppulu to Hyderabad to run its new research centre. Entrepreneurial overseas Indians, who had been running software companies in the US and elsewhere, also returned to tap local resources. 'The time to market is a key component in the dot.com business,' said Prasad Yenigalla, founder of California-based Magma Solutions, who had 35 employees in Hyderabad writing software to designs prepared by his US company. 'Here we can get new staff fast enough to build a portal in two to three months compared with six to nine months in the US, and we can do for $250,000 what would cost $1m in the US,' The number of units registered in Hyderabad's Software Technology Park rose from seven in 1991–92 to over 1,405 in 2004 and software exports rose from Rs 200,000 to Rs 180bn.[15]

To support this initiative and utilize the region's adept brainpower, Naidu set up various high-technology institutes and 180 engineering colleges (allegedly leaking their locations to friendly businessmen who bought land at nominal prices before announcements were made). One of his biggest coups was persuading the internationally recognized and supported Indian School of Business to set up in Hyderabad in the late 1990s. Previously there had been little large-scale industrial development apart from some public sector technology-based corporations that would never by themselves have become engines of economic growth. They now became significant because they helped provide a base for both the IT businesses and defence-oriented establishments plus a growing pharmaceutical industry.

The Electronics Corporation of India, which was set up in 1967, specialises in electronics for nuclear, space and defence industries, and Bharat Dynamics, established in 1970, develops guided weapon systems. These corporations have been the catalysts for a string of allied missile and defence research establishments. Hyderabad's other main industry is pharmaceuticals. It originated with the public sector Indian Drugs and Pharmaceuticals that was set up in 1961 to fulfil Nehru's (understandable) belief that there was 'far too much exploitation of the public in this industry' so the private sector should not be allowed to dominate.[16] Despite Nehru's view, IDPL's main contribution has been to spawn an extensive private sector industry, led by Dr Reddy's Laboratories, which was founded in 1984 by a former chemical engineer employee, Kallam Anji Reddy, and is one of India's leading pharmaceutical companies.

Naidu lost power in 2004, primarily because he focused too much on urban and technological development, and on extensive personal globetrotting and international publicity. This bred resentment in problem-ridden rural areas, and made him vulnerable politically. He was accused of ignoring rural development, and large numbers of farmers hit by heavy debt and other problems committed suicide. The rural landscape was in a shambles, wrote P. Sainath, a journalist and rural affairs expert, in 2004.[17] 'Agricultural credit and finance systems have collapsed. Taking their place are new entities [micro-credit schemes] that can make the village moneylender seem relatively less coercive. Prices have pushed most inputs beyond the reach of the small farmer. For many, a move from food crops to cash crops proved fatal. In some cases, the shift was towards high-outlay, water-guzzling crops such as sugar cane. All this, in an era of huge power tariff hikes. A steady shrinking of local democracy further deepened the chaos.'

YSR and Jagan

Y.S. Rajasekhara Reddy became a member of the Andhra Pradesh state assembly in 1978 when he was just 29 and, after a spell as a minister, was made Congress state chief in 1984 by Rajiv Gandhi, then the Congress prime minister and party leader. He fell out of favour when Narasimha Rao was prime minister (1991–96), but later bounced back. When he defeated Naidu and led the Congress party to victory in May 2004, he took over a state that had developed markedly during Naidu's nine years in terms of industrial and high technology. Economic growth was around 9 per cent in 2003–04, up from 5.6 per cent in 1994–95,[18] but the rural and agricultural economy was suffering badly.[19] Learning from Naidu's failures, YSR introduced programmes to help the poor and boosted growth to a peak of around 12 per cent in 2007–08, falling to near 7 per cent in 2008–09.

He proved himself to be one of India's most skilful regional politicians, seemingly working for the good of the state and the rural poor, while building himself an unassailable Congress power base by providing the Gandhi family with strong loyalty and support. That won him a comfortable re-election victory five months before he was killed, despite reports of widespread corruption and corporate cronyism that had been circulating about him and his son Jagan for some time. There were allegations of nepotism, with friends and relatives being allotted land far below market prices and also being informed about infrastructure projects in advance so that they could buy the land at low prices[20] (a frequent ploy in many states).

YSR's significance was demonstrated by the huge mass of mourners – from Sonia Gandhi and Manmohan Singh to the rural poor – who gathered to pay their last respects at his funeral.[21] Large crowds are often assembled in India by political parties and other interests, so it can be difficult to assess the extent of real grief on such occasions. There were, for example, vastly exaggerated reports of suicides and heart attacks around the state just after YSR was killed – some party officials were reported to be claiming, almost certainly bogusly, that a total of over 400 people had died.[22] Families were paid Rs 5,000 by local Congress politicians to hide the real cause of their relatives' deaths, according to local reports.[23] Temples were quickly erected to honour YSR. 'Some see the temples as desperate measures of sycophants keen to score brownie points with YSR's son Jaganmohan Reddy – others say the temples immortalise the man they worshipped,' said the *Mail Today*.[24]

There were two distinct views of YSR's time as chief minister. Admirers are typified by 'Shanti S', who wrote a comment on my blog in December 2009, saying: 'Every time I return to visit my relatives in Kurnool, I am touched by the programs YSR put in place for the poor. People can allege all they want, they have to also rationalize that progress at the very poor segments cannot come about just driven by greed – the leaders have to have some vision, which YSR had. The state was on a decent growth trajectory & I would take that over politicians who hoarded their coffers, paving the roads to their homes with gold and leaving absolutely no trace of the benefits of their power on the poor & neglected. I despair that we don't have anyone to fill his shoes now'.[25] This was despite the fact that Jagan's personal wealth was rocketing. Income-tax returns before the 2004 elections showed he had assets of Rs 9.18 lakh and the total value of family assets declared by YSR during the 2004 elections was only Rs 50 lakh. Jagan's declared wealth shot up to Rs 77 crore at the 2009 election, and a massive Rs 365 crore in 2011.[26]

Opponents' views have been evocatively summarized by Kancha Ilaiah, a social activist, writer and political science professor at Hyderabad's Osmania University. 'Money was mobilised like water and was distributed through various channels like water,' he told me, echoing the banker that Anvar Alikhan had mentioned. During YSR's rule in Andhra, Ilaiah wrote: 'Private palaces were built for the family use. Thousands of acres of land were given to private industrialists. His [YSR's] family started various industries, media networks and money was mobilised into those companies from the industrialists who took land, minerals, water, power, etc. from the state without giving anything to the state. The state resources were just plundered ... No dissent and difference of opinion was allowed to exist within the state structure.'[27] This was 'accumulation of private "property as theft", relocating the French experience of

Proudhon's time (1840s). When Proudhon wrote his book, *What Is Property?* the French monarchs were robbing the state resources for palace building and luxury living.'

Congress Benefits

The allegations of corruption, along with reports suggesting there were handsome payments to the Congress party nationally, were secondary to YSR's mass popularity. Indeed, if YSR had lived, it is reasonable to assume that the projects, corruption, kickbacks and funding would still be continuing today, with grateful Congress party leaders in Delhi doting on their loyal and valuable friend. No doubt there would have been more corruption allegations against him, and some deals would have been the subject of inquiries and could have come unstuck, but it is unlikely there would have been any major police investigations. Taking that a stage further, if Jagan had not tried immediately after his father's death to become the chief minister, the subsequent crisis might have been averted and he would not have been in jail three years later, accused of massive corruption.[28] And if Sonia Gandhi and the Congress party had handled his succession bid more adeptly, it would not have suffered the drubbing from Jagan's breakaway YSR Congress party in June 2012, and the official moves to form a Telangana state might not have been needed in 2013.

Sonia Gandhi and her fellow national party leaders appear to have done nothing during YSR's rule to stop the corrupt deals, even though they would have been fully aware of them. There were reports that YSR was 'sending huge sums of money for the Congress in Delhi every month in the name of "organisational expenses".[29] Yet, when it suited them politically, they picked on Jagan. The CBI only began to investigate his activities when he became a serious political problem for Congress nationally, and it then put him in jail just before the 2012 by-elections (exposing how governments manipulate the agency for political ends). It is hard to believe that

39-year-old Jagan's jailing[30] was not intended to remove him, as it did, from canvassing in the run-up to the elections that took place shortly after. A leading Indian business newspaper commented: 'While Mr Reddy may certainly turn out to be guilty, that the CBI has woken up to the strength of the case against him just as his party is in a position to threaten the Congress politically will strike many as further proof that India's premier investigative agency can no longer even pretend to independence'.[31]

I echoed that in my blog: 'Such are the ways of politics and corruption in India that those who stay loyal to their political chiefs and allies rarely go to prison, whereas trouble makers suddenly find their misdeeds, that had been condoned in the past, being splashed across the newspapers and the police knocking on their door'.[32] But the tactic misfired. Jagan was seen as a martyr and the Congress did appallingly in the by-elections[33] – albeit after voters had reportedly been bribed with massive amounts of cash, gold, jewellery and other gifts[34] that helped swell the turnout to an astonishingly high total of around 80 per cent.[35]

Missionary in Mining Ganglands

YSR came from a tough and feudal society background in Rayalaseema, which is frequently named for its 'bad lands', and his rise reflects how many of India's regional politicians have grown rich and powerful from poor origins. His family mixed Christian missionary work with business in the rough mining industry and there is death and brutality in the family's history. YSR's grandfather had converted to Christianity in the 1920s to escape poverty. His father, Raja Reddy, had started as a construction contractor on missionary projects and sent YSR first to missionary school and then to medical college in nearby Karnataka. YSR then returned home and began working in a missionary hospital.

This was explained in media reports (*Economic and Political Weekly*, 12 June 2004 and *The Times of India* Crest edition, 11 December 2010) that criticized YSR's record before he became chief minister, and said his political rise had been 'accompanied by more bloodshed than that of any other politician in this state – not bloodshed for some avowed "higher cause", but bloodshed for the narrowest possible cause: the rise of one individual to political power and prominence'. His father had 'made a name for himself as a rough and violent man with whom one had better not get into a quarrel'. He had 'become richer and "very ruthless" – his name evoked considerable fear in Cuddapah', a district in Rayalaseema now called Kadapa (and sometimes YSR Kadapa), where Jagan became the MP.

Raja Reddy started mining barytes, a mineral whose price increased sharply in the mid-1970s when it began to be used in petroleum. 'The mines in Mangampeta were owned by one Venkatasubbaiah, but Raja was quickly able to cajole the mine owner into becoming his junior partner,' reported *The Times*. 'A few years later, or so the story goes, Raja wanted to buy the mines and, when Venkatasubbaiah refused, the latter was mysteriously found murdered. Who murdered him was a question that was debated for long, but Raja went on to take full control of the mines. Raja then convinced YSR to help him out in his business.' An elderly villager who went to court in 1992 to stop his nephew's 1.8 acre mineral-rich land being mined by YSR 'had his hands and legs broken,' reported the *EPW*. 'With the money flowing from the barytes mines in his pockets, YSR was in a position to undertake the transformation of "village factions" into full-fledged instruments of political and economic domination at the highest level'. Raja Reddy was killed in a bomb attack on his car in 1998 that was allegedly carried out by political and business rivals. His death led to riots and one of his attackers was hacked to death.[36]

YSR answered the *EPW* article with an extraordinary letter that spent more time paraphrasing the accusations than rebutting them. It started by saying that the article had depicted him as 'a man who created terror and involved in bloodshed for the narrowest possible cause for rising in public life and gaining prominence and political power', and 'as one person who is up to any crooked enactment in gaining political benefits with an ultimate goal of gaining power in the state and as one of the pioneers of creating a nexus between politics, crime and money.'[37] He wrote that 'all the allegations and imputations made against me are totally false.'

Father, Son and Cronies

While he was chief minister, YSR moved on from the usual pattern of corruption – politicians and bureaucrats taking bribes in return for favours – and secured the loyalty of his supporters by providing business opportunities for contractors in unregulated, over-priced and scam-ridden irrigation, highways and other projects. The contractors and developers showed their gratitude by taking stakes in companies run by Jagan, mainly in a media business called Sakshi, and politicians and others cronies invested in the development and real estate schemes. Instead of just taking kickbacks, YSR's family and political associates became joint investors and stakeholders with their business contacts.

'He converted his key supporters into businessmen, industrialists, contractors and realtors,' wrote Bharat Bhushan, then the editor of India's *Mail Today*, in an article titled 'Money backs "Son-rise" in Andhra'[38] in September 2009. Their loyalty to the party or the leader was based on pure economic interest, and the loyalty of a majority of the 156 Congress MLAs who had just been elected was secured through similar largesse. Others benefited through smooth approvals of business ventures.

To expedite such deals, a chief minister would staff his office with selected bureaucrats, who would do his bidding and were skilful at writing carefully worded tenders and other official documents that favoured certain businesses. They would also steer project approvals through government departments and, local sources allege, ensure that owners of land wanted by YSR and Jagan did not succeed if they complained to the police and other authorities.[39]

Naidu's Deals

These activities escalated a style of operating that had been used to a far lesser degree in some other states, and by YSR's predecessor as chief minister, Chandrababu Naidu, whose friends and relatives benefited from projects. 'Bureaucrats and their business friends explained to politicians the potential of this sort of public-private partnership (PPP) that led to a flurry of investment projects,' says a local journalist. Projects in Naidu's tenure included the internationally famous Hi-Tec City. Well-known companies such as Microsoft, Infosys and Wipro were given generous terms to build facilities, and local real estate companies were encouraged to make parallel investments on the basis of advance inside information. Another project initiated by Naidu was the Hyderabad international airport, developed by a consortium led by GMR. The deal was completed during YSR's time and the consortium was given a large land allocation of 5,400 acres that triggered a property bubble in the nearby area of Shamshabad.

Relatively few formal allegations of corrupt deals came to light during Naidu's time as chief minister, despite his real estate links. Observers were surprised that the YSR government did not build up formal inquires and court cases against his predecessor, as often happens when state governments change. Only in two cases was any action initiated. One involved suggestions that the state government took bribes on alcohol sales from 1999 to 2003 (after a period of prohibition from 1995 to 1997), with AP Beverages Corporation, the government-run (and sole) liquor agency in the state, buying from distilleries at a large premium. A Congress supporter went to court with the allegations, but investigations were stopped on an appeal from Naidu, then the chief minister. When YSR came to power, there was talk of reviving the case, but nothing was done.

The other case arose in 2004 when Naidu, who was acting as caretaker chief minister in the run-up to elections, approved the allocation of 850 acres in two locations at a throwaway price of Rs 50,000 per acre to IMG Bharata for a sporting academy, along with other sports management activities. In preparation, Naidu created a sporting image for the state by hosting India's National Games in 2002 and the Afro-Asian Games in 2003. It was alleged that P. Ahobala 'Billy' Rao, who ran the company in an arrangement with IMG, a US-based international sports and events management agency, was acting in a benami role for Naidu. In 2005, the YSR government stopped the deal and cancelled the allocation of a 400-acre site.[40] It asked the CBI to investigate, but the agency did not do so, claiming a lack of available personnel. The case was later reopened on the basis of two private petitions and remains a subject of political controversy.[41]

Looking back, it may seem surprising that there was not more opposition to what YSR and Jagan were doing, and that Chandrababu Naidu's Telugu Desam Party (TDP) did not pro-actively do more to build up a political campaign against them. One of the reasons may be Naidu's poor political standing following his massive defeat in 2004. He had lost his credibility and was widely criticized by farmers who had suffered four years of devastating droughts. He was probably also constrained by the fact that his regime had run its own corrupt deals, so he did not want to provoke the government into ordering tit-for-tat police inquiries. Also, politicians and officials did not think it was in their interest to rock the boat and challenge such a determined minister as YSR, and most of the media played its accustomed pliant role. YSR built a climate of euphoria among the people about welfare projects that Naidu could not challenge. 'See, I brought you rain,' YSR said, when his election was followed by good monsoon rains, building an image that helped him five years later in the 2009 election.

YSR's 15–20 per cent Corruption

The level of corruption under YSR was described in 2007 as 'an open secret' and 'beyond the pale' even for India by David Hopper, then the US consul general for southern India. 'We thought Naidu was bad, but that was child's play compared with what is happening now,' he wrote in a cable to the US State Department that was published by WikiLeaks in September 2011.[42] 'Typically, five to seven per cent is lost to corruption, but in Reddy's irrigation programme that figure is more than 15 to 20 per cent,' said the cable. 'The sheer size of Reddy's signature programmes, with literally billions of dollars at play every year, leaves much room for "leakage" to Congress party officials and their allies.' The cable also pointed out that the chief minister and his party took a bigger cut from promoters wanting to put up multi-crore projects in the state.

YSR linked politicians, businessmen and bureaucrats by selling government-owned land around key centres such as Hyderabad, the industrial and port city of Vizag, and the temple town of Tirupati to raise money for infrastructure projects, notably a mega-irrigation scheme called Jalayagnam. He gave government funds as 'mobilization advances' to private sector contractors for the projects, many of which made little progress. 'Many of the contractors were cronies and they parked the money in real estate, and YSR added to the hype to it by announcing the new projects, many of which were located at places where the cronies had already bought land,' says a local journalist.

Politicians whose real-estate businesses thrived during the YSR years included Lagadapati Rajagopal and his Lanco group, whose family businesses include power projects, real estate, infrastructure and one of the country's biggest real estate mixed-development projects costing $1.5bn and covering 108 acres.[43] Congress politicians who were reported to have been awarded irrigation contracts during the YSR regime included three more MPs – T. Subbarami Reddy, Kavuri Sambasiva Rao and Rayapati Sambasiva Rao. Irrigation projects of various sizes and associated road works contracts also went to state ministers and other MLAs. Andhra Congress MLAs' real estate business also thrived. Other Congress leaders benefited from a Rs 3,000 crore Hyderabad outer ring road project and won other contracts for roads and building works.

State-owned sites were auctioned at extraordinarily high prices, triggering a real estate frenzy and enabling what one source calls 'influential people', who had already bought nearby land at low prices from mostly poor private owners, to sell at massive prices. In July 2006, for example, an auction of undeveloped land at the Golden Mile project in Kokapet, near Hyderabad's financial district, yielded Rs 14 crore per acre, which matched prices in the city's long-established prime central district of Jubilee Hills.[44] Many of these land deals are now in litigation. The government started an astronomically high number of 103 special economic zones that drove up real estate values.[45] A project called Fab City in Maheshwaram near Hyderabad was given a high-profile launch in 2005 as a centre for international semi-conductor companies, which led to land being bought at inflated prices. The lead company in this project, SemIndia, was to have brought in $3bn to make this a hub of microchip manufacturing, but after all the hype, the project was gradually watered down.

A month after he came to power, YSR flagged off his regime with a project called Jalayagnam (*jal* meaning water, and *yagnam* being an offering to the gods), which was exceptionally large-scale and ambitious with an estimated cost of some Rs 46,000 crore.[46] It included constructing dams, canals, water supply systems, power plants and lift irrigation schemes to pump river water from the Krishna and Godavari rivers up gradients and irrigate seven million acres of dry land in the state, mostly in the Rayalaseema and Telangana areas.

YSR, in effect, had planned Jalayagnam both to boost his populist image as a chief minister who cared for the rural poor by building long-delayed irrigation schemes promised in his election manifesto, and as a sop to contractors who were part of broader schemes with his son Jagan. Many of the projects had not received environmental clearances, and some were subject to disputes with neighbouring states over sharing river waters. Tens of thousands of people were to be displaced. Financing was helped by allocations from the central government, plus state funds from real estate auctions around big cities.

The leaked US cable said that an economist who had been studying the effectiveness of the state government's programmes had reported that 'with only four to five companies executing the projects through numerous subcontractors and little oversight, there are many opportunities for graft in the irrigation schemes'. India's Comptroller and Auditor-General criticized cost and time over-runs in a report, which was submitted to the government early in February 2013.[47] None of the contractors had met project completion dates, and only 16 out of the 86 projects had been finished. In a draft report submitted in July 2012, the CAG said that the state had neither enough funds nor water to implement the plans.[48] Jalayagnam appeared to consist of a large number of contracts that were awarded without any assurance on the completion of works within specified time periods and budgets, said the report. On one project, four firms obtained 16 contracts worth Rs 22,885 crore by forming joint ventures in 16 different combinations.

Jagan's Companies

Jagan Reddy entered business in 2001, taking over the Bengaluru-based Sandur Power Company, which handled small-scale power generation and distribution projects. By 2008, four years after YSR became chief minister, Sandur had spun off an investment company and expanded into real estate and other ventures including Jagan's Jagati Publications.[49] Working with his father, Jagan built up a media, cement and mining (the family's original business area) empire, including Sakshi TV, Bharathi Cement and Raghuram Cement in addition to Sandur and Jagati.

Along with other key companies that he controlled with investments totalling Rs 797 crore, Jagati Publications became a focal point in 2012 and 2013 for investigations into money laundering by India's Enforcement Directorate, and for separate corruption inquiries by the CBI into Jagan's alleged 'disproportionate assets'. Companies caught up in the assets case included Tamil Nadu-based

India Cements, run by N. Srinivasan, who has been a dominant figure in the politics of Indian cricket as the chairman of the Board of Control for Cricket in India (BCCI) from 2011. He was also involved in the IPL championship controversies as chairman of Chennai Superkings, one of the teams. The CBI alleged that India Cements had invested Rs 100 crore in Raghuram Cements and Rs 40 crore in other Jagan companies and, in return, was allowed by the Andhra Pradesh government to draw additional river water for cement manufacturing plants and also received a favourable limestone mining lease in YSR family's base of Kadapa.[50]

The allegations were published by Chandrababu Naidu's TDP. on the party's website[51] with companies such as Matrix Group, Penna Cements, Ramky Group, Aurobindo Pharma, Hetero Group and Mantri Developers listed as allegedly providing funds for Bharathi Cement, Jagati Publications, Carmel Asia Holdings and other businesses run by Jagan, and receiving favours in return.[52] The documents allege that Jagan and his father created 49 dummy companies around the country to launder the money they received in bribes. 'The modus operandi was very simple: investors favoured with land allocations in exchange for their buying shares of the dummy companies at exorbitant premiums fixed by Jagan and Co,' says the TDP website,[53] quoting a First Information Report (FIR) filed by the CBI.

The CAG said in its annual report in March 2011 that a total of 88,500 acres of land was allotted on an ad hoc and arbitrary manner to private parties, 'depriving the state revenue of nearly Rs 1 lakh crore (Rs 1bn)'. Among the companies named were Vanpic, Obulapuram Mining and Aurobindo Pharma, all of which were already being investigated in Jagan's cases. 'Alienation and allotment of land by the state government during 2006–11 was characterized by grave irregularities, involving allotment on an ad hoc, arbitrary and discretionary manner to private persons/entities at very low rates, without safeguarding the financial and socio-economic interests of the state,' said the CAG. 'The rates proposed at different established levels of the government hierarchy were disregarded and substantial benefits were unduly granted to private parties. Audit scrutiny revealed that in the test-checked cases, undue benefit of Rs 1,784 crore was given to various entities and persons due to the difference in the rates at which land was allotted and the market value as recommended by the district collector and empowered committee. In many cases of land allotment, the state government ignored the prescribed procedures and disregarded canons of financial propriety.'

In 2012, a 28,000-acre ports and industrial zone development in the state's Guntur and Prakasam districts called Vanpic (Vadarevu and Nizampatnam ports) became the main focus of inquiries by the CBI, which said it was 'nothing but a criminal conspiracy to loot the public assets in order to help private parties'.[54] Vanpic was promoted by Nimmagadda Prasad, a businessman, through one of his group companies, Matrix Enport. Prasad's original business was Matrix Labs, a prominent pharmaceutical company that was acquired by Mylan Labs of the US in 2006–07. Known locally as 'Matrix Prasad', he has interests in media and is chairman of Maa Television.

In addition to generous tax concessions, the government committed in 2008 to give Vanpic an excessive amount of land totalling some 18,000 acres, according to the CAG,[55] allegedly in return for Prasad investing $300–400m in Jagan's businesses including Sakshi. Investors in Vanpic, besides the Andhra government and Matrix Enport, included Ras Al Khaimah (RAK), one of the United Arab Emirates. (RAK also obtained controversial rights along with the state's mining corporation and a branch of the Jindal family business group, one of India's largest steel producers, to mine for bauxite in a protected tribal area, the Araku Valley, where only state agencies are allowed to work[56]). Prasad was jailed in 2012 while inquiries continued. In March 2013, CBI counsel alleged in court that, between 2006 and 2009, the government had provided assets worth Rs 17,000 crore for Vanpic ports, an industrial corridor, a greenfield airport project and a shipyard and put the total land awarded at 28,000 acres. In return, said the counsel, Prasad invested heavily in Jagan's companies.[57] In November 2013, the state government cancelled the project,[58] claiming it was doing so because it had not been properly cleared with the central government, which sounded like a neat excuse.

Big Names

A clutch of Andhra companies that thrived during the years when Chandrababu Naidu and YSR were chief ministers went on to run big projects in the rest of India and then abroad. They include names such as Satyam in software, and GMR, GVK and Lanco in infrastructure. GMR and GVK each run two of India's main airports and were responsible along with 13 other companies, at their peak, for a third of the power projects and half the highway concessions.[59]

They were using the skills and resources that had been built up in Andhra Pradesh over previous decades. These included the close connections with politicians in Hyderabad, Delhi and elsewhere that seemed to encourage risky expansion rather than business caution. Many of the politicians involved are believed to have invested in the projects, channelling accumulated bribe money through sources such as off-shore equity funds. They have all hit problems. Satyam collapsed in a fraud scandal. The others have suffered from over-rapid expansion in the boom years that led to heavy indebtedness, plus India's general problems of project delays caused by slow land approvals, environmental blockages and shortages of coal for power projects. Today, GMR, GVK and Lanco are among the country's most heavily indebted companies.[60]

Satyam and Maytas

The biggest collapse came in January 2009 when Satyam, India's third biggest software company with 53,000 employees and customers and operations in 66 countries, imploded. This was a rare case of the lid being lifted on India's rocky corporate governance. It was especially worrying for the country's international image because it happened in the new software information technology industry. Until the Satyam case, it had been assumed that these companies had better standards than many of India's old family-controlled groups that habitually switched funds between businesses and into personal accounts. It can now be seen, however, with the subsequent exposure of widespread corruption, to be a prime example of what was wrong.

Satyam, which means 'truth' in Sanskrit, was controlled by the family of its then chairman, Ramalinga Raju,[61] who was closely linked with various politicians, including Chandrababu Naidu and YSR. Raju inherited a family textiles business and then moved into construction. In 1987, he set up Satyam, which became one of the first to use India's low-cost software engineers to work at home and abroad for US and other companies. Satyam expanded rapidly as a market leader in the 1990s software boom, and in 1998 launched Satyam Infoway (Sify), one of India's first private sector internet service providers that was also the first to be floated on the US stock market (and was later sold to private equity firms).

The Rajus' infrastructure company, Maytas, received favours on contracts from the state government including YSR's Jalayagnam projects, and eventually drained funds out of Satyam for real estate speculation. This business tainted Raju's and his companies' reputations. Questions were being asked by potential investors in the early 2000s about his business ethics, with allegations of tax evasion and over-pricing in a 1999 takeover of IndiaWorld.com, an Internet portal. In 2001, a stock market official told me that he did not expect Sify's membership of the American NASDAQ stock exchange would stop Ramalinga 'falsifying its subscriber base figures in order to boost its share price'.

The reports and allegations of unethical operations tended to disappear without any legal action, and official inquiries came to nothing. In the over-hyped investor enthusiasm of the time, these worries were mostly overlooked, and were partially allayed in the early 2000s by assurances that Raju was improving the company's governance with new board members. Rumours continued to circulate in the following years, but Raju emerged in 2006 from his relatively low-key life to become chairman of NASSCOM, the software industry's national trade body, which boosted his and Satyam's image.

With hindsight, it can be seen that Raju's crony business practices were revealed publicly when YSR's government was heavily criticized in September 2008 for awarding a Hyderabad metro railway contract to Maytas.[62] E. Sreedharan, who built and ran the Delhi Metro and is regarded as an international expert, alleged that there was a possible land scam on the proposed public-private-partnership project that Maytas had secured on a build-operate-transfer (BOT) basis from YSR's government. In a letter to Montek Singh Ahluwalia, deputy chairman of the Planning Commission, Sreedharan cautioned against using BOT deals, which Ahluwalia favoured, for building such railways.[63] Sreedharan alleged that Maytas 'has a hidden agenda which appears to be to extend the metro network to a large tract of his private land holdings so as to reap a windfall profit of four to five times the land price'. Sreedharan's views, however, were swept aside by the YSR government which, unsuccessfully, demanded an apology from him and threatened legal action. (The Maytas contract was cancelled in July 2009 and the project was awarded a year later to L&T.)

The next sign of trouble came on 16 December 2008 when the markets forced Raju to reverse a sudden move by Satyam to take over Maytas. That evening (India time), after local stock markets closed, Satyam announced it was spending $1.6 bn surplus cash to buy out two privately held Maytas real estate and construction companies, Maytas Properties for $1.3bn and 51 per cent of Maytas Infra for $300m. The market reaction was swift – Satyam lost 55 per cent of its value on the New York stock market and there were strong attacks from investors and analysts. By the end of the day (US time), Satyam had cancelled the deal. Raju claimed implausibly that the Maytas companies would have helped 'de-risk' Satyam against a downturn in the software business, though that made little sense when construction and real estate businesses were harder hit than information technology outsourcing companies that were conserving cash to help weather the global economic slowdown. Rarely had a company been brought into line so rapidly and publicly – and it might not have happened if Satyam had not been quoted in the US because in India it might have merely caused some headlines and then been shuffled out of the news.[64]

A few weeks later, Raju resigned and admitted in a letter to the company's board that he had been inflating Satyam's profits for several years. Cash and bank balances and other favourable figures had been overstated, resulting in artificial balances of Rs 5.88bn in the three months ending the previous September. His attempt to merge Maytas into Satyam 'was the last attempt to fill the fictitious assets with real ones', aimed at filling the fraudulent holes in Satyam's balance sheet with genuine Maytas assets. 'It was,' wrote Raju, 'like riding a tiger, not knowing how to get off without being eaten'.[65] In July 2010, however, he retracted his statement while appealing for bail.

Satyam was rescued with the initiative led by the Indian government and is now part of the Mahindra group, capitalizing on the software skills that Raju had squandered in his family's race for Maytas's infrastructure projects. Both companies, and the Raju family, became the subject of extended inquiries by the finance ministry's Enforcement Directorate, which handles foreign exchange and money laundering cases, and the CBI. Raju was in jail from January 2009 till November 2011 when he was released on bail.[66]

In October 2013, the Enforcement Directorate filed charges against Raju and 47 other people, plus 166 companies, for offences under money laundering legislation.[67] The charges included selling and pledging of Satyam shares at inflated prices, receiving bonus shares under employee stock option schemes, and dividends on the inflated shares through inter-connected transactions involving 327 front companies 'which were used to layer the proceeds of crime'.

GMR, GVK and Lanco

GMR has one of the highest profiles among the large Andhra-originated infrastructure companies, stemming from multiple interests in India and abroad. Founded by G. Mallikarjuna Rao, the chairman, it is a classic example of entrepreneurial drive mixed with effective project management and assiduous cultivation of contacts among politicians and bureaucrats. Rao started in the family's jute and gold businesses and moved on to work in Andhra's public works department before setting up a company to produce cotton ear buds, and then a brewery and a sugar mill. Next, he bought shares in the Bengaluru-based Vysya Bank, where he became chairman before selling his stake to ING of the Netherlands for a reported Rs 350 crores.[68]

He began in infrastructure with power plants in Tamil Nadu and Karnataka in the mid-1990s, and highway projects on the Golden Quadrilateral highway programme in the early 2000s. Mobilizing his widespread contacts, he obtained the contract to build and operate Hyderabad airport, with a 63 per cent stake in partnership with the Indian and Andhra governments and Malaysia Airports Holdings. The airport opened in 2008 and was followed by a concession for the New Delhi airport, plus airports in the Maldives (which it later lost in a contract dispute) and Istanbul. At its peak, GMR had 17 power projects operating or under construction, four airports, nine highways totalling over 700 km and interests in coal mining – all achieved in less than 20 years. This led the group to become over-extended by 2011 when it was also running into delays on various projects, and financial problems on the Delhi airport.[69] It began shedding assets, including stakes in a Singapore-based energy business, the Istanbul airport, plus highway and power projects that were hit by delays[70] – though it did pick up a new Philippines airport contract in December 2013.

The biggest controversy to hit GMR concerned the Delhi airport, which its consortium won after a contentious bidding process presided

over by Praful Patel as aviation minister. The deal was criticized in
a CAG report in April 2012, which estimated that there were losses
in government taxes and passengers' charges totalling some Rs 3,750
crore, partly caused by commercial development arrangements on the
4,800-acre site.[71] It also criticized the consortium's right unilaterally
to extend its 30-year concession for another 30 years, which had not
been in the initial government plans but had been approved by Patel.
These findings were challenged by GMR, which denied obtaining
any special benefits.

GVK was founded by G.V. Krishna Reddy, who comes from a
family that in the past has held top posts in the Andhra government,
as well as carrying out irrigation and road contracts. He owns
several of Hyderabad's leading hotels run by the Taj group, and
since the mid-1990s has developed power projects, the Bengaluru
and Mumbai airports, and a special economic zone in Tamil Nadu.
More recently, he has taken on two airports in Indonesia and
bought a $1.26 bn controlling stake in Australian coal mines with
plans for a total investment of $10bn to create one of the world's
largest thermal coal mining operations. Hit with heavy debts, the
group has been selling stakes in its airport business and power
businesses.

The third leading company, Lanco, is the most politically high
profile of the three companies, having been led initially by Lagadapati
Rajagopal, the Congress MP and a key YSR supporter. His brother
L. Madhusudan Rao and brother-in-law G. Bhaskara Rao now run
the group, which claims to be India's largest private sector power
producer and also has coal mining interests in Australia. To improve
its image, Lanco moved its headquarters from Hyderabad to Gurgaon
on the outskirts of Delhi but it became over-extended and lost large-
scale projects for lack of funds, pulled out of others, dismissed a large
number of employees, and formally announced a debt-restructuring
process in 2013.

Some time in the future, Andhra's years of fraud and deception
will almost certainly be seen, in the traditions of early American

business, as merely one of the stepping stones that a new economy takes when it suddenly enjoys unexpected riches, and the prospect of much more, if politicians are suborned, rules bent and the state cheated.

For now, the Andhra companies have fallen from favour with more conventional investors. Barring the sort of scandals that emerged with Satyam and the YSR investigations, they should recover though, even if it is some time before they and their business families can regain credibility with savvy Indian and foreign investors. Too many private equity and other firms have been caught by what looked like sound deals and honest entreprenreurs for this to happen quickly, especially with the current investigations and pending court cases. Yet one should never under-estimate investors' ability to turn a proverbial blind eye when offered the prospect of quick profits – a thought that no doubt brings a glimmer of hope to such companies.

Notes

1.   http://ridingtheelephant.wordpress.com/2009/01/07/satyam%E2%80%99s-raju-lifts-the-lid-on-indian-corporate-fraud/
2.   http://ridingtheelephant.wordpress.com/2009/09/04/a-chief-minister%E2%80%99s-death-highlights-contradictions-of-indian-politics/
3.   http://ridingtheelephant.wordpress.com/2009/09/04/a-chief-minister%E2%80%99s-death-highlights-contradictions-of-indian-politics/
4.   http://ridingtheelephant.wordpress.com/2009/12/18/hyderabad-sinks-from-software-to-scams-as-greed-and-wealth-swamp-politics/
5.   Conversation with JE, July 2013
6.   Harish Damodaran, *India's New Capitalists*, p. 92 and following, Permanent Black, Delhi 2008
7.   Jawaharlal Nehru, *The Discovery of India*, p. 307 http://www.scribd.com/doc/31927774/The-Discovery-of-India-Jawaharlal-Nehru
8.   Swaminathan Aiyar, 'Declassify report on the 1948 Hyderabad massacre', *The Times of India*, 25 November 2012, http://blogs.

timesofindia.indiatimes.com/Swaminomics/entry/declassify-report-on-the-1948-hyderabad-massacre

9. 'Rock Formations of Hyderabad', Society to Save Rocks, http://www.hyderabadgreens.org/rocks.html

10. 'Telangana is more advanced than the rest of AP', http://www.indianexpress.com/news/backward-telangana-is-a-myth/734444/

11. *India's New Capitalists* by Harish Damodaran p 121, Permanent Black, Delhi 2008

12. http://www.indianexpress.com/news/centre-says-a-guarded-yes-to-telangana/552114/

13. 'Jagan is president of YSR Congress', 2 February 2011 http://www.thehindu.com/todays-paper/tp-national/tp-andhrapradesh/article1479332.ece

14. JE, 'India Calling: East Meets West at the Internet Frontier', *Fortune* magazine, 17 April 2000.

15. www.aponline.gov.in/Apportal/HumanDevelopmentReport2007/APHDR_2007_Chapter4.pdf

16. IPDL website http://www.idpl.gov.in/about_us.html

17. P. Sainath, 'Why Farmers Die', June 2004, http://www.indiatogether.org/2004/jun/psa-farmdie.htm

18. http://planningcommission.nic.in/data/datatable/0512/databook_117.pdf

19. P. Sainath, 'Why Farmers Die', June 2004, http://www.indiatogether.org/2004/jun/psa-farmdie.htm

20. 'Reddy in the Rough', http://indiatoday.intoday.in/story/ys-reddy-guarding-off-corruption-charges/1/156002.html

21. http://ridingtheelephant.wordpress.com/2009/09/04/a-chief-minister%E2%80%99s-death-highlights-contradictions-of-indian-politics/

22. 7 Sept 2009, http://www.in.siasat.com/english/news/clp-claims-417-die-wake-ysrs-deathpolice-could-not-confirm

23. 16 Sept 2009, http://indiatoday.intoday.in/story/Families+paid+to+cl aim+YSR+shock+deaths/1/61917.html

24. 'Deifying YSR', 14 September 2009, https://www.google.co.in/search?q=deifying+YSR&ie=utf-8&oe=utf-8&aq=t&rls=org.mozilla:en-US:official&client=firefox-beta&channel=fflb

25. http://ridingtheelephant.wordpress.com/2009/12/18/hyderabad-sinks-from-software-to-scams-as-greed-and-wealth-swamp-politics/

26. A. Srinivasa Rao, 'How Jagan Reddy became the richest Lok Sabha MP in India, and what is his real worth?', *Mail Today*, 28 May 2012, http://indiatoday.intoday.in/story/how-jagan-reddy-became-the-richest-mp-in-india-and-what-is-his-real-worth/1/197981.html

27. 'How did democratic values collapse?', 15 June 2012, http://millenniumpost.in/NewsContent.aspx?NID=4022

28. http://ridingtheelephant.wordpress.com/2012/06/15/andhra-pradesh-political-corruption-hits-sonia-gandhi-and-congress/

29. 11 December 2010, http://www.timescrest.com/society/mavericks-myth-money-4235

30. 'Jagan Mohan Reddy sent to jail as special prisoner', *The Times of India*, http://articles.timesofindia.indiatimes.com/2012-05-29/hyderabad/31887391_1_vijay-sai-reddy-sakshi-newspaper-odarpu-yatra

31. 'Andhra leader's arrest shows CBI reform is essential' http://www.business-standard.com/india/news/arrested-independence-/475828/

32. http://ridingtheelephant.wordpress.com/2012/06/15/andhra-pradesh-political-corruption-hits-sonia-gandhi-and-congress/

33. 15 June 2012, http://www.ndtv.com/article/south/election-results-jagan-sweeps-polls-will-be-chief-minister-in-2014-predicts-sister-231640

34. 8 June 2012, 'Costliest elections ever in State', http://www.thehindu.com/news/states/andhra-pradesh/article3501694.ece

35. 12 June 2012, http://www.ndtv.com/article/south/80-per-cent-turnout-in-andhra-pradesh-by-polls-jagan-mohan-reddy-on-trial-230500

36. 'CongressMP'sfatherkilledinbombblast',*IndianExpress*,24May1998,http://expressindia.indianexpress.com/ie/daily/19980524/14450754.html   and http://www.hindu.com/2004/04/13/stories/2004041305380500.htm

37. 'Beyond Media Images', a letter from YSR, *EPW*, 31 July 2004, http://www.epw.in/system/files/pdf/2004_39/31/Beyond_Media_Images.pdf

38. 'Money backs "Son-rise" in Andhra', *Mail Today*, 3 October 2009 (no internet link working)

39. JE conversations with Hyderabad sources

40. 'Andhra Pradesh cancels land allotment to IMG', IANS, 29 September

29, 2006 http://www.india-forums.com/news/business/3852-andhra-pradesh-cancels-land-allotment-to-img.htm

41. *The Times of India*, 4 November 2012, *http://timesofindia.indiatimes. com/city/hyderabad/IMG-Bharatas-Rao-defends-MoU-with-state-govt/ articleshow/17081258.cms*

42. 'YSR's "sheer size" of corruption shocked US diplomats', *First Post*, http://www.firstpost.com/politics/ysr-reddys-sheer-size-of-corruption-shocked-us-diplomats-85356.html

43. Company website: http://www.lancohills.com/

44. Golden Mile plots sold at Rs 55,000 a square yard, *The Hindu*, 21 July 2006, http://www.hindu.com/2006/07/21/stories/2006072120400400.htm

45. P Sainath, 'A short history of messing up', 8 June 2012, *The Hindu*, http://www.thehindu.com/opinion/lead/article3501815.ece

46. AP government website for Jalayagnam scheme: http://jalayagnam. org/index1.php?action=home

47. 'Jalayagnam delay: CAG raps State government', *The Hindu*, 7 February 2013, http://www.thehindu.com/todays-paper/jalayagnam-delay-cag-raps-state/article4387789.ece

48. 'Rs 186,000 Crore Illusion', *Down to Earth*, 15 July 2012, http://www.downtoearth.org.in/content/rs-186000-cr-illusion

49. TDP political party website: http://www.telugudesam.org/tdpcms/scams/rajaofcorruption/Chapter16.pdf

50. http://www.thehindubusinessline.com/news/jagan-assets-case-india-cements-md-srinivasan-other-accused-appear-in-court/article5304110.ece

51. '"Raja" of Corruption', http://www.telugudesam.org/tdpcms/scams/rajaofcorruption/

52. 'Flow of Funds', http://telugudesam.org/jagancorruption/?page_id=13

53. Ibid.

54. '3 mantris cleared Vanpic in a day', TNN, 6 June 2012 http://articles.timesofindia.indiatimes.com/2012-06-06/hyderabad/32078329_1_cbi-court-cbi-counsel-vanpic

55. CAG report for the year ending 31 March 2011; tabled in the Andhra Pradesh Assembly March 2012

56. The Andhra Pradesh Mineral Development Corporation obtained mining rights because it is a state corporation but a clause in its contract

enabled it to bring in the private sector if it lacked the technology, so it joined up with Jindal and RAK. 'Cancel bauxite mining leases in Vizag: House panel', *The Hindu*, 9 January 2013, http://www.thehindu.com/news/national/andhra-pradesh/cancel-bauxite-mining-leases-in-vizag-house-panel/article4289962.ece

57. 'Nimmagadda roped in RAK to bag Vanpic project: CBI counsel', *The Times of India*, 21 March 2013, http://articles.timesofindia.indiatimes.com/2013-03-21/hyderabad/37901956_1_aj-jagannadham-qatar-massad-nimmagadda-prasad

58. 'AP cabinet cancels Rs 16,000 crore port, industrial corridor project', *Mint*, 19 November 2013, http://www.livemint.com/Industry/BdV9O249hA3Q6RI0yWJ1MP/AP-cabinet-cancels-Rs16000-crore-port-industrial-corridor.html

59. 'Why the big four Andhra Pradesh-based infrastructure companies GMR, GVK, Lanco & IVRCL are in trouble?', *Economic Times*, 24 June 2012, http://articles.economictimes.indiatimes.com/2012-06-24/news/32382929_1_gayatri-projects-airport-business-gmr-infrastructure

60. 'Top Indian Companies Burdened With Debt', Forbes.com report on Credit Suisse report, 'House of Debt–Revisited', 19 August 2013, http://www.forbes.com/sites/meghabahree/2013/08/19/top-indian-companies-burdened-with-debt/

61. http://ridingtheelephant.wordpress.com/2009/01/07/satyam%E2%80%99s-raju-lifts-the-lid-on-indian-corporate-fraud/

62. http://ridingtheelephant.wordpress.com/2008/09/22/%E2%80%9Cfamily-silver%E2%80%9D-at-risk-on-hyderabad-metro-project/

63. 'Delhi Metro MD smells a scam', http://articles.economictimes.indiatimes.com/ 2008-09-21/news/27718987_1_hyderabad-metro-vgf-viability-gap-funding

64. http://ridingtheelephant.wordpress.com/2008/12/17/markets-kick-satyam-into-line-%E2%80%93-but-india%E2%80%99s-reputation-for-corporate-governance-is-hit/

65. 'Text – Satyam chairman Ramalinga Raju's letter', Reuters, 7 January 2009, http://www.reuters.com/article/2009/01/07/satyam-text-idINBOM36807220090107?rpc=44&sp=true

66. 'Ramalinga Raju gets bail after two years, eight months in jail', *Mint*, 5 November 2011, http://www.livemint.com/Companies/

NbnGDBW3olCdkKtcpHjo2M/Ramalinga-Raju-gets-bail-after-
two-years-eight-months-in-ja.html

67. 'Enforcement Directorate files charges in Satyam case – Seeks
    prosecution of Raju brothers, 45 others and 166 alleged front companies
    for laundering ill-made money', *Business Standard*, 29 October 2013,
    http://www.business-standard.com/article/current-affairs/ed-files-
    charge-sheet-in-satyam-case-113102800502_1.html

68. Sanjaya Baru, 'Breakfast with G.M. Rao – "Runway" success', *Business
    Standard*, 6 July 2010, http://www.business-standard.com/india/
    news/breakfastbs-g-m-rao/400446/

69. 'GMR's Shattered Dreams', *Forbes India*, 13 June 2011, http://
    forbesindia.com/article/boardroom/gmrs-shattered-dreams/25792/0
    and 'GM Rao: Fighting For His Dreams', *Forbes India*, 23 March
    2012, http://forbesindia.com/article/worlds-billionaires-2012/gm-
    rao-fighting-for-his-dreams/32570/1

70. 'GMR Infra to sell road toll projects to pare Rs 33k cr debt',
    MoneyControl.com, 6 August 2013, http://www.moneycontrol.com/
    news/cnbc-tv18-comments/gmr-infra-to-sell-road-toll-projects-to-
    pare-rs-33k-cr-debt_931375.html

71. 'Implementation of Public Private Partnership at Indira Gandhi Inter-
    national Airport', CAG Performance Audit Summary, 21 August 2012,
    http://www.prsindia.org/administrator/uploads/general/ 1345638508-
    ~CAG%20Report%20on%20the%20Indira%20Gandhi%20
    International%20Airport.pdf

VI

INDIA ABROAD

19

Uncertain Convictions

India has never recovered from its devastating defeat by China in a brief 1962 border war, which shattered its significant role on the international stage and still affects its overall stance on foreign policy. There have, of course, been moments when it has successfully reasserted itself internationally since then, notably with its nuclear tests in May 1998 and its growing economic importance in the 2000s, plus a new constructive relationship with the US. These positive developments, however, have been offset by other events, and India has never rebuilt anything near the international self-confidence and presence that Jawaharlal Nehru displayed immediately after independence in 1947.

Pakistan matched India's nuclear capability by testing weapons (developed with China's help) two weeks after India's tests in 1998. This diluted the regional significance of what India had done, although, on a broader international front, the tests did lead to the new interest from the US. Predictably, this did not lift India's international clout for long, and indeed it complicated relations with China. India's economic ebullience of the 2000s then floundered by 2011 in a morass of corruption scandals, populist politics, weak government leadership, and declining rates of economic growth. Corrupt and democracy-fettered decision-making had by this time also dashed any hope of matching China as an international economic power.

Here then is a country rich in culture, history, natural resources and brains, which has experienced the prospects of increasing economic importance but has not attempted to assert itself internationally since Nehru's idealism was crushed. Overall, its self-esteem is diminished by the extent of its poverty – it accounts for one-third of the world's poor. Its power is also restricted by limited economic and financial clout. Nevertheless, it is failing to rise to the potential that it does have, and it does not perform the international role that many outsiders, and some Indian experts, believe that it should be doing. Nor does it equip a desperately under-resourced external affairs ministry with the ability to do so. The Indian Foreign Service has only about 700 officers, which is ludicrously inadequate. (The number is being doubled over the next 10 years, but it probably needs to be nearer 3,000, with broader expertise and less elitist disdain for other government departments.)

Internationally, India's voice is rarely heard on major issues and was not even taken significantly into account when the country had a two-year term from 2011 to 2013 as a non-permanent member of the UN Security Council. Humphrey Hawksley, a BBC correspondent, emailed me during that period saying, 'Just come out of a half hour editorial meeting on Syrian crisis. India not mentioned – despite being on the UN – India doesn't have a voice'. That fits with an often-heard view that India is more focused on the prestige and the glory of joining clubs than what to do when it gets there – 'it has no apparent strategy at the UN except intervene less,' said another journalist.

President Obama tried, and largely failed, to get India to abandon some of its reticence when he addressed the Indian parliament in November 2010.[1] In a powerful speech, he came down firmly on India's side in relation to Pakistan terrorism and involvement in Afghanistan, and broadly backed its ambition to become a permanent member of the UN Security Council.[2] But as soon as he had drawn applause from the assembled members of India's two houses of parliament, he bluntly stated: 'Now, let me suggest that with increased power comes increased responsibility'[3] for those (implicitly, like India) 'that seek to lead in the 21st century'. He was, however, knocking on a closed door.

Such an approach does not fit precisely into the jugaad concept of turning shortages, chaos and adversity into some sort of order and success, nor precisely the chalta hai attitude of 'anything goes'. But, though few in India's foreign policy establishment would agree, there is a chalta hai sense that India's foreign relations will somehow fall into place, whatever is said or done. 'We have to change the absurdity that is our foreign service if we are to help shape the world rather than merely fend the world off,' says Kanti Bajpai, a leading policy analyst.[4]

Nehru's Vision

It all looked so different in 1947, when Nehru led India into an idealistic vision of non-alignment that was based on each country's right to decide issues as it saw fit and not because of commitment to either bloc. This was in tune with Mahatma Gandhi's approach of passive resistance and non-cooperation in India's independence movement, but was developed separately to handle the foreign policy realities of the time. It caught the mood of the world's 'whiff of idealism' after the 1939–45 war and led to the founding of the Non-Aligned Movement (NAM), with India as prime mover of independence for all countries, which Nehru felt could only be fully achieved if decisions were taken independently and not under pressure.

'We were accused of putting ourselves on a high moral plane, but we weren't trying to be better than anyone else – we were groping our way in a world we didn't understand,' says K. Shankar Bajpai, who was ambassador to Pakistan, China and the US between 1976 and 1986 and chairman of the prime minister's National Security Advisory Board in 2008–11.[5] 'Nehru felt that the greater the polarisation of states between the two blocs, the greater the risk of war. Non-alignment was thus an ancillary to his search for preventing war, with the United Nations as the real forum for sorting out conflicts. It was this faith in, or at least an urge for, a set of multilateral institutions and the development of international laws as the basis for a new world order, that coincided with the 'whiff of idealism,' says Bajpai, who was a young Ministry of External Affairs official in the 1950s and so is reflecting the view of diplomats at the time.

Nehru shunned a 'quest for dominance' – a phrase that prime minister Rajiv Gandhi used in the 1980s to illustrate India's limited ambitions, according to Mani Shankar Aiyar. 'Such an India was not content to merely not be non-partisan in the Cold War. It also had something different to tell the world. And it was precisely because India had something to say which no one else was saying that the world paused to listen. Thus, an asymmetrical foreign policy gave an asymmetric influence hugely disproportionate to the material strength of an India which, in conventional terms, would have been paid little heed to if it were merely parroting the words and postures of others,' Aiyar said in a foreign affairs lecture in Melbourne in 2011.[6]

Jaswant Singh, who held three top portfolios as external affairs, finance and defence minister in the 1998–2004 NDA government, talks about a 'mentality of separateness' that existed from the time of independence.[7] It was this that led Nehru to reject an informal suggestion from America in the mid-1950s that India should join the United Nations Security Council when it was formed. In practical terms, Nehru's reply avoided India upstaging and upsetting China, which was being left out in favour of Taiwan, but it also fitted with his approach, especially at a time when the world was splitting into two Cold War camps. The result, of course, was that India was excluded from the inner workings of the UN, which it is now trying to rectify with embarrassingly persistent cries to become a permanent member of the Security Council.

Nehru did not want an alliance with any single country or power block, but he did want India to play a leading role in a large constituency, which NAM provided when it was founded in 1961. For a time Nehru's voice was heard, and India had a significant influence on major international issues in the first decade of independence. Aiyar summed this up in his Melbourne lecture: 'On the major international issues of the first decade of India's independence – Palestine, Korea, Indo-China, Suez – so influential was the differential Indian voice that India was included in both the UN committees set up in 1947 to bring about the transition in Palestine from Mandate to Partition... In Korea,[8] precisely because India asymmetrically refused to see right as belonging only to one side or the other, she was invited to become the chairman of the Neutral Nations Repatriation Commission without which the Korean War could not have been brought to an end.'

Although not invited to the Geneva Conference on Indo-China in 1954, writes Aiyar, Krishna Menon installed himself in the Hotel Beau Rivage on the banks of Lake Leman and played such a crucial role brokering accords between the principals[9] that the former French premier, Pierre Mendes-France, referred to the Geneva Conference as 'this ten-power conference – nine at the table – and India'. In consequence, India was invited to chair the three International Commissions for Supervision and Control set up to monitor the implementation of the accords on Vietnam, Laos and Cambodia.[10]

India was at this time 'punching above our weight, measured strictly in realist balance of power terms', as Shivshankar Menon, India's national security adviser from 2010 in the Manmohan Singh government, and a former foreign secretary, put it in August 2011 in a wide-ranging exposition on India's foreign policy.[11] 'This was possible because of the strategic space that the Cold War opened up for us, and because of the eminent good sense and reasonableness of what Nehru was doing and advocating. During the fifties, India stood higher in the world's (and her own) estimation than her strength warranted'. Menon went on to admit rather elliptically what happened after that: 'During the sixties the reverse was the case. After 1971 there has been a greater correlation between India's strength and prestige, and this seems likely to continue for the foreseeable future'. This was a neat diplomatic way of saying (correctly) that India's defeat by China in 1962 ended both its clout and Nehru's international attempts at leadership. India then displayed regional strength when it helped Bangladesh to be carved out of Pakistan in 1971, but it has not been able to extend that on a wider international plane because of its relative economic and military weakness, despite the 1998 nuclear tests and economic growth in the 2000s.

After Nehru

In any case, India no longer has the will to be heard, nor does it seem confident, as it was in Nehru's time, that it has something different to say, apart from believing in non-intervention in other countries' affairs and therefore opposing the sort of regime change led by the US and UK in Iraq and elsewhere. Implicitly criticizing the West's military intervention in Libya and support for Syrian rebels, Manmohan Singh said at the UN in September 2011: 'The observance of the rule of law is as important in international affairs as it is within countries. Societies cannot be reordered from outside through military force. People in all countries have the right to choose their own destiny and define their own future'.[12]

That said, India is now much more focused on its own concerns, as Menon explained in his 2011 lecture: 'Our primary task now and for the foreseeable future is to transform and improve the life of the unacceptably large number of our compatriots who live in poverty, with disease, hunger and illiteracy as their companions in life. This is our overriding priority, and must be the goal of our internal and external security policies. Our quest is the transformation of India, nothing less and nothing more.' India had 'sought the strategic autonomy that nuclear weapons bestow upon us' so that it could pursue that goal 'without distraction or external entanglement', he added, diplomatically stopping short of naming China and Pakistan as the potentially distracting entanglements.

'So, while India is already a major economy in terms of size and ability to influence prices and supply and demand in certain markets, it will still be a country of poor people with overwhelming domestic priorities for an extended period of time. This will certainly be true for the foreseeable future which is, at best, fifteen years,' said Menon. 'That is why it is important to peg our goals and use of power to our immediate and overriding interest in our domestic transformation. In other words, our condition and the state of the world require us not to seek hegemony, or domination, or expansion, or strategic depth. None of these serve our basic interest, even in a defensive sense. Being a bridging power, or a swing state might, in certain circumstances. Power is the ability to create and sustain outcomes. Weight we have, our influence is growing, but our power remains to grow and should first be used for our domestic transformation.'

From Nehru to the present day (with Menon presumably reflecting the views of Manmohan Singh), it can be presented as a noble, well-honed and gradually developing cause – though Menon admitted it could also be seen as a 'very selfish policy'. In this view of history, India has moved logically and coherently from being an independent opinion-leader under Nehru, to a pragmatic domestic-oriented player in the twenty-first century's era of globalization, guarding and promoting its internal interests and staying out of trouble abroad when it does not need to be involved. This means that it does not think it should seek alliances with other countries (for example, as the UK does with the US), and it should oppose interference in other nation's affairs, especially interference that is aimed at regime change. If it is sometimes as selfishly hypocritical in choosing whom it supports as the West is when it goes for regime change in unfriendly oil-rich states while ignoring the lack of democracy in Bahrain or Sudan, so be it!

A Narrow Focus

Indian officials define the country's foreign focus as primarily on the neighbourhood, stretching from the Middle East across South Asia to China and Southeast Asia and, further away and to a lesser extent, the US. The actual focus is really much narrower and is driven by a sometimes proactive (and more often reactive) policy in relation to Pakistan, which stems from post-partition border disputes and tensions, plus the threats and reality of cross-border terrorism. In South Asia generally, India has failed so badly to get onto co-operative terms with any of its neighbours (apart from Bhutan) that China has seduced them and, in so doing, has gradually encircled India.

With the US, it has in recent years become an almost-partner (though not an ally), but it is Washington, not Delhi, that drives the relationship or allows it to drift. With China, which is its biggest and potentially most threatening neighbour, India is constantly on the back foot and allows Beijing to set the agenda. With the Gulf states and the rest of West Asia (broadly the Middle East), India only showed what some officials admit was 'benign neglect' till the late 2000s. This was despite the presence there of some six million Indians who send home $35bn remittances annually, and the fact that the region supplies about 60 per cent of India's oil and gas.[13] The same applied to Southeast Asia. Elsewhere, India is beginning to take more notice of Africa (with $5bn three-year aid and other initiatives announced in May 2011), the Gulf and eastern Asia, especially as it searches abroad for sources of energy and other essential supplies, realizing the need to counter China's growing international influence. It has also begun to develop an important relationship with Japan that was marked by the first-ever visit to India by an emperor and empress at the end of 2013. Japan is interested because it is attempting to counter aggressive diplomacy from Beijing, and there are potentially big gains for India in terms of development finance and other assistance.

India has always felt comfortable with the old Soviet Union, its ally in the Cold War; Indira Gandhi and other top leaders used to say that Moscow 'has never let us down'. India was directly affected when the Soviet Union collapsed in 1990–91 because the economic support it had been receiving stopped. But the relationship has continued with Russia, certainly on international affairs, though Moscow is uneasy about India's growing defence and other links with the US, and there have been problems with Russian defence contract delays and cost over-runs.

Formal links with Europe have not developed across a wide front since they were established in 1963 with the then European Economic Community (EEC), though they were given a boost in the 1990s and early 2000s.[14] India prefers to deal with individual countries and does not rate the European Union as a top priority or vital entity[15] even though, taken together, the countries involved are its major trading partner and it has been trying to negotiate a trade treaty. France is primarily seen as a useful and flexible supplier of defence and nuclear equipment. The UK is treated as a friendly, once-significant but now over-eager and occasionally condescending player. It is important at a business and people level – there are 1.5m residents of Indian origin in the UK along with substantial investments, including the Tata group, which is the largest private sector employer. Prime Minister David Cameron hopes unrealistically for a 'very special partnership' and for the two countries to be 'inextricably linked', as he spun it on a public relations-oriented trip to India.[16]

Losing the Argument

It is, of course, easy to take a negative view of India's approach, and especially the sanctimonious way that its foreign affairs have often been conducted with attitudes of arrogant pomposity that have little clear end-purpose. I irritated the external affairs ministry with a column in the *Business Standard* in 2001 at a time when India was losing arguments internationally, especially in the US and UK, over its problems with Pakistan and the future of Kashmir. 'India's failure to get its message across internationally is, of course, not new. Pakistan has for years had more pro-active and effective diplomatic and public relations, especially in Washington and London,' I wrote. 'While India strutted pompously for years on the world stage, irritating other countries by self-defensively protesting its importance but failing to follow through with sound diplomacy, Pakistan has won hearts and minds'.[17] When diplomats did get into negotiations, they characteristically became bogged down in agreement-defying detail.

My view was based partly on comments I had heard for a long time from many of the neighbouring countries' diplomats about ineffectual posturing and personal arrogance – a word that has been picked up by Antonio Armellini, a former Italian ambassador to India in a book, *If The Elephant Flies*.[18] He wrote about India's 'arrogance – or the exaggerated self-confidence if one prefers – that can adversely affect the country's decision-making and its overall ability to correctly assess opportunities and limitations'. He scathingly coupled that with 'the tendency to take one's expectations for facts' which 'influences political orientations and often leads to errors that are regularly ascribed to the hostility of others rather than one's own misjudgements'.

Such a critique was harsh but, taken point by point, it was accurate and is borne out by others. Susan Rice, Obama's national security adviser from June 2013, is reported to have said that she had become a 'lot less patient' with India after having a 'tough relationship' over votes on Libya and Syria with her Indian counterpart (Hardeep Singh Puri, a blunt Indian diplomat), when she was the US ambassador at the UN during the first Obama administration.[19] Having watched Indian diplomats perform at the UN, David Malone, a former Canadian high commissioner in Delhi, has written, 'The cleverest person in the room may win many arguments, but still not win the game'.[20] A retired senior Indian diplomat admitted to me that 'we have to give up our unrealistic pretensions that we have a monopoly of wisdom'.[21] Adding to that, a retired British diplomat told me that India had 'neither the will nor mechanisms to look at internal issues and pursue them', adding wearily, 'it takes offence at the slightest excuse and is slow to forgive and forget'.

In Washington, says a seasoned American foreign affairs expert and diplomat, Indian ambassadors rarely show the diplomatic and social aplomb of top European countries and the Israelis, and thus lack the access, opportunity and ability to influence decision-making.[22] Even though India was by mid-2012 well established and popular in the American capital, he said that 'it is hard to find an example of a US policy where India has had real influence – not on Pakistan, nor Afghanistan nor China'. Some foreign diplomats suggest that their Indian counterparts do not have a sense of direction or purpose and are reluctant to discuss issues, maybe because they are under-briefed and (or) are ambivalent about India's role in the world. India has also disappointed countries in Southeast and eastern Asia by not doing enough to build relationships beyond routine diplomatic exchanges, despite a look-east policy adopted in the 1990s. In practice, India is drawn in different directions by its wish to be a player, as it has been, for example, on climate change, and still carry the non-involved tag.

There is also criticism inside India as well as outside that the country lacks internationally recognized foreign affairs think tanks that could produce consistent analysis comparable to America's Brookings Institute and the Heritage Foundation. The importance of an occasional thematic speech like Menon's in August 2011 illustrates the potential. There are many small policy institutes in Delhi on defence as well as foreign policy issues, happily headed by retired foreign secretaries and other diplomats and the occasional admiral or general, but none has the authority at home or abroad of a major centre of thought and analysis. The Observer Research Foundation in Delhi, founded and partially funded by the Reliance Industries of Mukesh Ambani, fills some gaps but it has a far wider remit than foreign affairs, while the long-established Centre for Policy Studies has small rooms housing bright experts but does not aspire to collective clout.

Brahma Chellaney, a Delhi-based strategic affairs specialist, criticizes India from a different angle, arguing that it 'gives, and gets nothing in return', and does not recognize that 'reciprocity is the first principle of diplomacy'. He lists India's generosity on land issues ranging from surrendering British-inherited extra-territorial rights in Tibet in 1954, to giving back strategic gains after the 1965 and 1971 Pakistan wars and, more recently, facing pressure to cede control on the Siachen Glacier where the two countries have had a high altitude confrontation since 1984. Chellaney is an expert on the region's river water disputes and says that the 'world's most generous water-sharing pact is the 1960 Indus Waters Treaty, under which India agreed to set aside 80.52 per cent of the waters of the six-river Indus system for Pakistan, keeping for itself just the remaining 19.48 per cent share'.[23]

Power of the States

India's relations with its neighbours are becoming disrupted by the politics and attitudes of its states that border the other countries and increasingly interfere in national diplomacy. This raises the question of how much – or how little – support Delhi can expect from regional politicians, and whether it has the will, patience and skill to involve them in the development of foreign affairs. It is a question that has yet to be tackled by the policy makers and it risks weakening India's already poor handling of neighbourhood diplomacy. This is not new, but it has become more serious in recent years.

There have always been inevitable links between Jammu and Kashmir and India's policy on Pakistan because Kashmir is disputed territory, and between Tamil Nadu and policy on Sri Lanka because of links with the island's Tamil minority. India's north-eastern states and West Bengal have interests in India's relations with neighbouring Bangladesh and Myanmar, as do Bihar and Uttar Pradesh with Nepal. Further afield and less controversially, the southern state of Kerala has interests in policy on the United Arab Emirates and other Middle East countries because of its people working there and its dependence on the money they send home.

Such issues have become a bigger problem now that state-level political parties are members of India's coalition governments. The parties have become more assertive and independent-minded, usually pushing populist policies that win support in their states, irrespective of whether they gel with national priorities. The central government has failed to respond to this and has not developed an approach that would maintain its leading role on foreign policy. The problems were clearly stated by K. Shankar Bajpai in a December 2010 article: 'Drowning national needs in local politics, emotional or outdated ideological illusions, playing to the galleries or simple ignorance is mortally dangerous. Consider some random instances: Tamil Nadu's parties competed to embarrass Delhi's handling of Sri Lanka, states around Bangladesh connive at illegal immigration, Uttar Pradesh has no thought for its responsibilities vis-à-vis Nepal.'

Bajpai's Tamil Nadu reference stemmed from the way that, in order to protect the Congress party's political relationships in the state, India's 2004–2014 government allowed two rival regional political parties to affect diplomacy with Sri Lanka. The parties sought local popularity by objecting to India working with the island's chauvinistic Sinhalese-dominated government, and disrupted sporting and other links. Their influence even led to Manmohan Singh staying away from a Commonwealth heads of government meeting in Sri Lanka in November 2013. These political sensitivities left space for China and Pakistan (and Israel) to strengthen ties after they provided aircraft and other weaponry and training to help Sri Lanka defeat Tamil separatists in the 2000s.[24] China was then able to make the island one of its 'string of pearls' by building a port and airport and other projects with soft loans and other assistance.

A cross-border treaty with Bangladesh on the Teesta river waters was upset by Mamata Banerjee, the irascible and unpredictable chief minister of West Bengal, just as it was about to be signed in 2011 by Manmohan Singh.[25] This held up work on other issues affecting the two countries' 4,000-km border, including India possibly having transit rights across northern Bangladesh to its north-eastern states. On the other side of India, Narendra Modi, the BJP chief minister of Gujarat, objected just before his state's last assembly elections to negotiations on a possible settlement of a disputed part of Pakistan at Sir Creek on the Gujarat-Sindh maritime border.[26]

Banerjee's opposition seems to have stemmed at least partly from pique that she was not consulted. Sumantra Bose, a political scientist who knows her, says he believes that her opposition was 'due as much to her resentment of the Congress-ruled Centre's failure to adequately involve her state government in the process as it is to her substantive concerns that the treaty could prove to be detrimental to West Bengal's interests'.[27]

This opens up the question of what rights a state has to influence and dictate national foreign policy in federal India.[28] It also points to the need for the central government actively to recognize and involve the states when new policies and treaties are being developed. That was done in 1995 by I.K. Gujral, when he was foreign minister (H.D. Deve Gowda was prime minister). Gujral encouraged Bangladesh's Awami League government to liaise with Jyoti Basu, the communist leader of West Bengal's government, on negotiations over a barrage at Farakka on the River Ganga.[29] His sort of pragmatic statesmanship was not displayed by Manmohan Singh.

Inadequacies

Many senior officials are severely critical – sometimes publicly after retirement and confidentially before that. One of the most outspoken is K. Shankar Bajpai. 'Our apparatus for interacting with the world is inadequate, in concepts and in mechanics,'[30] he wrote shortly after Obama's address to the Indian parliament in November 2010.[31] Obama had listed issues that he must have known India would not find easy to accept. He specifically mentioned the Nuclear Non-Proliferation Treaty that India has always refused to sign, and challenged India to forsake its friendship with Iran – which it would not do for historic and oil-supply reasons – and condemn the military regime in its neighbouring country of Myanmar, which it was rightly loath to do because of China's growing role in that country.

Bajpai said that Obama's message was 'welcome to the high table, now show us what you can bring to it'. India's problem however was an inability, indeed refusal, to project its views persuasively. 'Issuing statements, or rushing around canvassing at the last minute, cannot substitute for timely, sustained advocacy,' wrote Bajpai. 'Our missions abroad mostly glean our stand from the press. Briefings, if given, are like the banalities we get away with at home, ineffectual with hard-headed foreign offices or media analysts. Our domestic vices spoil our international image. Others treat you as they estimate you: a strong, well-organised state, seen as knowing what it is doing and able to do it efficiently, inspires respect, circumspection, even cooperativeness — an invaluable shield against mischief. The shorter we fall of such stature, the greater our vulnerabilities.'

Jan Egeland, a Norwegian politician and a former senior UN official, has been even more blunt. 'You can't be a superpower in the Security Council in the morning and a poor development country in the afternoon,' he says.[32] 'You can't behave like an eagle and sweep into the Security Council and then behave like a chicken.' Egeland's view reflects frustration that India expects to win a permanent seat on the Security Council but is not prepared to play a role – a euphemism for taking sides – on major issues such as Syria with its human rights abuses and Iran's nuclear ambitions. Such critics argue that Nehru understandably wanted to stay neutral in the Cold War while tilting towards the Soviet Union, but India should behave differently now that the NAM justification for inaction no longer exists. India sees it differently and, as Menon said, wants to pursue its domestic goals 'without distraction or external entanglement'.

While its critics complain that it does not pull its weight in the Security Council and other international forums, Indian diplomats say they have a coherent policy at the UN – for example, pushing development as a leading priority, calling for a global anti-terrorism campaign, pushing human rights issues and humanitarian operations, plus individual concerns like the Middle East (where it backs Palestine). It has also had a leading role in UN peacekeeping since the 1950s, having taken part in 46 operations with a total of 130,000 troops, the third largest number among the countries involved.

India is perhaps more comfortable playing an international role in economic affairs, though its domestic-oriented agenda inevitably means that it does not line up with the West on issues such as trade negotiations and climate change – both areas where it has played an opposition role. There has also been frustration that, while refusing to break off relations with Iran, India neither developed a diplomatic strategy for dealing with the country, nor tried to lead an international attempt at compromise which, many diplomats say, it has been uniquely positioned to do. This often goes back to a basic criticism that India finds it easier to block initiatives than lead constructive coalitions – suggesting that as a country, and like its people, it is not basically a consistent team player.

Many Indian diplomats, especially younger ones, think that India should be more robust, especially in the UN, and less proselytizing, as do various pundits. 'It is time for us to give up moralistic pretensions assuming we have a monopoly of wisdom,' says a retired top diplomat. C.Raja Mohan, a leading foreign affairs analyst and journalist, argues that it is time for India to stop behaving like a weak power and 'learn to be the regionally active – not war-mongering but showing strength.'[33]

The biggest external pressure on India to shake off its current approach is coming from the US, which sees it primarily as a counterweight, and maybe one day an ally, against China's growing power, so wants to edge it into a wider role. Obama aired the frustration during his 2010 visit, though he showed little sensitivity for India's priorities, calling for it to be tougher on Iran without acknowledging India's historic links and need for Iranian oil. He also wanted it to condemn the military regime in neighbouring Myanmar, without even partially recognizing that India needed to have some form of bilateral relations to counter China's growing role and to deal with cross-border problems. 'If I can be frank, in international fora, India has often avoided these issues,' said Obama. 'But speaking up for those who cannot do so for themselves is not interfering in the affairs of other countries. It's not violating the rights of sovereign nations. It's staying true to our democratic principles. It's giving meaning to the human rights that we say are universal. And it sustains the progress that in Asia and around the world has helped turn dictatorships into democracies and ultimately increased our security in the world.'

The basic differences were paraded in Delhi two years later at a joint India-US dialogue run by FICCI, a business federation, and America's Brookings Institution. Menon said that the two countries shared the same goals in the Middle East (West Asia) of stopping Iran gaining nuclear weapons and helping the development of a moderate and democratic Syria, but that they differed on the method. He teased the West about its interventions and regime-change tactics for seeming to 'empower extremist, fundamentalist and even terrorist groups'.[34] Brookings' president Strobe Talbott countered this robustly, saying it 'would be helpful if India would focus a little more on Iran's dangerous side', adding provocatively that the country 'is in your neighbourhood'.

On Syria, Talbott said inaction had 'its own consequences' and that 'letting that situation burn itself out or play itself out' was not a good option. India had voted in favour of sanctions against Syria, but abstained from a vote at the United Nations General Assembly denouncing the government because the resolution was ultimately aiming at regime change, which India, opposes on principle.[35] By the end of 2013 however, India was becoming more involved in international moves to find a peaceful Syrian solution. This may turn out to be one of the first signs that it is prepared to play a more active role in world affairs, while opposing intervention in other countries' internal policies.

'Please remember that a people cannot be forced to be free or to practise democracy. They have to come to these values themselves if they are to be lasting. Such a crusade for one's values is often mistaken by others as the pursuit of self-interest couched in high tone words', said Menon in his 2011 lecture. Officials such as Menon argue that India did not create the mess and muddle caused by the West's involvement in places like Syria. Reflecting that view, a senior Indian official told me:[36] 'We didn't manufacture the problem. We don't supply weapons there. We are not involved and we don't have the right to be. We have watched their [US, UK and others] game in Libya and Syria, turning the clock back in the region'. When I asked why India did not make its voice heard widely and publicly with such a potentially popular line, I was told, with a smile: 'We have a view but our friends are happy we keep quiet about it publicly'.

It is not enough though, for India to stay silent. With its depth of experience in international issues such as terrorism, religious fundamentalism, poverty and climate change, it needs to make its voice heard with reasoned argument and leadership. Only then, with the world welcoming a new, strong, independent voice, will it gradually win the international recognition and status that it craves.

Notes

1. Remarks by President Obama to the Joint Session of the Indian Parliament in New Delhi, India, 8 November 2010, http://www.whitehouse.gov/the-press-office/2010/11/08/remarks-president-joint-session-indian-parliament-new-delhi-india
2. http://ridingtheelephant.wordpress.com/2010/11/09/obama-ends-his-india-visit-on-a-high-but-challenges-it-to-change/
3. Remarks by President Obama to the Joint Session of the Indian Parliament, supra.
4. Kanti Bajpai, 'Foreign Policy on a shoestring', *The Times of India*, 13 October 2012, http://articles.timesofindia.indiatimes.com/2012-10-13/edit-page/34414274_1_ifs-foreign-policy-bigger-service
5. In conversation with JE
6. Mani Shankar Aiyar, 'India's foreign policy – from Jawaharlal Nehru to Manmohan Singh', Australia-India Institute, University of Melbourne, 22 September 2011; Aiyar says Prime Minister Rajiv Gandhi used the phrase several times, including at the 9th Non-Aligned Summit in Belgrade, see *Selected Speeches and Writings*, 1989, Vol. V, Publications Division, New Delhi, p. 277
7. Jaswant Singh talking to JE October 2012; see also his book surveying

the country's foreign policy since independence: *India at Risk: Mistakes, Misadventures and Misconceptions of Security Policy*, Roli Books, Delhi 2013, and a television discussion when it was published on http://www.ndtv.com/video/player/the-big-fight/india-s-security-concerns/296592?pfrom=home-topstories

8. Aiyar's lecture footnote: In 1952, Nehru told a press conference that while 'there was no question of our being a mediator or anything like that', it was 'well-recognized that we are in a special position because we have friendly contacts with the Governments concerned', adding that 'we will be very happy to use those contacts in furtherance of the settlement'. *Selected Works of Jawaharlal Nehru*, Second Series, Vol. 19, p. 583, Jawaharlal Nehru Memorial Fund, 1996, distributed by OUP. In 1953, India's principled stand, which had annoyed the Soviet Union when India voted at the UN in favour of the resolution finding North Korea to be the aggressor and then the Americans by refusing to side with the US on China crossing the Yalu river, was eventually vindicated when India was requested to chair the Neutral Nations Repatriation Commission which enabled the armistice to come into being and hold over the next sixty years and more. Earlier, the Indian representative had been Chairman of the United Nations Commission on Korea since late 1947, yet recognition of India's special role in world affairs. See *India After Independence*, Bipan Chandra et al., Penguin Viking, 1999, pp. 152-154

9. Aiyar's lecture footnote: Jawaharlal Nehru to the Indonesian Prime Minister, *Selected Works of Jawaharlal Nehru*, Vol. 25, p. 468, Jawaharlal Nehru Memorial Fund, 1996

10. Aiyar's lecture footnote: Chandra et al.

11. Shivshankar Menon, National Security Adviser, 'Our ability to change India in a globalised world', The Prem Bhatia Memorial Lecture, IIC, New Delhi 11 August 2011, full video with Q&A: www.iicdelhi.in/webcasts/play_webcast/16th-prem-bhatia-memorial-lecture-2011---india-and-the-global-scene/; full text http://www.prembhatiatrust.com/ click on Lecture 16. Partial text: http://www.claws.in/index.php?action=master&task=930&u_id=36

12. 'Manmohan slams West for using force to change regimes', *The Times of India*, 25 September 2011, http://articles.timesofindia.indiatimes.com/2011-09-25/india/30200524_1_libya-sovereignty-countries

13. India and West Asian Security conference, Delhi, 15 February 2015 http://www.idsa.in/keyspeeches/IndiaandWestAsianSecurity

14. This report gives a concise 50-year review of the relationship. Dr Radha Kumar, 'The EU and India: Common Interests, Divergent Policies', Delhi Policy Group, March 2013, http://www.delhipolicygroup.com/pdf/The-Eu-and-India-%20Common-Interests-Divergent-Policies. pdf

15. Shashi Tharoor, 'there are few visible "wins" in India-EU co-operation', *Pax Indica*, pp. 245-247, Allen Lane India, 2012

16. http://ridingtheelephant.wordpress.com/2013/02/20/pr-man-turned-prime-minister-cameron-pays-respect-but-over-plays-his-hand/

17. JE, 'India's flatfooted diplomacy', 'Bystander' column, *Business Standard*, 19 October 2001, http://www.business-standard.com/india/news/india 8217s-flatfooted-diplomacy/100162/

18. Antonio Armellini, *If the Elephant Flies,* Har-Anand Publications, Delhi, 2012 http://www.haranandpublications.com/history&politics. html

19. Seema Sirohi, 'India-U.S: Last chance to salvage ties', by Gateway House, 11 September 2013, http://www.gatewayhouse.in/india-u-s-last-chance-to-salvage-ties/?utm_source=MadMimi&utm_medium=email&utm_content=Weekly+Briefing&utm_campaign=20130906_m117144040_Weekly+Briefing&utm_term=Read+more

20. David M. Malone, *Does the Elephant Dance? Contemporary Indian Foreign Policy,* OUP India 2011, http://www.oup.co.in/product/academic-general/politics/international-relations/207/does-elephant-dance-contemporary-indian-foreign-policy/9780198073833

21. Conversations with the author, 2012

22. Conversation with JE

23. Brahma Chellaney, 'Parched and Thirsty, yet Most Generous in Water Diplomacy', *The Times of India*, 3 July 2012 http://chellaney. net/2012/07/03/parched-and-thirsty-yet-most-generous/

24. Brahma Chellaney, 'Behind The Sri Lankan Bloodbath', *Forbes*, 10 September 2009, http://www.forbes.com/2009/10/08/tamil-tigers-rajiv-gandhi-opinions-contributors-sri-lanka.html

25. 'Federal foreign policy: Mamata Banerjee has raised an important point', *Business Standard*, 7 September 2011, http://www.business-standard. com/article/opinion/federal-foreign-policy-111090700061_1.html

and also see http://www.economist.com/blogs/banyan/2013/01/bangladesh-and-its-near-abroad

26. http://indiatoday.intoday.in/story/sir-creek-dispute-gujarat-chief-minister-narendra-mod-rann-of-kutchmaritime-boundary/1/237992.html

27. Sumantra Bose conversation with JE after the launch of his book, *Transforming India: Challenges to the World's Largest Democracy*, Picador India, December 2013

28. http://www.thehindu.com/opinion/lead/india-needs-a-federal-foreign-policy/article4591675.ece

29. 'I.K. Gujral: A tribute from Bangladesh', *The Daily Star*, 13 December 2012   http://archive.thedailystar.net/newDesign/news-details.php?nid=260907

30. K. Shankar Bajpai, *Knowing what's good for us*, *Indian Express*, 24 December 2010, http://www.indianexpress.com/news/knowing-what-s-good-for-us/728788/

31. Remarks by the President to the Joint Session of the Indian Parliament in New Delhi, India, 8 November 2010, http://www.whitehouse.gov/the-press-office/2010/11/08/remarks-president-joint-session-indian-parliament-new-delhi-india

32. Jan Egeland was speaking at the Foreign Correspondents' Club in Delhi, October 2012, when he was deputy director of Human Rights Watch. He became Secretary General of the Norwegian Refugee Council in August 2013

33. Speaking at the Observer Research Foundation in a discussion on Tharoor's *Pax Indica*, July 2012

34. JE was at the meeting which took place in October 2012

35. 'General Assembly, in Resolution, Demands All in Syria "Immediately and Visibly" Commit to Ending Violence', http://www.un.org/News/Press/docs/2012/ga11266.doc.htm

36. JE 'background chat' conversation with Indian source

20

India and China
Himalayan struggles

Wen Jiabao, China's premier from 2003 to 2013, was unexpectedly fulsome. Speaking in Delhi's rather drab Indian Council of World Affairs' conference hall in December 2010, he was full of talk about China's and India's joint aspirations, their friendship, their co-operation, and about how their two-way trade would almost double to $100bn a year by 2015. He had brought a weirdly large posse of 400 businessmen[1] with him on a two-to-three day visit to India and had presided with Manmohan Singh over a flourish of $16bn business deals and joint agreements. In his speech, there was even a personal tribute to Mahatma Gandhi that rivalled a similar line President Barack Obama had deployed in Delhi a month earlier.[2]

The Chinese and Indian civilizations had 'once added radiance and beauty to each other and deeply influenced the process of human civilization,' he said. 'The great Chinese and Indian nations which have suffered all kinds of hardships but strived unceasingly will definitely glow with vitality, shoulder the historical mission and join hands to shape new glory of oriental civilizations.' As I sat there and listened to him, it seemed that Wen meant it and that, sometimes almost adlibbing, he was using this relatively low-key moment in his visit to establish China as a friend.

Suddenly his tone and even his demeanour changed, and he put India firmly in its place as an unequal neighbour, taking China's usual rigid line on the two countries' decades-old dispute over its mountainous 3,488-km border. Lecturing like a stern headmaster, he said: 'It will not be easy to completely resolve this question. It requires patience and will take a fairly long period of time', adding that 'only with sincerity, mutual trust and perseverance can we eventually find a fair, reasonable and mutually acceptable solution'. The tone and phrases were typical of China's patronising style of negotiation – I had heard it 20 years earlier when I was in Hong Kong and Beijing was stalling British negotiators on the terms for the territory's return in 1997 to Chinese sovereignty.

This dashed any hopes India may have had of making progress on the border issue. It sounded as though Wen was reflecting sharply differing views inside China's government over how to treat India, as he moved from the more constructive approach to that of the hardliners in the Peoples' Liberation Army (PLA). Perhaps significantly, China's foreign ministry website carried only the co-operative remarks,[3] while the *Xinhua* official news agency led its story with the tough line, headlined 'Patience needed to resolve boundary question'.[4]

The mood was strikingly different when China's next premier, Li Keqiang, visited India in May 2013 and conducted a charm offensive, albeit just after a serious confrontation on the border. Never once did he deflect from friendly and practical remarks about sowing 'the seeds of friendship'. On the border, he said the two sides had 'agreed to push forward with negotiations', which contrasted sharply with the line taken by Wen Jiabao. It is the Wen Jiabao cameo, however, that goes to the heart of India's foreign policy dilemma, which dates from its defeat by China in the 1962 war.

China has become the biggest foreign policy challenge facing India and the most bewildering worry, not least because the entire 3,488 km (2,167 mile) border, called the Line of Actual Control (LAC), is disputed and is not defined on the ground or on maps. (By contrast, most of the India-Pakistan Line of Control – LoC – is delineated and is accepted as a temporary arrangement). China also weighs heavily on the Indian consciousness because of 1962, and it has a physical presence everywhere that India is or wants to be – ranging from disputed mountains and valleys in the Himalayas to potentially insecure shipping lanes in the South China Sea. China also controls the flow of river waters that India needs, and it wields growing power across South Asia as well as influence in the UN and other international forums where India is represented.

This potentially explosive range of differences is partially offset by growing trade and economic links, which have boomed in recent years so that China has become India's largest trading partner with bilateral trade of around $70bn.[5] The target for 2016 is $100bn. Together, the two countries now account for 40 per cent of the world's population and their rivalry has grown as they have emerged from past constraints – China from the Cultural Revolution of the late-1960s, and India from British colonialism and subsequent centralized economic controls.

There is intense competition for oil and other energy and natural resources in Asia, Africa, the Gulf and South America. With an economy that has grown nearly ten-fold in 30 years, China is far ahead of India. Its GDP is already four times larger and some forecasts say it will overtake America by 2017. It has enormously greater involvement in international investment, trading and financial markets than India. Its military budget is almost three times larger and its armed forces are much better equipped, while its physical infrastructure, especially highways, is far more advanced. It has become the world's second largest oil importer after the US, taking roughly 5.5m barrels per day (BPD), while India at number four imports approximately 2.3m BPD.

What is certain is that there is no prospect of India and China being at ease with each other. Looking back, there never was, from the time of India's independence, because China saw itself as a future regional and world power and was not prepared for India to be in the same league. There is however broad stability, despite increasing militarization on the Himalayan border, with rapidly growing economic ties, tedious and literally endless border negotiations, and occasional constructive bilateral co-operation on international issues.

'India–China relations are complex and require careful management. There is need for firmness but also prudence. The Chinese are sometimes contemptuous of India but at times there is a respectful wariness. This is matched by our own ambiguous posture on China. This is likely to continue,' says Shyam Saran, a former Indian foreign secretary.

Nehru's Dream

Nehru idealistically saw India and China as parallel civilizations that could work together and did not realize till it was too late that this clashed with China's ambition to achieve regional supremacy. On the ground, his attitude may have been indicated by the size of the 30-acre plot allocated for China's embassy compound on Shanti Path, New Delhi's diplomatic boulevard, which is bigger than any other country's. 'He didn't understand China,' says Jagat Mehta, who was a young Indian diplomat in the 1950s and later became foreign secretary.[6] 'He thought that anti-imperialism would smother nationalism but it didn't', so the two countries lacked the common bond that Nehru envisaged. Mehta says that Nehru did not consult his officials sufficiently: 'He lacked in that he did not know how to ask questions, and we in the civil service did not have the courage to tell him'.

In what must have been the biggest mistake of his foreign policy, Nehru was persuaded to turn down an offer from China in 1959–60 to settle the disputed Himalayan border. Based on what is known as the McMahon line, it had been drawn up by Britain and agreed with China and Tibet in 1914. China now rejects that agreement because it does not accept that Tibet, which it annexed in 1950–51, was a sovereign country qualified to settle border disputes.

Initially, Nehru's strategy of friendship appeared to be working and he signed the Five Principles of Peaceful Co-existence with China, known as the Panchsheel Agreement, in 1954. But Nehru went too far and appeared, in Chinese eyes, to be patronizing Chou en-Lai, the premier, when he introduced him in 1955 at an international conference of African and Asian nations in Bandung, Indonesia. Relations soured and Nehru, by now himself feeling patronized, is said to have told India's ambassador to Peking in 1958: 'I don't trust the Chinese one bit. They are a deceitful, opinionated, arrogant and hegemonistic lot'.[7] Relations steadily worsened, especially after the flight of the Dalai Lama from Tibet to sanctuary in India in 1959.

There were also increased Chinese incursions along the border, which culminated in its troops walking into what is now the Indian state of Arunachal Pradesh (then called the North-East Frontier Agency) at the strategically sensitive Buddhist monastery town of Tawang in 1962. Four devastating (for India) weeks later, in what was never formally declared a war, China withdrew from all the land that it had occupied to the current disputed Line of Actual Control.[8] China could have marched as far as it liked into India because it would have faced little resistance, so ill-prepared were the defences, but it had taught India a lesson and that was enough. People in Tawang still talk of the sudden invasion, the panic among Indian forces, the burning of bridges and houses by the retreating army, and the relative good behaviour of the invader.[9]

The invasion coincided with the Cuban missile crisis. 'Just as Mao Zedong started his invasion of Tibet while the world was preoccupied with the Korean War, so he chose a perfect time to invade India, as recommended by the ancient strategist Sun Tzu,' wrote Brahma Chellaney.[10] 'The attack coincided with a major international crisis that brought the United States and the Soviet Union within a whisker of nuclear war over the stealthy deployment of Soviet missiles in Cuba. China's unilateral ceasefire coincided with America's formal termination of its naval blockade of Cuba, marking the end of the missile crisis.'

Zhou Enlai, communist China's first and longest serving premier (1949–1976) who was admired internationally as a charming and urbane but also tough statesman, said at the time that his aim was 'to teach India a lesson'. As Brahma Chellaney put it on the 50th anniversary of the defeat, 'such have been the long-lasting effects of the humiliation it imposed that China to this day is able to keep India in check'.[11]

China in Charge

From 1962, China has left India metaphorically dangling on the end of a rope. 'It has been their policy since 1962, to restrain India, partly through support for Pakistan – that policy began long before China's economic opening up but it has been especially hostile in the last two years since the US-India nuclear agreement,' Brajesh Mishra, a retired diplomat who was national security adviser and principal secretary to Prime Minister Atal Behari Bajpayee from 1998 to 2004, told me in 2009.[12] Mishra had been posted to Beijing as charge d'affairs to open a diplomatic mission in 1969 when China was beginning to relax its international isolation. At a diplomatic event in Beijing in May 1970, Mao Zedong unexpectedly turned to Mishra and said, 'How long are we going to go on quarrelling like this. Let us be friends again'.[13] India posted an ambassador in 1975, and Atal Bihari Vajpayee went on a visit as foreign minister in 1979. But there was no real breakthrough till Rajiv Gandhi visited Beijing as prime minister in December 1988. 'The high point of the visit came when Deng Xiaoping smiled and shook his hand for eight and a half minutes in the Great Hall of the People in full view of the world's cameras to signal the start of a new era in India-China relations,'[14] says Mani Shankar Aiyar, who was with Gandhi. Deng called Gandhi 'my young friend'.[15]

Since then, China has played at alternately confronting and co-operating with India. It teases with friendship, with trade, with border talks that make little progress, and occasionally with international co-operation on multilateral issues such as climate change, banking reform and anti-piracy ship patrolling in the Gulf of Aden. Simultaneously, it taunts with warnings and incursions on the border, tripping India up in international forums such as the Geneva-based Nuclear Suppliers' Group where India wants to become a member.

Border Dispute

The border dispute has been exacerbated by China's lack of confidence about the security of Tibet. It calls Arunachal Pradesh 'Southern Tibet' and basically refuses to settle the border with India unless India hands over Tawang, which it occupied in 1962. Tawang lies in an area that was administered remotely by Buddhist monks from Tibet till it was annexed into British India in 1914. It was here that the Dalai Lama first fled in 1959, and the monastery town has become a focal point of the two countries' differences.

Talks in the early 1980s and 1990s did not produce an agreement, despite some optimism at the time though no lives have been lost in confrontations on the border since an Agreement on the Maintenance of Peace and Tranquillity in 1993 that was followed by new 'confidence building measures'. The mood changed in 2005 when China became far more strident after India's co-operation agreements with the US that included defence and sales of armaments. China then hardened its demands, claiming in particular that Arunachal Pradesh is not part of India, and objecting when Manmohan Singh visited the state during campaigning for assembly elections in 2009. It has refused visas to Arunachal people, including official visitors, and condemned India's increased militarization and highway construction activity in the area. In tit-for-tat measures late in 2012, China launched passports with maps showing Arunachal (and Aksai Chin, the second disputed border area in the Ladakh area of Jammu and Kashmir) as part of its territory, and India printed its own version of maps on visas issued to Chinese nationals.

Throughout these years, China 'has used Pakistan as a cat's paw to keep India distracted,' says Shyam Saran.[16] China uses Pakistan as a 'proxy' – for example, by helping it to develop a nuclear bomb to counter India's capability. Pakistan is its primary customer for conventional weapons and the two countries' defence and industrial co-operation includes co-production of fighter aircraft and jet trainers, air-to-air and other missiles, frigates and battle tanks according to a US Pentagon report in May 2013.[17]

China's support for Pakistan runs alongside assistance from the US, which has its own Afghanistan-oriented reasons for helping. Between 1982 and 2011, the US provided $13.5 bn in economic aid and $17 bn in military assistance to Pakistan which included fighter aircraft and other weaponry.[18] The US is in effect therefore condoning the nuclear and military supplies that China gives to Pakistan – it has sometimes told Beijing that it knows about Chinese missile companies' sales (revealed by WikiLeaks[19]), but has apparently done nothing to stop the trade. There are however limits to how far China will go. It surprised Pakistan by not being supportive during its Kargil near-war with India in 1999, presumably realizing that to have done so would have upset the equilibrium with the US, and may have escalated the confrontation into an unnecessary crisis. China is also wary of Pakistan-based terrorists' possible links with Muslims in its restive western Xingjian province.

The messages from China come from different sources which often conflict with each other. In August 2009, a Chinese strategic issues website was claiming China could 'dismember the so-called "Indian Union" with one little move'.[20] It said that 'there cannot be two suns in the sky – China and India cannot really deal with each other harmoniously'.[21] The following March, a westernized Beijing adviser called at a Delhi conference for China and India to see their disputed Himalayan mountain border 'not as an insurmountable barrier' but as a 'bridge linking these two ancient civilizations together, for mutual benefit, and for mutual enrichment'.[22] In April 2012, after India launch-tested an AGNI V missile with a 5,000-km range that could strike Beijing or Shanghai, China's Communist Party-owned

Global Times newspaper warned aggressively that India 'would stand no chance in an overall arms race with China'.[23]

China knows that India will not over-react to whatever happens because Delhi realizes it is unlikely to win an argument, and is also aware it might have problems gaining diplomatic support from other countries in a dispute. 'Overt tensions with China only constrain our foreign policy choices vis-à-vis other powers,' wrote Kanwal Sibal, former foreign secretary, in December 2012.[24]

India Encircled

China has encircled India with a 'string of pearls'[25] by establishing its presence in neighbouring countries – not just its traditional targets of Pakistan, Nepal, Bangladesh and Myanmar, but also Sri Lanka and the Maldives archipelago in the Indian Ocean. Activities range from military, infrastructure and economic aid to intelligence co-operation and encouraging anti-India activities (as it has also done, directly or indirectly, in India's north-eastern states).[26] In Nepal, a key buffer country, there is constant rivalry for internal political and economic influence, and China is reported to be making territorial inroads across its border in the north of the country.

Problems possibly created, or at least accentuated, by China have emerged in the Maldives. This tiny nation of some 1,200 islands is generally regarded internationally as a serene tourist destination, but it is facing a tide of Islamic conservatism that is creating social and political instability and makes it open to diplomatic meddling. China opened a mission in Male, the capital, in March 2012, and the country's president, Mohamed Waheed, met Wen Jiabao in China a month later, when $500m aid was agreed. Towards the end of 2012, the government cancelled a long-term build-and-operate airport contract with GMR, the Indian infrastructure company.[27] That happened just after China's defence minister, Liang Guangli, visited the islands. Mohammed Nazim, the Maldives minister for defence, national security and transport, who handled the airport, had also just been to Beijing. This showed a distinct pro-China tilt by the Maldives following a change of its government. Previously the islands had relied on Indian assistance, as was well illustrated in 1988 when Indian troops quickly quelled a coup attempt by Sri Lankan Tamil mercenaries.[28] Unsurprisingly India, which is rarely adept at handling its neighbours, failed to deal smartly with the airport situation and the contract was lost, which was widely seen as a gain for China.

In neighbouring Sri Lanka, where India has had an uneasy relationship for decades because of links between the Tamil communities in both countries, China has become an increasingly good friend and large financial donor at a time when the country is desperately short of international support. The island's government has been widely condemned in the United Nations and elsewhere for alleged human rights violations and mass killings in 2009, when it was fighting a guerrilla war that had been running for 26 years over a separate homeland for its minority Tamil community. Chinese companies have built infrastructure contracts worth some $4bn including the island's second international airport, opened in March 2013, a port and highways, all funded with Chinese soft loans.[29] That makes China a more valuable ally than India, which also helps with a variety of projects[30] but whose relations with the island are complicated by the politics of Tamil Nadu.

Bhutan's Happiness

The remote kingdom of Bhutan squeezed in the Himalayas between India and China is Beijing's latest target. With a tiny population of fewer than 700,000, Bhutan has been a virtual protectorate of India since September 1958 when Nehru rode there on a horse and yak through high mountain passes for a prime ministerial visit. It remains the only totally pro-India country on the subcontinent, though India's de facto control of its external links, especially of communications, has weakened in the past 25 years or so. In the mid-1980s, when I first went there,[31] air flights and even telex messages were routed via Calcutta. Now Bhutan has air links to other nearby countries, as well as internet and satellite television, but the economy is still heavily dependent on exports to India, dominated by sales of hydroelectric power.

China wants to settle 4,500 sq km of land on disputed sections of its 470-km border, and is using that to persuade Bhutan to let it open formal diplomatic links and an embassy in the capital of Thimpu. Only a few countries, ranging from Bangladesh to Finland and Switzerland, have embassies and consulates in Thimpu and, till recently, Bhutan firmly resisted China's approaches with India's encouragement. China's main aim is to extend its territory in the Chumbi Valley, a strategically important 'v' shaped area of Tibet between the Indian state of Sikkim to the west and Bhutan to the east.[32] This would be extremely sensitive for India because the 3,000 m (9,500 ft) high valley juts down towards a strip of Indian territory called the Siliguri Corridor, which is the only land route – known as the 'chicken's neck' – from the broad mass of India to its north-eastern states.[33]

So sensitive is India about China's links that the word went round that I was possibly a British spy when I was in Thimpu for a literature festival in early 2011.[34] I thought it was natural for a foreign correspondent making a rare visit to Bhutan to ask about China's diplomatic activities and its access and incursions on the northern and western borders. India's diplomats, however, seemed to think differently. The spy rumour was circulating by about the second or third day of my visit – I heard it (unofficially) when I went to a dinner in the garden of India's resident army general.

Bhutan's royal family and officials did not seem to have the same worry. I am credited there as the first foreign correspondent to be told (for the *FT* in 1987) by the then King Jigme Singye Wangchuck about his plans for Gross National Happiness or GNH. 'We are convinced we must aim for contentment and happiness,' he said when I interviewed him in 1987 at his Dechencholing Palace in

Thimphu. He put this above more usual targets of economic growth and GNP, and listed the parameters: 'Whether we take five years or ten to raise the per capita income and increase prosperity is not going to guarantee that happiness, which includes political stability, social harmony, and the Bhutanese culture and way of life,' he said.[35]

He had been working on the idea since the mid-1970s and this was the first time that he had opened up on the theme to a foreign reporter. 'Independence through an independent culture' was one of the aims, he said. 'We are fortunate in developing late at a time when other countries, which went through our present stage of development 30 or 40 years ago, are becoming aware of what they have done wrong. Many have developed a modern society but none has kept its strong traditions and culture which we want to do'. For example, he added, 'corruption began when development started in 1961, maybe not seriously compared with other countries, but serious by our standards.' That led on to the four principles of GNH: fair socio-economic development including education and health, conservation and promotion of the country's culture, environmental protection, and good governance.[36]

In 2006, having just introduced democratically elected governments, King Jigme Singye Wangchuck (or K4 as he is often known) abdicated in favour of one of his sons, 28-year-old Oxford-educated Jigme Khesar Namgyel Wangchuck, who was crowned in 2008. Here was a dynasty that was protecting the country's heritage while also looking for ways to encourage economic growth. The idea of GNH caught the world's imagination and Bhutan's first elected government, which came to office in 2008, tried to quantify and measure various indicators. It also pushed the topic internationally at the UN with a resolution titled 'Happiness: towards a holistic approach to development.'[37] A new government, elected in August 2013, took a more measured approach. When he visited Delhi, the new prime minister Tshering Tobgay and his officials told me that, while it was good for academics to study GNH, he would personally adopt a simpler approach and test every decision against the original basic aims.

China achieved a breakthrough on the fringes of a UN conference in Rio de Janeiro in June 2012 when Wen Jiabao secured his first meeting with Jigme Yoser Thinley, then the prime minister. This was followed by other contacts. Thinley's nationalist views made him less India-centric, and therefore more open to flattery and proposals from China than the Bhutanese monarchy which was traditionally India-oriented. King Jigme Khesar Namgyal (K5), is also believed to be more open-minded on the subject than his father, whom he succeeded in 2006 but who still has influence on international affairs.

Both King Jigme and the prime minister discussed China and the border issues during visits to Delhi early in 2013, but the urgency eased later in the year when Tshering Tobgay adopted a more pro-India stance[38]. Indian officials say privately that they recognize that China will gain increased diplomatic access in Thimpu, and possibly full recognition, some time in the future. When that happens, it will increase India's sense of encirclement, and will test its questionable ability to move from hegemony to partnership.

Business Security Risks

There are security risks in China's growing economic involvement with India because its companies are supplying telecom networks and power generation and other infrastructure equipment. Bilateral trade totalling $70bn is heavily weighted in China's favour. Indian manufacturers do not find it easy to break into the market, whereas Chinese goods, from cheap toys to heavy engineering equipment, sell well. In May 2013, the total value of Chinese companies' completed contracts and those in progress was $55 bn.[39] Some experts argue that such economic activity makes war between the two countries less likely because they would have too much to lose, but that is surely as realistic as Nehru thinking that China and India could become partners. If China decided a war was essential for some greater purpose, it would surely not be put off by the economic links.

Substantial trading ties did not, for example, stop it dangerously escalating a confrontation with Japan in 2013 over possession of disputed islands in the East China Sea, though the counter view is that China would not eventually allow such a row to escalate too far.

Telecom imports from China in 2010–11 totalled $6.7bn, ranging from phones and attachments to networks, with two Chinese companies, Huawei and ZTE, becoming major suppliers of low-cost networks and other equipment.[40] Huawei was founded in 1998 by Ren Zhengfei, a former officer in the People's Liberation Army, and it is hard to believe that he can now have a totally independent existence, even though he has said he has cut ties. The company has a five-year $2bn investment plan in India and is the second biggest provider of networks after Ericsson, with a 25–30 per cent market share. It supplies all of the country's top telecom operators and individual companies and also has a substantial share of the market for devices such as data cards and phones. Huawei is also active in the Maldives, Nepal and other neighbouring countries. I have asked various Indian officials and policy pundits about the extent of the national security risks of such a Chinese presence in India's communications. Most have ducked the issue, offering no solution and taking the same line as India's telecom operators – that the products are irresistible. Huawei says, for example, that its total costs of ownership (purchase prices plus maintenance) are 25–30 per cent lower than rival companies such as Alcatel-Lucent, Ericsson and Nokia Siemens[41].

The potential international threat was highlighted in October 2012 by a US Congress intelligence committee, which warned that companies such as Huawei and GTE could disrupt America's information networks and send sensitive data secretly back to China.[42] Huawei and others denied the allegations and explained how they co-operate with governments and other users to screen and secure their equipment. Huawei responded in 2013 by suggesting it might be cutting back on its US business plans, but also suggested that the US view was a protectionist ploy encouraged by its telecom companies. Other countries such as Canada, Australia and the UK are also worried and there have been some blocks on the companies obtaining government network contracts.[43]

China also has orders for potentially sensitive power plant equipment exceeding 44,000 MW[44] and is backing up its contracts with financing deals, sometimes with financially vulnerable companies that urgently need help. The debt-strapped Reliance Group controlled by Anil Ambani, for example, placed two orders totalling $10bn for power equipment from Shanghai Electric Group in 2010 and raised $2bn financing from Chinese banks for that order and for some refinancing of its telecoms business. There are also security concerns about Chinese bids for Indian power transmission grids. The State Grid Corporation of China has been looking for contracts in India.[45] Other areas include engineering and construction projects.

Future Contours

The contours of the likely long-term relationship between the two countries began to emerge as Wen Jiabao finished his 2010 visit to Delhi and flew on to Pakistan.[46] Economic and cultural ties would grow and trade would boom, but China would continue indefinitely to rattle India's nerves in a variety of ways, not least by becoming closer to Pakistan and claiming territory on the Himalayan border. Beijing would not see this economic carrot and diplomatic stick approach primarily as a bilateral matter because India is merely a (rather large) pawn in its overall ambition to become a superpower, alongside, and one day replacing, the US. That ambition necessitates keeping India in check because China is determined that it should not become a rival.

A key to these contours, as seen from Beijing, came from a Chinese official who told a former top Indian bureaucrat and ambassador in 2010 that India needed to understand three things.[47] First, political differences would not impede economic growth and trade relationship between the two countries. Second, India should not meddle with its neighbours (meaning presumably that China would meddle in places like Myanmar, Sri Lanka, Nepal and Bangladesh, but that India should neither object nor try to counter its efforts). Third, India should accept China's growing links with Pakistan, which would continue (presumably because arming and aiding a nuclear Pakistan is a key way to keep India in check). This meant that, while China was content to see India's prosperity grow and to participate in its economic growth, India should not expect to become a regional power, even though the US might like it to do so. It also probably meant that, though China was surprised and rather taken aback by India's rapid economic and industrial advances in the first decade of the twentieth century, and was rattled by growing close ties (and the 2008 nuclear deal) with the US, it knew that it was way ahead in terms of overall development and as a regional power.

King Goujian's Revenge

The contours laid down for India by the Chinese official – which, of course, India would not accept – tie in with the long-term question for the whole world of whether China will be a 'Friend or Foe', to quote the title of a special report in *The Economist*.[48] Did China's (rather clumsy) regional belligerence, which was developing in 2010, indicate that the 'foe' angle was gaining supremacy in Beijing as the country became economically powerful and the PLA's influence grew? The magazine's foreign editor wondered whether a story about Goujian, a fifth century king of Yue in what is now Zhejiang, was an alarming parable about China's ambitions, as it could indeed well be. Goujian was defeated and humiliated by another king, but bided his time as a meek prisoner and then wreaked revenge. The story of how he 'slept on brushwood and tasted gall is as familiar to Chinese as King Alfred and his cakes are to Britons, or George Washington and the cherry tree are to Americans,' said the article. 'In the early 20th century he became a symbol of resistance against the treaty ports, foreign concessions and the years of colonial humiliation'.

It looks as though Goujian-style revenge may have begun, but with an economic and strategic slant. China has been aggressively stepping up the confrontation with Japan over the oil-rich, uninhabited Senkaku islands in the East China Sea, as it has also done with Vietnam, the Philippines, Malaysia and Brunei over the Spratly and Paracel islands in the South China Sea. It has also argued with Vietnam over oil rights, in which Indian companies have been involved, and unilaterally announced an air defence identification zone that laid claims to international airspace over the East China Sea covering territories that China did not control. This 'Chinese art of creeping warfare', as Chellaney calls it, [49] is supported by extensive academic research into supportive historical maps and documents.[50] It shows a greater willingness to disrupt relations with neighbouring countries than in the past.

Other points of potential conflict are developing over China's 'hydro-hegemony' which could affect one-third of India's yearly water supply that comes from Tibet. Chellaney says that 'in contrast to the bilateral water treaties between many of its neighbours, China rejects the concept of a water-sharing arrangement or joint, rules-based management of common resources'.[51] There is a large-scale dam building programme on international rivers originating on China's Tibetan plateau and flowing to southern and southeastern Asia, including the mighty Brahmaputra river which India relies on for its water. China, however, has not been consulting India and has not given details of its plans as requested by India.

There was a sudden worsening of relations in April 2013 when 30 PLA troops not only crossed the LAC and moved 19 km inside what India regarded as its territory on the 16,000ft-high Depsang Plain in the Ladakh sector of the disputed border. This was in the no-man's land, or the red zone as it is called, which is the overlapping area between the two countries' perception of their territory. It is quite common for troops from both sides to cross into this area and then withdraw, but on this occasion the Chinese pitched tents and stayed. A procedure agreed in 2005 for solving such a face-off was not operated by China so, after some characteristically nervous indecision and delay, India reacted to heavy domestic political and media pressure and moved its troops and tents into the disputed area in a face-off with the Chinese. India also strengthened its previously soft diplomatic stance. After three weeks, both sides removed their troops and withdrew from Depsang, but the terms of the truce were not revealed.[52] This confrontation was totally unexpected in Delhi, especially coming soon after China's new president, Xi Jinping, had put forward five proposals for improving ties and said that 'peace and tranquillity' should be maintained on the border in order to help solve the border issue, a task that 'won't be easy'.[53]

India avoided condemning China for the incursion because it did not want to upset the visit to Delhi a month later by China's new premier, Li Keqiang. Though the visit was a presentational success, no firm commitments were made by either side. He repeated China's usual line about the border issue being 'a question left over by history' but added that the two sides had 'agreed to push forward with negotiations', which contrasted sharply with the line taken by Wen and most Chinese leaders in recent years.[54]

That apparent change of mood was the most notable point to emerge from the visit, especially coming at the start of the ten-year term in office of the new leadership, but it prompted questions about China's motives. Did it really want to solve disagreements over the border, which seemed unlikely, or did it have other aims? It was certainly teasing the US – Li quoted a Chinese proverb that 'a distant relative may not be as useful as a near neighbour,' appearing to be trying (fruitlessly of course) to wean India away from America. Or it could have decided that it had sent the wrong signals with the recent border row, and that it should not fall out with its biggest neighbour at the same time as it was aggressively confronting Japan and the Philippines.

Problems over the border, and over China possibly blocking

India's river waters with new upstream dams, had been dodged during Li's visit by talking about mechanisms rather than potentially more controversial substance. That fitted with India's traditionally low-key approach to foreign diplomacy everywhere, and of course played into China's hands. It also fitted with what C. Raja Mohan describes despairingly as India's 'ideological romanticism and political timidity' and 'relentless mystification of Chinese policies'.[55] It remained to be seen whether India would push for real movement, not just presentational mechanisms, and whether China would be willing to respond. Manmohan Singh visited Beijing a few months later and signed a border defence co-operation agreement aimed at preventing upsets with regular exchanges of information, and China agreed to share hydrological data. These were small steps of debatable significance.[56]

It looks as though this uncertain see-saw relationship will continue indefinitely, certainly so long as both countries are preoccupied with their internal economic development and growth, and consequently have neither the time nor inclination to interfere extensively in each other's affairs. There are, however, two problems with this approach, and India does not seem to be prepared for either because – chalta hai – it has no apparent overall plan for its dealings with China on a range of issues from infrastructure investment and corporate loans to border and river water issues.

First, what will China do when it has achieved what Deng Xiaoping described as its first priority of achieving an 'orderly rise' in economic and development terms? Deng is reported to have said – and India agrees – that modernization needed 'two prerequisites – one is international peace, and the other is domestic political stability'.[57] When the development goals have been achieved, will globalization have developed so far that China continues with that orderly rise, or will it then want to settle scores with its neighbours? The second problem is that likely differences over international oil and gas rights, access to sea-lanes and river waters, and maybe other issues could be seen by China as affecting its orderly economic development and modernization, and could therefore upset the equilibrium. Already there are the signs that it is moving on from another Deng dictum – 'hiding strengths and biding time' – and will be asserting itself internationally.

There is nothing to suggest that the border issue, which lies at the heart of the current differences, will be resolved any time soon. China will want to keep India on edge on the mountain peaks and passes, and it will also continue to develop close economic and defence relations in the neighbourhood. The best solution for India would be to keep talking with Beijing without expecting any agreements, while also strengthening border defences, improving liaison with Japan and other Asian countries, and watching out for King Goujian mustering his armies.

Notes

1. 'Chinese PM Wen Jiabao begins bumper Indian trade trip' – useful background here: http://www.bbc.co.uk/news/world-south-asia-11997221

2. http://ridingtheelephant.wordpress.com/2010/12/17/china-and-india-quarrel-despite-16bn-economic-carrots/

3. China's Ministry of Foreign Affairs website, Wen Jiabao Addresses the Indian Council of World Affairs, http://www.fmprc.gov.cn/eng/topics/wenjiabaofangwenyinduhebjst/t779524.htm

4. 'Wen: Patience needed to resolve boundary question', Xinhua News Agency, http://www.chinadaily.com.cn/china/2010wenindia/2010-12/16/content_11714501.htm

5. Website of the Embassy of the Republic of India in Beijing, China, http://www.indianembassy.org.cn/DynamicContent.aspx?MenuId=3&SubMenuId=0

6. Jagat Mehta, speaking in Delhi at the launch of his book *The Tryst Betrayed*, Penguin Viking, 2010

7. B.G. Verghese, 'The War We Lost', *Tehelka*, 13 October 2012, http://tehelka.com/the-war-we-lost/; Verghese writes that Nehru said this to India's new ambassador to China, G. Parthasarathi (according to

Parthasarathi's son Ashok), on 18 March 1958 prior to his departure for Peking

8.   Ajai Shukla, 'The LAC is not the LOC', *Business Standard*, 19 September 2012, http://www.business-standard.com/article/opinion/ajai-shukla-the-lac-is-not-the-loc-112091800050_1.html,   and *Broadsword* blog http://ajaishukla.blogspot.in/

9.   Adam Roberts of *The Economist* graphically described a visit to the area in October 2012 on the magazine's 'Banyan' blog – http://www.economist.com/blogs/banyan/2012/10/indias-remote-north-east

10. Brahma Chellaney, 'The Lessons of the China-India War', 14 October 2012, http://www.project-syndicate.org/commentary/why-china-india-tensions-are-growing-by-brahma-chellaney# 2lvQQFMAHUiTL1VW.99

11. Ibid.

12. As recounted by Brajesh Mishra to JE, August 2009

13. Ibid

14. Mani Shankar Aiyar, 'India's foreign policy – from Jawaharlal Nehru to Manmohan Singh', Australia-India Institute, University of Melbourne, 22 September 2011

15. Nicholas Nugent, *Rajiv Gandhi Son of a Dynasty*, BBC Books 1990, UBS Delhi 1991

16. Conversation with JE

17. Annual Report to Congress: Military and Security Developments Involving the People's Republic of China 2013, Office of the Secretary of Defense, http://www.defense.gov/pubs/2013_China_Report_FINAL.pdf

18. 'Can Pakistan survive without US aid?', *Dawn*, 15 February 2012, http://dawn.com/2012/02/15/can-pakistan-survive-without-us-aid/; this article quotes a *Guardian* (UK) newspaper report http://www.theguardian.com/global-development/poverty-matters/2011/jul/11/us-aid-to-pakistan – on six decades of US aid to Pakistan compiled by Wren Elhai of the Center for Global Development in Washington, DC. Since 1948, US assistance to Pakistan had largely been for civilian purposes – out of $61.7bn total assistance 1948-2010 (in constant 2009 dollars), $40.4bn was economic and $21.3bn military.

19. 'Wiki: China helping Pak upgrade its missiles', *Indian Express*, 12 September   2011,   https://www.google.co.in/search?q=Wiki%3A

+China+helping+Pak+upgrade+its+missiles&ie=utf-8&oe=utf-8&aq=t&rls=org.mozilla:en-GB:official&client=firefox-a

20. 'Break India, says China think-tank', TNN, 12 August 2009, http://articles.timesofindia.indiatimes.com/2009-08-12/india/28195335_1_dai-bingguo-state-councillor-chinese-website – Chinese website www.iiss.cn now not accessible on internet

21. http://ridingtheelephant.wordpress.com/2009/08/13/china-aims-to-block-india%E2%80%99s-place-in-the-sun/

22. http://ridingtheelephant.wordpress.com/2010/03/21/china-out-guns-the-us-in-friendliness-at-a-delhi-conference/

23. http://www.dnaindia.com/world/report_deluded-india-stands-no-chance-in-arms-race-china-s-reaction-to-agni-v_1677979

24. Kanwal Sibal, 'Bested by China's strategy', *Mail Today*, 11 December 2012

25. 'Fear of influence' – *Financial Times* article with interactive map of 'string of pearls' published 2009 (so lacking later information) http://www.ft.com/cms/s/0/84a13062-6f0c-11de-9109-00144feabdc0.html#axzz26ibsc8AR

26. 'NIA chargesheet: NSCN got arms from Chinese firms', *Indian Express*, 1 April 2012, http://www.indianexpress.com/news/nia-chargesheet-nscn-got-arms-from-chinese-firms/770069

27. 'Untangling the GMR-Male row: Timeline of incidents that lead to the scrapping of the $500 million airport development deal', *Business Standard*, 16 December 2012, http://www.business-standard.com/article/current-affairs/special-untangling-the-gmr-male-row-112121600022_1.html

28. 'An insensitive political class: Public anger at the decline of governance', G. Parthasarathy, http://www.tribuneindia.com/2013/20130116/edit.htm#4

29. http://www.reuters.com/article/2013/10/27/us-srilanka-china-highway-idUSBRE99Q06G20131027 and http://www.asianews.it/news-en/Sri-Lanka%E2%80%99s-inaugurates-second-highway,-%27made-in-China-%27-29389.html

30. http://mea.gov.in/Portal/ForeignRelation/India_-_Sri_Lanka_Relations.pdf

31. JE, 'The Modern Path to Enlightenment', *Financial Times*, 2 May 1987

32. Govinda Riza, 'Bhutan-China Border Mismatch', Bhutan News Service, 1 January 2013, www.bhutannewsservice.com/column-opinion/commentry/ bhutan-china-border-mismatch/ – analysis with maps
33. Virendra Sahai Verma, 'Dances with dragons', 21 August 2012 http://www.thehindu.com/opinion/op-ed/article3800096.ece – article with map
34. http://ridingtheelephant.wordpress.com/2011/05/29/bhutan-climbs-a-learning-curve-for-happiness/
35. JE, 'The Modern Path to Enlightenment', *Financial Times*, 2 May 1987, and on http://ridingtheelephant.wordpress.com/2008/11/05/bhutan%E2%80%99s-king-told-me-about-his-plans-for-gross-national-happiness/
36. 'The background of Gross National Happiness: A development path with values', GNH Centre Bhutan, http://www.gnhbhutan.org/about/a_development_path_with_values.aspx#sthash.7iUeemoF.dpuf
37. Omair Ahmad, 'The Royal Pleasure Index', *Sunday Guardian*, 2 March 2013, http://www.sunday-guardian.com/artbeat/the-royal-pleasure-index. Omair Ahmed is the author of *The Kingdom at the Centre of the World – Journeys into Bhutan*, Aleph Book Company, Delhi, 2013
38. C. Raja Mohan, 'The faraway neighbour', *Indian Express*, 17 July 2013, http://www.indianexpress.com/news/the-faraway-neighbour/1142653/0
39. Briefing by India's Ministry of External Affairs, 18 May 2013, http://www.mea.gov.in/media-briefings.htm?dtl/21718/Transcript+of+media+briefing+on+Chinese+Premiers+Forthcoming+Visit
40. http://ridingtheelephant.wordpress.com/2012/10/15/huawei-poses-risks-for-india-50-years-after-chinas-himalayan-victory/
41. Figures supplied by Huawei to JE
42. 'Huawei and ZTE pose security threat, warns US panel', BBC, 8 October 2012 www.bbc.co.uk/news/business-19867399 – and the US report is here: http://intelligence.house.gov/sites/intelligence.house.gov/files/documents/Huawei-ZTE%20Investigative%20Report%20%28FINAL%29.pdf
43. 'Huawei – A matter of procedure', *The Economist*, 6 June 2013, http://www.economist.com/blogs/schumpeter/2013/06/huawei
44. http://articles.economictimes.indiatimes.com/2012-08-28/

news/33450461_1_mega-power-projects-joint-economic-group-chinese-commerce-minister

45. 'China power major eyes transmission projects in India, sets alarm bells ringing', *Indian Express*, 15 October 2012, http://www.indianexpress.com/news/china-power-major-eyes-transmission-projects-in-india-sets-alarm-bells-ringing/1016828/0

46. http://ridingtheelephant.wordpress.com/2010/12/17/china-and-india-quarrel-despite-16bn-economic-carrots/

47. Related to JE in December 2010 by Abid Hussain (died June 2012), former Commerce Secretary, Member Planning Commission, and Ambassador to the US (1990-92); http://ridingtheelephant.wordpress.com/2010/12/17/china-and-india-quarrel-despite-16bn-economic-carrots/

48. Edward Carr, 'Brushwood and gall', *The Economist*, 2 December 2010, www.economist.com/node/17601499?story_id=17601499

49. Brahma Chellaney, 'The Chinese art of creeping warfare – By altering territorial 'facts' on the ground, China is successfully altering its borders without resorting to war', *Mint*, 24 December 2013, http://www.livemint.com/Opinion/bG5qzeOSsJRZ7dERHuuV6I/The-Chinese-art-of-creeping-warfare.html

50. 'China wages a quiet war of maps with its neighbors', *Washington Post*, 15 February 2013 http://www.washingtonpost.com/world/asia_pacific/china-wages-a-quiet-war-of-maps-with-its-neighbors/2013/02/14/d682b704-76b3-11e2-aa12-e6cf1d31106b_story.html?wpisrc=nl_cuzheads

51. Brahma Chellaney, 'China's Hydro-Hegemony', 8 February 2013, http://www.nytimes.com/2013/02/08/opinion/global/chinas-hydro-hegemony.html?_r=0 and http://chellaney.net/2013/02/08/chinas-hydro-hegemony

52. Indrani Bagchi, 'Depsang Bulge incursion accidental, Chinese military thinktank says', *The Times of India*, 15 July 2013, http://timesofindia.indiatimes.com/india/Depsang-Bulge-incursion-accidental-Chinese-military-thinktank-says/articleshow/21088756.cms

53. 'Xi Jinping unveils 5 proposals for improving Sino-India ties', PTI, 19 March 2013, www.indianexpress.com/news/xi-jinping-unveils-5-proposals-for-improving-sinoindia-ties/1090268/

54. http://ridingtheelephant.wordpress.com/2013/05/21/china-turns-friendly-with-india-but-why/

55. C. Raja Mohan, 'With China, keep it real, *Indian Express*, 20 May 2013, http://www.indianexpress.com/news/with-china-keep-it-real/1117966/

56. Brahma Chellaney, 'Singh's Sham Water Accord, A new agreement between China and India doesn't require Beijing to institutionalize rules-based cooperation on shared resources', *The Wall Street Journal*, 31 October 2013, http://chellaney.net/2013/10/30/singhs-sham-water-accord/

57. Quoted in Martin Jacques, *When China Rules the World*, p. 180, Penguin Books, Second Edition, 2012, http://www.penguinbooksindia.com/en/content/martin-jacques

21

Pakistan and the Neighbourhood
Few Friends

India does not get on well with most of its South Asian neighbours. This is partly because of its often heavy-handed diplomacy, but also because of problems left over by history, notably the partition of Pakistan from India in 1947 and the two countries' subsequent territorial dispute over Kashmir. The turbulent relations between the two have upset the development of South Asia as a region of trade and economic co-operation, as well as helping to blight India's position with other neighbours.

The seven countries of the subcontinent – India, Pakistan, Nepal, Bhutan, Bangladesh, Sri Lanka and the Maldives – have a total population of 1.7bn and share much of the brainpower and many of the other attributes and natural resources that have helped to fuel India's economic success. Yet the India–Pakistan stand-off, and the looming and interfering presence of China, have meant that they largely fail to co-operate and share in India's relative success. The South Asian Association for Regional Cooperation (SAARC), which was founded in 1985 to emulate South East Asia's ASEAN trade bloc, has achieved little. The great potential that could be achieved by a unified approach to subjects like climate change, hydro power and the environment as well as counter-terrorism, trade and joint investments has not even been tackled.

India's relations with Pakistan have greater explosive acrimony and hostility than they do with China, even though the border is less complicated because most of it is clearly defined. There is a Line of Control (LoC) along a 776 km section in Jammu and Kashmir, which is clear and is administered as a temporary arrangement, even though it is not formally accepted by either country as a permanent border, and there are exchanges of fire between the armies on either side. To the south, a 2,308-km formal border stretching down to the Indian state of Rajasthan and Pakistan's Sindh province is undisputed and peaceful. There is only a 110 km stretch, known as the Actual Ground Position Line (AGPL), which is undefined like the LAC with China. This is around the Siachen glacier in Kashmir[1] and Sir Creek. Lives are sometimes lost in the firings across the LoC (whereas none has been lost in border disputes with China since 1993) and there have been three wars and one near-war between the two countries since 1947.

The basic dispute between the two nuclear powers has existed since independence. Pakistan claims Kashmir, a predominantly Muslim area centred on the 5,2200-ft high Srinagar valley, as its territory. In response, India claims (but has never expected to get or seriously pursued) Pakistan's Azad Kashmir, immediately to the west of the LoC, and its Northern Areas that stretch up to the border with China at the 15,400-ft high Khunjerab Pass in the Karakoram mountains.

Mainstream politicians on both sides recognize that the only logical settlement is to abandon their claims and accept the Line of Control as the formal border, but long-standing passions make it difficult to put this into practice. On the Pakistan side, it would be firmly resisted by the army, backed by the Inter-Services Intelligence (ISI), which pursues an aggressive policy on India in order to justify its existence and political authority, and to extend Pakistan's regional reach. It would probably be accepted in India, provided there was a strong government in power, though it could be difficult to gain political acceptance. There is also rivalry for influence in Afghanistan and there is a China factor – Beijing enjoys India being destabilized by uncertain borders with Pakistan.

Kashmir

For the first 35 years or so after independence, the Pakistan–India confrontation focused on the claims for Kashmir territory. Cross-border terrorism then developed in the 1980s when Pakistan trained and helped infiltrators to cross the border into India's state of Punjab during Sikh extremists' unsuccessful Khalistan (independence) movement, and then into Kashmir across the LoC from around 1989–90 to foment an insurgency against India. Later there were major terror attacks in other parts of India.

The internal Kashmir insurgency stemmed from demands for some form of autonomy from Delhi, with extremists wanting full independence, or to become part of Pakistan, and a majority wanting a special semi-autonomous status. India would never agree to independence or a Pakistan takeover, and there is no prospect in the foreseeable future of the semi-autonomous demands being met in any sort of settlement between Delhi and the Kashmiris. That is partly because of an unwillingness in the Indian capital to grapple with the issue, and partly because no settlement is possible without the involvement of Pakistan.

Consequently, Kashmir regularly has periods of serious unrest, as happened in 2010 when protests were driven primarily by discontented youth.[2] The army was called in to quell clashes between security forces and stone-throwing and mostly young demonstrators. Kashmir seemed doomed to many more years of uncertainty, with periods of violence alternating with relative calm.[3] Prospects for the state's youth were bleak, with serious risks of them becoming increasingly militant. After two decades of trouble, generations had grown up in a stone-throwing culture where baiting and attacking security forces, and being viciously attacked and even killed in return, had become part of regular life from the age of nine or ten. This led to a declining work culture with poor job opportunities because there was no significant private sector investment.

There has been little improvement since then and some facets of the insurgency continue, with Pakistan continuing to allow and facilitate militants to cross its border into Kashmir. Despite poor performance in the official economy, however, Srinagar shows signs of growing consumerism. The city is thriving both on black money that circulates widely, much of it flowing across the LoC from Pakistan. There is also widespread corruption involving the security forces as well as the state government. This means there are strong vested interests that see no need to bring normalcy to the state.

Peace Talks

Politicians, businessmen and many others in both India and Pakistan increasingly want to move ahead and normalize relations, and to put aside the primary issue of Kashmir and the LoC that they know will not be settled in the foreseeable future. India's two prime ministers since 1998 – Atal Bihari Vajpayee and Manmohan Singh – both pursued the cause of peace with Pakistan, even though their efforts were disrupted by terror attacks and cross-border incidents triggered by Pakistan. Manmohan Singh spelt out the reasons for his initiatives in May 2010 at one of his rare formal press conferences in Delhi, when he stated that India 'cannot realize its full development potential unless we have the best possible relations with our neighbours – and Pakistan happens to be our largest neighbour'.

He missed an opportunity here to give shape and logic to his often criticized determination to have talks with Pakistan. Imagine the headlines if he had done, such as 'Pakistan peace will boost India, to 12 per cent growth', or 'Singh adds econ logic to Pak peace bid'.[4] There might have been one or two negative pitches such as 'Singh tacitly admits Pakistan stunts India's economy', but the positive message would have won through, and Singh might have been mocked less for his (unrealizable) wish to be written into the history books as the prime minister who made peace with Pakistan. People would have begun to understand why he – and Vajpayee before him – were so keen on mounting seemingly futile bids with India's increasingly dangerous neighbour. Peace, however, is not essential for economic success – there was strong growth in the 1990s and 2000s when there were extensive conflicts with Pakistan and cross-border terrorism.

Shivshankar Menon picked up the theme in his August 2011 lecture, saying: 'We need to work for a peaceful periphery. We have an interest in the peace and prosperity of our neighbours, removing extremism and threats from their soil, as we are doing successfully with Bangladesh, Sri Lanka and Bhutan'.[5] The aim was not just to stop terrorism and cross-border insurgencies but jointly to develop South Asia.

Ironic though it may seem, the best progress on a deal in recent years came after General Pervez Musharraf, who had engineered a near-war on the LoC at Kargil in 1999 when he was Pakistan's army chief of staff, became president. The start, though, was not auspicious. Vajpayee organized summit talks in July 2001 in Agra, the Taj Mahal tourist city, and Musharraf used his public relations skills and apparent friendliness to upstage Vajpayee with an unscheduled televised breakfast briefing for newspaper editors. The summit ended in confusion and failure, with hardline ministers on both sides upsetting whatever the two leaders had hoped to agree. India's BJP leaders felt it was not sellable, politically.[6]

This was followed by an agreement on Line of Control 'ceasefire' in November 2003, which dramatically reduced the cross-border clashes and general violence in Jammu and Kashmir. (Official figures show that the number of incidents came down from 3,401 in 2003 when 795 civilians, 314 security forces and 1,494 militants were killed to 118 incidents in 2012 with 23 civilians, 14 security forces and 58 militants killed.[7])

Vajpayee had more talks with Musharraf in 2004 and then Manmohan Singh picked up on the initiatives when he became prime minister. The solution that was being worked out would not have led to any change on the borders, but aimed to make the Line of Control irrelevant with gradual demilitarization and devolved government. There would have been a 'soft border' with relaxed visa restrictions, cross-border travel and trade, the reunification of divided families and friends, and liaison arrangements on economic policy and other matters. Musharraf has said that the four-point agenda was not complete, but that wide agreement had been reached despite some hitches.[8] This was, however, not approved (and might never have been) by the Pakistan army, nor by hard-line lobbies in either country, and the talks faded away when Musharraf faced increasing political problems in Pakistan and was ousted from office in 2008. Such a solution is not feasible now because India could not accept a soft border when Pakistan is wracked by the uncertainties of Taliban terrorism.

Relations next seemed to improve after the appointment of a young and personable 34-year-old Pakistan foreign minister, Hina Rabbani Khar. Visiting Delhi in July 2011, she spoke of a 'mindset change' in both countries and of a new generation seeing the relationship differently from the past.[9] 'It is our desire to make the dialogue process uninterrupted and uninterruptible,' she said. It sounded like 23 years earlier when Benazir Bhutto and Rajiv Gandhi, then young prime ministers of Pakistan and India, met in 1988 and brought a fresh but short-lived focus. Would this be any different? It was not clear what weight Khar's words carried because of power being divided in Pakistan between the government, the military and the ISI – the signals were mixed and were undermined regularly by Pakistan's aggressive and voluble interior minister, Rehman Malik.[10]

Some progress was made on visas, foreign direct investment, and India potentially receiving 'most-favoured nation' trading status (which it had given Pakistan 15 years earlier). Bilateral trade officially totals only some $2.5bn a year, plus perhaps another $3bn in informal links, mainly routed through the Gulf. There is an official target of $6–8bn, but that is unlikely to be realized because policy decisions are rarely implemented fully or quickly and there are only two cross-border airline flights a week – a fact that illustrates the tortuous relations.

Terrorism

The perennial question in India is how and why peace initiatives should be continued when they are regularly disrupted by actions allegedly originating in Pakistan – either terror attacks or clashes on the border – and when Pakistan does not rein in terrorists such as Hafiz Saeed, who roamed freely in the country despite being held responsible (by the US among others) for organizing attacks. 'Pakistan is determined to confront us bilaterally, regionally and internationally. It inflicts wounds on us, through jihadi terrorism, for instance,' says Kanwal Sibal, a former Indian foreign secretary, who favours a tough line.[11] 'There is no other country that uses terrorism as an instrument of state policy towards us, or where jihadi groups openly exist and incite hatred towards India.'

Terrorism drove the countries close to full military conflict in December 2001, when there was an attack on the Indian parliament building in Delhi, significantly (and humiliatingly in Indian eyes) just five months after Vajpayee had hosted the Agra summit. The US and UK feared in December 2001 that India would stage a retaliatory attack that could have sparked a nuclear war, and the UK advised its nationals living in Delhi to be prepared to evacuate – a move that India condemned as diplomatic pressure to make it back off from a confrontation. On 26 November 2008, in a much bigger attack, now remembered as 26/11, terrorists arrived by sea in Mumbai and shot their way into the Taj and Oberoi hotels and other targets, killing 166 people. This led to increasing pressure in India, escalated by media coverage, to respond strongly in response to such threats and terrorism.

One method has been spelt out by G. Parthasarathy, a former senior diplomat and high commissioner to Pakistan (1998–2000), who says that during the Narasimha Rao government in the mid-1990s, 'acts of terrorism in India resulted in violence in populated centres like Karachi and Lahore'. As a consequence, 'terrorism in Indian urban centres virtually ended'.[12] Benazir Bhutto, then Pakistan's prime minister, had ended a dialogue with India, so it might have been assumed that terrorist attacks would build up again in India, says Parthasarathy, but that did not happen. 'Pakistan-sponsored terrorism in Punjab ended and was virtually non-existent across India, except in Jammu and Kashmir. This was largely because of measures by Narasimha Rao to ensure that Pakistan paid a high price on its territory for sponsoring terrorism in India'. I also remember from my time in India in the 1980s that, within a few days of a major atrocity in the Indian state of Punjab, there would frequently be civil unrest and bomb attacks in the Pakistani city of Karachi that exploited local sectarian, ethnic and other divisions.

Musharraf admitted such mutual attacks in a speech in India after he had been ousted from the presidency. In characteristically bombastic but semi-jocular style, he said that the two countries had done 'a lot of meddling' in each other's internal affairs.[13] 'Your RAW does exactly what the ISI does, and the ISI does exactly what RAW does,' he said, referring to both countries' secret services. 'The past has been dirty ... the past has been bad, but don't put the blame on Pakistan'.

A new factor for the Indian government is growing pressure from an excitable media, especially television chat show hosts who have become more strident in recent years and demand retribution rather than peace initiatives. Frequent cross-border clashes in 2013, after a ten-year lull, led to the beheading of an Indian soldier and other deaths.[14] There was a media frenzy after the beheading with the chat shows raising the tempo to such a pitch that Manmohan Singh was forced to declare that it 'cannot be business as usual' with Pakistan.

There has also been pressure from the parliamentary opposition and it is likely that a BJP-led government, if elected in 2014, would take a tough stance. It would probably refuse to continue talks after terror attacks and instruct the army to react more aggressively to Pakistan firing across the LoC. 'The biggest problem in our dealing with Pakistan has been our defensive attitude, our unwillingness to retaliate against Pakistan so that a price is imposed on it for its infractions,' says Kanwal Sibal. He also lists as part of the problem 'our reluctance to assume risks accompanying a tougher policy, our concerns about the reaction of the international community if we acted against Pakistan, our fear that if we did that, our policy of treating our differences with Pakistan bilaterally would be compromized as the issues would get internationalised'. Pakistan is also a factor in India's internal politics because politicians believe that moderating reactions is assumed to win votes among India's large Muslim population and 'denote a more "secular" and less "anti-Muslim" bias', says Sibal.

My Missed Kargil Scoop

It is not clear how much a civilian government in Pakistan knows about what its army and the ISI are doing. There has never been any doubt that the army dominates the government, sometimes from behind the scenes and sometimes openly. This became especially pertinent when Nawaz Sharif was re-elected prime minister in June 2013 – having been ousted from an earlier period in office in October 1999 by a coup organized by General Musharraf, the then army chief of staff, who made himself president. About seven months before he removed Sharif, Musharraf staged a mini-invasion in the mountains above the Indian town of Kargil, between the Kashmir capital of Srinagar and the Buddhist region of Ladakh.[15]

Musharraf claims that Sharif was briefed three times about the plans, but Sharif has always insisted that he was not told in advance, and that he had not therefore been deceiving India's prime minister, Atal Bihari Vajpayee, when he welcomed him on a dramatic peacemaking trip on 20 February, 15 days after one of Sharif's alleged briefings on 5 February. Vajpayee crossed the land border at Wagah, between the Indian city of Amritsar and Lahore in Pakistan, and was feted by Sharif and other leaders, though the visit was boycotted by the armed service chiefs including Musharraf.[16] The two prime ministers initiated a diplomatically significant cross-border bus service and signed the Lahore Declaration that started with the words: 'Sharing a vision of peace and stability between their countries …'.[17]

If Sharif was briefed on 5 February, I missed the scoop of my career. I had joined him on a day-long helicopter tour so that I could catch a quick interview on the country's politics and economy for *Fortune* magazine. We landed at Kel, a Pakistan army camp some 6,000ft up in the Himalayas, beside the Line of Control. I was introduced to Musharraf, who looked at me quizzically, and I chatted to more approachable army officers, asking about the mood in the country and the government's stability, without a thought that I ought to be checking on an invasion. Musharraf took Sharif into a conference room with other aides and officers for what I was told was a routine border briefing, and it lasted about an hour or so. They then went for prayers in the base's mosque – it was a Friday – while I chatted to some of the more Westernized looking officers who declined to join them, and we flew off.

Musharraf started secretly sending infiltrators (out of uniform) across the LoC a few weeks later, and maybe had already been doing so for two months according to some reports.[18] In his autobiography, *Line of Fire,* he says that the aim was to 'fill large gaps between our defensive positions', and that this had been approved in January 1999.[19] 'Freedom fighters' were moving across the border 'from March onwards' and by 'the end of April' over 100 new posts had been secured by Pakistani troops. India's intelligence and military failures meant that the Indian army did not react to what was happening till early May. A border battle followed, involving 1,000 fighters from Pakistan (its own troops and Afghan and other Islamic militants or 'freedom fighters') that brought the two nuclear powers to the brink of war. The action ended when Sharif went to see President Bill Clinton in Washington in July and agreed, apparently contentedly, to withdraw Pakistani troops, having already been refused help on a visit to Beijing, which remained neutral.[20]

Since then, Sharif has repeatedly said he was not informed in advance,[21] but Musharraf claimed in *Line of Fire*[22] that he had been briefed on three occasions, the second time at Kel.[23] An Indian report in 2006, based on alleged Indian phone tap transcripts, however supports the Sharif line and says he was not told till May[24]. Mani Dixit, a former Indian foreign secretary, wrote in a book published in 2002 that Sharif was briefed 'at the general headquarters of the Pakistan Army in Rawalpindi in January 1999'.[25] The controversy continues – as recently as January 2013, a retired Pakistani army general claimed Kargil was planned by a 'four-man show' run by Musharraf, though Sharif had 'not' been kept totally in the dark.[26]

A Novelist's War Secret

As a footnote to the story, having missed my scoop at Kel, I was forewarned of the Kargil offensive by Humphrey Hawksley, an old friend and a BBC journalist. He was in Pakistan at the end of February 1999 researching a novel called *Dragonfire* that was published a year later[27]. He came to Delhi on 1 March and told me confidentially that (as a novelist researching material) he had been informed in Pakistan that there would soon be a cross-border invasion. I laughed and said that could not be correct because, just eleven days earlier, Vajpayee had done his bus trip to Lahore, but Hawksley was sure.

He later explained what happened in a (non-fiction) book,[28] where he wrote that a former head of the ISI had told him that 'Pakistan needed to conduct military operations inside India and that would happen very soon'. (This was an intriguing example of how journalists are trusted more when they switch roles and become novelists!). In *Dragonfire,* Hawksley utilized the former ISI chief's briefing, and Pakistan invaded India. He also included a nuclear attack on India, which derived from another conversation with a former top Pakistani diplomat, who told him that 'although we say the use of the [nuclear] bomb would be our last resort, it would in fact be our first resort'.[29] The Pakistani diplomat's argument was that, because India's conventional forces would be so overwhelming, the only way they could be stopped would be with nuclear weapons. 'Therefore last resort becomes first resort,' says Hawksley.[30]

The extent of the Pakistan civilian government's prior knowledge and approval of the Kargil affair is significant because it goes to the heart of how much India can now trust peace initiatives from Sharif, as well as other civilian leaders. Would Sharif have taken a foreign correspondent on the trip if he had known how sensitive it was? And even if he thought it safe with a business-oriented *Fortune* reporter, his spokesman had also invited Ken Cooper of *The Washington Post*.[31] Cooper did not come because of an appointment elsewhere, but might have been more focused on border questions. So maybe Sharif did not know what he would be told, or at least not its full extent and implications – and maybe, as others have suggested, he was not fully briefed.

Distant Peace

There is no chance of the main dispute over Kashmir and the Line of Control being solved permanently in the foreseeable future, and military and other sensitivities on both sides make it difficult to settle the border at Siachen and Sir Creek. That situation could continue, without severe disruption to either country, so long as extremists in the ISI and terrorist groups based in Pakistan do not seize power or escalate attacks. Almost inevitably, however, a terrorist attack in India, or a major border incident, will raise tensions. The risk, says Ahmed Rashid, a leading Pakistani writer on terrorism and diplomacy, is that 'the proxy wars' that India and Pakistan wage could escalate. 'Terrorist groups who have been sponsored by the Pakistani military in the past and are not under any control now could create a war syndrome on the border, just as the 2008 suicide attack in Mumbai by Lashkar-e-Taiba did when 166 Indians were killed. Likewise, India is needling Pakistan by allegedly backing separatists in Baluchistan'.[32]

Policy planners should not expect the two countries to make

peace for many years ahead. It is inconceivable that China would allow Pakistan to make a deal while it continues to have border and other differences with India. There will be constructive periods, as there have been, when successful attempts are made to build ties, though there will always be the risk that extremists in Pakistan will launch terror attacks to destabilize talks if they seem to be successful. What is needed in parallel is leadership from the prime ministers in both countries to develop the exchanges and possible agreements on trade, investment, visas and cross-border links. If these help Pakistan's economy to develop, optimists believe that its army might realize that it should slow down militancy and border clashes in order not to disrupt trade co-operation. At the same time, India would have to tolerate Pakistan regularly (but ineffectually) raising the issue of Kashmir in international meetings such as the United Nations.

India would need to develop a more coherent and tough policy than it has displayed in recent years, when Manmohan Singh's determination to keep talks going has undermined the ability of his government and army to retaliate. This is a neighbourhood example of how India needs to toughen up its habitually soft approach to international diplomacy and set firm boundaries for co-operation that Pakistan can accept or reject. A consensus would have to be reached in India with other political parties and with the states. International pressure could help to persuade Pakistan's civilian government and the military to co-operate. Unless that happens, it will be business as usual, with occasional trouble on the LoC, possible terrorist attacks, and some talks – and with Pakistan being unable to reap the benefits of trade and investment co-operation with India.

Notes

1. http://www.business-standard.com/article/opinion/ajai-shukla-the-lac-is-not-the-loc-112091800050_1.html
2. 'Protests in Indian Kashmir – Stony ground – A new round of anti-government unrest', 8 July 2010, http://www.economist.com/node/16542619?story_id=16542619

3. http://ridingtheelephant.wordpress.com/2010/07/07/security-forces%E2%80%99-bullets-for-stones-bring-death-and-disaster-to-kashmir/

4. http://ridingtheelephant.wordpress.com/2010/05/28/manmohan-singh-displays-his-own-and-his-government%E2%80%99s-limitations/

5. Shivshankar Menon, National Security Adviser, 'Our ability to change India in a globalised world', The Prem Bhatia Memorial Lecture, IIC, New Delhi 11 August 2011; full text http://www.prembhatiatrust.com/ click on Lecture 16

6. 'Summit ascended, but Kashmir not yet broached – The Indo-Pakistani summit came close to success, and may yet achieve it if the hardliners on both sides can be restrained', The Economist, 19 July 2001, http://www.economist.com/node/702471

7. Shekhar Gupta 'National Interest' column, 'On the LoC, in fact', Indian Express, 19 January 2013; the figures were sourced from the Ministry of Home Affairs and the J&K Government and appear in a table in the newspaper headed 'The Ceasefire Dividend', http://www.indianexpress.com/news/national-interest-on-the-loc-in-fact/1061720/0

8. 'Manmohan Singh, Musharraf came close to striking Kashmir deal: WikiLeaks', The Times of India, 3 September 2011, http://articles.timesofindia.indiatimes.com/2011-09-03/india/30109679_1_pervez-musharraf-president-musharraf-pakistani-president and Musharraf speaking at Hindustan Times Leadership Summit, Delhi, November 2012 http://www.youtube.com/watch?v=dh30ffA4-6k

9. http://ridingtheelephant.wordpress.com/2011/07/28/a-new-young-face-brings-hope-to-pakistan%E2%80%99s-tortured-india-relationship/

10. http://ridingtheelephant.wordpress.com/2012/12/18/pakistan-minister-fuels-a-bad-relationship-with-india/

11. Kanwal Sibal, 'India's Options in Dealing with Pakistan', Indian Defence Review, 7 August 2013, http://www.indiandefencereview.com/spotlights/indias-options-in-dealing-with-pakistan/0/

12. G. Parthasarathy, 'India's Pakistan policy comprising uninterrupted dialogue and getting US to pressure Pakistan on terrorism is falling apart', The Hindu Business Line, 13 February 2013, http://www.

thehindubusinessline.com/opinion/columns/g-parthasarathy/composite-dialogue-with-pak-a-failure/article4411449.ece

13. http://ridingtheelephant.wordpress.com/2009/03/08/musharraf-walks-a-delhi-tightrope-%E2%80%93-in-a-time-warp/

14. 'Pak army kills 5 soldiers in raid, tests India's patience yet again', *The Times of India*, 7 August 2013, http://articles.timesofindia.indiatimes.com/2013-08-07/india/41166744_1_poonch-sector-indian-soldiers-pakistan-troops

15. 'Just a small skirmish in Kashmir? John Elliott on why the India-Pakistan border is suddenly the world's most dangerous place', *New Statesman*, 7 June 1999, http://www.newstatesman.com/node/134912

16. 'Pak military chiefs boycott Wagah welcome', Rediff.com, 20 February 1999, http://www.rediff.com/news/1999/feb/20bus2.htm and http://www.rediff.com/news/1999/feb/20bus1.htm

17. The Lahore Declaration, a Memorandum of Understanding, and a Joint Statement issued at the end of Prime Minister Atal Bihari Vajpayee's visit to Lahore, 20-21 February 1999, Stimson Research Papers http://www.stimson.org/research-pages/lahore-summit/

18. Mani Dixit, former India Foreign Secretary, *India and Pakistan in War and Peace*, p 43, Books Today (India Today Group), India, and Routledge, USA, 2002, http://www.routledge.com/books/details/9780415304726/ and online at http://books.google.co.in/books?id=XnzRttnqExUC&pg=PA25&source=gbs_toc_r&cad=4#v=onepage&q&f=false

19. Pervez Musharraf, *In the Line of Fire, A Memoir*, pp 87-93, Simon and Schuster, London, 2006, Simon and Schuster Pocketbook paperback, 2008, Free Press, India, 2008, extracts on line http://www.amazon.co.uk/In-Line-Fire-Pervez-Musharraf/dp/074329582X (also sold on Delhi and Mumbai streets in pirated edition for Rs 200)

20. Swaran Singh, 'The Kargil Conflict: Why and How of China's Neutrality', *Strategic Analysis Volume* 23, Issue 7, 1999, IDSA, http://www.idsa-india.org/an-oct9-3.html

21. Sohail Warraich, 'Ghaddar Kaun?', http://bookcentreorg.wordpress.com/2012/02/21/ghaddar-kaun-author-sohail-warraich-price-us-28-50-price-pak-rs/

22. Pervez Musharraf, *In the Line of Fire, A Memoir*, p. 96

23. Pervez Musharraf produced photographs of Nawaz Sharif's visit on

a Pakistan TV channel, http://www.businessplustv.pk/ in July 2006. 'Look at these pictures,' said Musharraf. 'In one of these pictures, I am receiving him.' 'Musharraf says Sharif knew about Kargil', *DNA*, 13 July 2006, http://www.dnaindia.com/world/report_ghaddar-kaun-musharraf-says-sharif-knew-about-kargil_1041540

24. ''99 phone tapes show General kept Sharif in dark on Kargil, in book he says opposite', *Indian Express*, 26 October 2006, http://www.indianexpress.com/news/-99-phone-tapes-show-general-kept-sharif-in-dark-on-kargil-in-book-he-says-opposite/15422/0

25. Mani Dixit, *India and Pakistan in War and Peace*

26. 'Kargil adventure was four-man show', *Dawn*, 29 January 2013 http://dawn.com/2013/01/29/kargil-adventure-was-four-man-show-general/

27. Humphrey Hawksley, *Dragonfire*, Macmillan, London, 2000. George Fernandes, India's Minister of Defence at the time said: 'The political and historical backdrop against which he [Hawksley] writes is real. The dramatis personae couldn't have been more real. The fictional denouement stands out as a call for reason to assert before time runs out. I commend this book to every Indian.'

28. Humphrey Hawksley, *Democracy Kills*, p. 168, Macmillan, London, 2009

29. Ibid., pp. 167-168

30. Humphrey Hawksley in conversation with JE, September 2013

31. http://multimedia.journalism.berkeley.edu/people/kencooper/

32. Ahmed Rashid, 'Beware Pakistan's small nuclear weapons', Blogs FT.com, http://blogs.ft.com/the-a-list/2013/10/22/beware-pakistans-small-nuclear-weapons/#axzz2iQHAMoKG

22

India and the US
Sometimes Partners, Not Allies

India's relations with the US were transformed in 2008 with a deal on the civilian use of nuclear energy that gave it a new level of acceptability in Washington and international respectability, plus access to nuclear energy and freedom to trade internationally in sensitive technologies. In terms of the history of independent India, this stood alongside the economic liberalization reforms that began in 1991, which were the biggest positive event since the British left in 1947.[1] Its effect has not been as instantly dramatic as those of 1947, nor yet as progressive as 1991, but it helped to change India's potential place in international affairs and laid the foundations for the world's most powerful and largest democracies to become allies one day, though progress is slow.

There have been ups and downs since 2008 as both sides have begun to learn about each other's priorities and limitations, but there are strong bilateral links. Nearly three million people of Indian origin live in America, forming the second largest Asian community there and playing a significant role in politics and business, and there are almost 100,000 Indian students studying in the country.[2] There is a $100bn target for annual two-way trade and there is substantial direct investment in businesses and projects – $50bn from the US into India and over $11bn from India into the US.[3]

From the Indian side, the nuclear deal was achieved primarily because of three men who saw the historic potential of ending a half-century stand-off. The first two were Jaswant Singh, who was India's external affairs minister from 1998 to 2002 in the then NDA government, and Brajesh Mishra, a retired diplomat who was a central figure in that government, pulling the strings of power for Prime Minister Vajpayee. With Vajpayee and Singh, Mishra led a transformation of foreign (and security) policy, not just with the US but also Israel and Pakistan.[4] The third person was Manmohan Singh. Though largely seen from 2009 as an ineffectual prime minister, he had had the vision to revive the nuclear deal when it appeared to be collapsing in 2008[5] and to drive it through a parliamentary confidence vote (amid allegations of bribery) on the floor of the Lok Sabha[6]. In terms of personal initiative, this far exceeded his role as finance minister in 1991. All three men had to overcome extreme scepticism in India because of a deep distrust of America, especially in the self-consciously leftward-leaning Congress party where it has never been politically correct to display pro-US tendencies.

The US Turns

The change in US attitudes began with India's 1998 nuclear tests. Within a month, Bill Clinton, the US president who till then had tilted towards Pakistan rather than India, sent Strobe Talbott, a senior state department official, to Delhi to start a dialogue with Jaswant Singh[7]. In Washington, there was a surge of interest and access for Indian diplomats that had not been seen before.[8] Clinton then supported India during its potentially dangerous conflict with Pakistan in 1999, when he told Nawaz Sharif to withdraw troops from the mountain peaks above Kargil. He had a triumphant visit to India in 2000, saying he welcomed 'India's leadership in the region and the world', adding that he knew it must be difficult to be 'bordered by nations whose governments reject democracy'.[9] But Clinton did little more. In particular, he did nothing to lift a multitude of nuclear-linked sanctions on India. This was partly because his Democratic Party took a strong line on nuclear non-proliferation after the 1998 tests, and partly because the state department did not want to upset Pakistan which it saw as its more important ally.

The next moves came after two major terrorist attacks in 2001 – 9/11 on the New York twin towers in September that year and on the Indian parliament in December. By this time, George W. Bush had become US president and he decided to launch an initiative to build a new relationship. Officials from both sides, including Mishra and Robert Blackwill, the then US ambassador in Delhi, began to look for a policy idea that would be a game-changer in the bilateral relationship and enable India gradually to become a counterweight to China[10]. They chose the nuclear deal which was, as Geoffrey Pyatt, a senior US official, said later, 'a single big issue ... which captured everybody's attention and made clear that we were changing the rules of engagement'.[11] Without China as a potential common adversary, these moves might never have happened.

Tensions remained, however, especially over America's closeness with Pakistan, and also because Washington viewed its relations with India through what was known as the India–Pakistan prism and did not see India as an individual subject. The tensions were underlined in July 2002 when Kanwal Sibal, who had just become India's foreign secretary and describes himself as a 'hard-nosed foreign policy realist', accused America of intentionally giving Pakistan's President Pervez Musharraf 'a lot of room to play with ambiguities on terrorism'. Sibal said that this gave Musharraf 'an alibi' when terrorist attacks originating from Pakistan took place in Jammu and Kashmir. American priorities on the fight against terrorism, he added, were 'not quite in phase' with India's because the US was less concerned about stopping terrorism in Kashmir than elsewhere in the world.[12]

Relations improved in June 2005, when a 'New Framework for India-US Defence Relationship' was agreed, followed a month later by a visit to Washington by Manmohan Singh, who was flattered and feted by Bush. The two leaders agreed to 'transform the relationship' between their two countries, with discussions on trade, science, technology and other areas, including defence.[13] Three years later, after many setbacks, this led on to the 2008 nuclear deal. The nuclear potential was then stalled because India's parliament insisted on foreign contractors taking a degree of liability for equipment failures, which was unacceptable internationally, especially for the US, which did not like India trying to re-write established international rules.

It is arguable how much this matters overall because the deal was never really about energy, even though it was paraded by the Indian and US governments in those terms with contract-hungry US nuclear power companies that used their lobbying clout and pushed for it in Washington. Ultimately, the contractor liabilities issue will be solved – US officials in favour of the deal hope this will happen soon because it would remove a negative point in the relationship that is often cited by powerful India-sceptics in Washington. India will then benefit long term from supplies of nuclear technology and uranium fuel from France, Russia and Australia as well as the US. Meanwhile a new 'Strategic Dialogue' was launched by the two countries in July 2009, following on from the nuclear deal, and that led to a range of consultations and links straddling subjects from counter-terrorism and space to clean energy and climate change, education and health.

Progress – and Myths

The relationship is still developing, sometimes bumpily, and it is not as deep as its supporters would like to claim. India has learned that it can say 'no' to the US, for example, by not breaking relations with Iran or with Myanmar (before both regimes softened their stance in 2013 and 2012), and by voting against the US (and Israel) on Palestine's status in the UN.[14] The US has learned – maybe with some surprise – that India is not prepared to become an obedient ally, and that it will not dutifully follow American wishes on foreign policy or on quickly opening up foreign investment regulations to hungry US companies. Another show of India's independence came in April 2011 on a billion-dollar multi-role combat aircraft fighter contract that the US had virtually assumed its companies would eventually win until India short-listed Dassault of France and Eurofighter, not Lockheed Martin or Boeing.[15] The US had, however, by mid-2012 received defence orders approaching $9bn over the previous ten years, with almost another $10bn in the pipeline, which made defence the most active area of co-operation.

The positives were neatly listed by Hilary Clinton, then the US Secretary of State, at the end of talks in India in July 2011.[16] 'We have worked together for the important task of preventing cyber attacks on our respective infrastructures. We are talking about a new bilateral investment treaty that will build on the 20 per cent increase in trade we've seen just this last year. And we have watched as trade is increasingly flowing in both directions. We have new initiatives linking students and businesses and communities, and one of my personal favourites is the Passport to India, a programme designed to bring more American students to study in India to match the great numbers of Indian students that come to America to study, because we want to create those bonds between our young people and our future leaders'. Her talks on that visit also covered anti-terrorism, economic ties, nuclear projects and defence co-operation. An American foreign affairs specialist said in Delhi a year later: 'We are better off if you are free and confident. Even if India annoys the US all the time, it's still better to have a strong India... Even if we don't get returns and the balance is in the red on nuclear contracts, Iran and the MRCA (the Indian fighter jet contract), it's better we are aligned and work on our common world view'.[17]

There are however sceptics about the relationship in India, as well as those in the US who strongly believe India should be more docile and subservient. There will always be headlines about differences. Usually these will be on issues such as Iran and there is also concern in India about how determined the US is to support Asian countries against the sort of Chinese aggression seen in the East China Sea. There will also be unexpected rows, as happened in December 2013 when US law officers suddenly arrested Devyani Khobragade,

India's 39-year-old deputy consul general in New York, just as she was dropping her daughter at school. Accused of visa fraud over an Indian maid who had worked in her home, she was handcuffed, strip-searched, underwent DNA swabbing, and was held in a cell with others accused of crimes including drugs till she was released on $250,000 bail.[18]

This led to a dispute over Khobragade's diplomatic status and provoked a furious reaction from India, which cancelled various diplomatic privileges that the US enjoyed in India but did not give to India's diplomats in America. Security barricades that blocked a road adjacent to the embassy in Delhi's diplomatic area were dramatically removed. India's foreign service officials were united in condemning the US, led by Sujatha Singh, India's new foreign secretary, who had been in Washington for talks the day before the arrest and was apparently not consulted.

The sharp reaction – and media frenzy – in India flushed out a latent anti-America feeling born of resentment of the way the US threw its weight around. As Stephen Cohen of the Brookings Institution in Washington was reported saying in the *Financial Times*, 'we have created a myth that India is pro-America and that is not the case'.[19]

Before this row broke out, the relationship had been drifting because of a lack of care in both countries with a weakly-led Indian embassy in the US and an American ambassador in Delhi who, though able, could not excite political support back home. There were few, if any, committed supporters in the Obama administration, and there were many officials and commentators in India who enjoyed taking a more aggressive stance. The drift had increased as the Indian government and the country's economy became weaker. The strategic dialogue was continuing but no top leader in either country was consistently pushing it ahead. Officials also said that there were not enough senior diplomats and other experts, especially in India, to run all the areas of co-operation effectively. Adding to the problem was what two policy analysts had earlier called the 'inertia of the mid-level bureaucracy on both sides' steeped in 'residual institutional memories'.[20] President Barack Obama had other priorities, though the US had had India in its sights when he responded to China's growing regional ambitions by launching a new 'pivot' towards Asia in November 2011 (later softened to a 'rebalancing' of America's Asia focus). Manmohan Singh also had other priorities in India, so it was back to chalta hai.

Kanwal Sibal, while recognizing the benefits of the new relationship, reflected the continuing wariness of America felt by many when he told me a year before the Khobragade row that the US had done more than any other country to damage India strategically over the previous 60 years. It had done this 'directly by curbing the development of India's strategic capabilities, by imposing nuclear and space and missile related sanctions, and by applying stringent export controls on transfers of high-technology'.[21] It had also pressured India on territorial issues by backing Pakistan on the disputed territory of Kashmir. 'Now the US is undoing a lot of those negative attitudes and expect us to be pro-them, but we say "you are only undoing things you did against us, so we owe you little". By contrast, says Sibal, who was ambassador in Moscow after retiring as foreign secretary, 'Russia has rarely let India down'.

Much has however been achieved, and a lasting 'strategic partnership, not an alliance' (as Menon put it[22]) is in place after a decade of work. How it develops will depend largely on how America's initiatives in the Asia-Pacific region play out, especially with China. India's role will depend on its reactions as those events unfold, and whether it has the will – and maybe one day the economic strength – to play a leading role in world affairs. Either way, the new relationship with the US has to be seen as a positive development, provided India maintains its independence as a friend and occasional partner but not an ally.

Notes

1. http://ridingtheelephant.wordpress.com/2008/10/02/manmohan-singh-leads-india-into-a-nuclear-%E2%80%9Ctryst-with-destiny%E2%80%9D/

2. Open Doors Data, Institute of International Education, http://www.iie.org/Research-and-Publications/Open-Doors/Data/Fact-Sheets-by-Country/2013

3. 'India and the USA', Speech by National Security Advisor Shri Shivshankar Menon, Aspen Institute India, 20 September 2013, http://www.mea.gov.in/Speeches-Statements.htm?dtl/22238/Speech+by+National+Security+Advisor+Shri+Shiv+Shankar+Menon+on+India+and+the+USA+at+Aspen+Institute+India+September+20+2013

4. Shekhar Gupta, 'Vajpayee's Atal', *Indian Express,* 6 October 2012, http://www.indianexpress.com/news/national-interest-vajpayee-s-atal/1012767

5. http://ridingtheelephant.wordpress.com/2008/07/09/manmohan-singh-wins-the-first-stage-of-his-nuke-gamble/

6. http://ridingtheelephant.wordpress.com/2008/07/23/bribery-claims-cloud-india-parliament-ahead-of-us-nuke-deal/

7. Lalit Mansingh, former India foreign secretary, writing in *The Economic Times*, 26 December 2010 http://articles.economictimes.indiatimes.com/2010-12-26/news/27609758_1_foreign-policy-global-stage-nuclear-tests

8. Indian diplomat posted to Washington DC after nuclear tests, in conversation with JE, October 2012

9. JE, 'How Clinton began a new love affair: Not long ago, China was America's big friend in Asia. All of a sudden, it's India', *New Statesman*, 28 March 2000, http://www.newstatesman.com/node/137270

10. Robert Blackwill in conversation with JE, October 2012

11. Geoffrey R. Pyatt, US Principal Deputy Assistant Secretary South and Central Asian Affairs (posted as senior official in US Embassy Delhi in early 2000s), speaking at Brookings-FICCI Dialogue on the India-US. Strategic Partnership, Delhi, 10 October 2012, http://newdelhi.usembassy.gov/sr101612.html; http://ridingtheelephant.wordpress.com/2008/07/09/manmohan-singh-wins-the-first-stage-of-his-nuke-gamble/

12. 'New tensions in Kashmir – What the peacemakers can expect', *The Economist*, 12 July 2002, http://www.economist.com/node/1227915

13. Joint Statement Between President George W. Bush and Prime Minister Manmohan Singh, The White House Office of the Press Secretary, 18 July 2005, http://georgewbush-whitehouse.archives.gov/news/releases/2005/07/20050718-6.html

14. 'World embraces Palestine; snubs US, Israel', TNN, 1 December 2012, http://articles.timesofindia.indiatimes.com/2012-12-01/us/35530380_1_observer-state-palestinian-authority-palestinian-victory

15. http://ridingtheelephant.wordpress.com/2011/04/28/india-takes-a-nam-route-on-11bn-fighter-contract/

16. Hilary Clinton, 'India and the United States: A Vision for the 21st Century', 20 July 2011, Chennai, http://www.state.gov/secretary/rm/2011/07/168840.htm

17. Speaking in September 2012 at an Observer Research Foundation seminar in Delhi on 'Chatham House' rules

18. https://ridingtheelephant.wordpress.com/2013/12/18/anti-america-and-anti-corruption-are-key-issues-as-india-general-election-looms/

19. 'Maid in Manhattan drama exposes rift', *Financial Times*, 20 December 2013, http://www.ft.com/intl/cms/s/0/e0bfdc54-6999-11e3-aba3-00144feabdc0.html#axzz2otaUNY9F

20. Seema Sirobhi and Samir Saran, 'Looking beyond the honeymoon', *The Hindu*, 29 September 2012, http://www.thehindu.com/opinion/op-ed/looking-beyond-the-honeymoon/article3946259.ece

21. Conversation with JE, September 2012

22. Speaking at Brookings-FICCI Dialogue on the India-US Strategic Partnership, Delhi, 10 October 2012

VII

INDIA'S TRYST WITH REALITY

Conclusions

India has been in a state of denial for years. It is rightly proud of its vibrant and chaotic democracy that has survived and been accepted almost without question across this vast and diverse country for over 65 years. But it is in denial because it has not been prepared to recognise that the vagaries of democracy are providing smokescreens that obfuscate many of the negative aspects of how the country works. Democracy creates an environment where jugaad fixes are easy, and where the failures of the system in terms of poor governance and weakened institutions make the fatalism of chalta hai a welcome safehaven. Democracy has therefore become an unchallengeable fig leaf covering what is not achieved. It allows the negative and under-performing aspects of Indian life to flourish, and it blocks changes and acts as an excuse for what is not being achieved.

The country can no longer afford to allow this to continue. If it does, systems will deteriorate further, possibly leading to implosions as the functioning of institutions is undermined and destroyed. India is far too large and diverse for a revolution to gain hold and dramatically change the way that it is run, but implosion, where government authority crumbles, systems break down, society becomes more lawless, and investment and growth slumps, can already be seen.

This is not an argument for doing away with democracy, but to recognise and change the negative way in which it operates. Democracy has helped to hold India together since independence, providing an outlet for people's frustrations and anger, sometimes ousting prime

447

ministers, chief ministers and their governments. Though far from perfect, it has given the great mass of the population a feeling that they have a say in how the country is run, however faint and rare that may be and however much they are cheated and maltreated by those they elect. But it has also provided an excuse and a cover for the gradual criminalisation of politics that has been allowed to grow for decades to such an extent that election campaigns are distorted, large bribes are paid when coalitions are being formed, and many members of parliament and state assemblies have criminal charges pending against them, often for serious offences.

Democracy is also used as an excuse for ineffective government. The most recent examples of this have come with the coalitions of the past two decades, especially in the past ten years. Manmohan Singh has attempted to pass off prime ministerial vacillation in policy and questionable decision-making as the inevitable result of the 'compulsions of coalition government',[1] and has allowed opposition from other parties to become an excuse for years of policy delays. But, while the recent years have been bad, the problems are deeper and will not be solved simply by switching to another prime minister or political party that carries the baggage of the past. The mission of legitimate governments should be to create inclusive economic development with a sharing of wealth and governance by strong, impartial institutions. On that count, India has failed as corruption and bad governance have facilitated the emergence of a self-serving political system, a politicised bureaucracy, an unprofessional judiciary, and mindless and often cruel policing.

Consequently, the role of politics, democracy, governments, institutions, laws and regulations, which were lauded 20 to 30 years ago as India's special strengths, have been progressively undermined. They have been replaced by arbitrary powers wielded by individuals, be they ministers, bureaucrats, policemen, or regional politicians and gang bosses. Speaking with the experience of having worked with India's oil and other ministries as a former chairman of Shell India, Vikram Singh Mehta says institutions are 'so hollowed out that there is a vacuum and we don't know who is exercising power'.[2] Senior bureaucrats talk about the difficulty of getting officials down the line to follow established procedures and implement decisions. Ministers and officials are reluctant to write notes on policy papers and take decisions because of possible later accusations, fair or unfair, of corruption or other faults, as was seen in the coal and other scandals. Democracy is also a drag on development because, while it has rightly opened the way for dissent and opposition to projects, no effort had been made to curb its misuse by vested interests who corruptly manipulate policies and government action. This has contributed to India becoming an increasingly unpredictable, unreliable, uncompetitive and even difficult place to live and do development and business.

Ungovernable India

'India has always been ungovernable – the only difference now is that we want it to be so', a leading newspaper editor said to me, only half-jokingly, when I was writing an article for the *New Statesman* in 2002 and a BJP-led government was in power.[3] The first part of that remark reflected the view that India has always been too large to be run efficiently from the national capital and that partnership was needed, but rarely achieved, with state governments.

There has also always been a sense that India's massive problems of poverty and backwardness defy effective government and are too big to be solved – a problem that is growing as aspirations expand and several million people flood the job market every year. I suggested that acceptance of the ungovernable idea stemmed from the country's 'fatalistic and (traditionally) easy-going Hindu culture' – a suggestion that provoked intense criticism when the article was reprinted in *Outlook* magazine. In this book, I have taken that view further with the theme that jugaad and chalta hai provide the approaches of quick fixes and fatalism that resist basic change.

It is, of course, possible to put a positive spin on India's way of doing things. Shivshankar Menon, Manmohan Singh's national security adviser, tried to do this in his November 2011 lecture on foreign policy. Answering a question about the turmoil in Indian politics and government, he said: 'We love arguing about it [India's problems]. We love bringing ourselves down ... that's up to us. It's part of the way we do our business. We make a huge amount of noise ... I tell my Chinese friends, "We do in public everything that you do in private – all the arguing, all the policy making". At the end of it, after getting to all the extremes, we come somehow to the middle and we find our way through, and we normally find a good solution, so I'm not worried by turmoil – turmoil is creative, tension is creative, and it works.'

The second part of the editor's remark raised a more vital point – that powerful vested interests do not want India's problems to be tackled and therefore impede effective government. The elite, I suggested in the article, had shuddered since 1947 at the prospect of the poorly fed and poorly educated half of the population rapidly entering mainstream society. That elite has expanded massively in recent years to include the newly rich and powerful, who have their own vested interests in resisting change. Sooner or later, I wrote, the electorate would tire of non-performing governments. Then a new grouping would emerge, led by younger politicians 'probably involving the Congress without Sonia Gandhi in the lead'. India would then move forward again, as it always does. Quite possibly, a national crisis would suddenly trigger change and help to set the country on a new course, as had happened in 1991. I thought, however, that the dominant picture would continue to be the dichotomy of a country that was becoming internationally important in geo-political and economic terms, but whose democracy was becoming anarchic. That was not the India I had seen when I arrived in India in the 1980s when newspaper headlines and politicians' speeches were peppered with phrases saying the country was 'poised for take-off' and 'on the springboard for success'.

The question now is whether India has reached that point when it will move forward. Certainly, the government of Manmohan Singh and Sonia Gandhi has led people to 'tire of non-performing governments'. There is a generational change in prospect with Rahul Gandhi, 42, emerging at the top of the Congress party to challenge Narendra Modi, the 63-year-old controversial and abrasive chief minister of Gujarat who is the BJP's prime ministerial candidate. But they are both being challenged by a popular movement that started with the country-wide anti-corruption protests three years ago and led on to the mass demonstrations over rape and the treatment of women at the end of 2012. Out of this emerged the Aam Aadmi Party, led by Arvind Kejriwal, 45, which has provided a platform for people to become part of a movement that could be an alternative to self-serving and corrupt national and regional political parties. India's middle classes – especially the young – are not (yet) cohesive enough to be mobilised to fight collectively for change, but they are angry enough to spread the AAP's presence. How far Kejriwal can go, having conquered New Delhi and become chief minister, is hard to judge. The AAP's best chance of making a difference would be to grow as a minority party that maybe forces established politicians to change the way they behave.

In his independence speech in 1947, Jawaharlal Nehru used the memorable phrase 'tryst with destiny'. India is now facing its tryst with reality, not just over immediate problems of economic growth and a weak government, but over its long-term failure to tackle mounting problems in the way that democracy functions. On my first visit to India in 1982, my driver from the Taj Hotel in Bombay had gone up the wrong side of a central reservation on the road to Pune. When I asked him why, his charming reply was, 'Don't worry, sahib, both roads go same place'. That, I had soon learned, was a metaphor for the way India likes to work, but it is no longer apt. There are choices to be made about which way India will go – whether democracy will continue to provide a cover for the country's inequality, injustice, corruption and appalling governance, or whether new and younger political leaders and a more vocal expanding middle class will ensure that India, with all its advantages of history, culture, brain power and aspiration, avoids the risk of implosion.

Notes

1. Examples of Manmohan Singh using the phrase are here http://www.mydigitalfc.com/news/i-am-not-blocking-deal-jpc-says-pm-750 and http://indiatoday.intoday.in/story/upa-government-bows-to-allies-mamata-banerjee-m-karunanidhi/1/178501.html

2. Vikram S. Mehta, now chairman, Brookings India, in conversation with JE, and in an article, 'Dimming of Brand India, Indian Express', 2 September 2013, http://m.indianexpress.com/news/dimming-of-brand-india/1163302/

3. JE, 'A BMW kills six, no questions asked. India has become ungovernable. But who cares? Good government might threaten the elite', New Statesman, 22 April 2002, http://www.newstatesman.com/node/ 142790?quicktabs_most_read=0

Index

About the Author

John Elliott is a former *Financial Times* journalist who is now based in New Delhi and writes a blog on South Asia current affairs – http://ridingtheelephant.wordpress.com/. He also writes for the Asia Sentinel in Hong Kong and his blog appears on *The Independent* newspaper website in the UK. He has been in Asia since 1983, initially for the *FT* in India (1983–88) and then in Hong Kong (1988–91) covering the territory, Taiwan and southern China. In 1991, he left the *FT* and spent three years in the Hong Kong government as public affairs adviser to the Chief Secretary before returning to India in 1995. Since then, he has written mainly for *The Economist, Fortune* magazine and the *New Statesman*.

He lead-edited an anthology, *Foreign Correspondent: 50 years of Reporting South Asia*, published by Penguin Books India in 2008. In 1995, he wrote one of the first India-China comparative studies, 'India and China – Asia's New Giants: Stepping Stones to Prosperity', for the Rajiv Gandhi Institute of Contemporary Studies.